NEW PULSE 4
Teacher's Book

Tim Bowen

macmillan education

Macmillan Education
4 Crinan Street
London N1 9XW
A division of Springer Nature Limited

Companies and representatives throughout the world

New Pulse Level 4 Teacher's Book ISBN 978-1-380-02034-5
New Pulse Level 4 Teacher's Book Premium Pack
ISBN 978-1-380-02745-0

This edition published 2019
First edition entitled "Pulse" published 2014 by Springer Nature Limited

Teacher's Book credits:
Designed by emc design ltd
Original design by James Osborne
Page make-up by SPi Global

The publishers would like to thank the following teachers for their contribution to the Project:
Alexia Vidal Seguí, Col·legi Sant Ferran, Barcelona; Amaya Eizaguirre Bolumburu, IES Lauiazeta BHI, San Sebastián – Donostia, Gipuzkoa; Anna Martín Rauret, Escola Isabel de Villena, Esplugues de Llobregat, Barcelona; Aurora Hernandez Martínez, Institut La Mallola, Esplugues de Llobregat, Barcelona; Beatriz Sayalero Martín, IES Gran Capitán, Madrid; Cristina Ceide Ramírez, Institut Ítaca, Sant Boi de Llobregat, Barcelona; Esther Valbuena Ibáñez, Colegio Hijas de la Caridad. Nuestra Señora de Begoña, Bilbao, Bizkaia; Eva Farreny Mata, Col·legi Jesus María Claudina Thévenet, Barcelona; Julio César Fernández García, IES Galileo Galilei, Navia, Asturias; M.ª Ángeles Jimenez Fernández, Institut Centre d'Alt Rendiment, Sant Cugat del Vallès, Barcelona; M.ª Covadonga Gaitero Suarez, IES Parque de Lisboa, Alcorcón, Madrid; Mª Purificación Pascual Mateos, Colegio Fundación Santamarca, Madrid; M.ª Teresa Gil Yanguas, IES Rafael Frühbeck de Burgos, Leganés, Madrid; Marta Ponti Alemany, Institut Menéndez y Pelayo, Barcelona; Olga Mata Burillo, Institut Les Corts, Barcelona; Rebeca Gorostieta López, C.P.E.I.P.S. SANTA MARIA H.L.B.H.I.P., Portugalete, Bizkaia; M.ª Jesús Páramo, Intitut Ernest Lluch, Barcelona; Yolanda Pérez Iborra, Colegio Calasancio, Alicante; Helena del Pico del Palacio, IES Julio Caro Baroja BHI, Algorta, Bizkaia.

Student's Book credits:

Additional material by Laura Clyde

Original design by Andrew Oliver
This edition design and page make-up by emc design ltd
Illustrated by Mark Draisey pp12; Arpad Olbey (Beehive Illustration) p40-41; Nathalie Ortega (Beehive Illustration) pp24, 62, 121
Cover design by Andrew Magee Design Limited

Cover illustration/photographs by Corbis; Flickr RF; Getty Images/iStockphoto; Getty Images/Radius Images; Westend61.
Picture research by Julie-anne Wilce and Penelope Bowden

Full acknowledgements for illustrations and photographs in the facsimile pages can be found in the Student's Book ISBN 978-1-380-02032-1.

The authors and publishers are grateful for permission to reprint the following copyright material:

Page 14 Fact from National Citizen Service Trust, 2019.

Page 34 Fact from Gov.UK, Crown copyright, 2018.

Page 44 Fact from *The College Administrator's Survival Guide* by C. K. Gunsalus, Harvard University Press, 2006.

Page 44 Data from What Next Consultancy, What Next Consultancy Limited, 2019.

Page 61 Data from Comparitech, 2018.

Page T61 Data from SplashData, 2019.

Page 64 Fact from Australian Communications and Media Authority, 2013.

Page 74 Statistic from Mobile Marketing Magazine online, 2017.

Page 74 Data from Global Music Report 2017, IFPI, 2017.

Page 74 Data from We Are Happy Media PTY Limited, 2017.

Page 74 Data from Essential Facts about the Computer and Video Game Industry Report, Entertainment Software Association, 2015.

Page 74 Data from Big Fish Games, Inc, 2017.

Page 74 Statistic from Stephen Follows, 2017.

Page 74 Data from Netflix on 2017 – A Year in Bingeing Press Release, Netflix, 2017, 2017.

Page 74 Data from Technology for Publishing, 2016.

Page 74 Data from Merch Dope, 2018.

Page 74 Statistic from Inc., 2017.

Page 74 Data from UNESCO, 2019.

Page 81 Fact from Red Crow Marketing, 2015.

Video footage supplied by BBC Studios Distribution Ltd on pp.14, 34, 54, 74, 93.

New Pulse conforms to the objectives set by the Common European Framework of Reference and its recommendations for the evaluation of language competence.

Printed and bound in the UK

2023 2022 2021 2020 2019
10 9 8 7 6 5 4 3 2

CONTENTS

INTRODUCING NEW PULSE

New Pulse is a four-level Secondary course which offers teenagers a wide variety of real-world topics and engaging activities, as well as a range of highly motivating videos.

With *New Pulse*, students fully develop their language competence and create personal strategies for lifelong learning at the same time as acquiring valuable exam skills for Secondary and beyond.

Meaningful learning

Videos

New Pulse's vibrant new video content (**Getting started**, **Flipped classroom** grammar presentations, **Speaking sketch** and **Culture byte**) adds variety to classes and makes learning relevant and fun.

Mixed ability

New Pulse caters for a range of learner profiles and helps teachers to provide extra support (digital **Grammar basics** and **Vocabulary basics**) or to level up the material (**The longer read** and **Advance your vocaulary**) when necessary.

Vocabulary and Grammar in context

New Pulse's extensive **vocabulary** syllabus (two vocabulary sets per unit, **Words in context** and **Word builder**) is presented in context and prepares students to communicate in the real world.

Grammar structures are presented through a range of texts that provide context for understanding meaning. One of the two grammar sections in each unit begins with a Flipped classroom grammar video which offers a flexible approach to teaching grammar.

Scaffolded skills work

There is a rich variety of appropriately graded and structured contemporary **reading** texts, with teen-appropriate topics.

Writing is highly structured as students first interact with model texts and are then guided through a scaffolded writing task, with a focus on analysing language and structure.

New Pulse provides students with the support they need before and during **listening** activities to aid comprehension and improve confidence.

Students participate in personalized **speaking** tasks which provide frequent opportunities to interact and exchange opinions.

Using a model video dialogue, the **Integrated skills** pages in the Student's Book provide fully integrated reading, listening, writing and speaking practice to prepare students to use English in real-life situations.

Lifelong learning skills

Life skills

Macmillan is at the forefront of promoting extracurricular **life skills** which are vital for success in the classroom and for full participation in everyday life.

New Pulse Student's Book 4 has three **Life skills** pages which extend the unit topic and preview grammar while teaching students skills such as decision-making or negotiating.

Evaluation material and exam preparation

New Pulse provides teachers with ample resources for the continuous evaluation of linguistic skills and key competences. Learning outcomes can be evaluated using the **Tests and exams** in the Teacher's Resource Centre and the **CEFR Skills Exam Generator**.

The **External exam trainer** offers essential practice material to prepare students for Cambridge B1 Preliminary, or Cambridge-style exams, in line with the new 2020 format. The Student's Book focuses exclusively on speaking, with the other skills featuring in the Workbook.

Self-study and self-evaluation

New Pulse promotes learner autonomy by encouraging students to take an active role in their own learning. A **Study guide** is provided in the Student's Book with all of the unit grammar and vocabulary. The **Self-study bank** in the Workbook contains **Grammar reference**, **Advance your vocabulary** and **Writing hub** sections to reinforce and expand upon what students learn in class, plus a **Wordlist** and **Pronunciation reference**.

Critical thinking

Critical thinking tasks which encourage students to analyse and process information, for example by evaluating advantages and disadvantages of a situation, appear alongside all the main reading texts of the Student's Book. The **Analyse** questions on the grammar pages help activate students' learning potential by encouraging them to notice form and structure and to draw comparisons with their own language.

Socio-cultural awareness

New Pulse equips students with the socio-cultural awareness and skills they need to become more informed global citizens, with a focus moving from **cultural awareness** (levels 1 and 2) to **social awareness** and **life skills** (levels 3 and 4). The Culture byte videos on these pages offer a window onto relevant cultural and social issues.

Digital competence

New Pulse promotes digital competence in numerous ways, including **Web quest tips** and online research tasks as well as supporting students in using software packages and web tools in the **Collaborative projects**. Students expand their knowledge of these tools through the **Digital competence worksheets**.

Council of Europe and key competences

New Pulse has been developed following the legal guidelines set out by the Council of Europe, whose curricular objective is not just teaching a language itself, but teaching how to communicate through it. Following the Council of Europe's Common European Framework of Reference for Languages (CEFR), students must be able to carry out progressive communication tasks in order to gradually develop their communicative competence in a foreign language.

The course contents of *New Pulse* have been designed to develop skills in all key competences:

CAE Cultural awareness and expression
CLC Competence in linguistic communication
CMST Competence in mathematics, science and technology
DC Digital competence
L2L Learning to learn
SCC Social and civic competences
SIE Sense of initiative and entrepreneurship

Support and solutions for teachers

New Pulse has a full range of components to support teachers and offer solutions to classroom challenges. These include:

Teacher's Book

Teacher's Presentation Kit

COURSE COMPONENTS

Student's Book

New Pulse Student's Book offers a starter revision unit, nine core units, a Study guide section, three Collaborative projects and an External exam trainer focusing on speaking tasks.

Vocabulary

The **Getting started video** sets the unit topic and introduces target vocabulary and grammar in an appealing way for teens.

Vocabulary is presented in real-life contexts using a variety of techniques and activities.

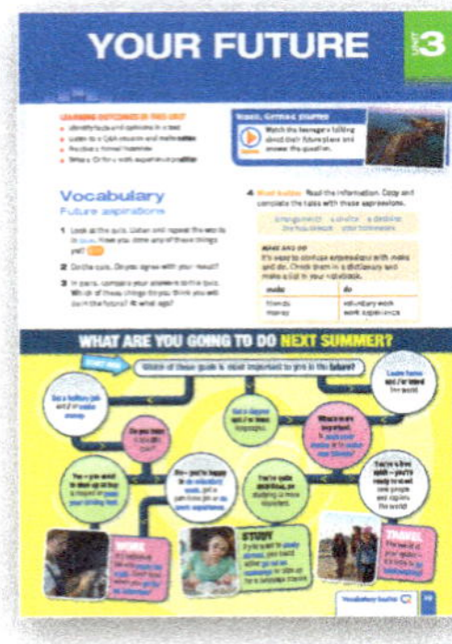

A short speaking task gives students the opportunity for personalized practice.

Reading

Contemporary real-world reading texts capture students' attention and present new language in context.

Students develop strategies for recognizing and learning new vocabulary through the **Words in context** and the **Word builder** features.

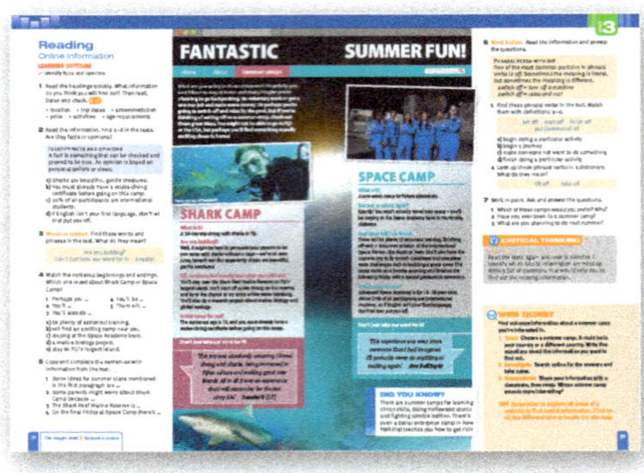

Real-life skills are developed through the **Critical thinking** sections, while the **Web quest** gives students the opportunity to investigate the reading topic further.

Grammar

Flipped classroom videos with teenage peer 'teachers' provide a flexible learning tool for grammar presentation.

Carefully graded exercises help students practise what they learn, and the **Analyse** feature encourages them to compare English grammar with their own language.

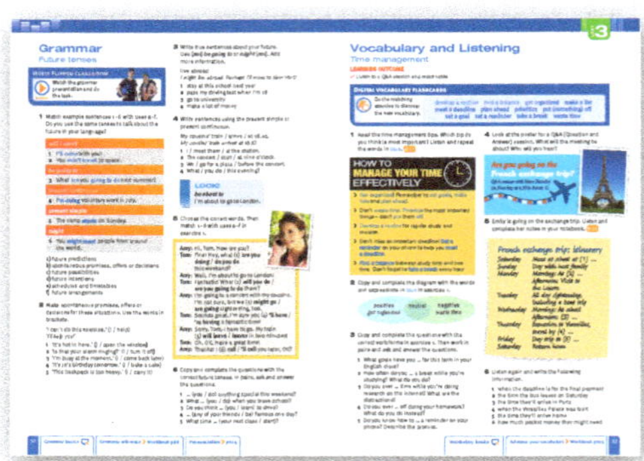

Vocabulary and Listening

The Presentation Kit has optional **Digital vocabulary flashcards** which provide a fun alternative for teaching vocabulary.

An extended listening text develops listening skills and recycles the target language in context.

Social awareness / Life skills

The four **Social awareness** pages broaden students' knowledge of culture in English-speaking countries, and the four **Life skills** pages provide useful strategies for life both now and in the future.

In alternate units these pages are supplemented by a **Culture byte** video.

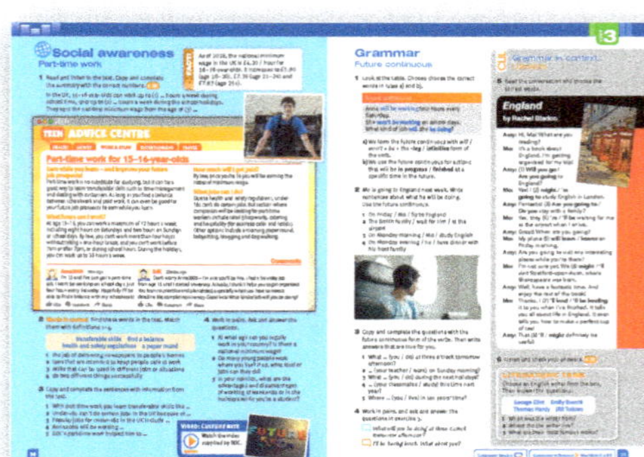

Grammar

Grammar modelled on the Social awareness / Life skills page is presented and practised on the second grammar page.

All grammar presented in the unit is reviewed in the extended **Grammar in context** activity with a CLIL focus.

Integrated skills

A reading text introduces the topic, practises comprehension and provides ideas for the final speaking task.

The **Speaking sketch video** dialogue serves as a model for the student's own dialogue.

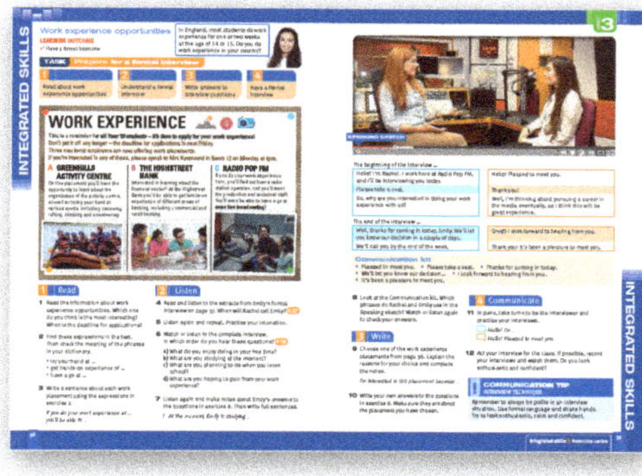

Students write and practise their own guided conversation with the option of preparing and filming a more open conversation.

Writing

The writing page provides a model for different text types. Students practise relevant language in the **Focus on language**, while the **Focus on content** helps students to structure the text and include relevant content. The **Writing kit** guides students through the preparation and production of their own text.

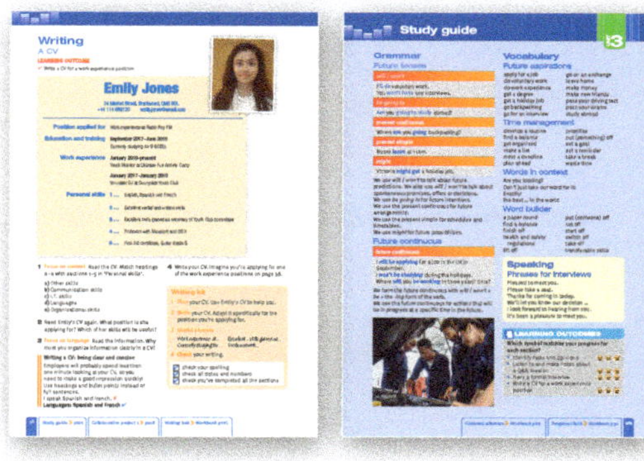

Study guide

The **Study guide** for each unit, at the end of the Student's Book, is a useful quick reference for all vocabulary, grammar and functional language presented in the unit and helps students revise and consolidate what they have learnt.

Collaborative projects

Collaborative projects provide an opportunity for students to work cooperatively and to develop their digital competence.

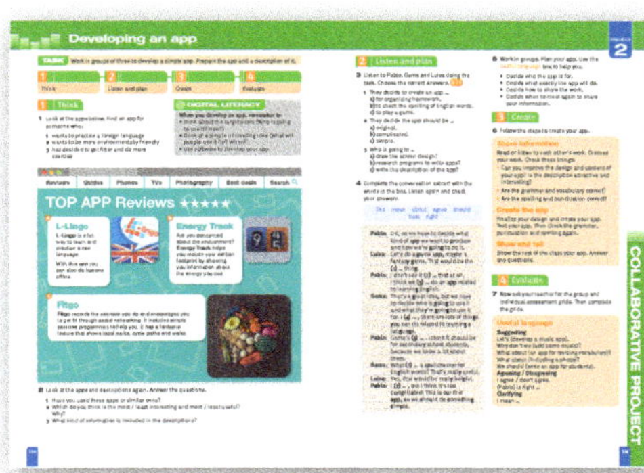

External exam trainer

The **External exam trainer** presents a clear example of a model speaking exam question and answer, with exam advice and tips, followed by a guided practice exam task.

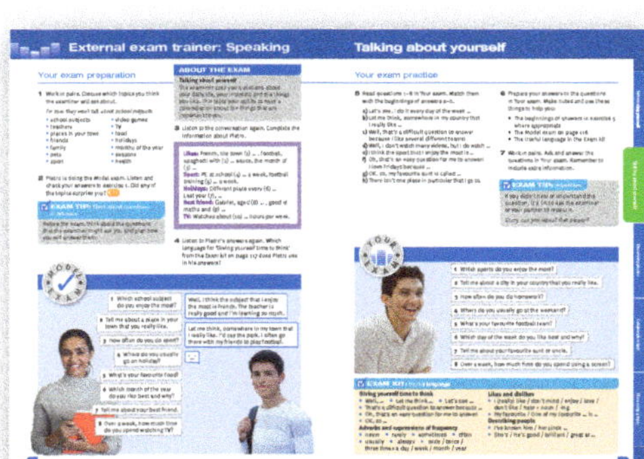

Workbook

New Pulse Workbook consolidates all the core language presented in the Student's Book, and includes a Progress check and Extension for each unit.

The full-colour Self-study bank includes further practice, extension activities and reference material.

Vocabulary

A variety of activities ensures successful revision of the first vocabulary set from the Student's Book. Activities are graded from one star ★ to three stars ★★★ to indicate the level of difficulty.

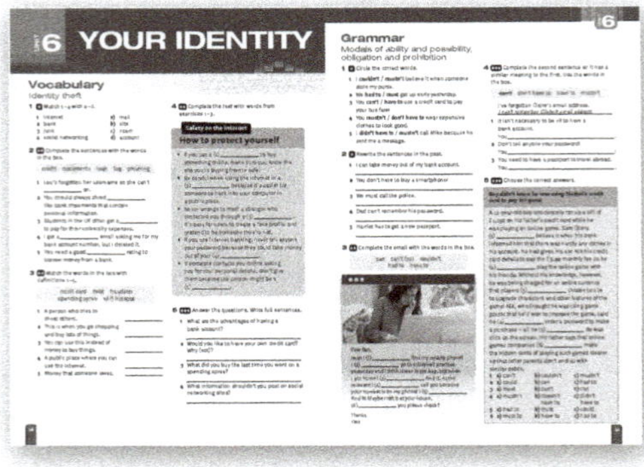

Grammar

Easy-to-follow, graded exercises provide students with extensive practice of the first Grammar page in the Student's Book.

Vocabulary

The vocabulary from the Vocabulary and Listening page in the Student's Book is practised with a range of graded activities.

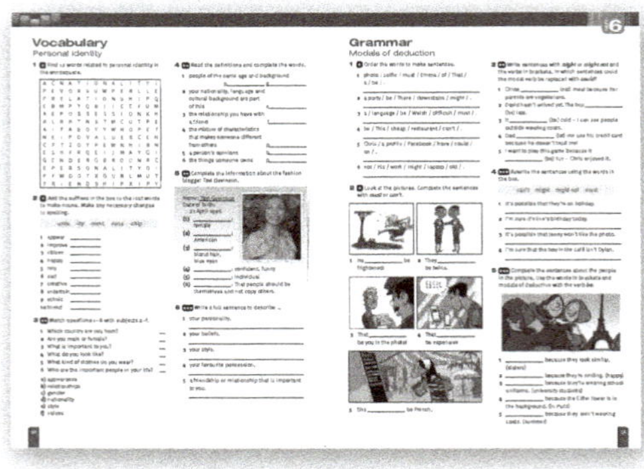

Grammar

The second grammar page of the Student's Book is thoroughly practised in carefully graded exercises.

Reading

Students work with a wide variety of reading texts on theme-related topics and have comprehensive practice of varied task types.

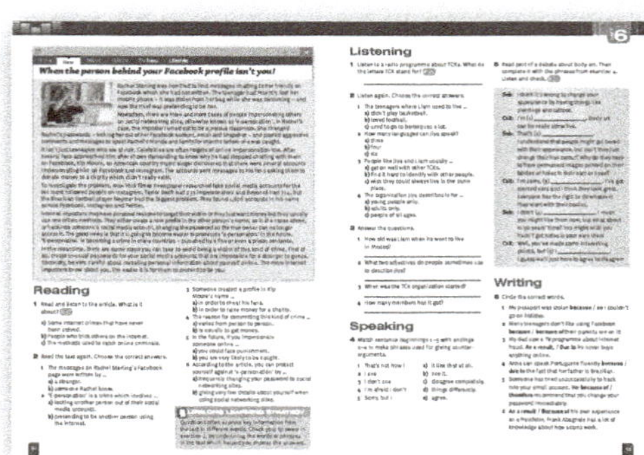

Listening, Speaking and Writing

A broad range of listening, speaking and writing texts and tasks link thematically to the units and train students to correctly use the language presented in the Student's Book.

Progress check

The Progress check provides an in-depth test of all core vocabulary and grammar covered in the unit.

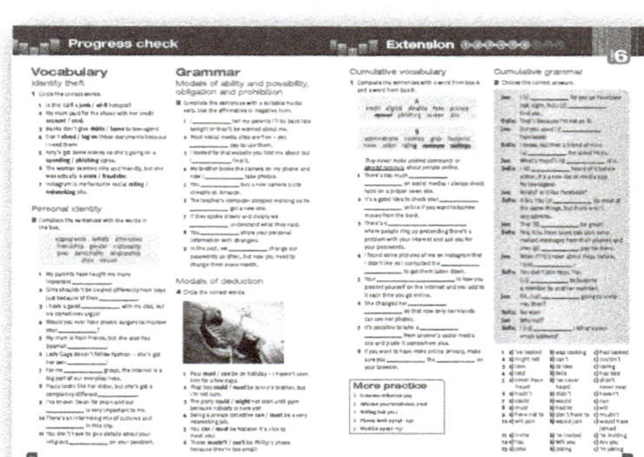

Extension

The extension page provides cumulative practice of vocabulary and grammar covered throughout the book and of the non-core Word builder in the unit.

Grammar reference

The **Grammar reference** section provides grammar tables and explanations of all grammar covered in the Student's Book. A downloadable PDF is available in Castilian and Catalan in the Teacher's and Student's Resource Centres.

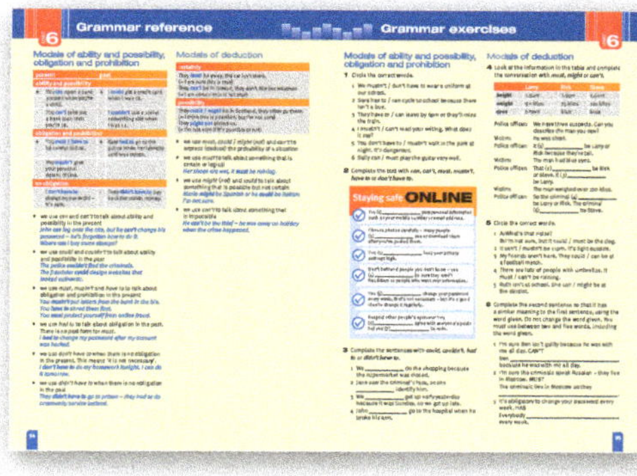

Grammar practice exercises are provided opposite the relevant Grammar reference pages.

Advance your vocabulary

The **Advance your vocabulary** pages use visuals to present a new lexical set related to the topic of each unit.

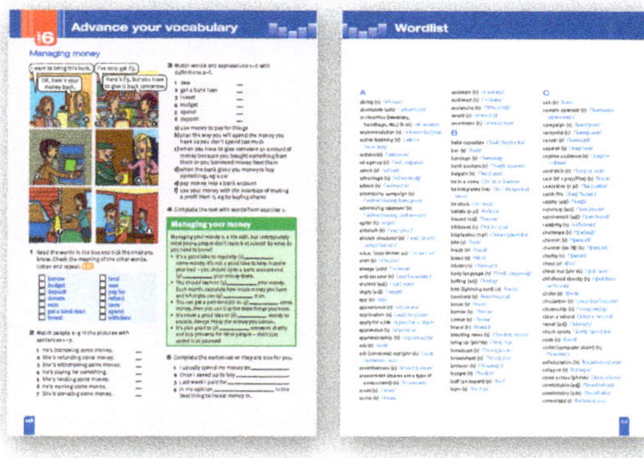

Wordlist

A complete **Wordlist** in alphabetical order helps students review vocabulary and check pronunciation. Bilingual versions are provided in the Teacher's and Student's Resource Centres for download.

Writing hub

An **annotated model text** linked to the unit topic shows students what they need to include in their own written work, covering a wide range of genres.

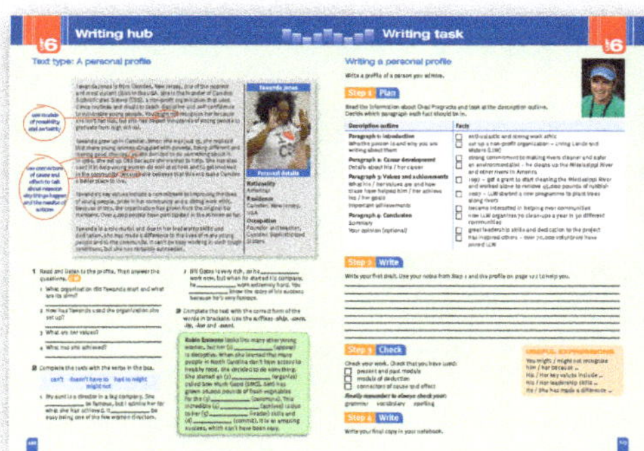

Writing tasks are broken down into steps to help students plan, prepare, produce and review their own writing texts at home.

External exam trainer

Your exam preparation provides a model question and answer, and **Your exam practice** then gives students the opportunity to put their exam strategies into action.

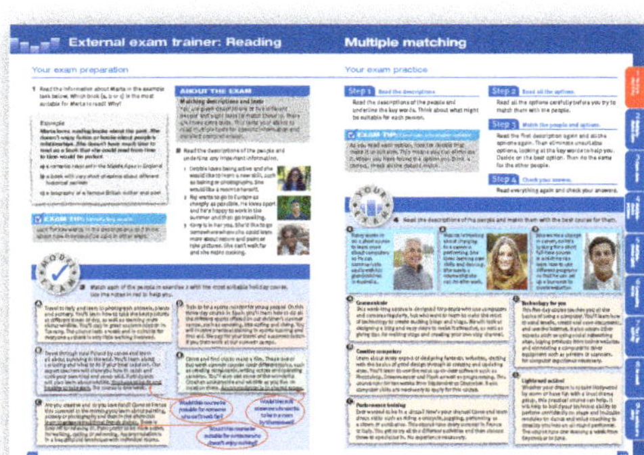

Exam tips offer advice and techniques to help students answer exam questions successfully.

Digital resources

Teacher's Presentation Kit

The Teacher's Presentation Kit fulfils all your digital classroom requirements in one place, with digital solutions to suit all teaching environments. The course contains:

- Digital versions of the Student's Book and Workbook with audio, video and answers for use with interactive whiteboards
- Digital Vocabulary and Grammar basics exercises for additional lower-level practice in class
- Built-in tools to customize your presentations
- Markbooks to automatically keep track of students' progress

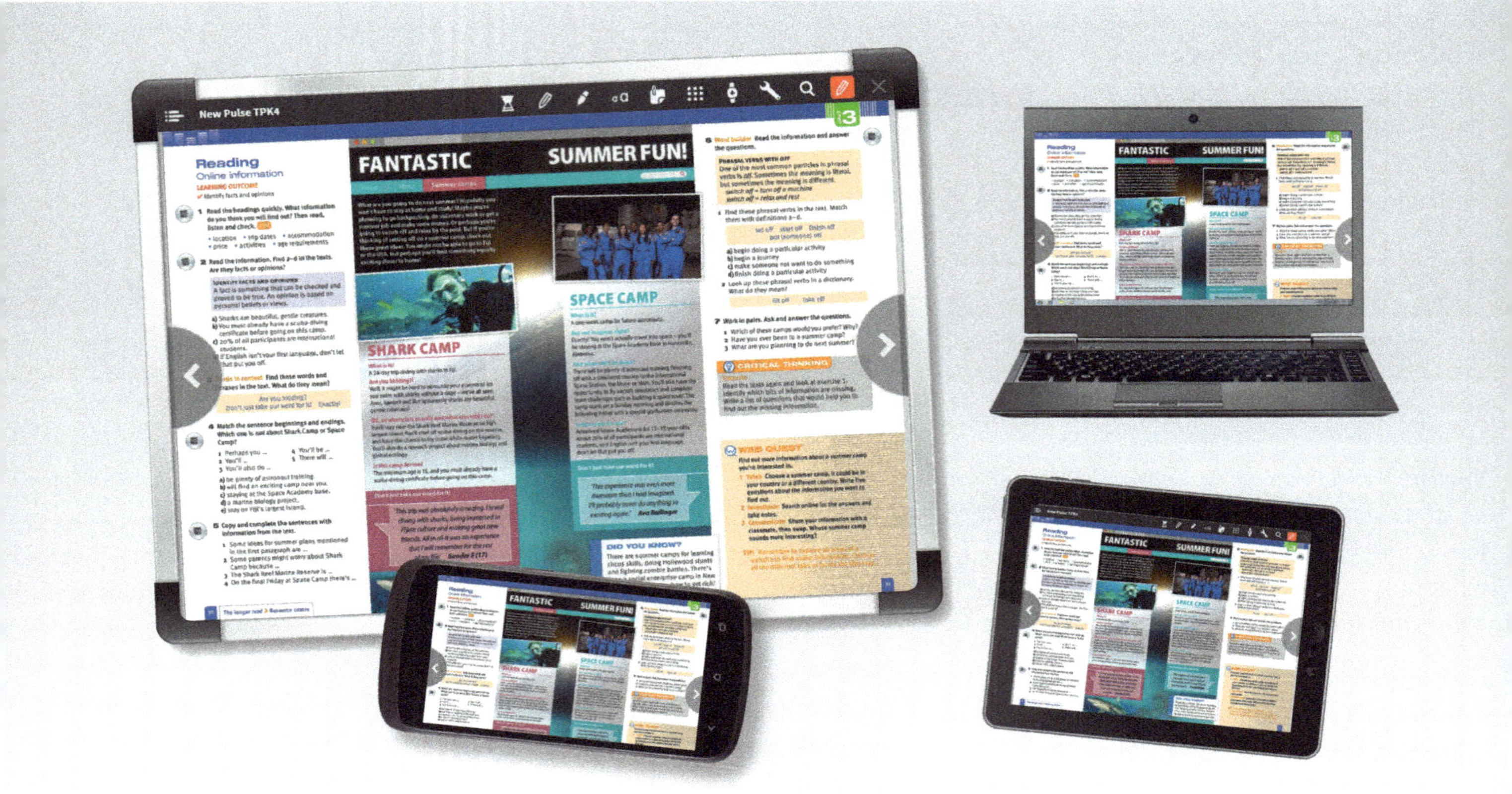

Teacher's Resource Centre

The **Teacher's resource file** features a wealth of downloadable and photocopiable worksheets, MP3 audio files and resources to recycle and practise language, develop skills, and evaluate and assess your students. **Tests and exams** can be downloaded from the Teacher's Resource Centre as editable Word documents as well as PDFs.

CEFR Skills Exam Generator

The CEFR Skills Exam Generator gives teachers the opportunity to generate their own skills-based exams. Covering CEFR levels A1+/A2, A2, A2+ and B1/B1+, the exams include a range of reading, writing and speaking tasks typical of external exams.

Digital components

Markbooks, linked to the Digital Student's Book and the Online Workbook, facilitate correction and help to evaluate students' progress.

An enhanced eBook of the Student's Book is also provided.

All audio recordings from the Student's Book and Workbook can be downloaded as MP3 files, and video files are available to view on the Teacher's and Student's Resource Centres.

Videos

Each unit of *New Pulse* offers an array of videos to encourage, engage and energise your students:

- **Getting started** videos feature interviews with British teens giving their views on a question related to the unit topic
- **Speaking sketch** videos model the functional language of the unit and help students create their own dialogue

- **Flipped classroom** grammar presentation videos in which teenage peer 'teachers' present the new grammar point
- The Social awareness pages also feature **Culture byte** videos, which extend students' cultural knowledge of the unit topic

Additional resources for students

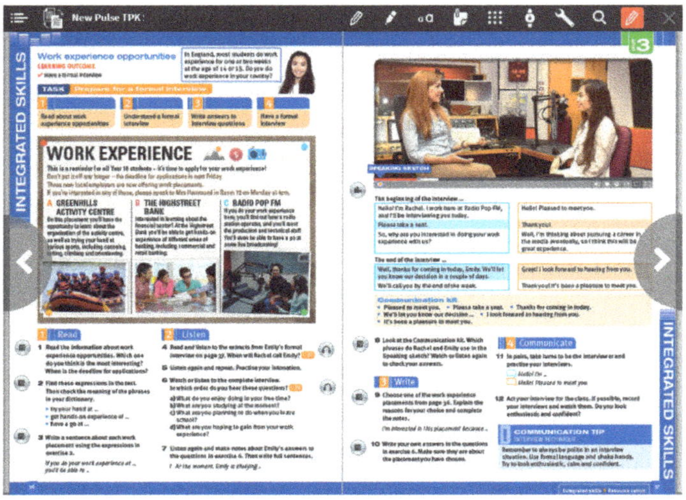

The **Digital Student's Book** is a versatile learning tool compatible with all devices and includes class audios and videos, while the **Online Workbook** contains all the Workbook material. Scores for both of these are automatically recorded in the Markbooks.

The **Student's Resource Centre** provides students with supplementary materials to enhance learning and promote learner autonomy, including access to the Student's Book videos.

MACMILLAN DICTIONARY

Search

Dictionary Thesaurus

www.macmillandictionary.com

The **Macmillan Dictionary Online** is a free English dictionary and thesaurus. The website presents users with clear definitions, word sets and useful synonym boxes in addition to grammar information, example sentences, common phrases, and recorded British and American pronunciations.

Teacher's Book

The Teacher's Book contains a variety of different features and tasks to help make the best use of the *New Pulse* materials.

A comprehensive unit overview details and provides cross-references to the unit objectives and key competences, linguistic contents, skills, lifelong learning skills, evaluation, digital material, digital competence, reinforcement material, extension material and the Teacher's Resource Centre.

Clear **Lesson objectives** provide a useful summary of the new language that will be presented in class and the tasks that students will perform.

Optional **Warmer** activities are short and practical, helping to prepare students for the lesson ahead.

Language notes provide extra information about pronunciation, vocabulary, grammar or idiomatic use of English.

The **Background** and **Culture note** sections provide additional cultural context and useful information about the people, places or events mentioned in the Student's Book.

The **Extra activity** and **Finished?** boxes provide extra tasks for fast finishers and help with multi-level classroom situations.

Teacher's resource file

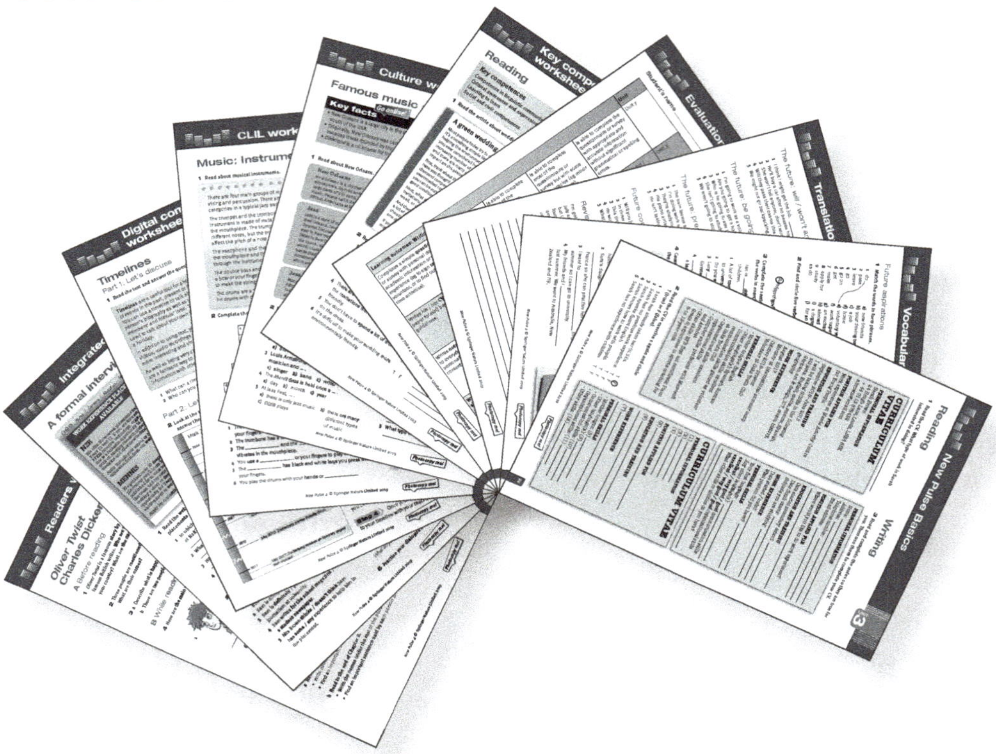

With more than 310 pages of downloadable material, answer keys and audioscripts, the Teacher's resource file provides all the extra materials you need to ensure your students have a meaningful and thorough learning experience.

New Pulse Basics – six worksheets per unit tailored to lower-level students – provides an ideal solution for classroom diversity, revising the key vocabulary, and reading and writing skills-work from the Student's Book.

Vocabulary and grammar consolidation and extension – with two Consolidation worksheets and two Extension worksheets per unit – provides revision and extended practice of all vocabulary and grammar covered in the Student's Book.

Translation and dictation worksheets are linked to each unit. MP3 audio files for the dictation exercises can be downloaded from the Teacher's Resource Centre.

Evaluation rubrics include criteria to evaluate levels of achievement of specific reading, writing, listening and speaking learning outcomes in the course.

The **Key competences** worksheets provide further work on relevant competences related to the four skills.

Culture worksheets are based around the history and culture of different places in the English-speaking world. **CLIL** worksheets link cultural topics with other areas of the school curriculum.

Digital competence worksheets promote digital competence and support students in using online tools. Accompanying **Teacher's notes** provide more information and explain how to use the tools to carry out the tasks.

The **Culture byte** worksheets test students' comprehension of the Culture byte videos. The worksheets are accompanied by optional homework web quests. Teacher's notes explain how to make the most of the worksheets in class.

The **Integrated skills** worksheets feature reading, listening, writing and speaking exercises that build on the Integrated skills section in the Student's Book through at-home practice.

The longer read worksheets extend the main reading texts and exercises in the Student's Book and provide a more challenging option for higher-level students.

The **Macmillan Readers** worksheets include comprehension activities to accompany the Macmillan Graded Readers and provide a useful focus on literature.

Tests and exams

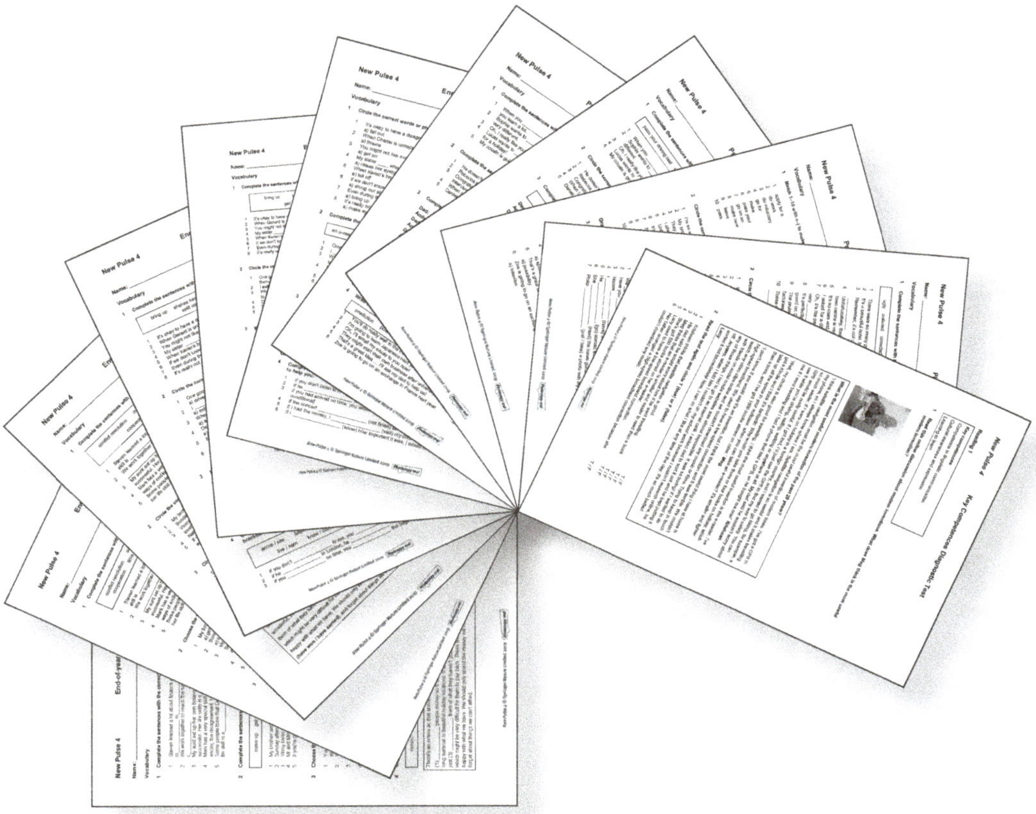

The photocopiable Tests and exams can be downloaded from the Teacher's Resource Centre as editable Word documents as well as PDFs. The material includes:

- A placement test and key competences diagnostic test which can be used to assess the language level and key competences of students
- Tests available at three levels: basic, standard and extra. Each level has:
  - nine unit-based progress tests
  - three end-of-term tests
  - an end-of-year exam
- Answer keys, downloadable MP3 files and audioscripts for all the tests and exams

Other resources

The Teacher's Resource Centre also includes the Workbook answer key and translated versions of the Student's Book Grammar reference and Wordlist.

	READING Culture Byte VIDEO SUPPLIED BY THE BBC	LISTENING	INTEGRATED SKILLS Speaking Sketch	WRITING
	• Gerunds and Infinitives • Holiday activities: verb + noun collocations • Question tags			
	• **A feature article:** *As if by Magic!* **Critical thinking:** Suggest reasons **Social awareness:** NCS (National Citizen Service) Culture Byte video	• A discussion about a life skills workshop	**A youth club committee** • Speaking: An informal interview • Reading: A job advertisement	• A personal blog **Focus on language:** Adverbs of degree
	• **News stories:** *Lucky escapes* **Critical thinking:** Create a timeline **Life skills:** Problem-solving (risk assessment)	• A news report about an emergency incident	**A survival game** • Speaking: A group discussion • Reading: Instructions for a game	• A news report **Focus on language:** Connectors of sequence
	• **Online information:** *Fantastic summer fun!* **Critical thinking:** Enquire **Social awareness:** Part-time work Culture Byte video	• A Q&A session about a foreign exchange	**Work experience opportunities** • Speaking: A formal interview • Reading: Information about work experience opportunities	• A CV **Focus on language:** Writing a CV: being clear and concise
	• **A profile and song:** *With a little help from his friends ...* **Critical thinking:** Create **Life skills:** Effective listening	• A radio phone-in about non-verbal communication	**Moral dilemmas** • Speaking: A group debate • Reading: A quiz	• Instant messages **Focus on language:** Informal expressions
	• **A science article:** *STEM stars at 'The Big Bang'* **Critical thinking:** Imagine **Social awareness:** Virtual classrooms Culture Byte video	• A TV technology show about 3D printing	**Great innovations** • Speaking: A presentation • Reading: A timeline	• A formal letter **Focus on language:** Writing a formal letter
	• **An article and advice:** *Stolen phone, stolen life ...* **Critical thinking:** Judge **Life skills:** Digital competence	• A radio discussion about ID cards	**Your online identity** • Speaking: A class debate • Reading: An article	• A personal profile **Focus on language:** Connectors of cause and effect
	• **A forum:** *Virtual teen forum* **Critical thinking:** Decide **Social awareness:** Entertainment and technology Culture Byte video	• Phone calls and messages about a rock festival	**An entertainment survey** • Speaking: A survey • Reading: An entertainment survey	• A report **Focus on language:** Expressing statistics
	• **An article with comments:** *Purrfectly persuasive ...* **Critical thinking:** Categorize **Life skills:** Critical thinking	• Adverts about different products and services	**Charity adverts** • Speaking: A presentation • Reading: Adverts	• A for and against essay **Focus on language:** Connectors of addition and contrast
	• **A leaflet:** *How to ... keep calm and pass exams!* **Critical thinking:** Summarize and evaluate information Culture Byte video		**Assessment methods** • Speaking: A debate • Reading: A website	• Formal emails **Focus on language:** Formal and informal language

STARTER

ON HOLIDAY

Exercise 1
positive: comfortable exciting lively peaceful pretty romantic safe
negative: crowded dangerous dirty expensive polluted ugly
neutral: ancient

Vocabulary
Describing places

1 Listen and repeat the adjectives. Do they have a positive, negative or neutral meaning? 2

ancient comfortable crowded dangerous dirty exciting expensive lively peaceful polluted pretty romantic safe ugly

2 Read the quiz. How many adjectives in exercise 1 can you find? Then answer the questions.

Quiz Holiday destinations around the world

1 Spending a weekend in New York is always exciting! More than 50 million people visit the USA's biggest city every year. In which district would you find Times Square and Central Park?

a Brooklyn b Manhattan

2 Come to this peaceful national park if you want to get away from it all! The Rocky Mountains span almost 5,000 km between two countries. Which countries are they?

a Canada and the USA
b Mexico and the USA

3 The ancient region of Cappadocia has got amazing rock formations and cave hotels. Where is it?

a Australia b Turkey

4 Do you enjoy sunbathing? It's easy to find space on the sandy beach at Praia do Cassino – it isn't crowded. It's the longest beach in the world! Where is it?

a Brazil b Portugal

Exercise 2
exciting crowded peaceful ancient
1 b) – Manhattan
2 a) – Canada and the USA
3 b) – Turkey
4 a) – Brazil

3 Read the Look! box. Write comparative and superlative forms of the other adjectives in exercise 1.

LOOK!
Comparatives and superlatives
safe – safer – the safest
expensive – more expensive – the most expensive

4 Write sentences about places that you know. Use comparative and superlative forms of the adjectives in exercise 1.

The Turkish Riviera is more peaceful than Istanbul.

My town is the prettiest place in Mexico.

Exercise 4
Students' own answers

Exercise 3
ancient – more ancient – the most ancient
comfortable – more comfortable – the most comfortable
crowded – more crowded – the most crowded
dangerous – more dangerous – the most dangerous
dirty – dirtier – the dirtiest
exciting – more exciting – the most exciting
lively – livelier – the liveliest
peaceful – more peaceful – the most peaceful
polluted – more polluted – the most polluted
pretty – prettier – the prettiest
romantic – more romantic – the most romantic
ugly – uglier – the ugliest

Vocabulary
Describing places

LESSON OBJECTIVES
In this lesson students will:
- revise adjectives to describe places
- revise comparatives and superlatives

WARMER
Play a spelling game to revise the English names of different countries around the world. Put students into pairs. Write the letter *A* on the board. Ask students to write down the name of a country beginning with that letter, eg *Argentina*. Continue with the other letters of the alphabet. The pair with the most correctly spelt countries is the winner.

1 🔊 2
- Play the audio. Students listen and repeat the words chorally and individually.
- They work in pairs and sort the adjectives into three categories – positive, negative and neutral (neither positive nor negative).
- Check answers as a class. Make sure students pronounce comfortable/ˈkʌmftəbəl/ correctly with three syllables.

2
- Explain that some of the adjectives from exercise 1 can be found in the quiz.
- Students read the quiz and note down the adjectives.
- They read the quiz carefully and answer the four questions.
- They compare answers in pairs.
- Check answers as a class.

LOOK!
Students read the information in the LOOK! box. Elicit rules for the formation of comparatives and superlatives and write them on the board. (See the LANGUAGE NOTE in the next column.)

3
- Students write the comparative and superlative form of the other adjectives in exercise 1.
- Check answers as a class. Point out that we never use *more* or *the most* with short comparative or superlative adjectives with -er or -est endings.

LANGUAGE NOTE
Short adjectives (adjectives of one or two syllables) form their comparatives by adding *-er* and their superlatives by adding *-est*, eg *long – longer – the longest*. If a short adjective ends in *-e*, only *-r* or *-st* is added, eg *safe – safer – the safest*. In short adjectives ending in *-y*, this letter changes to an *i* in the comparative and superlative forms, eg *easy – easier – the easiest*. Short adjectives ending in vowel-consonant double the consonant in the comparative and superlative forms, eg *big – bigger – the biggest*. Two-syllable adjectives ending in *-ing*, *-ed*, *-ful* and *-less* and adjectives with more than two syllables form their comparatives with more and their superlatives with the most. The form of these adjectives does not change, eg *expensive – more expensive – the most expensive*. The three main adjectives with irregular comparative and superlative forms are *good – better – the best*, *bad – worse – the* worst and *far – further – the furthest*.

4
- Read the example sentences aloud to the class.
- Remind students that comparative adjectives are followed by *than* and that *the* is always used with superlatives.
- Students work individually and write at least five sentences about places they know using comparative and superlative forms of the adjectives in exercise 1.
- Invite students to come to the board and write a sentence. Check for correct spelling and use of comparative and superlative forms.

Grammar

Present simple and present continuous

LESSON OBJECTIVES
In this lesson students will:
- revise the present simple and the present continuous
- revise gerunds and infinitives

WARMER
Books closed. Write the sentence *More than 70 million people visit Paris every year* on the board with the words in the wrong order: *70 million visit Paris people every year more than.* Students work in pairs and write the sentence in the correct order. Write the correct sentence on the board.

1 • Students read the information in the grammar table.
• They work individually and answer the four questions.
• They compare answers in pairs.
• Check answers as a class. Highlight *usually* and elicit other adverbs of frequency used with the present simple to describe habits and routines, eg *never, rarely, occasionally, sometimes, often, always.*

2 • Read the example sentences aloud to the class. Highlight the use of the present continuous with today.
• Explain the task. Students should write one negative and one affirmative sentence for each example using the present simple or present continuous tense as appropriate, eg 1 *We don't study English six times a week. We study English twice a week.* 2 *Our teacher isn't telling us about her holiday at the moment. She's writing on the board.*
• Students work individually and write their sentences.
• They compare answers in pairs.
• Check answers as a class.

3 • Make sure students understand the task. If necessary, do the first question with the whole class as an example to show how the question is made from the prompts (*What are you doing at the moment?*).
• Remind students that time expressions indicate which tense to use.
• Students work individually and write the questions. They write true answers.
• Check the questions as a class but do not listen to their answers at this stage. In question 2, the present simple is used because the class starts and finishes according to a timetable, (a type of routine).

Gerunds and infinitives

4 • Students read the information in the table.
• They work individually and match rules a–f with sentences 1–6.
• They compare their answers in pairs.
• Check answers as a class. Point out that to explain purpose (rule f) means *to say why you did, do or are going to do something.*

5 • Encourage students to refer to the rules in exercise 4 to help them complete this exercise individually.
• Check answers as a class.

EXTRA ACTIVITY
Students work in pairs, asking and answering the questions in exercise 5, using the answers they wrote.

6 • Students copy the text into their notebooks and fill the gaps using gerunds or infinitives.
• Check answers as a class.

Grammar reference > Workbook page 82

Grammar

Present simple and present continuous

Exercise 1
1 present continuous
2 present simple
3 every year, once a year, usually
4 at the moment, now, today

1 Look at the table and answer the questions.

present simple
More than 70 million people visit Paris **every year.**
Many British people go abroad **once a year.**
Where do you **usually** go on holiday?
present continuous
We're studying **at the moment.**
I'm not lying on the beach **now.**
Is it raining **today?**

1 Which tense is for actions in progress?
2 Which tense is for habits and routines?
3 Which time expressions do we use with the present simple?
4 Which time expressions do we use with the present continuous?

Exercise 2
Students' own answers

2 Change the words in bold to make them true for you. Write one negative and one affirmative sentence for each statement.

We're visiting a museum today.
We aren't visiting a museum today.
We're learning English today.

1 We study English **six times a week.**
2 Our teacher **is telling us about her holiday** at the moment.
3 Our summer holidays start in **April.**
4 I'm wearing **a swimsuit** today.
5 My best friend lives in **New York.**
6 We're finishing **exercise 4** now.

Exercise 3
1 What are you doing at the moment?
2 What time does this class finish?
3 What are you learning in English today?
4 What time do you usually get up?
5 Who are you sitting next to now?
6 How often do you go to the beach?

3 Write questions using the present simple or present continuous. Then write answers that are true for you.

1 What / you / do / at the moment?
2 What time / this class / finish?
3 What / you / learn / in English / today?
4 What time / you / usually / get up?
5 Who / you / sit / next to / now?
6 How often / you / go to the beach?

Gerunds and infinitives

4 Look at the table. Match rules a–f with sentences 1–6.

We use gerunds:
a) after certain verbs (*like, love, hate, enjoy, finish, avoid, stop …*)
b) after prepositions (*in, at, for, before …*)
c) as the subject of a sentence
We use infinitives:
d) after certain verbs (*decide, want, hope, remember, afford …*)
e) after adjectives (*easy, happy …*)
f) to explain purpose

1 **Spending** a weekend in New York is exciting!
2 Do you enjoy **sunbathing**?
3 It's easy **to find** space on the beach.
4 Do you want **to get away** from it all?
5 Are you interested in **visiting** ancient sites?
6 Go to Cappadocia **to see** the rock formations.

Exercise 4
1 c
2 a
3 e
4 d
5 b
6 f

5 Copy and complete the questions with the gerund or infinitive form of the verbs. Then write answers that are true for you. Give extra information.

Do you like … (travel)? *travelling*
I love travelling! My favourite place is …

1 Where do you want … (go) on holiday next year?
2 Do you enjoy … (visit) quiet, peaceful places?
3 What do you usually pack before … (go) on holiday?
4 … (practise) your English, where is the best place to go on holiday?

Exercise 5
1 to go
2 visiting
3 going
4 To practise
Students' own answers

6 Copy and complete the text with the gerund or infinitive form of the verbs in brackets.

Let's get organized!

Summer's over. Are you happy (1) … (be) back at school? Here are some tips for (2) … (get) organized:

- Use a planner (3) … (organize) your time.
- When you finish (4) … (do) your homework, remember (5) … (put) it in your school bag immediately.
- (6) … (study) effectively at home, it's important (7) … (create) a study space. Make sure it's calm so that it's easy (8) … (concentrate).
- Avoid (9) … (rush)! (10) … (get) up ten minutes earlier in the morning is a good idea.

Exercise 6
1 to be
2 getting
3 to organize
4 doing
5 to put
6 To study
7 to create
8 to concentrate
9 rushing
10 Getting

Grammar reference > Workbook p82

Vocabulary

Holiday activities: verb + noun collocations

Exercise 1
swim in the sea
lie on the beach
get a suntan
get sunburnt
go snorkelling
go abroad
go sightseeing
take a photo
hire a bike
visit a museum
wear sun cream

1 **Word builder** **Read the information. Then match the verbs in A with the words in B. You can use some verbs more than once. Use your dictionary to help you.**

Collocations
A collocation is two or more words that often go together. When you learn a new collocation, write examples of other words you could use.
hire a car / jet ski
have a barbecue / picnic

A	B
get go hire lie swim take visit wear	abroad a bike a museum a photo a suntan in the sea on the beach sightseeing snorkelling sunburnt sun cream

Exercise 2
Students' own answers

2 **Listen, check and repeat.** 3

Exercise 3
1 a picnic
2 football
3 a photo
4 swim
5 get

3 **Which collocation is incorrect in each of 1–5?**

1 visit **a castle** / **a picnic** / **a museum**
2 go **sightseeing** / **ice-skating** / **football**
3 hire **a bike** / **a photo** / **a car**
4 **relax** / **lie** / **swim** on the beach
5 **travel** / **get** / **go** abroad

Exercise 4
1 travel; By plane
2 voyage; America
3 trip; About 40,000 km
4 journey; Two and a half hours

4 **Read the Look! box. Then complete questions 1–4 with *journey*, *trip*, *voyage* or *travel*. Can you answer the questions?**

1 What is the quickest way to ... from New York to San Francisco?
2 Where did Christopher Columbus and his crew go on their ... in 1492?
3 If you take a ... around the world, how many kilometres will you fly?
4 How long is the train ... from London to Paris?

LOOK!
journey (n) = one occasion when you travel from one place to another
trip (n) = the process of going somewhere and returning
voyage (n) = a long journey by boat or into space
travel (v) = go from one place to another, usually in a vehicle

5 **Read and listen to the text about holiday nightmares. How many collocations in exercise 1 can you find? Write a list.** 4

We hired bikes, ...

Exercise 5
go sightseeing
visit a museum
swim in the sea
lie on the beach
get sunburnt
wear sun cream
go snorkelling
take a photo

HOLIDAY **NIGHTMARES!**

Home About News Comments

Our school trip to Amsterdam a few years ago was a great adventure! We hired bikes to go sightseeing round the city, went to Anne Frank's house and visited the Van Gogh museum. But while we were waiting to fly home, the airport workers went on strike so we had to get the train and ferry. We finally got home 24 hours later!

Annie Share Reply

We used to go abroad every summer to visit my grandparents. Once, we were at the beach and we were all swimming in the sea except my dad. He was lying on the beach because he wanted to finish his book. But while he was reading, he fell asleep and got really sunburnt. Now, he always wears sun cream and stays in the shade!

Jake Share Reply

We had a holiday nightmare last year. On the website, our campsite looked really pretty and peaceful. But when we arrived, builders were constructing a new hotel next door. It was really noisy. Anyway, on the second day, we decided to go snorkelling. I had a special underwater camera, but while I was taking photos of all the colourful fish, a jellyfish stung me. It was so painful!

Georgia Share Reply

Advance your vocabulary > Workbook p102

Vocabulary

Holiday activities: Verb + noun collocations

LESSON OBJECTIVES

In this lesson students will:

- revise a set of collocations related to holiday activities
- read about holiday nightmares

WARMER

Write *summer holiday* on the board. Elicit that this is often a holiday that involves beach-related activities such as sunbathing and swimming. Ask students to work in pairs and write down six things to take on a summer holiday. Listen to their ideas as a class and make a list on the board, eg *a swimsuit*, *sun cream*, *sunglasses*, *mobile phone*, *a camera*, *a book*, *a towel*, *goggles* etc.

1 Word builder

Collocations

- Write the word *collocation* on the board.
- Ask students to read the Word builder and find out that a collocation is two or more words that often go together, eg *make a phone call* (not *do a phone call*).
- They work individually and match the verbs in A with the words in B.
- They compare answers in pairs.

2 3

- Play the audio so that students can check their answers.
- Play the audio again. Students repeat the collocations individually and chorally.
- Check the answers as a class. Point out that go is often followed by activities ending in *-ing*, eg *go swimming*, *go running*, *go cycling*.

LANGUAGE NOTE

Highlight that the main stress in these collocations is never on the verb but is on the noun or adjective, eg *take a photo*, *get sunburnt*.

3
- Point out that in each example, two of the collocations are correct and one is not possible.
- Students work individually to complete the task.
- They compare answers in pairs.
- Check answers as a class.

FINISHED?

Ask fast finishers to write the correct word or phrase that collocates with the words that are incorrect in 1–5 in exercise 3. (**Answer key**: **1** have a picnic, **2** play football, **3** take a photo, **4** swim in the sea, **5** get a suntan / sunburnt)

LOOK!

Ask students to read the definitions in the LOOK! box carefully. Highlight the difference between a *journey* (one way) and a *trip* (away somewhere and back home) and point out that *travel* is a verb.

4
- Students work individually and use the four words in the LOOK! box to fill the gaps in sentences 1–4.
- They answer the questions.
- They compare their answers in pairs.
- Check answers as a class.

5 4

- Explain the task. Students should write a list of the collocations from exercise 1 that they find in the text. Highlight the phrase *We hired bikes* in the text and the example collocation *hire a bike*.
- Play the audio. Students listen and follow the text in the books.
- They find the collocations and write a list.
- Check answers as a class. Eight other collocations are in the text.

Advance your vocabulary > Workbook page 102

Grammar

Past simple and past continuous

LESSON OBJECTIVES
In this lesson students will:

- revise the past simple and the past continuous
- revise *used to*

WARMER

Write on the board: *go*, *come*, *think*, *teach*, *buy*, *tell*, *write*, *find*, *make*, *swim*. Ask students to work in pairs and write the past simple forms of these verbs.

1 • Students read the information and answer questions 1–3. Check answers.

LANGUAGE NOTE

While is normally followed by the past continuous, eg *She got sunburnt while she was lying on the beach. When* can be followed by the past continuous, eg *I saw an accident when I was walking home from school* if the action that follows it is a continuous one in progress at the time. It can also be followed by the past simple if the action that follows it is a single one, eg *I was walking home when I saw an accident.*

2 • Complete the first gap with the whole class as an example (*was studying*). Elicit that we use the past continuous here because the verb comes after *while*.
- Students copy and complete the text. Check answers.
- Elicit which verbs are irregular. Explain that although *spend* is not irregular in the past simple negative (*didn't spend*), it is irregular in the past simple affirmative (*spent*).

3 • Read the example question and the answer *I went to Croatia on holiday* aloud to the class.
- Point out that the tense of each question will be the same as the tense in each answer.
- Students write the questions. Check answers.
- Students write answers to the questions. Listen to some answers.

used to

4 • Students read the information in the table and answer the questions. Check answers.

LANGUAGE NOTE

Used to refers to past habits or states. It cannot be used to talk about single actions in the past. There is no present form of *used to*. To talk about a present habit we use the present simple and the adverb usually, eg *I usually play tennis on Sundays.*

ANALYSE

Highlight the use of *used to* to talk about past habits and ask students how they say this in their language. Ask students to translate the three example sentences in the table in exercise 4 into their language to check they fully understand the concept.

5 • Encourage students to read the whole text first and to refer to the table in exercise 4 to help them with the form. Check answers.

6 • Point out that the short answer to questions with used to is *Yes, I / you / he / she / it / we / you / they did* or *No, I / you / he / she / it / we / you / they didn't.*
- Show how the question is formed from the prompts and the interrogative of *used to*.
- Students write the questions and short answers, using the information in the text. Check answers.

Grammar reference > Workbook page 82

Grammar

Past simple and past continuous

Exercise 1
1 a
2 b
3 past simple after *when*; past continuous after *while*

1 **Look at the table. Read the sentences and answer the questions.**

past simple and past continuous
a) She was taking photos.
b) A jellyfish stung her.
She was taking photos when a jellyfish stung her. = A jellyfish stung her while she was taking photos.

1 Which action was longer, a) or b)?
2 Which action happened at a specific point in time?
3 Which tense do we use after *when*? Which tense do we use after *while*?

Exercise 2
1 was studying
2 asked
3 said
4 had
5 was waiting
6 was staying
7 visited
8 didn't spend
have and *spend* are irregular

2 **Copy and complete the text with the past simple or past continuous form of the verbs in brackets. Which verbs are irregular?**

My best holiday was a trip to New York last summer. While I (1) … (study) for my GCSEs, my parents (2) … (ask): 'Do you want to visit Uncle David in the USA after your exams?' Of course I (3) … (say) yes! David was living in Manhattan because he (4) … (have) a job there. I flew to JFK airport and David (5) … (wait) for me. While I (6) … (stay) there, we went sightseeing. We (7) … (visit) the Statue of Liberty and the Empire State Building. I (8) … (not spend) long in New York, but it was fantastic!

Exercise 3
1 What were you doing last May?
2 When did school start again?
3 What time did you get up?
4 What were you doing at midnight last night?
Students' own answers

3 **Write questions for the phrases in bold. Use the past simple or past continuous. Then write answers that are true for you.**

I went **to Croatia** on holiday. (Where …?)
Where did you go on holiday?

1 I was **lying on the beach** last May. (What …?)
2 School started again **on 1st September**. (When …?)
3 I got up **at six o'clock**. (What time …?)
4 I was **doing my homework** at midnight last night. (What …?)

used to

Exercise 4
1 infinitive without *to*
2 It changes to *did/didn't use to.*

4 **Look at the table. Read the sentences and answer the questions.**

used to
They used to go abroad every summer.
They didn't use to stay at home.
Did you use to go abroad on holiday?

1 What is the form of the verb after *used to*?
2 How does *used to* change in the negative and question forms?

ANALYSE

In English, we use *used to* to talk about habits in the past. How do you say *used to* in your language?

Exercise 5
1 didn't use to go
2 used to stay
3 used to rain
4 didn't use to stay
5 used to go
6 used to come

5 **Copy and complete the text with the correct form of *used to* and the verbs in brackets.**

Holiday memories

Last summer, I went to France with my parents. But when I was younger we (1) … (not go) abroad. We (2) … (stay) in a caravan in Blackpool and it (3) … (rain) all the time. I was always jealous of my friend Marie. Her family (4) … (not stay) in England. They (5) … (go) to a villa in Spain. Marie always (6) … (come) home with a suntan and stories about exotic places.
Katy, 17

Exercise 6
1 Did Katy use to go to Blackpool? Yes, she did.
2 Did Katy use to stay in a hotel? No, she didn't.
3 Did Marie use to go abroad? Yes, she did.
4 Did Marie use to stay in a caravan? No, she didn't.
5 Did Katy use to get a suntan? No, she didn't.

6 **Write questions with the correct form of *used to*. Then write answers with information from the text in exercise 5.**

Katy / go abroad?
Did Katy use to go abroad?
No, she didn't.

1 Katy / go to Blackpool?
2 Katy / stay in a hotel?
3 Marie / go abroad?
4 Marie / stay in a caravan?
5 Katy / get a suntan?

Grammar reference > Workbook p82

Comparatives and superlatives

1 **Match sentences a–f with 1–6. Then write answers to the questions with your opinions.**

Exercise 1
1 e
2 a
3 b
4 f
5 c
6 d

comparatives and superlatives
a) Which is more comfortable, a car or a bus?
b) Which is better, a vacation or a 'staycation*'?
c) What is the most popular tourist attraction in your region?
d) Where can you eat the best local food in your town?
e) Which is faster, a train or a plane?
f) Where is the longest bridge in the world?

*A 'staycation' is when you stay at home for your holiday!

1 regular comparative (short adjective)
2 regular comparative (long adjective)
3 irregular comparative
4 regular superlative (short adjective)
5 regular superlative (long adjective)
6 irregular superlative

2 **Look at the information. Then copy and complete the sentences with one word only.**

Exercise 2
1 as
2 not
3 than
4 less

LOOK!
= as ... as
≠ not as ... as
› more ... than
‹ less ... than

1 Florence is interesting. Venice is interesting. Florence is as interesting ... Venice.
2 Ankara is big. Istanbul is bigger. Ankara is ... as big as Istanbul.
3 Cádiz is ancient. Athens is more ancient. Athens is more ancient ... Cádiz.
4 Edinburgh is expensive. London is very expensive. Edinburgh is ... expensive than London.

LOOK!
In English we can use comparative structures with the verb *get* to show a changing situation.
Our English is getting **better and better**.
These exercises are getting **more and more difficult**.
We use *...er and ...er* with short and irregular adjectives. We use *more and more* ... with long adjectives.

Question tags

3 **Look at the table and choose the correct words in rules a–c.**

Exercise 3
a negative
b affirmative
c subject pronouns

question tags
Question tags are small questions that we often use at the end of sentences to check information when we're speaking. The longest bridge in the world **is** in China, isn't it?
If the first verb has got a modal, we use the same modal in the question tag. Cars **can't** travel across it, can they?
If there's no auxiliary verb in the first part, we use the correct form of *do* in the question tag. The bridge **starts** in Shanghai, doesn't it? They **built** more than 160 km, didn't they?

a) If the sentence is affirmative, the question tag is **affirmative** / **negative**.
b) If the sentence is negative, the question tag is **affirmative** / **negative**.
c) We always use **names or nouns** / **subject pronouns** in question tags.

4 **Copy and complete question tags. Use the auxiliary verbs in the correct affirmative or negative form, and remember to use subject pronouns.**

Exercise 4
1 is it
2 hasn't she
3 are there
4 can't you
5 isn't it

1 The Brooklyn Bridge isn't the longest bridge in the USA, ...?
2 Your sister has been to New York, ...?
3 There aren't any beaches in Austria, ...?
4 You can speak German, ...?
5 It's your birthday soon, ...?

5 **Copy and complete question tags. As there are no auxiliary verbs, use the correct form of *do*.**

Exercise 5
1 didn't she
2 doesn't it
3 do they
4 don't they
5 didn't they
6 didn't you

1 Your sister went to Edinburgh last year, ...?
2 It often rains in Scotland, ...?
3 People don't speak Spanish in Brazil, ...?
4 They dance samba there, ...?
5 Your cousins lived in China, ...?
6 You saw the Danyang–Kunshan Bridge, ...?

Grammar reference > Workbook p83

Grammar

Comparatives and superlatives

LESSON OBJECTIVES
In this lesson students will:

- revise comparatives and superlatives
- revise question tags

WARMER

Write three questions on the board: **1** *What's the highest mountain in the world?* **2** *What's the biggest city in the world?* **3** *What's the most beautiful city in your country?* Students discuss the answers in small groups. (**Answer key: 1** Mount Everest **2** The Nile **3** Students' own answers.)

1 • Explain the task. Students match the sentences with the different types of comparatives and superlatives.
• They work individually and write answers to the questions. Check answers as a class.

CULTURE NOTE

The world's longest bridge is the Danyang–Kunshan Grand Bridge in China, which is part of the high-speed railway from Beijing to Shanghai. It opened in 2011 and is 165 kilometres long.

LOOK!

Refer students to the information in the LOOK! box. Remind them that *less than* is the opposite of *more than*. Explain that *as ... as* means the two things you are comparing are the same. *Not as ... as* means they are not the same. e.g. *Sara is as tall as Josh*, this means they are the same height. *Josh isn't as old as Sara* means that they aren't the same. Josh is younger than Sara.

2 • Students read the Look! box.
• They copy the sentences into their notebooks and write in the missing words.
• Check answers as a class.

LOOK!

Refer students to the information in the LOOK! box. If necessary add some more examples, e.g. *It's getting colder and colder. Air travel is getting more and more popular.*

Question tags

3 • Ask students to read the information in the table and then choose the correct answers to complete the rules about question tags.
• Highlight the fact that the form of the question tag will change depending on the type of verb used before it (modal/auxiliary verb or normal verb).
• Emphasise the fact that positive sentences have negative question tags and negative sentences positive question tags.

4 • Point out that these sentences all use auxiliary verbs or modal verbs so the question tag will use the same auxiliary or modal verbs.
• Students work individually to complete the task. Check answers as a class.

5 • Emphasise that these sentences, with one exception, don't use auxiliary verbs, so the correct form and tense of *do* must be used in the question tags.
• Students work individually to complete the task.
• They compare answers in pairs.
• Check answers as a class.

Grammar reference > Workbook page 83

UNIT 1

TEAMWORK

UNIT OBJECTIVES AND KEY COMPETENCES

In this unit the student will learn …

- to recognize, understand, and correctly use vocabulary related to skills and abilities and words associated with life skills **CLC SCC CAE**
- to recognize, understand and correctly use the present perfect with *just, yet, already, for and since* **CLC L2L**
- to understand and correctly use the present perfect and past simple and to know when to use which **CLC L2L**
- what social awareness is and how it relates to their own life **CLC CMST SCC SIE**
- about attending informal interviews **CLC DC SCC**

In this unit the student will learn …

- to understand reference words in a text about illusionists **CLC SCC CAE**
- to look online for more information about magic tricks and illusions **CLC DC SCC CAE SIE**
- to listen for specific information in a discussion about life skills **CLC CMST SCC**
- to read job descriptions, listen to an informal interview, prepare for and practise an informal interview **CLC CMST SCC SIE**
- to write a blog post **CLC SCC SIE L2L**

LINGUISTIC CONTENTS

Main vocabulary

- Skills and abilities: *bake cupcakes, learn to juggle, design a website*, etc
- Life skills: *creative thinking*, *self-awareness*, *respect for others*, etc

Extra vocabulary

- Words in context: *assist, illusion, blade, audience, a.k.a., levitate*
- Word builder: Suffixes for people: *assist (v) › assistant (n), illusion (n) › illusionist (n)*
- Word families: *self awareness (n) / be self-aware (v), problem-solving (n) / solve problems (v)*

Grammar

- Present perfect with *just, yet, already, for* and *since*
- Present perfect and past simple

Functional language

- Talking about your skills and interests

Pronunciation

- *-tion* endings

SKILLS

Reading

- Read an article about illusionists
- Read a text about social awareness
- Read a notice about committee roles at a youth club
- Read a pop band's blog

Writing: Interaction and production

- Write notes and answers to prepare for an interview for a committee role
- Learn how to use adverbs of degree

Listening

- Listen to people making a video blog about a life skills day
- Listen to a model interview

Spoken interaction

- Exchange information about experiences of life skills
- Ask and answer questions using *How long …?* and the present perfect

Spoken production

- Prepare and act out an informal interview

LIFELONG LEARNING SKILLS

Self-study and self-evaluation

- Study guide: Student's Book page 99
- Progress check: Workbook page 14
- Extension: Workbook page 15
- Grammar reference and practice: Workbook pages 84–85
- Wordlist: Workbook pages 151–157

Learning strategies and thinking skills

- Understanding reference words
- Critical thinking: suggesting reasons
- Study strategies for effective revision and developing efficient study habits

Social awareness

- National Citizen Service
- The importance of using life skills at school and at home

Cross-curricular contents

- Literature: *Slumdog Millionaire* by Vikas Swarup
- ICT: searching the internet for information about an author and his/her works

EVALUATION

- Unit 1 End-of-unit test: Basic, Standard and Extra
- CEFR Skills Exam Generator

KEY COMPETENCES

CLC	Competence in linguistic communication
CMST	Competence in mathematics, science and technology
DC	Digital competence
SCC	Social and civic competence
CAE	Cultural awareness and expression
L2L	Learning to learn
SIE	Sense

DIGITAL MATERIAL

New Pulse Digital Course including:

- Interactive vocabulary presentation
- Grammar and Vocabulary basics exercises
- Getting started video
- Flipped classroom grammar video: Present perfect
- Culture byte video: Sleep to success
- Speaking sketch video: An informal interview

DIGITAL COMPETENCE

- Web quest: Find out more about tricks and illusions
- Digital competence worksheet: Online posters

REINFORCEMENT MATERIAL

- New Pulse Basics: Teacher's Resource Centre
- Vocabulary and grammar consolidation worksheets: Teacher's Resource Centre
- Grammar and Vocabulary basics exercises: Teacher's Presentation Kit

EXTENSION MATERIAL

- Vocabulary and grammar extension worksheets: Teacher's Resource Centre
- Advance your vocabulary: Workbook page 103
- The longer read: Teacher's Resource Centre
- Writing hub: Workbook page 112

TEACHER'S RESOURCE MATERIAL

- Translation and dictation
- Evaluation rubrics
- Key competences worksheets
- Culture and CLIL worksheets
- Culture byte video worksheets
- Digital competence worksheets
- Macmillan Readers worksheets
- Integrated skills

Vocabulary

Skills and abilities

LESSON OBJECTIVES

In this lesson students will:

- learn words related to life skills
- ask and answer questions about their experiences of life skills
- read a bucket list

Video: Getting started

In this video the speakers answer the question: *Do you have a bucket list? What's on it?*

Focus the students on the unit title *Teamwork*.

- Write the following sentences on the board:
  1 Who played in a band at a school concert?
  2 Who wants to climb Mount Everest?
  3 Who has never been abroad before?
- Students watch the video and answer the questions on the board.
- Students watch the video again to check answers.
- At the end of the lesson, ask students to answer the question from the video: *Do you have a bucket list? What's on it?*

Answer key: 1 Olivia **2** Josh **3** Emily

WARMER

Use lines to represent the letters of *bucket list* and write them on the board: _ _ _ _ _ _ _ _ _ _. Students suggest letters of the alphabet to guess the phrase. Check they understand the meaning: a list of things you want to do during your life.

1 5

- Students read the phrases in blue.
- Play the audio. Students listen and repeat.
- Elicit the skills shown (*bake cupcakes, perform on stage*).
- If you are using the TPK and your students need more work on the meaning of the words, do the Vocabulary basics exercise.

Vocabulary basics

Key: 1 baking cupcakes **2** learning a foreign language **3** performing on stage **4** writing a song **5** making a video blog **6** speaking in public

LANGUAGE NOTE

The verbs in the phrases in the box do not carry the main stress. In phrases like *play in a band, ride a unicycle, speak in public*, the main stress in each phrase is on the last word, eg *play in a band*. In compound nouns like *magic tricks, video blog* and *computer code*, the main stress is on the first word in the compound noun, eg *do magic tricks*.

2 • Students read the definitions and find the words in the bucket list.
• Check answers as a class.

3 • Elicit which of verbs are irregular.
• Students check the past participles of the irregular verbs in the Student's Book table on pages 126–127.

CULTURE NOTE

The first video blog (vlog) was posted in January 2000 when an American called Adam Kontras added a video to his blog. In the vlog, he informed his friends about his forthcoming move across the USA to Los Angeles. Video sharing is now one of the most popular activities on the Internet.

4 • Nominate two students to read aloud the example question and the two different answers. Highlight the use of the past simple in the follow-up statement to the affirmative short answer (*I baked them last summer*) and elicit that we use this tense because it describes an event at a fixed point in the past (*last summer*). Highlight the use of the present perfect in the follow-up statement to the negative short answers (*But I've made a pizza!*) and elicit that we use this tense because it describes a past action when no time is mentioned.
• Students ask and answer questions about the skills. Find out which students have done the different things.

EXTRA ACTIVITY

Students choose three activities they have never done that they would like to try and give reasons for their choices.

TEAMWORK

UNIT 1

LEARNING OUTCOMES IN THIS UNIT
- Understand reference words in a text
- Listen for specific information in a discussion
- Practise an informal interview
- Write a blog post about a talent contest

VIDEO: GETTING STARTED

WATCH

Watch the teenagers talking about skills and answer the question.

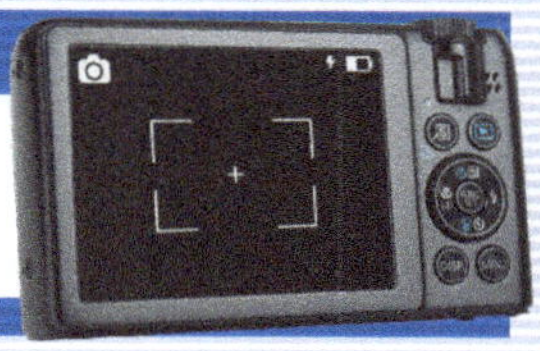

Vocabulary
Skills and abilities

Exercise 1
bake cupcakes, perform on stage

1 Look at the bucket list. Listen and repeat the words in blue. Which things can you see in the photos? 5

My Summer Bucket List

1 bake cupcakes
2 catch a fish
3 design a website
4 do magic tricks
5 do something for charity
6 edit photos
7 fly a kite
8 go to a concert
9 go to a museum
10 go to the beach
11 learn a foreign language
12 learn first aid
13 learn to juggle
14 make a new friend
15 make a video blog
16 perform on stage
17 play in a band
18 read three books
19 ride a unicycle
20 run a 5K race
21 speak in public
22 watch a sunset
23 watch ten films
24 write a song
25 write computer code

Exercise 2
1 unicycle
2 first aid
3 juggle
4 bake
5 perform

2 Find words in the bucket list that mean …

1 a bicycle with a single wheel (n)
2 basic medical treatment (n)
3 to keep objects moving through the air by catching them as they fall (v)
4 to make cakes or bread in an oven (v)
5 to do something in front of an audience in order to entertain them (v)

Exercise 3
do, learn, make, ride, speak, write
do – done
learn – learnt
make – made
ride – ridden
speak – spoken
write – written

3 Look at the verbs. Which ones are irregular? Check the past participle form of the irregular verbs on pages 126–127.

- bake
- design
- do
- edit
- learn
- make
- perform
- play
- ride
- speak
- write

do – done

4 Work in pairs. Ask and answer questions using the words in blue and *Have you ever …?* Give extra information.

Have you ever baked cupcakes?

Yes, I have. I baked them last summer. / No, I haven't. But I've made a pizza!

Exercise 4
Students' own answers

Q&A *Have you ever …*

1 baked cupcakes?
2 …

Exercise 1

Leah Mae Devine is a dance student. **Sarah Jade** is Leah Mae's younger sister. She's Leah Mae's assistant. **Dynamo** is an illusionist whose real name is Steven Frayne. He's the star of the 'Seeing is believing' tour. **Katherine Mills** is the first female magician to get her own show on British TV. She's a psychology graduate.

Exercise 2

It = magic
She = Leah Mae Devine
Her = Katherine Mills
Their = Leah Mae and Sarah Jade's mother
She = Leah Mae and Sarah Jade's mother
That = the cut her assistant in half magician trick
Who = Sarah Jade
Them = Leah Mae or Sarah Jade
He = Dynamo

Exercise 3

1 b
2 b
3 c
4 a

Reading

A feature article

LEARNING OUTCOME

✔ Understand reference words

1 Read and listen to the text. Who are these people? Make two sentences for each person, using information a–g. 6

- Leah Mae Devine
- Sarah Jade
- Dynamo
- Katherine Mills

a female illusionist *Leah Mae Devine is a female illusionist.*

a) Leah Mae's younger sister
b) an illusionist whose real name is Steven Frayne
c) a dance student
d) the first female magician to get her own show on British TV
e) a psychology graduate
f) Leah Mae's assistant
g) the star of the 'Seeing is believing' tour

2 Read the information. Who or what do the words in bold in the text refer to?

one = an illusionist

UNDERSTAND REFERENCE WORDS
Reference words refer back to people or things already mentioned, or add more information about someone or something. They are words like subject, object or possessive pronouns (*they*, *them*, *their*, ...), demonstrative pronouns (*this*, *these*, ...) or relative pronouns (*who*, *which*, ...).

3 Read the text again and choose the correct answers.

1 Leah Mae Devine has been a magician ...
a) all her life.
b) since she was eight.
c) since the age of ten.

2 Leah Mae's mother ...
a) loved doing card tricks.
b) used to do magic.
c) wasn't interested in magic.

3 Leah Mae and Sarah Jade ...
a) are both members of the Magic Circle.
b) have been hurt doing a trick.
c) work together during the magic show.

4 Dynamo and Katherine Mills have both ...
a) made illusionism more popular.
b) worked with David Blaine.
c) written a book about magic.

DID YOU KNOW?

The Magic Circle is a British organization dedicated to promoting the art of magic. It was set up in 1905 as a 'Gentleman's club' but changed its rules in 1991 to accept membership from female magicians. There are now 1,500 members and 100 of these are female. To become a member, you have to pass a magic exam, although there is also a Young Magicians Club which is open to anyone aged 10–18.

If you've ever been amazed watching illusionists like Dynamo on television, then Leah Mae Devine is **one** to watch out for in the future.

Leah Mae has already made history by becoming the first female magician to win the prestigious 'Young Magician of the Year' competition. 'The biggest myth about magic is that "girls can't do **it**",' says Leah Mae, talking to *The Independent* newspaper. **She** is now among the Magic Circle's around 7% of female members.

Just an illusion?

In recent years, illusionists like Dynamo and Katherine Mills have helped bring magic to a wider audience. Katherine Mills, a psychology graduate who was inspired by the American magician David Blaine when she was a teenager, became the first female magician to get **her** own show on British TV.

4 Words in context Find these words in the text. Match them with definitions a–f.

assist illusion blade audience a.k.a. levitate

a) 'also known as'
b) to rise and float in the air as if by magic
c) to help someone
d) the sharp part of a knife
e) an appearance or effect that is different from the way things really are
f) a group of people who have come to a place to see or hear a film, performance or show

Exercise 4

a) a.k.a.
b) levitate
c) assist
d) blade
e) illusion
f) audience

The longer read > Resource centre

Reading

A feature article

LESSON OBJECTIVES
In this lesson students will:

- understand reference words
- learn noun suffixes for people

WARMER

Write the words *magic* and *illusion* on the board and check students understand what they mean. Then elicit the words for people who *do magic* or *create illusions* – *magician* and *illusionist*. Highlight the difference in stress between *magic* and *magician*.

1 6

- Explain the task. Students should match the pieces of information (a–g) with the four people, making two full sentences for each person.
- Play the audio. Students read and listen to the text and write sentences in their notebooks.
- Check answers as a class.

READING STRATEGY

Understand reference words

Being able to recognize which words pronouns such as *one*, *this* and *which* refer to is an important skill as it enables students to read texts more effectively.

2
- Students read the information about reference words.
- They write down in their notebooks which words the ten reference words in bold in the text refer to. Check answers as a class.

3
- Students read the questions and the different possible answers first. They read the text again and find the answers.
- Students compare their answers in pairs.
- Check answers as a class.

4 Words in Context

- Students find the words in the box in the text to see them in context.
- They match the words to definitions a–f.
- Check answers as a class.

EXTRA ACTIVITY

Focus on the pronunciation of some of the other vocabulary in the text, eg *magician* /mə'ʤɪʃən/, *prestigious* /prə'stɪʤəs/, *illusion* /ɪ'lu:ʒən/, *audience* /ɔ:dɪəns/.

DID YOU KNOW?

Highlight the *Did you know?* box. Students read about The Magic Circle and concentrate on the figures.

5 • Students decide what the numbers and dates in the *Did you know?* box refer to.
• Check answers as a class.

6 • Students read the questions carefully first. Emphasise that they should try to answer the questions in their own words and not copy from the text.
• They work individually and write answers in their notebooks. Check answers as a class.

7 Word Builder
• Write the word *teach* on the board and elicit the suffix that forms the noun: *teacher*. Students read the information in the box and find the nouns in the text for *dance* and *magic*.
• Check answers as a class. Remind students that verbs ending in *'e'* only add *-r* as a suffix when forming nouns (e.g. *juggler*).

8 • Students read the three questions first and note down their ideas.
• Students work in pairs asking and answering the questions.
• Check answers as a class. Students report what their partner said.

CRITICAL THINKING

• Explain the task and highlight the different factors students should consider when answering the questions.
• They work individually and note down possible answers.
• Listen to their ideas as a class.

WEB QUEST

Students watch different magic trick videos and find illusions that they like.

1 **Investigate** Students choose which illusions they want to find out about and open the official website.
2 **Communicate** Students work in groups comparing their illusions.

TIP! Highlight the fact that students should search for the celebrity's official websites. Point out that some people make unofficial websites and that these might not be secure, might not be reliable for facts and should be avoided.

VIDEO: FLIPPED CLASSROOM

You may want to ask Students to watch the Flipped classroom video for unit 1 as homework in preparation for the following grammar lesson. The Flipped grammar presentation focuses on the present perfect with *just, yet, already, for* and *since*.

The longer read > Resource centre

As if by magic!

Assisted by her younger sister Sarah Jade, Leah Mae has been a magician for about ten years, since the age of eight. The sisters used to watch **their** mother doing magic – **she** did more illusions than card tricks – and Leah Mae always knew that she wanted to be a magician.

So what does the future hold for Leah Mae? At the moment, she is studying dance, and a future on the stage looks likely, either as a dancer or a magician, because she has always loved performing.

And what about the trick where the magician cuts her assistant in half – does Leah Mae do **that**? Yes – but with a difference. It's Leah Mae who goes into the box and her sister **who** holds the blade. But neither of **them** has ever been hurt – not yet, anyway!

Dynamo (a.k.a. Steven Frayne) has amazed audiences worldwide with his 'Seeing is believing' tour. **He** has 'levitated' above the Shard building in London and 'walked on water' across the River Thames. Now he has just published his first book of magic secrets, so if you haven't learnt any new tricks yet, what are you waiting for?!

Exercise 5
1,500 = the total number of members in the Magic Circle
10–18 = the ages accepted by the Young Magicians Club
1991 = the year the Magic Circle started accepting female members
100 = the total number of female members

5 Read the information in the 'Did you know?' box. What do these numbers and dates refer to?

• 1905 • 1,500 • 10–18 • 1991 • 100

1905 = the year when the Magic Circle was set up

Exercise 6
Students' own answers

6 Answer the questions in your own words.

1 How did Leah Mae 'make history'?
2 Give an example of how Sarah Jade assists her sister.
3 When did Katherine Mills become interested in magic and illusions?
4 Give two examples of Dynamo's illusions.
5 What is Dynamo's book about?

7 **Word builder** Read the information and answer the questions.

SUFFIXES FOR PEOPLE
We add suffixes like *-(e)r*, *-or*, *-ant*, *-ist* and *-ian* to nouns or verbs to make nouns for people.
assist (v) > *assistant* (n)
illusion (n) > *illusionist* (n)

1 Find nouns for people in the text that are related to these words.

dance magic

2 Which suffix do we use to make the nouns for people related to these words?

design juggle perform sing code

Exercise 7
1 dancer, magician
2 designer, juggler, performer, singer, coder

8 Work in pairs. Ask and answer the questions.

1 Can you do any magic tricks? If so, how did you learn?
2 Have you heard of any of these magicians before reading the text? Have you seen any of them on TV?
3 In your opinion, which trick or illusion mentioned in the text sounds the most interesting? Can you think of a logical explanation for it?

Exercise 8
Students' own answers

CRITICAL THINKING

SUGGEST REASONS

About 93% of Magic Circle members are male. What examples can you find in the text to show how opportunities for female magicians are changing?

Suggest reasons why only about 7% of Magic Circle members are female. Think about:

- the historical situation
- changing opportunities
- role models
- self-confidence
- ability

WEB QUEST

Work in groups of three. Find video clips of magic tricks and illusions online.

1 **Investigate** Each choose one of these illusionists. Go online and find videos of their illusions.
• Dynamo • Katherine Mills • David Blaine
2 **Communicate** Share your favourite illusion with your group.

TIP! When researching people, use official websites if possible. For example, the keywords 'Dynamo official website' will take you to Dynamo's own website.

Grammar

Present perfect with *just*, *yet*, *already*, *for* and *since*

VIDEO: FLIPPED CLASSROOM

WATCH

Watch the grammar presentation and do the task.

Exercise 1
1 Between the auxiliary verb *have* / *has* and the past participle.
2 recently
3 Students' own answers

1 Read the sentences in the table and answer the questions.

just
We've **just** read an article about magicians. Dynamo has **just** published a book.

1 Where does *just* go in the sentence?
2 Did these actions happen recently or some time ago?
3 How do you say expressions with *just* in your language?

Exercise 2
1 Because we've just watched a funny film.
2 Because I've just fallen off my unicycle.
3 Because my brother has just baked cupcakes.
4 Because the programme has just finished.
5 Because I've just finished this exercise.

2 Write answers using *just* and the words in brackets.

Why are you so happy? (I / learn a new trick)
Because I've just learnt a new trick.

1 Why are you laughing? (we / watch a funny film)
2 Why is your knee bleeding? (I / fall off my unicycle)
3 Why does the kitchen smell so good? (my brother / bake cupcakes)
4 Why did you turn off the TV? (the programme / finish)
5 Why are you so pleased? (I / finish this exercise)

Exercise 3
Yet usually goes at the end of the sentence. *Already* usually goes between the auxiliary verb *have* / *has* and the past participle.

3 Read the sentences in the table. Where do *yet* and *already* usually go in the sentence?

yet and *already*
Leah Mae has **already** joined the Magic Circle. She hasn't finished college **yet**. Have you seen her perform **yet**?

4 Look at the information and write sentences about Aisha and Ben.

Aisha has already learnt to juggle.
Ben hasn't learnt to juggle yet.

School of circus skills	Aisha	Ben
1 learn to juggle	✔	✘
2 ride a unicycle	✘	✔
3 do magic tricks	✔	✔
4 perform on stage	✘	✘

Exercise 4
2 Aisha hasn't ridden a unicycle yet. Ben has already ridden a unicycle.
3 Aisha has already done magic tricks. Ben has already done magic tricks.
4 Aisha hasn't performed on stage yet. Ben hasn't performed on stage yet.

5 Read the sentences in the table. Translate answers a) and b) into your language. How do you say *for* and *since* in your language?

for, *since* and *How long ...?*
How long has Leah Mae been a magician? **a)** She's been a magician **for** ten years. (= a duration of time) **b)** She's been a magician **since** she was eight. (= a point in time)

Exercise 5
Students' own answers

6 Write sentences with information that is true for you. Use *for* or *since* and the present perfect form of the verbs in brackets.

(be) in this classroom
I've been in this classroom for ten minutes / since ten o'clock.

1 (study) English
2 (have) this book
3 (know) my teacher
4 (be) at this school
5 (live) in this town
6 (be) a teenager

Exercise 6
Students' own answers

7 Write questions about the things in exercise 6. Use *How long ...?* and the present perfect. In pairs, ask and answer the questions.

How long have you studied English?
I've studied English for / since ...

Exercise 7
Students' own answers

ANALYSE

just yet already for since ever never

In English, we use the present perfect with all these time expressions. Which tenses do you use in your language?

Grammar reference > Workbook p84

Grammar

Present perfect with *just, yet, already, for* and *since*

LESSON OBJECTIVES
In this lesson students will:
- learn how to use the present perfect with *just*, *yet* and *already*
- revise the use of *for* and *since* with time expressions

WARMER

Write the sentence *He has just published his first book* on the board with the words in the wrong order. Students work in pairs and write the question in the correct order.

VIDEO: FLIPPED CLASSROOM

- If you set the video for homework, Students compare their Task time! answers and then check the answers as a class.
- If you didn't set it for homework, watch the video in class and answer the Task time! questions at the end of the presentation.

Answer key: 1 true **2** false **3** true

1
- Students read the sentences in the table.
- They answer questions 1–3.
- Elicit that *'ve* is the contraction of *have*.
- Students translate the two example sentences into their language.

2
- Highlight the example question and answer with the whole class.
- Students work individually to complete the task and compare answers in pairs.
- Check answers as a class. Point out that fallen is an irregular past participle.
- If you are using the TPK and your students need more practice of the grammar, do the Grammar basics exercise.

Grammar basics

Answer key: 1 Luke has just gone to bed. **2** I've just baked the cupcakes, now I need to make the sandwiches. **3** We've just had dinner, I'm not hungry. **4** Mason and Ava have just done the class on editing photos. **5** We've got maths in ten minutes and I've just finished my homework now! **6** Monica's plane has just landed now

LANGUAGE NOTE

Point out that we normally use the contracted form (*'ve / 's*) in speech after personal pronouns. The full form (*have / has*) is more common after nouns, as in the answers to questions 3 and 4 in exercise 2.

3
- Students work in pairs to answer the questions.
- Highlight the fact that we use *already* in positive sentences to say that something happened earlier than expected. Point out that we use *yet* in negative sentences and questions to talk about things we expect to happen.

4
- Highlight the example sentence and check students understand the task.
- Check answers.

5
- Elicit the translations of the answers from the class and how students say *for* and *since* in their language.
- Highlight that we use *for* followed by time expressions to describe a duration of time (eg *for ten minutes, for an hour*) and we use *since* to describe when the action started. (eg *since 8 o'clock, since Tuesday, since 2018*). We use *How long ...?* to ask a question about the duration of time.

FINISHED?

Write these time expressions on the board: *a long time, two weeks, 9.30, 2011, 15th January, six months, three hours, Tuesday*. Elicit which expressions go with *for* and which go with *since*. (**Answer key**: ***for***: a long time, two weeks, six months, three hours; ***since***: 9.30, 2011, 15th January, Tuesday)

6
- Students write complete sentences that are true for them in the present perfect with *for* or *since* using prompts 1–6.

7
- Students write questions. They then work in pairs and ask and answer the questions. Point out that in question 3, the pronoun *my* changes to *your*.

ANALYSE

Elicit the tenses used with *just, yet, already, for, since, ever, never* in the students' language. Highlight that we usually use the present perfect with these expressions in English.

Grammar reference > Workbook page 84

Vocabulary and Listening
Life skills

LESSON OBJECTIVES
In this lesson students will:
- learn some vocabulary related to life skills
- listen for specific information

WARMER
Write this word on the board with the letters all jumbled up: *t e v a c e i r*. In pairs students put the letters in the correct order to spell a word that collocates with *thinking*.
(**Answer key:** *creative*)

DIGITAL VOCABULARY FLASHCARDS
In this digital presentation, students match the vocabulary with definitions.
- Do the digital presentation with the class.
- Encourage students to repeat the words.

1 7
- Students read the text and note down which of the life skills they have used on this particular day.
- Play the audio. Students listen and repeat the words in blue. Make sure they stress the words correctly.
- If you are using the TPK and your students need more work on the meaning of the words, do the Vocabulary basics exercise.

Vocabulary basics
Answer key: 1 f **2** a **3** e **4** d **5** c **6** b

LANGUAGE NOTE
Highlight the main stress in the phrases with adjective + noun (*active listening, creative thinking*) and in those formed with noun + noun (*conflict resolution, money management, time management*).

CULTURE NOTE
As well as learning traditional academic subjects, students also need to learn life skills that will help them not just with their education, but also future employment and other areas of life. In the UK, school students are often taught these skills in PSHE (Personal, Social, Health and Economic Education) classes.

2 Word Builder
- Show how the nouns in the examples in the Word builder are changed into verb forms in the right-hand column.
- Students copy and complete the table. Check answers.

3
- Students discuss the questions in pairs.

4 8
- Read the three questions aloud to the class. Students read the information in the notice and note down their answers to each question.
- Play the audio. Students listen and check their answers.

For audioscript, see page T14

5
- Students have to match the names with the life skills they talk about. Play the audio again.
- Check answers as a class.

6
- Students read the questions first. Encourage students to give full answers.
- Students listen and check their answers.

EXTRA ACTIVITY
Put students into pairs. Ask them to take turns to dictate the two girls' reports from the workshop to their partner. Student A dictates Bella's report to Student B, who writes it down. Student B then checks his or her writing by comparing it with the original version. They then swap roles and Student B dictates Tessa's report to Student A.

Advance your vocabulary > Workbook page 103

Pronunciation lab > *-tion* endings > Student's Book page 124

Vocabulary and Listening

Life skills

LEARNING OUTCOME

✔ Listen for specific information in a discussion

DIGITAL VOCABULARY FLASHCARDS

Do the matching exercise to discover the new vocabulary.

active listening assertiveness conflict resolution cooperation creative thinking entrepreneurship money management negotiation problem-solving respect for others self-awareness time management

Exercise 1
Students' own answers

1 Read the text. Which of these life skills have you used today? Listen and repeat the words in blue. 7

What are life skills?

Life skills help us to participate in all aspects of our life successfully. Here are some different life skills:

- **SELF-AWARENESS:** understanding our own feelings and abilities
- **PROBLEM-SOLVING:** the process of finding solutions to problems
- **CREATIVE THINKING:** generating new ideas or new ways of doing things
- **TIME MANAGEMENT:** organizing our time effectively
- **COOPERATION:** when people work together
- **ACTIVE LISTENING:** the ability to listen effectively
- **NEGOTIATION:** trying to reach an agreement that everybody accepts
- **RESPECT FOR OTHERS:** treating other people with kindness and tolerance
- **CONFLICT RESOLUTION:** facilitating a peaceful end to conflict
- **ENTREPRENEURSHIP:** starting a new business or being innovative
- **ASSERTIVENESS:** the confidence to express our own opinions
- **MONEY MANAGEMENT:** being able to budget money effectively

Exercise 2
time management – manage your time
cooperation – cooperate
active listening – listen actively
negotiation – negotiate
respect for others – respect others
conflict **resolution** – solve conflicts
entrepreneurship – be enterprising
assertiveness – be assertive
money management – manage your money

2 Word builder Read the information. Then copy and complete the table with the other life skills in exercise 1. Use your dictionary to help you.

WORD FAMILIES: NOUNS AND VERBS

noun	verb
self-awareness	be self-aware
problem-solving	solve problems
creative thinking	think creatively

Exercise 3
Students' own answers

3 Have you ever learnt life skills at school? Which ones?

4 Look at the information below and guess the answers to questions 1–3. Then listen and check. 8

1 Who will you hear?
2 What will they talk about?
3 Will you hear a monologue, a dialogue or a discussion?

Exercise 4
Possible answers:
1 Young people who have attended the workshop to improve life skills.
2 What they have learnt.
3 Monologues.

LIFE SKILLS DAY

FRIDAY 27TH SEPTEMBER

at Newville Community School

A day of workshops to improve your life skills!

Final session (4–5pm)

In this final session we'll talk about what you've learnt, and you can give us your feedback.

Come and help us to make a vlog about your experiences!

5 Listen again. Match students 1–5 with five of the life skills in a–g.

1 Dan
2 Bella
3 Chris
4 Tessa
5 Joe

a) assertiveness
b) creative thinking
c) money management
d) time management
e) entrepreneurship
f) conflict resolution
g) active listening

Exercise 5
1 c
2 a
3 b
4 e
5 g

6 Answer the questions. Listen again to check your answers.

1 What did Dan learn to do?
2 What do we know about Bella's character?
3 What kind of game did Chris play?
4 What are Tessa and her friends planning to do?
5 What has Joe learnt from the workshop?

Vocabulary basics | Advance your vocabulary > Workbook p103 | Pronunciation > p124

Exercise 6
1 He learnt to make a personal budget.
2 She has always been quite shy.
3 He played a game with different coloured hats.
4 They are planning to enter a school competition and set up a business.
5 He's learnt how to listen better.

Social awareness

NCS (National Citizen Service)

FACT! Nearly 500,000 young people have taken part in NCS (National Citizen Service), with participants completing 12 million hours of community action.

Exercise 1
a) hiking
c) photography

1 Read and listen to the text. Which of these activities are mentioned? 9

a) hiking b) tennis c) photography

HOME FIND A PROGRAMME BLOG FAQS SIGN UP

Summer Ideas

SAY 'YES' TO NCS!

NCS is a four-phase programme that gives 16-17 year olds the chance to try new things and learn new skills. The programme can improve students' CVs when planning for their future at university, college or in the world of work. This is how it works:

NATIONAL CITIZEN SERVICE

PHASE 1: ADVENTURE

The first part is a residential break at an outdoor centre where you can try activities like canoeing, hiking and rock climbing, as well as making new friends and challenging yourself.

PHASE 2: DISCOVERY

In the second part, you live independently in university-style accommodation (including doing your own cooking!). You can learn a new skill such as photography or drama, and develop life skills such as teamwork, assertiveness and entrepreneurship.

PHASE 3: SOCIAL ACTION

In the third part of the programme, you put your new skills into action to design a social action project. You plan, fundraise and problem-solve your ideas as a team, then go and make a difference in your local community.

PHASE 4: CELEBRATION

Finally, NCS participants celebrate their triumphs together at one great event.

I've just finished @NCS – it was the most fun I've ever had and I've made some great new friends. It took me out of my comfort zone, and I've tried so many things I'd never done before.
Emily (Hull) REPLY SHARE

I admit I had my doubts at first, but I can't believe how much @NCS has shaped me as a person! This experience has changed me so much and has helped boost my confidence and self-awareness. The best part for me was definitely the outdoor adventures.
Jess (Ramsgate) REPLY SHARE

When I was at @NCS, we raised £3,000 for a kids' charity, and I've raised even more since then. NCS opened so many doors for me and I can honestly say that it has kick-started my life!
Ollie (London) REPLY SHARE

READ MORE REVIEWS

Exercise 2
'It took me out of comfort zone.'
'I've tried so many things I'd never done before.'
'This experience has changed me so much and has helped build my self-confidence and self-awareness.'
'The best part for me was definitely the outdoor adventure.'
'NCS opened so many doors for me and I can honestly say that it has kick-started my life!'

2 Read the reviews again. Copy and complete the list of positive feedback.

NCS positive feedback
'It was the most fun I've ever had.'
'I've made some great new friends.'

3 Words in context Find these words and phrases in the text. What do they mean?

hiking fundraise
out of (your) comfort zone boost
kick-start

4 Work in pairs. Ask and answer the questions.

1 Is there a scheme like NCS for teenagers in your country?
2 Do young people do voluntary work where you live? If so, what kind of work do they do?
3 Which part of NCS would you most / least like to do? Why?

Exercise 4
Students' own answers

VIDEO: CULTURE BYTE
Watch the video supplied by BBC.
WATCH

Exercise 3
hiking = an outdoor adventure activity
fundraise = raise money for charity or as part of your social action project
out of (your) comfort zone = try things that you wouldn't normally do
boost = increase
kick-start = helped move you to the next stage of your life

Social awareness

NCS (National Citizen Service)

LESSON OBJECTIVES

In this lesson students will:

- read a blog about National Citizen Service
- talk about voluntary work in their country

WARMER

Write these three adjectives and two verbs on the board: *active, confident, assertive, apply, cooperate*. Students work in pairs and write nouns form of these words. The first pair to find all five nouns is the winner. (**Answer key**: activity, confidence, assertiveness, application, cooperation).

FACT!

- Find out whether there is a similar institution to NSC in the students' countries.

1 9

- Focus on the Fact box. Then students read the three activities a–c.
- Play the audio. Students read and listen to the text and decide which activities are performed at the NCS programme.
- Check answers as a class.

2

- Students copy the information in the box into their notebooks.
- They read the text again and add more examples of positive feedback to the list.
- Check the answers as a class.

3 Words in context

- Students read the words in the box. Then ask them to find the words in the text and use the context to decide what they mean.
- Check the answers as a class.

4

- Students work in pairs and ask and answer the questions.
- Listen to their ideas as a class.

EXTRA ACTIVITY

Write these words on the board: **1** *do* **2** *make* **3** *solve* **4** *have* and **a)** *problems* **b)** *doubts* **c)** *voluntary work* **d)** *friends*. Students match verbs 1–4 with nouns and noun phrases a) – d) to make expressions from the text.

VIDEO: CULTURE BYTE

This video is about teenagers' body clocks. For exploitation and comprehension practice based on this video, see the Culture byte video worksheets on the Resource Centre.

8 Audioscript, page 13, exercise 4

Workshop facilitator: Hello everyone! Hope you've enjoyed the life skills workshops today!
Well, as you know this is the last session of the day, and we're going to make a short video blog about what you've all learnt today. So that will be great, if you can tell us a bit about what you've done – about your favourite session, maybe – about what you've learnt ... Just come up to the webcam when you're ready ...

1 **Dan:** Hi! My name's Dan, and I've just finished the workshop about managing your money. I've learnt to make a personal budget, so now I know how much I'm spending and I can set savings goals for the future. I've had a savings account since I was 14 but I didn't really use it, so now I'm going to use it more!

2 **Bella**: Hello, I'm Bella. I've learnt a lot today. I've always been quite shy and I don't like speaking in public, but today I did the assertiveness workshop and it's been really useful. I've learnt that assertiveness is about self-respect, really – about knowing what your own needs are and being able to express them clearly.

3 **Chris:** Hi – my name's Chris and in my favourite workshop today we played an interesting game. We all had a different coloured hat – each hat represented a different way of thinking. So, if you had the red hat, you had to think about everything from an emotional perspective, and with the black hat, you had to think of all the possible problems, and so on. This was the creative thinking workshop and it was really fun! I've definitely learnt to think outside the box!

4 **Tessa:** Hi there, I'm Tessa and I've just been to the workshop for young entrepreneurs. They told us all about a school competition that we can enter, where we set up a business and win prizes for our school. Me and my friends have already decided that we're going to do it – well, we haven't asked our teacher yet but I'm sure it'll be OK. She's always talking about having an entrepreneurial spirit!

5 **Joe:** Hello, I'm Joe. This workshop has been great! I've only been here for, like, a day, but I've learnt so much! I think the most useful workshop has been the one about active listening. Have you ever stopped to think about how you listen? Well, I've learnt how to listen better, and I know this will improve the way I communicate with people. It's been great!

Grammar

Present perfect and past simple

LESSON OBJECTIVES
In this lesson students will:
- contrast the present perfect and the past simple
- read a text about a novel

WARMER
Books closed. Write these gapped sentences on the board: *I have studied English _____ five years. We have been here _____ 9 o'clock. I haven't finished this exercise _____*. Elicit answers from the class (*for, since, yet*) and complete the sentences.

1 • Students read the sentences in the table and complete the rules.
• They compare their answers in pairs.
• Make sure students understand that the past simple is used for completed actions that have a specific time reference (*when I was at NCS*) and do not continue in the present.

2 • Check students understand the task.
• Point out the time expressions highlighted in bold in the texts. Remind students that some time expressions are used with the present perfect and others with the past simple.
• Students work individually to complete the task.
• They compare answers in pairs.
• Check answers as a class. Point out that answers 3, 4, 5 and 6 are in the past simple because they refer to a specific time in the past and have no connection to the present.
• If you are using the TPK and your students need more work on the meaning of the words, do the Grammar basics exercise.

Grammar basics
Answer key: 1 haven't performed **2** arrived **3** 's/has learned **4** 've/have been **5** didn't earn **6** did

3 • Explain the task. Check answers.

4 • Make sure students understand they should use either the present perfect or the past simple to write their true sentences with the time expressions in exercise 3.
• They work individually and then compare sentences in pairs.
• Listen to some of their sentences as a class.

FINISHED?
Ask fast finishers to write two sentences for each verb – one using the present perfect and one using the past simple.

CLIL

Grammar in context: Literature

5 10
• This activity practises the difference between the present perfect and past simple.
• Students read the whole text before they write the correct form of the verbs in brackets.
• Students work individually to complete the exercise.
• They compare answers in pairs.
• Play the audio. Students check their answers.

EXTRA ACTIVITY
Give students further practice by using the first paragraph of the text in exercise 5 as a dictation. Put students into pairs. One student dictates the first three sentences while the other writes. Then they swap roles for the remaining three sentences.

LITERATURE TASK
Students use the internet to find out more about the author Vikas Swarup and to answer the three questions. Check answers.

Grammar reference > Workbook page 84

Grammar

Present perfect and past simple

Exercise 1
a present perfect
b past simple

1 Look at the sentences in the table. Then copy and complete rules a) and b) with *present perfect* or *past simple*.

past simple
When I **was** at NCS, we **raised** £3,000 for a kids' charity.
present perfect
I**'ve raised** even more since then.

a) We use the … for actions that began in the past and continue in the present.
b) We use the … for completed actions in the past.

Exercise 2
1 haven't left
2 've just finished
3 was
4 wanted
5 left
6 started
7 've been
8 've already learnt

2 Copy and complete the texts with the present perfect or past simple form of the verbs.

I (1) … (not leave) school **yet**. I (2) … (**just** / finish) my third year. I don't know what I want to do next. **When** I (3) … (be) younger I (4) … (want) to be a maths teacher, but now I'm not sure!

I (5) … (leave) school a few months **ago**, **last** June. In September, I (6) … (start) a catering course at college. I (7) … (be) really happy **since** I started college. I (8) … (**already** / learn) a lot of new skills, such as time management and baking cupcakes!

Exercise 3
with the past simple: *when, ago, last*
with the present perfect: *yet, just, already*

3 Copy and complete the table with the time expressions in exercise 2.

with the past simple	with the present perfect
ago	*since*

Exercise 4
Students' own answers

4 Write sentences which are true for you. Use the time expressions in exercise 3 and these verbs.

• finish • live • study • start • play • have • try

I haven't finished this exercise yet.

CLIL

Grammar in context: Literature

Exercise 5
1 've just started
2 did he know
3 has loved
4 wrote
5 didn't become
6 Have you seen
7 watched
8 enjoyed
9 haven't finished

5 Complete the text with the past simple or present perfect form of the verbs in brackets. Then listen and check. 1.10

Slumdog Millionaire
by Vikas Swarup

BOOK REVIEW

I (1) … (just / start) reading *Slumdog Millionaire*. It's about a young man called Ram Mohammad Thomas, from the slums of Mumbai. When Ram wins the Indian TV quiz show *Who Will Win a Billion?*, people think that he has cheated. How (2) … (he / know) all the answers? This book tells the story of Ram's life, from his childhood in an orphanage to his marriage to the girl that he (3) … (love) since he was 18. In each chapter, we find out how Ram knew the answers because of the experiences he had during his life.

The Indian author Vikas Swarup (4) … (write) this story in 2005. Originally the book was called *Q&A* (Questions and Answers). The book (5) … (not become) famous until the film *Slumdog Millionaire* came out a few years later.

(6) … (you / see) the film yet? I (7) … (watch) it last year and I really (8) … (enjoy) it. I (9) … (not finish) the book yet, but I would recommend it because it's a very good story.

Literature task
1 He was born in India.
2 He's a diplomat and works for the Indian Foreign Service.
3 *Six Suspects, The Accidental Apprentice.*

LITERATURE TASK

Find out about the author Vikas Swarup.
1 Where was he born?
2 As well as being a writer, what job does he do?
3 Which other books has he written?

A youth club committee

LEARNING OUTCOME

✔ Have an informal interview

Today we're learning about the different roles on a committee. We're going to talk about our skills and interests, and explain why we're perfect candidates!

TASK Talk about personal skills and interests

1 Read a job advertisement
2 Understand an informal interview
3 Write answers to interview questions
4 Have an informal interview

SUNNYSIDE YOUTH CLUB

JOIN THE COMMITTEE!

- Have you ever wanted to have a bigger say in how your youth club is organized?
- Do you want to be part of a fantastic team?
- Are you well-organized, assertive and reliable?
- Then join the youth club committee!

Being on the committee is a great opportunity to initiate change and make new friends, as well as develop your own skills. It also looks good on your CV!

We're looking for the following people:

SOCIAL EVENTS ORGANIZER

Role: To organize trips, parties and events.
You need:
- Excellent interpersonal skills
- Good time management skills

SECRETARY

Role: To chair meetings and write minutes.
You need:
- Good listening skills
- Excellent organizational skills

TREASURER

Role: To assist the management with the annual budget.
You need:
- Good money management skills
- Experience of spreadsheets

WEBSITE COORDINATOR

Role: To design and update the new website.
You need:
- Code-writing and web design experience
- Photo editing skills

Exercise 1
1 website coordinator
2 secretary
3 social events organizer
4 treasurer
5 website coordinator
6 secretary
7 treasurer
8 social events organizer

Exercise 2
Students' own answers

1 Read

1 Read the information. Which committee role involves:

1 updating the youth club website?
2 keeping minutes of committee meetings?
3 organizing a party?
4 keeping records of the finances?
5 uploading photos to the website?
6 being the chairperson at meetings?
7 using spreadsheets?
8 planning trips to the cinema or sports centre?

2 Copy and complete the sentences so they are true for you.

1 The role I would prefer is ... because ...
2 I wouldn't like to be the ... because ...

2 Listen

3 Read and listen to the extract from Jack's informal interview on page 17. 11

4 Listen again and repeat. Practise your intonation.

5 Watch or listen to the complete informal interview. Does Jack answer all the questions? 12

6 Watch or listen again. Choose the correct answers.

1 Jack's been on the committee of his **football** / **judo** club.
2 Jack's interested in the position of **treasurer** / **social events organizer**.
3 He's good at **managing money** / **communicating with people**.
4 Jack would organize **weekly** / **monthly** trips to the cinema.
5 Kelly will phone Jack **before** / **after** the weekend.

Exercise 3
Students' own answers

Exercise 4
Students' own answers

Exercise 5
Yes

Exercise 6
1 judo
2 social events organizer
3 communi-cating with people
4 monthly
5 before

Integrated skills
A youth club committee

LESSON OBJECTIVES
In this lesson students will:
- work on all four skills
- read a poster advertising roles on a youth club committee
- watch or listen to an interview
- write and present an informal interview

WARMER
Write the phrase youth club on the board. Students work in pairs and write down what things they expect to do at a youth club (eg *do different sports, learn skills, have parties, dance*). Listen to their ideas as a class and make a list on the board.

1 Read

1
- Students read the eight questions carefully first.
- They look in the text and find the answers to the questions. Remind students that when we look at texts like this, we usually have some idea of what we are looking for first. We do not usually begin at the beginning of the text and read everything but we scan the text until we find what we are looking for.
- They compare answers in pairs.
- Check answers as a class. Make sure students understand the meaning of *minutes* (taking notes to show what happened in a meeting).

2
- Students complete the sentences.
- They compare sentences in pairs.
- Listen to their ideas as a class. Make sure they give reasons for their answers (eg *The role I would prefer is treasurer because I am good at money management.*).

EXTRA ACTIVITY
Write these words on the left of the board: **1** *minutes* **2** *assist* **3** *budget* **4** *spreadsheet*. On the right of the board, write these definitions: **a)** *a chart that shows numbers in a way that makes them easy to compare* **b)** *to help* **c)** *an official written record of what is discussed at a formal meeting* **d)** *the amount of money an organization or person has to spend on something*. Students match the words to the meanings. (**Answer key: 1** c, **2** b, **3** d, **4** a)

2 Listen

Video with audio option
The dialogue is also available to watch as an audio file. If you prefer to present it this way, play the audio and follow the teacher's notes as for the video.

3 11 REC
- Students watch, read and listen to the extract from Jack's informal interview on page 17.

11 Audioscript, page 16, exercise 3
Kelly: Hi Jack! I'm just going to ask you a few questions to start with.
Jack: OK, that's fine.
Kelly: Have you been on a youth club committee before?
Jack: No, I haven't. But I've had some experience of committees, because I used to be the secretary of the judo club.
Kelly: That sounds like good experience. Which position are you applying for?
Jack: Well, I'm really interested in the position of the social events organizer. I think I'd be good at that.
Kelly: OK, so what skills do you think you could contribute?
Jack: Well, I communicate really well with people ... For example, I'm good at talking to people on the phone and at negotiating. And I'm really good at organizing parties!
Kelly: They're useful skills! What else makes you a good candidate for the position?
Jack: People often say that I'm very sociable. For example, I love meeting new people, making new friends ...
Kelly: What do you think you would enjoy most about this role?
Jack: What I find most exciting about this opportunity is the chance to organize some amazing events. For example, I'd love to organize a talent contest at the youth club, maybe for singing and dancing ... that would be amazing!

4
- Play the video again. Students watch, repeat and practise their intonation.

5 12
- Students listen to the complete interview.
- Elicit the answer to the question.

For audioscript, see page T17

6
- Encourage students to read the sentences and the different choices carefully first.
- Students listen again, and choose the correct answers.
- Check answers as a class.

7 • Students look at the expressions in Communication kit: Talking about skills and interests on page 17.
- Elicit which of these expressions are in the complete interview.
- Play the audio again for students to check their answers.

3 Write

8 • Students choose one of the roles on page 16.
- They work individually and make notes under the four headings.
- Monitor while they are working and give help if necessary.

9 • Students work individually and write full answers to the questions in the extract from Jack's interview, using their notes from exercise 8 and expressions from the Communication kit.
- Monitor while they are writing and give help if necessary.

4 Communicate

COMMUNICATION TIP
INFORMAL INTERVIEW TECHNIQUES

Students look at the Communication tip box. Encourage them to give examples of their experience and say how their skills are relevant.

10 • Students practise their interviews in pairs.

11 • If possible, record the interviews. Then Students watch the interviews to identify how they can improve their style.

12 Audioscript, page 16, exercise 5

Kelly: That sounds like a great event – I'm sure everyone would love that! What other events would you organize?
Jack: I love going to the cinema, so I'd organize trips to the cinema once a month. I would ask everyone their favourite films and then plan the trips.
Kelly: I think cinema trips would be very popular. How about activities at the sports centre – do you think sports would be popular?
Jack: Oh yes, it's very important to do sports. You can play football, basketball and tennis at our local sports centre. I would definitely organize some sports days at the sports centre.
Kelly: Well, thank you Jack for coming in today and being so very enthusiastic! I'll phone you before the weekend.
Jack: Thank you for your time. Bye!
Kelly: Bye Jack, thanks!

Integrated skills > Resource centre

Hi Jack! I'm just going to ask you a few questions to start with.	OK, that's fine.
Have you been on a youth club committee before?	No, I haven't. But I've had some experience of ...
That sounds like good experience. Which position are you applying for?	Well, I'm really interested in the position of ...
OK, so what skills do you think you could contribute?	Well, I communicate ... For example, ...
They're useful skills! What else makes you a good candidate for the position?	People often say that I'm ...
What do you think you would enjoy most about this role?	What I find most exciting about this opportunity is ...

Communication kit

- I've had some experience of ...
- I'm really interested in ...
- For example, ...
- I'm good at ... and ...
- People often say that I'm ...
- What I find most exciting about this opportunity is ...

Exercise 7
All of them

7 Look at the Communication kit. Which expressions are in the Speaking sketch? Watch or listen again to check your answers.

3 Write

Exercise 8
Students' own answers

8 Imagine you're applying for one of the roles on page 16. Prepare your interview.

The role I'm interested in:
My personal qualities:
My relevant skills:
What I would enjoy in this role:

Exercise 9
Students' own answers

9 Read the Communication tip. Write answers to the questions in the Speaking sketch. Use expressions from the Communication kit to give examples.

4 Communicate

Exercise 10
Students' own answers

10 Work in pairs. Practise your interview using the model questions and your answers in exercise 9.

Have you been on a youth club committee before?
No, I haven't. But I've had some experience of ...

Exercise 11
Students' own answers

11 If possible, record your interviews. Work together to improve your style.

! COMMUNICATION TIP
GIVE EXAMPLES

Give relevant examples of your skills and experience, so the interviewer clearly understands why you have these skills.

INTEGRATED SKILLS

Writing

A personal blog

LEARNING OUTCOME

✔ Write a blog post about a talent contest

Latest posts   Photos

THE RED TRICKS

WELCOME TO OUR BLOG!

Archive   Select month < >

1 Hello! We're The Red Tricks – an indie pop band that makes pretty great music! We're Alex (on vocals), Ellie (on guitar), Matt (on guitar) and Chris (on drums). At the moment, we're preparing for the Sunnyside Youth Club Talent Contest.

2 **Getting ready for the talent contest …** 15th September, 20.45
Well, we're almost ready for the talent contest. We've practised our song a million times! We've decided to sing *Just Like Magic*. We've written a few songs since we started the band, and this one is our favourite. We haven't sung it in public yet, but we're quite confident that everyone will love it! So, the talent contest is tomorrow night … It's a bit scary, but we're up for the challenge! We're really looking forward to it …

3 **The verdict!** 16th September, 21.30
Well, the talent contest finished half an hour ago and the committee have counted all the votes. So we've just heard the amazing news – we came second! It was a really fantastic evening. We enjoyed all the performances, especially the hip-hop dance group and Kelly's juggling act. Tom's magic tricks were very funny! He deserved to win the contest. Well done, everyone!

4 **Check out our new video here!**
We've written some new songs – check them out here!
Just Like Magic   *Tricky Times*   *Media Circus*

Exercise 1
1 Alex, Ellie, Matt and Chris. / No

1 Read the blog. Who is in the band? Did they win the talent contest?

Exercise 2
1 c
2 b
3 d
4 a

2 Focus on content Read the blog again and match sections 1–4 with a–d.

a) links to their material
b) their preparations
c) about the band / their activity
d) the results of the talent contest

Exercise 3
five: a bit
quite
pretty
very
really

3 Focus on language Read the information. How many adverbs of degree can you find in the blog?

Adverbs of degree

We use adverbs of degree before adjectives to show the intensity of something.

✘	✔	✔✔
not very	a bit quite	pretty very really

Exercise 4
Students' own answers

4 Copy and complete the sentences so they are true for you.

1 I'm quite interested in …
2 I'm not very keen on …
3 I'm really good at …
4 I'd be really happy to …

5 Imagine you and your friend(s) enter a talent contest. Choose an activity and write a blog about your experience.

- sing
- play music
- do magic tricks
- do circus skills

Exercise 5
Students' own answers

Writing kit

1 **Plan** your blog. Answer these questions.
- Who is taking part?
- What are you going to perform?
- What have you done to prepare?
- Did you win the contest?

2 **Write** your blog. Write three paragraphs and include links to photos, video or audio.
1 an introduction (about you / your activity)
2 the first post (about your preparations)
3 the second post (about the results)

3 **Useful phrases**

Hello! We're …	We've decided to …	Check out …
At the moment, …	We've just heard …	Well done, everyone!

4 **Check** your writing.

- ☑ adverbs of degree
- ☑ past time expressions
- ☑ correct past tense (past simple or present perfect)
- ☑ three paragraphs

Study guide > p99   Writing hub > Workbook p112

Writing
A personal blog

LESSON OBJECTIVES
In this lesson students will:
- read blog posts
- use adverbs of degree
- write a blog

WARMER
Write *talent contest* on the board. Ask students if they ever watch talent contest programmes on TV. If they appeared in a talent contest, what would they do?

1
- Highlight the two questions. Students read the text. Check answers.

2 Focus on content
- Go through summaries a) to d) with the whole class.
- Students read the text again and match the summaries with the sections.
- Check answers as a class.

3 Focus on language
- Highlight that adverbs of degree show the intensity of something.
- Students look at the table. Point out that *not very* shows a negative intensity, *a bit* and *quite* show some intensity and *pretty*, *very* and *really* show a lot of intensity.
- Students write down examples of adverbs of degree they find in the blog.
- Check answers as a class.

4
- Remind students that if you are keen on something, you like it very much.
- Students complete the sentences.
- Listen to some sentences as a class.

5
- Read the instructions to the class.
- Students each choose one of the activities.

Writing kit
The aim of this activity is for students to write a blog about students' experience to enter a talent contest that includes the correct use of adverbs of degree. Ask the students to follow the stages in the Writing kit. Encourage them to use their plan and the blog in exercise 1 to help them. Monitor while they are writing and give help with vocabulary if necessary. At the Check stage, ask them to swap notebooks and check each other's writing.

Study guide > Student's Book page 99

Writing hub > Workbook page 112

UNIT 2

LUCKY ESCAPES

UNIT OBJECTIVES AND KEY COMPETENCES

In this unit the student will learn ...

- to recognize, understand and correctly use vocabulary related to rescue and survival and a set of extreme adjectives **CLC CMST SCC**
- to recognize, understand and correctly use the past perfect and the past simple, the time expressions used with the past perfect, and use both tenses in a short speaking activity **CLC L2L SIE**
- to recognize and understand the difference between subject and object questions **CLC L2L**
- about conflict resolution and how it relates to their own life **CLC CMST SCC CAE SIE**
- about having a group discussion by watching a short video **CLC DC SCC**

In this unit the student will learn how ...

- to identify topic sentences in a text about lucky escapes **CLC CMST SCC CAE**
- to look online for more information about extreme weather **CLC DC SCC CAE SIE**
- to identify specific information in a news report **CLC CMST SCC CAE**
- read a set of instructions, listen to a group discussion, prepare for and have a group discussion **CLC SCC CAE SIE**
- write a news story **CLC CAE**

LINGUISTIC CONTENTS

Main vocabulary

- Rescue and survival: *victims*, *casualties*, *firefighters*, etc
- Extreme adjectives: *freezing*, *starving*, *fascinating*, etc

Extra vocabulary

- Words in context: *flood*, *damage*, *strike*, *headset*, *bolt*, *blister*, *run by*, *emergency services*, *stuck*, etc
- Word builder: UK and US English; Extreme adjectives

Grammar

- Past perfect
- Subject and object questions

Functional language

- Using question tags
- Phrases for describing photos in an exam
- Phrases for narrating events in an exam

Pronunciation

- Difficult sounds /ʒ/ and /z/
- Word stress in multi-syllable words

SKILLS

Reading

- Read online information about two lucky escapes
- Read information about mountain rescue

Writing: Interaction and production

- Write notes to prepare for a discussion about objects to take on an expedition
- Write a news report in three steps
- Learn how to use connectors of sequence

Listening

- Listen to a news report about an accident
- Listen to a group discussion

Spoken interaction

- Ask and answer questions about the past
- Spoken production
- Prepare and participate in a group discussion

LIFELONG LEARNING SKILLS

Self-study and self-evaluation

- Study guide: Student's Book page 100
- Progress check: Workbook pages 22
- Extension: Workbook page 23
- Grammar reference and practice: Workbook pages 86–87
- Wordlist: Workbook pages 151–157

Learning strategies and thinking skills

- Using topic sentences
- Critical thinking: creating a timeline of events for a news story

Life skills

- Problem-solving (risk assessment)

Cross-curricular contents

- Accidents and disasters, survival stories
- Literature and history: *Touching the Void* by Joe Simpson
- Literature task: searching the internet for information about other survival stories

EVALUATION

- Unit 2 End-of-unit test: Basic, Standard and Extra
- CEFR Skills Exam Generator

KEY COMPETENCES

CLC	Competence in linguistic communication
CMST	Competence in mathematics, science and technology
DC	Digital competence
SCC	Social and civic competences
CAE	Cultural awareness and expression
L2L	Learning to learn
SIE	Sense of initiative and entrepreneurship

DIGITAL MATERIAL

New Pulse Digital Course including:

- Interactive vocabulary presentation
- Grammar and Vocabulary basics exercises
- Getting started video
- Flipped classroom grammar video: past tenses
- Speaking sketch video: A formal interview

DIGITAL COMPETENCE

- Web quest: Prepare a presentation of a survival story
- Digital competence worksheet: Web-based writing tools

REINFORCEMENT MATERIAL

- New Pulse Basics: Teacher's Resource Centre
- Vocabulary and grammar consolidation worksheets: Teacher's Resource Centre
- Grammar and Vocabulary basics exercises: Teacher's Presentation Kit

EXTENSION MATERIAL

- Vocabulary and grammar extension worksheets: Teacher's Resource Centre
- Advance your vocabulary: Workbook page 104
- The longer read: Teacher's Resource Centre
- Writing hub: Workbook page 114

TEACHER'S RESOURCE MATERIAL

- Translation and dictation worksheets
- Evaluation rubrics
- Key competences worksheets
- Culture and CLIL worksheets
- Digital competence worksheets
- Macmillan Readers worksheets
- Integrated Skills

Vocabulary
Rescue and survival

LESSON OBJECTIVES
In this lesson students will:
- learn words and phrases related to rescue and survival
- ask and answer questions about survival stories

Video: Getting started

In this video the speakers answer the question *Have you heard about any disasters in the news recently? What happened?*
- Focus the students on the unit title *Lucky Escapes*.
- Write these sentences on the board: **1** Who talks about a cave rescue? **2** Who discusses a place that was declared a disaster zone? **3** Who discusses the sadness of seeing people his / her age suffer?
- Students watch the video and decide whether the sentences are true or false.
- Students watch the video again to check their answers.
- At the end of the lesson, ask students to answer the question from the video: *Have you heard about any disasters in the news recently? What happened?*

Answer key: 1 Olivia **2** Leo **3** Naomi

WARMER

Write *disaster* in the middle of the board. Elicit words for different types of disaster from the class and write them round the central word, eg *earthquake, tsunami, flood.*

1
- Students copy and complete the diagram.
- They compare answers in pairs.
- Make sure they understand *capsize*. If a ship capsizes, it turns upside down in the water.
- Highlight the difference between a victim (someone who has been affected by a bad situation) and a casualty (someone who has been injured or killed in a bad situation).
- If you are using the TPK and your students need more work on the meaning of the words, do the Vocabulary basics exercise.

Vocabulary basics

Answer key: 1 crash **2** search and rescue workers **3** give first aid **4** capsize **5** paramedics **6** firefighters **7** victims **8** casualties

2 13
- Play the audio. Students listen, check their answers and repeat. Make sure students pronounce *casualties* /ˈkæʒʊəltɪz/ correctly.

LANGUAGE NOTE

In phrases like *catch fire, give first aid, receive compensation* and *send international aid*, the verbs do not carry the main stress. The main stress is towards the end of each phrase.

3
- Students look at the photos.
- They read the short extracts and match each extract with one of the photos.
- Check answers as a class.

4
- Highlight the three jobs in exercise 1 – *firefighter, paramedic, search and rescue worker.*
- Put students into pairs and ask them to decide whether they would like to do any of these jobs. Encourage them to say why or why not.
- Listen to their ideas as a class.

LUCKY ESCAPES

UNIT 2

LEARNING OUTCOMES IN THIS UNIT
- Use topic sentences
- Listen for specific information in a news report
- Take part in a group discussion
- Write a news report about a survival story

VIDEO: GETTING STARTED

WATCH Watch the teenagers talking about survival stories and answer the question.

Vocabulary
Rescue and survival

Exercise 1
1 firefighters
2 search and rescue workers
3 casualties
4 victims
5 catch fire
6 crash
7 receive compensation
8 send international aid

1 Copy and complete the diagram with the words in the box.

capsize casualties catch fire crash firefighters give first aid paramedics receive compensation search and rescue workers send international aid survivors victims

- people
  - people who help: paramedics, (1) ..., (2) ...
  - people who suffer: survivors, (3) ..., (4) ...
- verbs
  - verbs for disasters: capsize, (5) ..., (6) ...
  - verbs for assistance: give first aid, (7) ..., (8) ...

Exercise 2
Students' own answers

Exercise 3
1 c; firefighters, catch fire
2 d; Paramedics, first aid
3 a; crashed, capsized
4 b; search and rescue, survivors

Exercise 4
Students' own answers

2 Listen, check and repeat. 13

3 Match stories 1–4 with photos a–d. Then choose the correct words.

4 Work in pairs. Would you like to do any of the jobs in exercise 1? Why (not)?

a

b
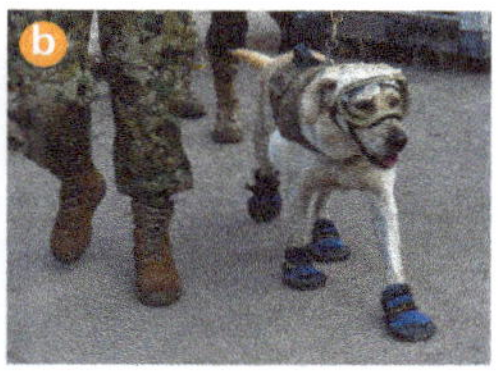
c

d

1 Firefighter dogs to retire

Toby will leave the London Fire Brigade when his handler retires. The dog has attended more than 2,000 incidents, helping (1) **paramedics / firefighters** to locate dangerous substances that might (2) **catch fire / capsize.**

2 PET SAVES OWNER

One very clever cat managed to call the emergency services the moment her owner collapsed at home. (3) **Paramedics / Rescue workers** arrived on the scene very quickly and were able to give life-saving (4) **compensation / first aid** to the casualty.

3 Ocean rescue

When his boat (5) **crashed / rescued** against rocks and (6) **caught fire / capsized**, Dimitry had a very lucky escape when a group of dolphins swam to the scene.

4 Frida: a Mexican hero

After disasters including the earthquake in Mexico City, (7) **search and rescue / casualty** dog Frida has found 12 (8) **victims / survivors** alive under collapsed buildings.

Vocabulary basics

Reading
News stories

LEARNING OUTCOME

✔ Use topic sentences

Exercise 1
1 the USA
2 extreme weather

1 Look at the headlines and photos. Before reading the text, guess the correct answers.

1 These news stories are from **the USA** / **the UK**.
2 Both stories are about **man-made disasters** / **extreme weather**.

Exercise 2
1 **Siri saves Texan teen** – *Tyler Frank*; **Lightning strikes** – *Faith Mobley*
2 **Siri saves Texan teen** – *Texas*; **Lightning strikes** – *Alabama*
3 **Siri saves Texan teen** – *Tyler was rescued from her roof*; **Lightning strikes** – *Faith survived being hit by lightning.*

2 Read the information. Then read only the topic sentences in each news story and answer questions 1–3 about each story.

1 Who is the main character?
2 Where did the story take place?
3 What happened in the end?

USE TOPIC SENTENCES
A topic sentence is usually the first sentence in a paragraph. It gives an idea of what the paragraph is about.

Exercise 3
1 b
2 a
3 c
4 b

3 Read and listen to both news stories and choose the correct answers. 14

1 Tyler was on the roof of her house because ...
 a) she was playing there with her brothers.
 b) the hurricane had caused a flood.
 c) rescue workers told her to go there.
2 Tyler ...
 a) asked Siri for help.
 b) called the helicopter herself.
 c) couldn't use her mobile phone.
3 Faith was hit by lightning while ...
 a) she was driving to work.
 b) her co-workers were talking to her.
 c) she was washing up.
4 Faith ...
 a) called the paramedics.
 b) was taken to hospital.
 c) suffered serious injuries.

Exercise 4
flood = noun
damage = noun
strike = verb / noun
headset = noun
bolt = noun
blister = noun

4 **Words in context** Find these words in the text. Are they nouns, verbs or adjectives? What do they mean?

flood damage strike headset bolt blister

Log in | Register

Home News Sport About

Lucky escapes

Siri saves Texan teen

Tyler Frank spent nearly two days on the roof of her house waiting for help after Hurricane Harvey had struck Houston, Texas. The 14-year-old had woken in the early hours with flood water surrounding her bed. Luckily Tyler was safe because her brother Joseph had carried her up to the roof with the rest of her family.

Fortunately Tyler hadn't forgotten to take her mobile phone with her! She had already tried calling the emergency services, but she was told that all the rescue workers were busy dealing with other casualties. With no sign of rescue, Tyler had an idea. 'Siri's smart, let me ask her!' she thought. The voice-activated software called the emergency services who sent a helicopter. Eventually, Tyler was flown to Texas Children's Hospital.

Like many survivors of Hurricane Harvey, Tyler's family have lost everything. 'Everything's gone,' she told *The Independent* newspaper. 'We have to start over.' At least 70 people lost their lives, and more than 176,000 homes were damaged or destroyed.

5 Are the sentences true or false? Correct the false sentences.

1 Tyler was 16 at the time of the hurricane.
2 Hurricane Harvey caused a lot of damage in Houston, Texas.
3 Tyler was taken to hospital by ambulance.
4 Faith worked full-time at McDonald's.
5 Faith was wearing earphones when the lightning struck.
6 The lightning went through Faith's shoe.

Exercise 5
1 **False** – She was 14.
2 **True**
3 **False** – She was flown to hospital in a helicopter.
4 **False** – She worked part-time.
5 **False** – She was wearing a microphone headset.
6 **True**

Reading
News stories

LESSON OBJECTIVES
In this lesson students will:
- read online news articles
- identify and use topic sentences
- study some word differences between UK and US English

WARMER
Write the phrase *bad weather* on the board. Elicit from the class examples of very bad weather and the problems for people that bad or extreme weather can cause and make a list on the board, e.g. *thunderstorm, heavy rain, fog, snow, drought,* etc.

1
- Students look at the headlines and the photos of the two articles. Encourage them to guess the answers to the two questions before they read the texts. Remind students that predicting content from features that accompany a text will help them to understand the text.
- They work individually and guess the answers to 1–2.
- Do not correct them at this stage.

2
- Remind students that the topic sentence of a news story is normally the first sentence.
- They work individually and answer questions 1-3.
- Do not correct them at this stage.

READING STRATEGY
Topic sentences
Students read the information about topic sentences and check that they understand the importance of recognizing these in a text.

3 14
- Students read the questions and the different possible answers first.
- Play the audio. Students listen and follow the news article in their books.
- They choose the correct answers.
- Check answers as a class.

CULTURE NOTE
There are a number of hurricanes every year around the world, and sometimes two or three hurricanes can happen at the same time. Giving these storms names makes it much easier for people such as weather forecasters, emergency workers and ships captains to communicate about specific hurricanes and to be clearly understood.

BACKGROUND
Hurricane Harvey was a major hurricane that hit parts of the Caribbean and southeast Texas, in the US, in August 2017. Over 100 people died in the storm. It also caused significant flooding in Houston and the surrounding area, which has placed it as one of the most expensive tropical storms in history.

4 Words in context
- Students find the words in the box in the text.
- Ask them to use the context to help them decide the word class and the meaning of each word.
- Check answers as a class.

5
- Students read the sentences carefully first.
- They work individually and read the text again to decide whether the sentences are true or false.
- Encourage students to write down key words, phrases or sentences to help them decide. Students correct the false sentences.
- Check answers as a class.

6 • Students read all the questions first. Check understanding.
• They work individually and answer the questions using the information in the text.
• Check answers as a class.

7 Word builder
• Write the words *smart* and *clever* on the board and tell students they have the same meaning but one is British and one is American. Students tell you which is which.
• They read the information in the box and find the American equivalents to a) and b). Point out that *through* can also be written *thru* in American English, but that this spelling is only used in informal written American English.
• Ask students if they know the British equivalents of the words in question 2. If there are any they don't know, ask them to use a dictionary to check.

FINISHED?

Students find the British English equivalents of these American nouns: *candy*, *potato chips*, *apartment*, *check*, *parking lot*, *trash*. (**Answer key:** sweets, crisps, flat, bill, car park, rubbish).

8 • Students read all the questions first and note down their ideas.
• Put them into pairs to ask and answer the questions.
• Listen to their ideas as a class.

DID YOU KNOW?

Students read the information in the *Did you know?* box. Ask if they find this information surprising and why.

CRITICAL THINKING

• Students read the two stories again and choose one.
• They work individually identifying the main events and writing a timeline for their chosen story.
• Listen to their ideas as a class and make sure they have included all the events in the correct order.

WEB QUEST

Students prepare a short news report about another extreme weather story.

1 **Investigate** Put students into pairs. Students open a search engine (eg *Google*) and search for news stories about extreme weather conditions in their own country.
2 **Collaborate** They find as much information as they can about what happened and work together to prepare a news story or a video clip. Monitor while they are working and give help with vocabulary if necessary.
3 **Communicate** They present their news story to the rest of the class.

TIP! Explain to students that online translation tools are not always accurate. They should be used as a guide, but not taken as foolproof. They can help you translate from a foreign language into your own, but should not be trusted for translations the other way round. It will always be more effective for students to use their own words and knowledge of a language than to depend on these.

VIDEO: FLIPPED CLASSROOM

You may want to ask Students to watch the Flipped classroom video for unit 2 as homework in preparation for the following grammar lesson. The Flipped grammar presentation focuses on the past perfect and past simple.

The longer read > Resource centre

DID YOU KNOW?
Worldwide, more than 2,000 people are killed by lightning every year.

Lightning strikes at McDonald's drive-thru

16-year-old student Faith Mobley from Haleyville, Alabama, had a lucky escape when she was hit by lightning at a McDonald's drive-thru.

The teenager, a part-time worker at the restaurant, had just started doing the dishes when she saw a flash of lightning outside. Before she could react, the lightning had already travelled through the building, through the washing-up water and through Faith's microphone headset, before passing through her body, down one leg, and out of her foot. When she was interviewed by reporters later, she showed them the hole in her shoe where the lightning bolt had left her body.

Faith's co-workers called the paramedics immediately and she was rushed to hospital. Dr James Hwang, who treated Faith, said she had been very lucky – lots of victims of lightning suffer more serious injuries, with clothes catching fire or the lightning causing permanent nerve damage.

By the following day, the small black blister on Faith's foot had disappeared. All that remained was the hole in her shoe and another strange phenomenon which her doctor had never witnessed before: before the lightning struck Faith had always worn glasses, but afterwards she could see perfectly well without them!

Exercise 6
1 Tyler had been asleep in her bed.
2 She used the assistant on her mobile phone to call for help.
3 At least 70 people lost their lives and more tan 176,000 homes were destroyed.
4 She felt it through her headset, down one leg and out of her foot.
5 Because lots of victims of lightning strikes suffer more serious injuries, like nerve damage or their clothes catch fire.
6 It restored her eyesight and she doesn't need to wear glasses anymore.

6 Answer the questions.

1 Where was Tyler when the hurricane arrived?
2 Why was her mobile phone so important in the story?
3 How much damage did Hurricane Harvey cause?
4 How did Faith feel the lightning in her body?
5 Why did Dr Hwang say that Faith had been very lucky?
6 What unusual effect did the lightning strike have on Faith?

7 **Word builder** Read the information and answer the questions.

UK and US English
Some words are different in British and American English.
smart (US) = *clever* (UK)
do the dishes (US) = *wash up* (UK)

1 Find the American English version of these phrases in the text.
a) 'We have to start again.'
b) a drive-through restaurant
2 How do you say these American words in British English? Use a dictionary to help you.

cab elevator movie subway soccer vacation

Exercise 7
1 **a)** 'We have to start over.'
b) a McDonald's drive-thru
2 **cab** = taxi
elevator = lift
movie = film
subway = underground
soccer = football
vacation = holiday

8 Work in pairs. Answer the questions.

1 What kinds of extreme weather can cause problems where you live?
2 Have you ever had a lucky escape?
3 Do you know anyone who has been in a dangerous situation caused by extreme weather?

Exercise 8
Students' own answers

CRITICAL THINKING

CREATE A TIMELINE
Choose one of the news stories. Identify the key events and write a list. Create a timeline of events for the story. Make sure you put them in the correct order.

WEB QUEST

Works in pairs. Find a news story related to extreme weather in your country. Prepare a news report or a video news clip.

1 **Investigate** Search online for news stories and decide which one to report on.
2 **Collaborate** Work together to create a news article or a script for your video clip.
3 **Communicate** Present your news report to the class.

TIP! Online translation tools can help you to get a general understanding of a text. Just be sure to use your own words afterwards!

Grammar

Past perfect and past simple

VIDEO: FLIPPED CLASSROOM

WATCH Watch the grammar presentation and do the task.

Exercise 1
1 past participle
2 before

1 Look at the table. Choose the correct words to complete rules a) and b).

past perfect and past simple
When the lightning struck, Faith had already started work. She hadn't finished washing up when the lightning went through her body. Had Faith always worn glasses before the lightning struck?

a) After *had* / *hadn't*, we use the **past participle** / **infinitive**.

b) The blue actions happened **before** / **after** the red actions.

Exercise 2
Already goes between *had* and the past participle.

2 Read the Look! box and look at the time expressions. Which one goes between *had* and the past participle?

> **LOOK!**
>
> **Time expressions with the past perfect**
> Tyler had called the emergency services **before** she asked Siri for help.
> = Tyler asked Siri for help **after** she had called the emergency services.
> **By the time** the rescue helicopter arrived, Tyler had **already** been on the roof for nearly two days.

Exercise 3
1 had heard
2 hadn't heard
3 happened
4 had already done
5 told

3 Copy and complete the sentences with the past simple or past perfect form of the verbs in brackets.

1 I ... (hear) about Hurricane Harvey before I read this news story.
2 I ... (not hear) about Tyler Frank before we read about her in class.
3 My cousins had planned to visit Texas before this disaster ... (happen).
4 I ... (already / do) my homework before this class started.
5 Had you heard the news before I ... (tell) you?

4 Read the text and choose the correct words. Then listen and check. 15

Exercise 4
1 hit
2 had already arrived
3 crashed
4 struck
5 After
6 decided
7 By the time
8 had already helped

SURVIVOR JOINS RESCUE EFFORT

When an earthquake (1) **hit / had hit** Nepal, 17-year-old Matt Moniz from Colorado, USA, was about to climb Mount Everest. He and his team (2) **already arrived / had already arrived** at base camp when an enormous avalanche suddenly (3) **crashed / had crashed** through the camp. There hadn't been any warning before the avalanche (4) **struck / had struck**, but Matt and his team were able to survive by taking cover behind a big rock. (5) **After / Before** he had survived the avalanche, Matt (6) **decided / had decided** to stay in Nepal to join the rescue operation. (7) **Already / By the time** he returned home, Matt (8) **already helped / had already helped** to build many temporary homes in the mountain villages affected by the earthquake.

Exercise 5
1 had climbed
2 went
3 hadn't climbed
4 happened
5 hadn't heard
6 read
The past perfect actions happened first.

5 Copy and complete the answers with the past simple or past perfect form of the verbs in brackets. Which actions happened first?

Q: Was Matt an experienced climber?
A: Yes, he (1) ... (climb) other mountains with his father before he (2) ... (go) to Nepal.
Q: Had he already climbed Everest?
A: No, he (3) ... (not / climb) Everest before the avalanche (4) ... (happen). But he returned three years later and reached the summit.
Q: Did you know anything about this avalanche before now?
A: No, I (5) ... (not hear) about it before I (6) ... (read) this text.

Exercise 6
1 Had you already studied English before you came to this school?
2 Had you already met your teacher before school started in September?
3 Which other English books had you used before you had this one?

6 Copy and complete the questions with the past perfect or past simple form of the verbs in brackets. In pairs, ask and answer the questions.

1 ... you ... (already / study) English before you ... (come) to this school?
2 ... you ... (already / meet) your teacher before school ... (start) in September?
3 Which other English books ... you ... (use) before you ... (have) this one?

Grammar

Past perfect and past simple

LESSON OBJECTIVES

In this lesson students will:

- learn the uses of the past perfect and the past simple
- Use time expressions with the past perfect

WARMER

Books closed. Students discuss what they remember about the two lucky escapes in the previous lesson. Elicit ideas from the class and make a list on the board, eg *There was a hurricane. She used Siri to call the emergency services. She was hit by lightning.*

VIDEO: FLIPPED CLASSROOM

- If you set the video for homework, students compare their Task time! answers and then check the answers as a class.
- If you didn't set it for homework, watch the video in class and answer the Task time! questions at the end of the presentation.

Answer key: 1 false **2** true **3** false

1
- Students read the sentences in the table and choose the correct answers.
- Check answers as a class.
- Highlight the form of the past perfect and point out that *have* / *has* in the present perfect simply changes to *had* in the past perfect.
- Point out that the clauses can be in either order in the example sentences, but the clause with the past perfect happened first, eg *When the lightning struck, Faith had already started work*. Sometimes the past simple can be used in both clauses, eg *I did my homework before this class started* but this changes the meaning, e.g. *When the lightning struck, Faith started work* would mean she started work after the lightning struck and not before.
- Students translate the three example sentences into their language.
- If you are using the TPK and your students need more practice of the grammar, do the Grammar basics exercise.

Grammar basics

Answer key: 1 A1 B2 **2** A2 B1 **3** A1 B2 **4** A2 B1 **5** A2 B1

2
- Students read the time expressions in the Look! box.
- Students answer the question. Then, they translate the expressions into their language.

LANGUAGE NOTE

Time expressions with the past perfect

The past perfect is used to emphasize that one action happened before the other. Words like *before*, *already* and *just* may be used with the past perfect. Highlight the fact that *already* is used with the past perfect in a similar way to how it is used with the present perfect, but it is used to refer to the past not the present.

3
- Complete the first sentence with the whole class as an example (*had heard*).
- Students work individually to complete the task.
- They compare answers in pairs.
- Check answers as a class. Point out that *had not* is usually contracted to *hadn't* in spoken English.

4 15
- This activity practises the difference between the past perfect and past simple.
- Students read the whole text before they choose the correct answers.
- Play the audio. Students listen and check their answers.

5
- Students choose the correct form of the verb in brackets to complete the three sentences.
- They compare answers in pairs and discuss which actions happened first.
- Check answers as a class.

6
- Remind students that the first action in each question will be in the past perfect tense. Students copy and complete the questions.
- Check the questions as a class.
- Students work in pairs and ask and answer the questions.

Grammar reference > Workbook page 86

Pronunciation lab > Difficult sounds: /ʒ/ and /z/ > Student's Book page 124

Vocabulary and Listening

Extreme adjectives

LESSON OBJECTIVES
In this lesson students will:
- learn a set of extreme adjectives
- listen to confirm predictions and listen for specific information

WARMER

Write the letter *a* on the board. Students tell you an adjective beginning with this letter and repeat for all letters of the alphabet.

DIGITAL VOCABULARY FLASHCARDS

In this digital presentation, students match the vocabulary with definitions.
- Do the digital presentation with the class.
- Encourage students to repeat the words.

1 16
- Ask students to read the headlines. Ask them what is special about headlines. Elicit that newspaper headlines use a special style – they do not normally contain articles.
- Students read the headlines again and decide which are positive.
- Play the audio. Students listen and repeat the words in blue in the headlines. Make sure they stress the words correctly, e.g. *unforgettable, disgusting*.
- If you are using the TPK and your students need more work on the meaning of the words, do the Vocabulary basics exercise.

Vocabulary basics

Answer key: Positive: delighted, fascinating, gorgeous.

Negative: disgusting, exhausted, freezing, furious, horrific, starving, boiling, terrifying

It depends: huge, tiny, unforgettable

2 • Students match adjectives 1–14 with the extreme adjectives in exercise 1. Encourage them to use a dictionary if necessary. Check answers as a class.

3 Word builder
- Students read the information in the Word builder box.
- Draw a vertical line on the board. At the bottom, write *warm*. In the middle, write *hot* and at the very top, write *boiling*. Emphasize that extreme adjectives come at the very top or very bottom of the scale.
- Highlight that we cannot use adverbs of degree (eg *quite*, *very*) with extreme adjectives but that we can use *absolutely*
- Do one example that is true for you to demonstrate the activity, eg *The most unforgettable day I've had was ...* Students complete the sentences.
- Listen to some sentences as a class.

FINISHED?

Write six more extreme adjectives on the left of the board: *awful*, *amazing*, *filthy*, *delicious*, *hideous*, *packed*. Then write these adjectives in random order on the right of the board: *dirty*, *ugly*, *tasty*, *bad*, *crowded*, *good*. Students match the two sets of adjectives.

4 17
- Students look at exercises 5 and 6 and predict which news story they think they will hear about. Play the audio. Students listen and check their answers.

For audioscript, see page T24

5 • Encourage students to read the questions again carefully. Point out that in question 2 the answer is the subject of the sentence. Play the audio again. Check answers.

6 • Students read all the questions again carefully. Make sure they understand *retrieve* (to get something back, especially if it is difficult to do so).

EXTRA ACTIVITY

Put students into pairs. They each take a part and read the interview section of the audioscript for exercise 4 (from Rachel: Hello!) aloud to each other. When they have finished, they swap roles and repeat the activity.

Advance your vocabulary > Workbook page 104

Pronunciation lab > Word stress in multi-syllable words > Student's Book page 124

Vocabulary and Listening

Extreme adjectives

LEARNING OUTCOME

✔ Listen for specific information in a news report

DIGITAL VOCABULARY FLASHCARDS

Do the matching exercise to discover the new vocabulary.

boiling delighted disgusting exhausted fascinating freezing furious gorgeous horrific huge starving terrifying tiny unforgettable

1 Read headlines 1–7. Which three headlines are for positive stories? Listen and repeat the words in blue. 16

1. Exhausted travellers return after terrifying helicopter crash
2. Family furious with disgusting holiday accommodation
3. Jungle explorer recounts fascinating trip in boiling temperatures
4. UN sends aid as huge famine leaves thousands starving
5. Family delighted with gorgeous new home
6. Horrific accident caused by freezing weather
7. Top 10 unforgettable films made on a tiny budget

Exercise 1

3 Jungle explorer recounts fascinating trip in boiling temperatures.
5 Family delighted with gorgeous new home.
7 Top 10 unforgettable films made on a tiny budget

2 Match adjectives 1–14 with the extreme adjectives in exercise 1. Use your dictionary to help you.

1 small	6 hot	11 bad
2 big	7 memorable	12 interesting
3 tired	8 angry	13 unpleasant
4 frightening	9 hungry	14 happy
5 cold	10 beautiful	

Exercise 2

1 tiny
2 huge
3 exhausted
4 terrifying
5 freezing
6 boiling
7 unforgettable
8 furious
9 starving
10 gorgeous
11 horrific
12 fascinating
13 disgusting
14 delighted

3 Word builder Read the information. Then copy and complete the sentences so they are true for you.

EXTREME ADJECTIVES

We use extreme adjectives to give emphasis.
very bad = horrific
We don't use normal adverbs of degree with extreme adjectives. We use *absolutely*.
~~*very horrific*~~ ✗ *absolutely horrific* ✔

1. The most unforgettable day I've had was …
2. It makes me absolutely furious when …
3. When I'm exhausted, I usually …
4. The most fascinating person I know is …

Exercise 3

Students' own answers

4 Read exercises 5 and 6. Do you think you will hear about news story a, b or c? Listen and check. 17

a) Paramedics assist accident victims
b) Teen receives compensation after disaster
c) Firefighters rescue 16-year-old from drain

Exercise 4

c

5 Listen again. Choose the correct answers.

1. When she dropped her phone, Rachel was …
   a) jogging in the park.
   b) walking the dog.
   c) going to school.
2. … called the emergency services.
   a) Rachel
   b) Rachel's friend
   c) A member of the public
3. Rachel had had her phone for …
   a) two days.
   b) two weeks.
   c) two months.
4. Immediately after the incident, Rachel …
   a) received first aid from the paramedics.
   b) uploaded photos on social media.
   c) went home to have a bath.

Exercise 5

1 b
2 b
3 b
4 c

6 Answer the questions.

1. How did Rachel try to retrieve her phone?
2. Who rescued her?
3. Was Rachel injured?
4. How long was she in the drain?
5. Could she use her phone afterwards?
6. Did Rachel mind that photos of her had gone viral on the internet?

Exercise 6

1 with her feet
2 firefighters
3 no
4 ten minutes
5 no
6 no

Vocabulary basics | Advance your vocabulary > Workbook p104 | Pronunciation > p124

Exercise 1
1 risks
2 risk assessment
3 putting yourself or others in danger
4 taking precautions

Life skills

Problem-solving (risk assessment)

FACT! **Risk assessment** is an important part of problem-solving. It involves identifying the possible **risks** before you do an activity, and **taking precautions** to avoid **putting yourself or others in danger**.

1 **Read the Fact box. Match definitions 1–4 with the words and expressions in bold.**

1 the possibility that something dangerous might happen
2 the process of calculating how much risk is involved in a particular action
3 acting in a way that could harm yourself or others
4 doing something to protect yourself or others against possible dangers

TO THE RESCUE!

FAQS: MOUNTAIN RESCUE

What is mountain rescue?

In the UK, Mountain Rescue teams are run by trained volunteers. They work with the emergency services when people call the number 999 with mountain-related emergencies.

Who do they help?

They help anyone who's in danger in the countryside. For example, one recent rescue involved two climbers stuck in freezing conditions on the Scottish mountain Ben Nevis.

What happens when there's an emergency call?

Volunteers are on call 24/7 – that is 24 hours a day, seven days a week. When there's an emergency, they leave their normal jobs and rush to the scene.

If it's a charity, who pays for the equipment?

Mountain rescue teams operate thanks to donations. Members of the public make a huge contribution every year to pay for their operation costs.

Who volunteers for mountain rescue?

Volunteers must be over 18, physically fit, and have good navigation skills and a first aid qualification.

***TOP TIP!** Mountain rescue recommends that people do a risk assessment before doing any outdoor activity, to avoid putting themselves and others in danger.

Essex teen Kiera Tippett knows all about risk and rescues. She was delighted to be one of six teenagers to take part in a reality TV programme called *Hero Squad*, working next to real-life lifesavers including firefighters, lifeboat crew and mountain rescue volunteers. The unforgettable experience took them all around Britain and ended with a simulated rescue operation. Speaking to Echo News she said, 'It was such a wonderful experience and I feel very lucky to have been one of very few to train with the emergency services.'

5 STEPS: RISK ASSESSMENT

1 Identify the dangers.
2 Who do the dangers affect, and how?
3 Evaluate the risks and decide on which precautions you can take.
4 Put your precautions in place.
5 Review the assessment regularly.

Exercise 2
run by = to organize and provide a service
emergency services = the organizations that deal with fire, accidents and injuries
stuck = to become difficult to move
equipment = things that you need for a particular job or activity
navigation = the skill of choosing a path

2 Words in context **Find these words in the text. What do they mean?**

run by emergency services stuck equipment navigation

3 **Read the text again and answer the questions.**

1 Who do mountain rescue volunteers help?
2 What do the volunteers do in an emergency?
3 What skills and qualities do volunteers need?
4 Who is Kiera Tippett and what did she do?

4 **Read the 5 steps. Have you ever done a risk assessment? In what situations would it be useful?**

Exercise 4
Students' own answers

5 **Work in pairs. Read the situation and do a risk assessment. Follow the 5 steps.**

You and some friends are planning to go hiking in the mountains next Saturday. None of you has been hiking in this area before.

Exercise 5
Students' own answers

Exercise 3
1 Anyone who is in danger in the countryside.
2 They leave their normal job and rush to the scene.
3 They must be over 18, physically fit, and have good navigation skills and a first aid qualification.
4 She was one of six teens who took part in a reality TV programme working with real-life lifesavers.

Life skills

Problem-solving (risk assessment)

LESSON OBJECTIVES
In this lesson students will:
- read a text about mountain rescue
- do a risk assessment

WARMER

Write the words *mountain rescue* on the board. Students make a list of reasons why mountains can be dangerous. Listen to their ideas and make a list on the board, e.g. *people can get lost*, *the weather can be bad*, *people can have accidents* etc.

FACT!

- Ask students to read the fact. Point out the difference between a *risk* and a *danger.* (A *danger* indicates a higher chance of more significant harm than a *risk*)

1
- Ask students to read the definitions carefully first.
- Students work individually matching the words in bold in the Fact! box with definitions 1-4.
- They compare answers in pairs.
- Check answers as a class.

2 Words in context
- Students find the words in the word box in the text. Encourage them to use the context to help them guess the meaning of the words.
- Check the answers as a class.

3
- Students read the questions carefully first.
- They read the text again and find the answers.
- They compare answers in pairs.
- Check answers as a class.

4
- Students read the five steps of risk assessment.
- They think about their answers to the two questions.
- Listen to their ideas as a class.

5
- Read the situation aloud to the class.
- Put students into pairs and ask them to follow the steps in exercise 4 to do a risk assessment of this situation.
- Listen to their ideas as a class.

17 Audioscript, page 23, exercise 4

Newsreader: ... And finally, here's the story of an unlucky accident, with a happy ending! Let's go over to Martha in Newville, to hear all about it ... Hello Martha?
Reporter: Hello! Yes, well we all know how difficult it is to separate teenagers from their mobiles, but last night 16-year-old Rachel Wright got into a very sticky situation right here! This is the drain where she – literally! – got stuck when her phone fell down there while she was out walking the dog with a friend. So she decided to remove this – very heavy! – drain cover, and reach down with her feet! When she couldn't get out, her friend started to panic and called 999. By the time the firefighters arrived, Rachel had been down there nearly ten minutes, and a crowd of people had gathered. By the time they pulled her out, photos had already gone viral on the internet! Fortunately, Rachel could see the funny side, and didn't lose her sense of humour. And she's joined us here now to tell us a bit more about her unforgettable experience ... Hello Rachel!
Rachel: Hello!
Reporter: Well, I'm glad to see you're well! You weren't injured, were you?
Rachel: No, I wasn't – it was just totally embarrassing!
Reporter: Hmm, I imagine! So, when you dropped your phone, why did you decide to go down there? I'm sure most of us wouldn't bother!
Rachel: Yeah – it was stupid. But I was furious because I'd only bought the phone two weeks before, so I hadn't had it very long at all. And I thought it'd be easy to get it back, you know ...
Reporter: But it wasn't that easy! They rescued you quite quickly, though, didn't they?
Rachel: Yes, the firefighters were amazing! They arrived in about ten minutes, and they just pulled me out straight away! They were going to send the paramedics but fortunately I didn't need any first aid!
Reporter: Hmm. So what did you do then, once you were out?
Rachel: Oh, I ran straight home and jumped in the bath! I'd been down the drain, so it was pretty disgusting!
Reporter: Yes, I imagine! And what about the phone – did you rescue it in the end?
Rachel: No – it was completely ruined!
Reporter: Hmm ... and how do you feel about these photos that've gone viral?
Rachel: Oh, they're hilarious! I don't mind really. Worse things could happen!
Reporter: Yes, indeed. Well, thanks for talking to us Rachel – I'm glad you're safe!
Rachel: Thank you!
Newsreader: Well, there's a story with a happy ending! Which is more than we can say for the weather forecast, I imagine! Let's go over to Susanna to hear more about that ...

Grammar

Subject and object questions

LESSON OBJECTIVES
In this lesson students will:
- contrast subject questions and object questions
- answer questions about a text on the RNLI
- read a text about a survival story

WARMER

Books closed. Write these words from the previous lesson with letters missing: *r_s_u_, e_e_g_n_y, f_e_z_n_, v_l_n_e_r, a_s_s_m_n_*. Students complete the spelling of the words. Elicit the correct spelling of each word from the class. (**Answer key:** rescue, emergency, freezing, volunteer, assessment)

1
- Students look at the table. They read the example questions and translate them into their language.
- They compare answers in pairs.
- Check the translations as a class.

ANALYSE

Highlight the use of the auxiliary verb *do / does / did* in object questions and emphasize that it is not used in subject questions.
Elicit the difference between subject and object questions in the students' language.

- If you are using the TPK and your students need more work on the meaning of the words, do the Grammar basics exercise.

Grammar basics

Answer key: 2 √ **4** √ **5** √ **6** √

2
- Read the two questions aloud to the class.
- Students work individually and find the answers by reading the text.
- They compare answers in pairs.
- Check answers as a class.

3
- Students work individually to match questions 1–4 with answers a–e. Point out that one answer isn't needed.
- They compare answers in pairs.
- Check answers as a class.

FINISHED?

Write the answers *237* and *140,000* on the board. Ask fast finishers to write questions for these answers (*How many lifeboat stations has the RNLI got? How many lives has it saved since it was set up?*).

CLIL

Grammar in context: Literature

4 18
- This activity practises the difference between the past perfect and past simple.
- Students read the whole text before they choose the correct tenses.
- They compare their answers in pairs.
- Play the audio. Students listen and check their answers.

5
- Students read the questions carefully first.
- They read the text again and answer the questions.
- Check answers as a class.

EXTRA ACTIVITY

Give students further practice by using the first paragraph of the text in exercise 4 as a dictation. Put students into pairs. One student dictates the first two sentences of the paragraph while the other writes. Then they swap roles for the last sentence of the paragraph.

LITERATURE TASK

Students use the internet to find out about the survival stories and decide which one is a true story. Check answers.

CULTURE NOTE

Although a work of fiction, *Robinson Crusoe* is believed to be based on the true story of Alexander Selkirk, a Scottish castaway who lived for four years on a Pacific island called Más a Tierra, now part of Chile. The island was renamed Robinson Crusoe Island in 1966

Grammar reference > Workbook page 86

Grammar
Subject and object questions

Exercise 1
Students' own answers

1 Look at the table. Read example questions a) and b). Translate them into your language.

subject questions

Volunteers help Mountain Rescue.
subject object
a) Who helps Mountain Rescue? Volunteers

object questions

Mountain Rescue helps people in danger.
subject object
b) Who does Mountain Rescue help? People in danger

ANALYSE

In English we don't use an auxiliary verb (such as *do*) in subject questions. Is there a difference between subject and object questions in your language?

Exercise 2
RNLI stands for Royal National Lifeboat Institution and is a charity that saves lives at sea. It has saved about 140,000 lives so far since it was set up.

2 Read the text. What does RNLI mean? How many lives has the RNLI saved since it began?

The RNLI: Saving lives at sea

The RNLI (Royal National Lifeboat Institution) is a charity that saves lives at sea. It helps all people who are in danger around the UK coasts, including swimmers, surfers and sailors.

The people that work for the RNLI are volunteers: there are about 4,600 crew members on the lifeboats, and thousands more that help in other ways.

The RNLI has got 237 lifeboat stations around the country and it operates 444 lifeboats. The charity has saved about 140,000 lives since it was set up in 1824.

Exercise 3
1 c
2 a
3 e
4 d

3 Match questions 1–4 with answers a–d. There's one answer that you don't need.

1 Who does the RNLI help?
2 Who works for the RNLI?
3 What happened in 1824?
4 How many lifeboats are there now?

a) Thousands of volunteers.
b) 4,600.
c) People who are in danger at sea.
d) 444.
e) The RNLI was founded.

CLIL
Grammar in context: Literature

4 Complete the text with the past simple or past perfect form of the verbs in brackets. Then listen and check. 18

Exercise 4
1 climbed
2 had already heard
3 had already taken
4 expected
5 ran out
6 fell
7 he decided
8 wrote

Touching the Void
by Joe Simpson

I've just finished reading *Touching the Void*. It's a true story about Joe Simpson and Simon Yates, who (1) … (**climb**) the Siula Grande mountain in Peru. I (2) … (**already** / **hear**) about this story because there's also a film about it. I think it's one of the greatest survival stories of all time!

When Simpson and Yates reached the summit of Siula Grande, their expedition (3) … (**already** / **take**) longer than they (4) … (**expect**) because of bad weather. Then they (5) … (**run out**) of fuel, so they couldn't melt snow to drink. Later, while they were descending, Simpson (6) … (**fall**). The two climbers were attached to the same rope and Yates had to make a terrible decision: cut the rope, or both fall to their death. What do you think (7) … (**he** / **decide**) to do? Perhaps you can guess by answering this question: Who (8) … (**write**) the book?!

5 Read the text again. Answer the questions.

1 Which mountain had Simpson and Yates climbed?
2 Who fell?
3 Who had to make a terrible decision?
4 Who wrote the book?

Exercise 5
1 Simpson and Yates had climbed the Siula Grande mountain in Peru.
2 Joe Simpson
3 Simon Yates
4 Joe Simpson

LITERATURE TASK

Find out more about other survival stories. Which one is a true story?
- *Robinson Crusoe* by Daniel Defoe
- *The Hunger Games* by Suzanne Collins
- *The Odyssey* by Homer
- *I'm Bahia, the Miracle Girl* by Bahia Bakari

Literature task
I'm Bahia, the Miracle Girl

Grammar basics | Grammar reference > Workbook p86

A survival game

LEARNING OUTCOME

✔ Take part in a group discussion

Today we're going to do a teamwork activity about survival. Which of these things do you think are the most useful?

TASK Explain the reason for your opinion

1 Read instructions for a game

2 Understand a group discussion

3 Write sentences with question tags

4 Present a group discussion

WHO WILL SURVIVE?

You and your team are going on a three-day trek in the desert.

- You each have basic food supplies, water, clothes and a map.
- Now choose five more items to take between you.
- Explain the reasons for your choices.
- How could the objects help you to survive?

Exercise 1
1 box
2 pack
3 pair
4 packet
5 bunch

Exercise 2
1 my team and I
2 the desert
3 three days
4 Students' own answers
5 Students' own answers
6 Students' own answers

1 Read

1 Read the instructions for the survival game. Complete 1–5 with these collective nouns.

- box • bunch • pack
- packet • pair

2 Work in groups. Answer the questions.

1 Who is going on the trek?
2 Where are you going?
3 How long will you be there?
4 Which five objects did you choose?
5 Which object do you think you need the most? Why?
6 Which is the least important object? Why?

2 Listen

3 Read and listen to the extract from a group discussion on page 27. Why is Emily unsure about the first aid kit? 19

4 Listen again and repeat. Practise your intonation.

5 Watch or listen to the complete group discussion. Which five objects do they mention? 20

6 Match 1–4 with question tags a–d. Then watch or listen again and check your answers.

1 We'd be in the middle of nowhere,	a) will we?
2 That's the most important thing,	b) wouldn't we?
3 I don't think we'll need it,	c) isn't it?
4 It'll be boiling hot,	d) won't it?

Exercise 6
1 b
2 c
3 a
4 d

Exercise 3
Because it's huge.

Exercise 4
Students' own answers

Exercise 5
the mobile phone
the first aid kit
the contact lenses and the bottle of cleaning solution
the pair of gloves
the packet of energy tablets

Integrated skills

A survival game

LESSON OBJECTIVES
In this lesson students will:
- work on all four skills
- read a set of instructions for a game
- watch or listen to a group discussion
- prepare and conduct a group discussion

WARMER
Write *Antarctica* on the board. Students tell you the most important things to take on a trip to Antarctica. Elicit examples and write them on the board, eg *boots*, *warm clothes*, *hat*, *gloves*, *sun cream*, *sunglasses*, etc.

1 Read

1 • Students read the instructions for the survival game and the labels for the items.
• They use the collective nouns to complete the labels.
• Check answers as a class.

LANGUAGE NOTE
The five gapped expressions in exercise 1 are examples of collocations. We cannot say *a packet of cards*. The only word that can fill the gap is *pack*. Point out that *pair* can be used with many different items, eg *a pair of shoes*, *a pair of trousers*, etc.

2 • Students work in groups and answer the questions.
• Check answers. Make sure students give reasons for their answers to questions 5 and 6.

2 Listen

Video with audio option
The dialogue is also available to watch as an audio file. If you prefer to present it this way, play the audio and follow the teacher's notes as for the video.

3 19 REC
• Students watch, read and listen to the extract from a group discussion. Elicit the answer to the question from the class.

4 • Play the audio again. Students listen and repeat and practise their intonation.

5 20
• Play the audio. Students listen to the complete discussion and note down their answers. Check answers.

6 • Students match sentences 1–4 with question tags a–d.
• They compare answers in pairs.
• Play the audio again. Students check their answers.

19 & 20 Audioscript, page 26, exercises 3, 4, 5 and 6

Emily: So, what do you think the most important thing is?
Oliver: Well, I had thought that the mobile phone would be the most useful thing, but then I realized it would be useless if the battery ran out.
Katy: Yes, and what if there was no signal? We'd be in the middle of nowhere, wouldn't we?
Oliver: Yes, I hadn't thought of that! I'm not sure if it's useful or not.
Jack: Well, I think we should take the first aid kit. That's the most important thing, isn't it?
Emily: I suppose so. But it's huge! Who's going to carry it?
Jack: Yeah, it's a bit heavy, but I think it would be really useful if someone had an accident.
Katy: Yes, I agree.
Oliver: Yes.
Emily: Me too.
Oliver: So, what about the things that we definitely don't need?
Katy: Like the contact lenses and the bottle of solution, for example!
Jack: Yes, that's a waste of space, isn't it?
Oliver: Yes, definitely.
Emily: Well, I don't know ... Didn't you hear about that boy who got lost in the Australian outback, and he survived by drinking contact lens fluid?
Jack: Really?
Katy: No way!
Oliver: Why had he taken contact lens fluid into the desert?
Emily: I've no idea. Anyway, I don't think we'll need it, will we? We've got water bottles, anyway.
Jack: Yeah. We don't need it.
Katy: No.
Oliver: What else? Things we don't need?
Emily: A pair of gloves?
Jack: Yes, who needs gloves in the desert? It'll be boiling hot, won't it?
Katy: Yes, let's get rid of the gloves. What else?
Oliver: Can I just say, let's take the packet of energy tablets. We'll need the extra energy. And if I'm starving, I don't want to eat disgusting things like insects!
Jack: Yeah – let's take the sweets.
Emily: OK. Right! So far we've got the first aid kit and the packet of sweets. What else ...?

7 • Students look at the Communication kit.
• Elicit which expressions are in the discussion.
• Play the audio again for students to check their answers.

3 Write

8 • Students look at the ten items in exercise 1 again.
• They work individually and rank them in order from 1–10, according to their importance.
• They make notes giving reasons for their choice.

9 • Students work individually and write full sentences with question tags for the five most important items in their list from exercise 8.
• Monitor while they are writing and give help if necessary.

4 Communicate

10 • Ask two students to read aloud the example question and answer.
• Students work in groups of three or four and discuss their ideas, using their notes from exercise 8. Remind them to use question tags.

11 • The purpose of this activity is for students to come to an agreement in their group about which five items are the most important.
• Set a time limit of five minutes for this activity.
• Ask each group to report back to the whole class giving reasons for their choices.

! COMMUNICATION TIP
QUESTION TAGS

Highlight that we use question tags to confirm information, check agreement, or just keep a discussion going.

Integrated skills > Resource centre

SPEAKING SKETCH

Emily: So, what do you think the most important thing is?

Katy: Yes, and what if there was no signal? We'd be in the middle of nowhere, wouldn't we?

Jack: Well, I think we should take the first aid kit. That's the most important thing, isn't it?

Oliver: Well, I had thought that the mobile phone would be the most useful thing, but then I realized it would be useless if the battery ran out.

Oliver: Yes, I hadn't thought of that! I'm not sure if it's useful or not.

Emily: I suppose so. But it's huge! Who's going to carry it?

Communication kit

- That's the most important thing, **isn't it?**
- I don't think we'll need it, **will we?**
- It'll be boiling hot, **won't it?**
- That isn't very useful, **is it?**
- We could use that for (cooking), **couldn't we?**
- We wouldn't use that, **would we?**

Exercise 7
That's the most important thing, isn't it?
It'll be boiling hot, won't it?
I don't think we'll need it, will we?

7 Look at the Communication kit. Which expressions are in the Speaking sketch? Watch or listen again to check your answers.

3 Write

Exercise 8
Students' own answers

8 Prepare your group discussion. Write the objects in order of importance, from 1 (most important) to 10 (least important). Prepare your reasons.

1 The most important object is … because …

Exercise 9
Students' own answers

9 Read the Communication tip. Practise using question tags. Write sentences for your five most important objects.

We could use the mirror for making a fire, couldn't we?

4 Communicate

Exercise 10
Students' own answers

10 In groups, discuss your ideas. Use your notes in exercise 8 and question tags.

Who thinks we should take the first aid kit?
I do! That would be really useful, wouldn't it?

Exercise 11
Students' own answers

11 In your group, make a final decision about your five objects. Compare your choices with the other groups, and explain your reasons.

! COMMUNICATION TIP
QUESTION TAGS

Use question tags to confirm information, check agreement or keep the discussion going.
That's the most important thing, isn't it?

Exercise 1
1 He was working on a farm in his gap year.
2 He didn't return.
3 After drinking a tiny bottle of water, he drank his own urine and contact lens solution.
4 A search and rescue helicopter found him.

Writing

A news report

LEARNING OUTCOME

✔ Write a news report about a survival story

1 Read the news report and answer the questions.

1 Why was Sam in Australia?
2 What happened when he went for a run?
3 How did he survive?
4 What happened in the end?

WORLD NEWS

NEWS | SPORT | WEATHER | EDUCATION | MORE

SURVIVAL IN THE AUSTRALIAN OUTBACK

① 18-year-old British student Sam Woodhead was working on a farm in Australia during his gap year. One afternoon, he went out for a run, but he got lost and didn't return. He hadn't told anyone where he was going. He was missing for three days and three nights.

② Sam had only taken a small rucksack, so he didn't have much water. It was boiling hot – over 40°C. At first, Sam drank the tiny bottle of water that he had taken. After that, he tried drinking his own urine (he had learnt this survival tip from a TV programme!). Then he found some packets of contact lens solution in his rucksack. He drank them slowly until they were finished. Finally Sam was exhausted and he thought he was going to die.

③ Eventually a search and rescue helicopter found Sam. 200 local volunteers had helped to look for him. By the time they found him, Sam was dehydrated and starving. He had lost 12 kg in three days. In the end, Sam recovered and he was delighted to survive his terrifying experience and be reunited with his family.

2 **Focus on content** Read the news report again and match paragraphs 1–3 with a–c.

a) narrates the sequence of events
b) explains how the story ends
c) introduces the people, place and time

Exercise 2
1 c
2 a
3 b

3 **Focus on language** Read the information. How many of the connectors can you find in the text? How do you say them in your language?

Connectors of sequence
At first Next Then Later
After that Finally
Eventually In the end

Exercise 3
At first
After that
Then
Finally
Eventually
In the end

4 Choose the correct connectors.

British paraglider Guy Anderson crashed while he was flying in Idaho, USA. (1) **In the end** / **At first**, he tried to use his radio, but it didn't work. (2) **Next** / **Eventually**, he checked his mobile phone, but there was no signal. Guy had some terrible injuries, and it was very difficult to walk. (3) **Eventually** / **At first**, after two days, he heard a search and rescue helicopter. Amazingly, the terrifying accident didn't put Guy off paragliding, and he returned to the sky (4) **in the end** / **then**!

Exercise 4
1 At first
2 Next
3 Eventually
4 in the end

5 Write a news report about a survival story.

Exercise 5
Students' own answers

Writing kit

1 **Plan** your story. Choose or invent a story and answer these questions.
- Who?
- When?
- Where?
- Why?
- What happened?

2 **Write** your news report using three paragraphs:
1 Introduce the people, place and time.
2 Narrate the sequence of events.
3 Explain how the story ends.

3 **Useful phrases**

One morning / day ...
At first, ...
After that / Then ...
In the end, ...

4 **Check** your writing.

☑ connectors of sequence
☑ extreme adjectives
☑ check that you've used the past tenses correctly
☑ three paragraphs

Study guide > p100
Writing hub > Workbook p114

Writing
A news report

LESSON OBJECTIVES
In this lesson students will:
- read a news report
- use connectors of sequence
- write a news report

WARMER
Write *Australian outback* on the board. Students tell you what they know about the Australian outback. Elicit ideas and write key words and phrases on the board.

1 • Students read the text and answer the questions.
• Check answers as a class.

2 Focus on content
• Students work individually and complete the task.
• They compare their answers in pairs.
• Check answers as a class.

3 Focus on language
• Students read the list of connectors of sequence.
• They work individually and find examples of these connectors of sequence in the text in exercise 1.
• Check answers as a class.
• Students translate the connectors of sequence into their language.

4 • Explain the task. Encourage students to read the whole text before they choose the connectors.
• Check answers as a class.

5 • Explain the task. Ask students to follow the stages in the writing kit.
• Encourage them to use connectors of sequence in their stories.
• Monitor while they are writing and give help if necessary.
• At the check stage, ask them to swap notebooks and check each other's writing.

Writing kit
The aim of this activity is for students to produce a piece of guided writing that includes the correct use of connectors of sequence and that uses extreme adjectives. It also gives them practice in using past tenses correctly. Ask the students to follow the stages in the Student's Book. Encourage them to use the texts in exercises 1 and 4 for ideas. Monitor while they are writing and give help with vocabulary if necessary. At the Check stage, ask them to swap notebooks and check each other's writing.

Study guide > Student's Book page 100

Writing hub > Workbook page 114

UNIT 3

YOUR FUTURE

UNIT OBJECTIVES AND KEY COMPETENCES

In this unit the student will learn ...

- to recognize, understand and correctly use vocabulary related to future aspirations and time management CLC CMST SCC CAE SIE
- to recognize, understand and correctly use different future tenses and use them in a short speaking activity CLC L2L SIE
- to recognize, understand and correctly use the future continuous CLC L2L
- about preparing for a formal interview and an interview technique CLC CMST SCC
- about attending formal interviews by watching a short video CLC DC SCC

In this unit the student will learn ...

- to identify specific information in a text about summer camps CLC CMST CAE
- to look online for more information about summer camps CLC DC CMST CAE SIE
- to identify specific information in a text about preparing for a formal interview CLC CMST SCC
- to read information about work experience placements, listen to a formal interview, prepare for and practise a formal interview CLC CMST CAE SIE
- to prepare for and do a speaking exam talking about a prepared topic CLC SCC L2L SIE
- to write a CV for a work experience programme CLC SCC SIE L2L

LINGUISTIC CONTENTS

Main vocabulary

- Future aspirations: *get a holiday job*, *do voluntary work*, *study abroad*, etc
- Time management: *set goals*, *meet a deadline*, *prioritize*, etc

Extra vocabulary

- Words in context: *are you kidding?*, *don't just take our word for it!*, *exactly!*, *find a balance*, *health and safety regulations*, *a paper round*, *the best ... in the world*, *transferable skills*
- Word builder: *make* and *do*, Phrasal verbs with *off*

Grammar

- Future tenses
- Future continuous

Functional language

- Phrases for interviews
- Phrases for answering questions about a prepared topic in an exam
- Phrases for talking about the future in an exam

Pronunciation

- Contractions *'ll* and *won't*

SKILLS

Reading

- Read online information about summer camps
- Read a text about part-time work
- Read a notice about work experience
- Read a CV

Writing: Interaction and production

- Write notes to prepare for an interview for a work experience placement
- Write a CV in three steps

Listening

- Listen to a Q&A session about a student exchange trip
- Listen to a text about part-time work
- Listen to a formal interview

Spoken interaction

- Ask and answer questions about future plans

Spoken production

- Prepare and act out a formal interview

LIFELONG LEARNING SKILLS

Self-study and self-evaluation

- Study guide: Student's Book page 101
- Progress check: Workbook page 30
- Extension: Workbook page 31
- Grammar reference and practice: Workbook pages 88–89
- Wordlist: Workbook pages 151–157

Learning strategies and thinking skills

- Learning to identify facts and opinions
- Critical thinking: Identifying missing information

Life skills

- Part-time work
- Preparing for an interview and practising interview technique

Cross-curricular contents

- Literature: *England* by Rachel Bladon
- Literature task: searching the internet for further information on other English writers

EVALUATION

- Unit 3 End-of-unit test: Basic, Standard and Extra
- End-of-term test: Basic, Standard and Extra
- CEFR Skills Exam Generator

KEY COMPETENCES

CAE	Cultural awareness and expression
CLC	Competence in linguistic communication
CMST	Competence in mathematics, science and technology
DC	Digital competence
L2L	Learning to learn
SCC	Social and civic competences
SIE	Sense of initiative and entrepreneurship

DIGITAL MATERIAL

New Pulse Digital Course including:

- Interactive vocabulary presentation
- Grammar and Vocabulary basics exercises
- Getting started video
- Flipped classroom grammar video: Future tenses
- Culture byte video: Choosing your future
- Speaking sketch video: A formal interview

DIGITAL COMPETENCE

- Web quest: Find out more about a summer camp
- Digital competence worksheet: Timelines

REINFORCEMENT MATERIAL

- New Pulse Basics: Teacher's Resource Centre
- Vocabulary and grammar consolidation worksheets: Teacher's Resource Centre
- Grammar and Vocabulary basics exercises: Teacher's Presentation Kit

EXTENSION MATERIAL

- Vocabulary and grammar extension worksheets: Teacher's Resource Centre
- Advance your vocabulary: Workbook page 105
- The longer read: Teacher's Resource Centre
- Writing hub: Workbook page 116

TEACHER'S RESOURCE CENTRE

- Translation and dictation
- Evaluation rubrics
- Key competences worksheets
- Culture and CLIL worksheets
- Culture byte video worksheets
- Digital competence worksheets
- Macmillan Readers worksheets
- Integrated Skills

Vocabulary
Future aspirations

LESSON OBJECTIVES
In this lesson students will:
- learn a set of phrases related to study, travel and work
- learn collocations with *make* and *do*
- read and answer a quiz

VIDEO: GETTING STARTED

In this video the speakers answer the question *Have you got any plans for the next five years? What are they?*

- Focus the students on the unit title *Your Future*.
- Write the following questions on the board: **1** Who wants to get a degree in Maths? **2** Who wants to pass his / her driving test? (2 speakers) **3** Who wants to be an actor?
- Students watch the video and complete the sentences on the board.
- Students watch the video again to check answers.
- At the end of the lesson, ask students to answer the question from the video: *Have you got any plans for the next five years? What are they?*

Answer key: 1 Kirsty **2** Kirsty, Will **3** Harry

WARMER

Introduce the topic. Write *future* on the board. Elicit words/phrases that refer to the future from the class and make a list on the board, eg *tomorrow, the day after tomorrow, next week, in two years' time*, etc.

1 21
- Students read the phrases in blue.
- Play the audio. Students listen and repeat.
- If you are using the TPK and your students need more work on the meaning of the words, do the Vocabulary basics exercise.

Vocabulary basics

Answer key: Work get a holiday job, make money, do voluntary work, do work experience, apply for a job, go for an interview; **Study** get a degree, pass your exams, study abroad; **Travel** go on an exchange, go backpacking, study abroad; **Other** leave home, make new friends, pass your driving test

LANGUAGE NOTE

In all the phrases in exercise 1, the main stress is not on the verbs, eg *apply for a job, do voluntary work.*

2
- Students do the quiz.
- They work individually to complete the task.
- Ask individual students if they agree with the results.

3
- Ask students to work individually and decide which of the things they think they will do in the future.
- They compare ideas in pairs.

4 Word builder
- Ask students to read the Word builder carefully.
- Point out that some words and expressions go with *make* and others go with *do*.
- Encourage students to copy the table and expressions into their notebooks and add collocations with *make* and *do* when they meet them.
- Students add the expressions in the box to the correct column in the table.
- They compare answers in pairs.
- Check answers as a class.

LANGUAGE NOTE

Highlight the fact that words and expressions that go with *do* are often words related to work, jobs or tasks, eg *do the housework, do a job, do a task, do business, do the shopping. Make* often has the sense of construct in collocations, eg *make a list, make a cake, make an appointment, make a telephone call.*

FINISHED?

Write these words on the board: *the washing-up, an effort, an exception, the cleaning, a good job, a noise*. Ask students to decide which three expressions that go with *do* and which three go with *make*. (**Answer key:** do the washing-up, the cleaning, a good job; make an effort, an exception, a noise.)

YOUR FUTURE

UNIT 3

LEARNING OUTCOMES IN THIS UNIT

- Identify facts and opinions in a text
- Listen to a Q&A session and make notes
- Practise a formal interview
- Write a CV for a work experience position

VIDEO: GETTING STARTED

WATCH Watch the teenagers talking about their future plans and answer the question.

Vocabulary
Future aspirations

Exercise 1
Students' own answers

Exercise 2
Students' own answers

Exercise 3
Students' own answers

1 Look at the quiz. Listen and repeat the words in blue. Have you done any of these things yet? 21

2 Do the quiz. Do you agree with your result?

3 In pairs, compare your answers to the quiz. Which of these things do you think you will do in the future? At what age?

4 **Word builder** Read the information. Copy and complete the table with these expressions.

arrangements a choice a decision the housework your homework

MAKE AND DO
It's easy to confuse expressions with *make* and *do*. Check them in a dictionary and make a list in your notebook.

make	*do*
friends money	voluntary work work experience

Exercise 4
Make:
a decision
arrangements
a choice
Do:
the housework
your homework

WHAT ARE YOU GOING TO DO NEXT SUMMER?

START HERE

Which of these goals is most important to you in the future?

Get a holiday job and / or make money.

Get a degree and / or learn languages.

Leave home and / or travel the world.

Do you have a specific goal?

What's more important: to pass your exams or to make new friends?

Yes – you want to save up to buy a moped or pass your driving test.

No – you're happy to do voluntary work, get a part-time job or do work experience.

You're quite ambitious, so studying is more important.

You're a free spirit – you're ready to meet new people and explore the world!

WORK
It's definitely time to apply for a job. Good luck when you go for an interview!

STUDY
If you want to study abroad, you could either go on an exchange or sign up for a language course.

TRAVEL
The world is your oyster – it's time to go backpacking!

Reading

Online information

LEARNING OUTCOME

✔ Identify facts and opinions

Exercise 1
Location, activities

1 Read the headings quickly. What information do you think you will find out? Then read, listen and check. 22

- location • trip dates • accommodation
- price • activities • age requirements

Exercise 2
a) opinion
b) fact
c) fact
d) opinion

2 Read the information. Find a–d in the texts. Are they facts or opinions?

IDENTIFY FACTS AND OPINIONS
A fact is something that can be checked and proved to be true. An opinion is based on personal beliefs or views.

a) Sharks are beautiful, gentle creatures.
b) You must already have a scuba-diving certificate before going on this camp.
c) 20% of all participants are international students.
d) If English isn't your first language, don't let that put you off.

Exercise 3
Are you kidding? = Are you being serious?
Don't just take our word for it! = You can discover for yourself that what we are saying is true.
Exactly! = That is correct!

3 Words in context Find these words and phrases in the text. What do they mean?

Are you kidding?
Don't just take our word for it! Exactly!

Exercise 4
1 b (this one is not about Shark Camp or Space Camp.)
2 e
3 d
4 c
5 a

4 Match the sentence beginnings and endings. Which one is *not* about Shark Camp or Space Camp?

1 Perhaps you ...
2 You'll ...
3 You'll also do ...
4 You'll be ...
5 There will ...

a) be plenty of astronaut training.
b) will find an exciting camp near you.
c) staying at the Space Academy base.
d) a marine biology project.
e) stay on Fiji's largest island.

5 Copy and complete the sentences with information from the text.

1 Some ideas for summer plans mentioned in the first paragraph are ...
2 Some parents might worry about Shark Camp because ...
3 The Shark Reef Marine Reserve is ...
4 On the final Friday at Space Camp there's ...

The longer read > Resource centre

FANTASTIC

Home | About | **Summer camps**

What are you going to do next summer? Hopefully you won't have to stay at home and study! Maybe you're planning to go backpacking, do voluntary work or get a summer job and make some money. Or perhaps you're going to switch off and relax by the pool. But if you're thinking of setting off on a summer camp, check out these great ideas. You might not be able to go to Fiji or the USA, but perhaps you'll find something equally exciting closer to home!

Photo courtesy of Broadreach

SHARK CAMP

What is it?
A 24-day trip diving with sharks in Fiji.

Are you kidding?!
Well, it might be hard to persuade your parents to let you swim with sharks without a cage – we've all seen *Jaws*, haven't we? But apparently sharks are beautiful, gentle creatures!

OK, so where is it exactly and what else will I do?
You'll stay near the Shark Reef Marine Reserve on Fiji's largest island. You'll start off scuba diving on the reserve, and have the chance to try some white-water kayaking. You'll also do a research project about marine biology and global ecology.

Is this camp for me?
The minimum age is 15, and you must already have a scuba-diving certificate before going on this camp.

Don't just take our word for it!

'This trip was absolutely amazing. I loved diving with sharks, being immersed in Fijian culture and making great new friends. All in all it was an experience that I will remember for the rest of my life.' **Sander E (17)**

Exercise 5
1 Some ideas for summer plans mentioned in the first paragraph are backpacking, volunteering or getting a summer job to make some money.
2 Some parents might worry about Shark Camp because you'll be swimming with sharks without a cage.
3 The Shark Reef Marine Reserve is on Fiji's largest island.
4 On the final Friday at Space Camp there's a special graduation ceremony.

Reading
Online information

LESSON OBJECTIVES
In this lesson students will:
- read online material
- identify facts and opinions
- formulate questions to get further information

WARMER
Mime scuba diving and ask students to guess the sport or activity. The student who guesses correctly then mimes another sport or activity. Write each word on the board.

1 22
- Students read the six words and check that they understand them.
- They read the headings in the texts and decide which of the six information categories they will find in the text.
- Do not check the answers at this stage.
- Play the audio. Students listen and follow the text in their books.
- They note down the answers.

READING STRATEGY
Identifying facts and opinions
It is a key skill for readers to be able to decide which parts of a text are facts and which are opinions. Facts are true and can be checked. Opinions are what people think and believe about a particular topic.

2
- Ask students to read the definitions and statements a)–d) carefully first.
- They read the text again and answer the questions.
- Check answers as a class.

BACKGROUND
A summer camp is a programme for children and teens during the school summer holidays. There are many different types of summer camps: sports camps, language camps, religious camps, music camps, etc. The thing they have in common is that they offer a wide range of outdoor and social activities. They can be day camps or those where the participants board for a number of days or weeks. Summer camps are very popular in the US and parts of Europe.

3 Words in Context
- Read the three words and phrases aloud to the class.
- Students find the phrases in the text and discuss their meaning in pairs.
- Check answers as a class.

4
- Explain the task and highlight the fact that one sentence is not in either of the texts.
- Students work individually to match the beginnings and endings and read the texts again to discover which sentence is not mentioned.
- Check answers as a class.

5
- Ask students to copy the sentence beginnings into their notebooks and then complete each sentence using information from the text.
- Note that sentence 2 will require students to use their own ideas rather than copying information from the text.
- Check answers as a class.

6 Word Builder

- Highlight the fact that phrasal verbs can sometimes have a literal meaning but also an idiomatic meaning.
- Students find the four phrasal verbs in the text and use the context to help them match the verbs with their meanings.
- Check answers as a class before asking students to use a dictionary to find the meanings of *lift off* and *take off*. Highlight the fact that *take off* has several meanings.

7
- Read the three questions aloud to the class.
- Students work in pairs and discuss the questions.
- Check answers as a class. Find out which of the camps is the most popular.

DID YOU KNOW?

Highlight the *Did you know?* box. Students read about four more types of summer camp.

CRITICAL THINKING

- Students look at exercise 1 again and decide which of the six pieces of information are not mentioned in the texts.
- Students work individually and write questions to help them find out that information (eg *How much does Space Camp cost?*).
- Check answers as a class.

WEB QUEST

Students find out more about summer camps.

1 Think Ask students to read the information in the *Did you know?* box again as this may give them ideas about the kind of summer camp they would like to research in the web quest. Give them time to write questions about the camp using the categories in exercise 1 if necessary.

2 Investigate They open a search engine (eg *Google*) and type in 'summer camp'. They find as much information as they can about the summer camp they have chosen and make notes. Monitor while they are working and give help with vocabulary if necessary.

3 Communicate They share their information with their partner.

Listen to the information pairs have found out as a class.

TIP! Point out that students should carefully study all of the different tabs on the menu bars of the website and any links at the bottom of the page. Often these will provide additional information that students will find useful. Some websites have a site map link which provides a quick glance at all of the content on the site.

VIDEO: FLIPPED CLASSROOM

You may want to ask students to watch the Flipped classroom video for unit 3 as homework in preparation for the following grammar lesson. The Flipped grammar presentation focuses on future tenses

The longer read > Resource centre

SUMMER FUN!

SPACE CAMP

What is it?
A one-week camp for future astronauts.

But not in space, right?
Exactly! You won't actually travel into space – you'll be staying at the Space Academy base in Huntsville, Alabama.

And what will I do there?
There will be plenty of astronaut training, finishing off with a simulated mission to the International Space Station, the Moon or Mars. You'll also have the opportunity to fly aircraft simulators and complete team challenges such as building a space rover. The camp starts on a Sunday morning and finishes the following Friday with a special graduation ceremony.

Is this camp for me?
Advanced Space Academy is for 15–18-year-olds. About 20% of all participants are international students, so if English isn't your first language, don't let that put you off.

Don't just take our word for it!

'This experience was even more awesome than I had imagined. I'll probably never do anything so exciting again.' ***Ava Ballinger***

DID YOU KNOW?

There are summer camps for learning circus skills, doing Hollywood stunts and fighting zombie battles. There's even a social enterprise camp in New York that teaches you how to get rich!

6 Word builder Read the information and answer the questions.

PHRASAL VERBS WITH *OFF*
One of the most common particles in phrasal verbs is *off*. Sometimes the meaning is literal, but sometimes the meaning is different.
switch off = turn off a machine
switch off = relax and rest

1 Find these phrasal verbs in the text. Match them with definitions a–d.

set off start off finish off put (someone) off

a) begin doing a particular activity
b) begin a journey
c) make someone not want to do something
d) finish doing a particular activity

2 Look up these phrasal verbs in a dictionary. What do they mean?

lift off take off

7 Work in pairs. Ask and answer the questions.

1 Which of these camps would you prefer? Why?
2 Have you ever been to a summer camp?
3 What are you planning to do next summer?

Exercise 6
1
a) start off
b) set off
c) put (someone) off
d) finish off
2
Students' own answers

Exercise 7
Students' own answers

CRITICAL THINKING

ENQUIRE
Read the texts again and look at exercise 1. Identify which bits of information are missing. Write a list of questions that would help you to find out the missing information.

WEB QUEST

Find out more information about a summer camp you're interested in.

1 **Think** Choose a summer camp. It could be in your country or a different country. Write five questions about the information you want to find out.
2 **Investigate** Search online for the answers and take notes.
3 **Communicate** Share your information with a classmate, then swap. Whose summer camp sounds more interesting?

TIP! Remember to explore all areas of a website to find useful information. Click on all the different tabs or locate the site map.

Grammar
Future tenses

VIDEO: FLIPPED CLASSROOM

WATCH

Watch the grammar presentation and do the task.

Exercise 1
1 b
2 a
3 d
4 f
5 e
6 c

1 Match example sentences 1–6 with uses a–f. Do you use the same tenses to talk about the future in your language?

will / won't

1 I'**ll come** with you!
2 You **won't travel** to space.

be going to

3 What **are** you **going to do** next summer?

present continuous

4 I'**m doing** voluntary work in July.

present simple

5 The camp **starts** on Sunday.

might

6 You **might meet** people from around the world.

a) future predictions
b) spontaneous promises, offers or decisions
c) future possibilities
d) future intentions
e) schedules and timetables
f) future arrangements

Exercise 2
1 'I'll open the window.'
2 'I'll turn it off.'
3 'I'll come back later.'
4 'I'll bake a cake.'
5 'I'll carry it.'

2 Make spontaneous promises, offers or decisions for these situations. Use the words in brackets.

'I can't do this exercise.' (I / help)
'I'll help you!'

1 'It's hot in here.' (I / open the window)
2 'Is that your alarm ringing?' (I / turn it off)
3 'I'm busy at the moment.' (I / come back later)
4 'It's Jo's birthday tomorrow.' (I / bake a cake)
5 'This backpack is too heavy.' (I / carry it)

Exercise 3
Students' own answers

3 Write true sentences about your future. Use (*not*) *be going to* or *might* (*not*). Add more information.

live abroad
I might live abroad. Perhaps I'll move to New York!

1 stay at this school next year
2 pass my driving test when I'm 18
3 go to university
4 make a lot of money

Exercise 4
1 I'm / I am meeting them at the station.
2 The concert starts at nine o'clock.
3 We're / We are going for a pizza before the concert.
4 What are you doing this evening?

4 Write sentences using the present simple or present continuous.

My cousins' train / arrive / at 18.10.
My cousins' train arrives at 18.10.

1 I / meet them / at the station.
2 The concert / start / at nine o'clock.
3 We / go for a pizza / before the concert.
4 What / you do / this evening?

LOOK!
be about to
I'm about to go to London.

Exercise 5
1 are you doing, f
2 are you going to do, d
3 might visit, c
4 'll have, a
5 leaves, e
6 'll call, b

5 Choose the correct words. Then match 1–6 with uses a–f in exercise 1.

Amy: Hi, Tom. How are you?
Tom: Fine! Hey, what (1) **are you doing** / **do you do** this weekend?
Amy: Well, I'm about to go to London!
Tom: Fantastic! What (2) **will you do** / **are you going to do** there?
Amy: I'm going to a concert with my cousins. I'm not sure, but we (3) **might go** / **are going** sightseeing, too.
Tom: Sounds great. I'm sure you (4) **'ll have** / **'re having** a fantastic time!
Amy: Sorry, Tom, I have to go. My train (5) **will leave** / **leaves** in two minutes!
Tom: Oh, OK. Have a great time!
Amy: Thanks! I (6) **call** / **'ll call** you later, OK?

Exercise 6
1 Are you doing
2 are you going to do
3 you'll learn
4 Will any of your friends be
5 does your next class start

6 Copy and complete the questions with the correct future tenses. In pairs, ask and answer the questions.

1 ... (you / do) anything special this weekend?
2 What ... (you / do) when you leave school?
3 Do you think ... (you / learn) to drive?
4 ... (any of your friends / be) famous one day?
5 What time ... (your next class / start)?

Grammar
Future tenses

LESSON OBJECTIVES
In this lesson students will:
- learn different ways of talking about the future
- ask and answer questions about the future

WARMER
Books closed. Ask students to work in pairs and discuss what they plan to do that evening. Listen to their ideas but do not correct their use of future forms if they make errors as this is the focus of this lesson.

VIDEO: FLIPPED CLASSROOM
- If you set the video for homework, ask students to compare their Task time! answers and then check the answers as a class.
- If you didn't set it for homework, watch the video in class and answer the Task time! questions at the end of the presentation.

Answer key: 1 two o'clock **2** a first-aid kit **3** a tent

1
- Students read the information in the table and match example sentences (1–6) with their uses (a–f).
- Highlight the use of *will* / *won't*. Point out that it is not used for future intentions or definite arrangements.

2
- Read the example sentence aloud to the class. Highlight the contracted form.
- Remind students to use the *will* form of the future here as the sentences are spontaneous promises, offers or decisions.
- Point out that they will need to add an object pronoun in questions 1 and 2.
- Check answers as a class.
- If you are using the TPK and your students need more practice of the grammar, do the Grammar basics exercise.

Grammar basics
Answer key: 1 won't (future predictions) **2** will (spontaneous promises) **3** might (future possibilities) **4** is going to go (future intentions) **5** arrives (schedules and timetables) **6** 're having (definite arrangements)

3
- Show how the example sentence is made from the prompt. Remind students that *might* is used for future possibilities and *going to* for future intentions.
- Students work individually and write true sentences using the prompts. Remind them to add more information.
- Check answers as a class. Correct any errors in the use of the future forms.

4
- Remind students that the present simple is used for schedules and timetables and the present continuous for definite arrangements.
- Students complete the exercise.
- Check answers as a class.

5
- This activity practises the different future forms.
- Ask students to read the whole dialogue before they choose the correct words and match 1–6 with uses a–f in exercise 1.
- Students work individually to complete the exercise.
- They compare answers in pairs.
- Check answers as a class.

LANGUAGE NOTE
Ask students to read the example sentence. Highlight that we use *be about to* for actions we are going to do very, very soon. Write one or two further examples on the board, eg *We're about to finish our exams. They're about to go on holiday.*

6
- Encourage students to refer back to the rules in exercise 1 to check that they are using the correct future tenses.
- Students complete the questions individually.
- Check answers as a class.
- Students work in pairs and ask and answer the questions.
- Check answers as a class.

Grammar reference > Workbook page 88

Pronunciation lab > Contractions *'ll* and *won't* > Student's Book page 124

Vocabulary and Listening

Time management

LESSON OBJECTIVES
In this lesson students will:

- learn phrases related to time management
- listen for specific information

WARMER

Write the word *time* on the board. Students work in pairs and think of three verbs that can go before *time* and three nouns that combine with *time* to make compound nouns, eg *save time*, *timetable*.

DIGITAL VOCABULARY FLASHCARDS

In this digital presentation, students match the vocabulary with definitions.

- Do the digital presentation with the class.
- Encourage students to repeat the words.

1 23

- Elicit the meaning of the words in blue.
- Highlight that different verbs collocate with the nouns in the phrases and that these are fixed expressions, eg we say *find a balance* (not *make a balance*).
- Play the audio. Pause after each of the words/ phrases in blue for students to repeat them.
- If you are using the TPK and your students need more work on the meaning of the words, do the Vocabulary basics exercise.

Vocabulary basics

Answer key: 1 develop **2** waste **3** off **4** meet **5** make **6** Plan

2 • Explain that a Venn diagram has three main areas and that the middle area contains items that could be in both of the other areas.
- Students copy the diagram into their notebooks and add the phrases to the correct part of the diagram.
- Check answers as a class.

3 • Students complete the gaps. Check answers.
- Students then ask and answer the questions in pairs.

4 • Students read the poster and answer the questions. Check answers.

5 24

- Play the audio. Students listen and complete the notes. Check answers as a class.

24 Audioscript, exercises 5 and 6

Teacher: Hello, everyone! Are we all here? Are you looking forward to the trip? OK! one important thing before we start ... Can I just remind everyone that the deadline for the final payment is Tuesday, OK? Right, well, I'm going to start with the itinerary, so you can see how we'll be organizing our time in Paris, OK? ... and then you can ask questions, all right? Any doubts you might have ... Right! So, the itinerary. Well, we leave on Saturday, and I'm afraid it's going to be a very early start ... You'll need to set your alarm 'cause we're meeting here outside school at quarter to six, OK? Got that? 5.45! Don't be late – the bus leaves at six o'clock. We're going to travel through the Channel Tunnel and we'll get to Paris about five o'clock in the afternoon. Then, Sunday will be a day with your host family – so you'll have time to get to know them. We won't all meet up again until Monday morning ... when you'll go to school with your exchange partners, OK? You're going to spend the morning with them, so you'll see what it's like to study abroad! Then on Monday afternoon we're visiting the Louvre. Anyone know what that is? Yes, Michael?
Michael: A gallery!
Teacher: That's right – a huge art gallery in the centre of Paris. OK, so on Tuesday we're going sightseeing ... We'll take a boat trip down the river, and you'll see all the landmarks as we go by ... Then, on Wednesday morning, you'll be at school again, and then in the afternoon we're going to go up the Eiffel Tower! So let's hope Wednesday's a fine day, and we'll get some great views! OK. Thursday ... err, on Thursday we're going on a trip to Versailles. What's Versailles, does anyone know?
Student 1: A palace?
Teacher: Yes – a 17th-century royal chateau! We're going to travel there by train, and we'll be there all day ... OK? Then, Friday – Friday is our trip to Disneyland! Another full-day excursion ... And that brings us to Saturday, when we travel back home ... Right, so that gives you an idea of what we're going to do. Now, any questions? Yes, Tom?
Tom: What time will we get home? On that final Saturday?
Teacher: Good question. We won't be back 'til about midnight, I'm afraid, so it'll be a late night for your parents to come and meet you! OK, anyone else? Yes, Tanya?
Tanya: Will we have to do lessons when we go to school there?
Teacher: I'm afraid so! But it'll be fun – you'll see!
Student 3: How much money will we need to take?
Teacher: Well, you'll need to plan ahead and work out what you think you'll use ... All the trips are already included, so you'll just need pocket money – about €50 should be fine? Any more questions? Yes, Sarah?

6 • Ask students to read the information carefully first. Play the audio again. Check answers.

Advance your vocabulary > Workbook page 105

Vocabulary and Listening

Time management

LEARNING OUTCOME

✔ Listen to a Q&A session and make notes

DIGITAL VOCABULARY FLASHCARDS

Do the matching exercise to discover the new vocabulary.

develop a routine   find a balance   get organized   make a list
meet a deadline   plan ahead   prioritize   put (something) off
set a goal   set a reminder   take a break   waste time

Exercise 1
Students' own answers

1 Read the time management tips. Which tip do you think is most important? Listen and repeat the words in blue. 23

HOW TO MANAGE YOUR TIME EFFECTIVELY

- Get organized! Remember to set goals, make lists and plan ahead.
- Don't waste time. Prioritize the most important things – don't put them off!
- Develop a routine for regular study and revision.
- Don't miss an important deadline! Set a reminder on your phone to help you meet a deadline.
- Find a balance between study time and free time. Don't forget to take a break every hour.

Exercise 2
Positive:
set goals
make lists
plan ahead
prioritize
develop a routine
meet a deadline
find a balance
Neutral:
set a reminder
take a break
Negative:
put off

2 Copy and complete the diagram with the words and expressions in blue in exercise 1.

positive	neutral	negative
get organized		*waste time*

Exercise 3
1 set
2 take
3 waste
4 put
5 set

3 Copy and complete the questions with the correct verb forms in exercise 1. Then work in pairs and ask and answer the questions.

1 What goals have you ... for this term in your English class?
2 How often do you ... a break while you're studying? What do you do?
3 Do you ever ... time while you're doing research on the internet? What are the distractions?
4 Do you ever ... off doing your homework? What do you do instead?
5 Do you know how to ... a reminder on your phone? Describe the process.

4 Look at the poster for a Q&A (Question and Answer) session. What will the meeting be about? Who will you hear?

Exercise 4
the French exchange trip, Mme Blanche answering students' questions

5 Emily is going on the exchange trip. Listen and complete her notes in your notebook. 24

French exchange trip: itinerary

Saturday	*Meet at school at (1) ...*
Sunday	*Day with host family*
Monday	*Morning: At (2) ...* *Afternoon: Visit to the Louvre*
Tuesday	*All day sightseeing, including a boat trip*
Wednesday	*Morning: At school* *Afternoon: (3) ...*
Thursday	*Excursion to Versailles, travel by (4) ...*
Friday	*Day trip to (5) ...*
Saturday	*Return home*

Exercise 5
1 5.45 (a quarter to six)
2 school
3 the Eiffel Tower
4 train
5 Disneyland

6 Listen again and write the following information.

1 when the deadline is for the final payment
2 the time the bus leaves on Saturday
3 the time they'll arrive in Paris
4 when the Versailles Palace was built
5 the time they'll arrive home
6 how much pocket money they might need

Exercise 6
1 Tuesday
2 6 o'clock
3 about 5 o'clock in the afternoon
4 17th century
5 about midnight
6 about €50

Vocabulary basics   Advance your vocabulary > Workbook p105

Social awareness

Part-time work

Exercise 1
1 12
2 35
3 16

1 Read and listen to the text. Copy and complete the summary with the correct numbers. 25

In the UK, 15–16 year-olds can work up to (1) ... hours a week during school time, and up to (2) ... hours a week during the school holidays. They earn the national minimum wage from the age of (3) ...

FACT! As of 2018, the national minimum wage in the UK is £4.20 / hour for 16–18-year-olds. It increases to £5.90 (age 18–20), £7.38 (age 21–24) and £7.83 (age 25+).

Exercise 2
1 a paper round
2 health and safety regulations
3 transferable skills
4 find a balance

Exercise 3
1 With part-time work you learn transferable skills like time-management and dealing with customers.
2 Under-16s can't do certain jobs in the UK because of health and safety regulations.
3 Popular jobs for under-16s in the UK include retail, catering and hospitality.
4 Anna2000 will be working four hours every Saturday.
5 Ed K's part-time work helped him to get organized.

TEEN ADVICE CENTRE

HEALTH | MONEY | WORK & STUDY | ENTERTAINMENT | TRAVEL

Part-time work for 15–16-year-olds

Earn while you learn – and improve your future job prospects!
Part-time work is no substitute for studying, but it can be a great way to learn 'transferable' skills such as time management and dealing with customers. As long as you find a balance between schoolwork and paid work, it can even be good for your future job prospects to earn while you learn.

What hours can I work?
At age 15–16, you can work a maximum of 12 hours a week, including eight hours on Saturdays and two hours on Sundays or school days. By law, you can't work more than four hours without taking a one-hour break, and you can't work before 7am or after 7pm, or during school hours. During the holidays, you can work up to 35 hours a week.

How much will I get paid?
By law, once you're 16 you will be earning the national minimum wage.

What jobs can I do?
Due to health and safety regulations, under-16s can't do certain jobs. But sectors where companies will be looking for part-time workers include retail (shop work), catering and hospitality (for example cafés and hotels). Other options include a morning paper round, babysitting, blogging and dog walking.

Comments

Anna2000 3hrs ago
I'm 15 and I've just got a part-time job. I won't be working on school days, just four hours every Saturday. Hopefully I'll be able to find a balance with my schoolwork!
Like Comment Share

EdK 25mins ago
Don't worry Anna2000 – I'm sure you'll be fine. I had a Saturday job from age 15 until I started university. Actually, I think it helps you to get organized. You learn to prioritize and plan ahead, especially when you have to meet a deadline like completing an essay. Good luck! What kind of job will you be doing?
Like Comment Share

2 Words in context Find these words in the text. Match them with definitions 1–4.

transferable skills find a balance health and safety regulations a paper round

1 the job of delivering newspapers to people's homes
2 laws that are intended to keep people safe at work
3 skills that can be used in different jobs or situations
4 do two different things successfully

3 Copy and complete the sentences with information from the text.

1 With part-time work you learn transferable skills like ...
2 Under-16s can't do certain jobs in the UK because of ...
3 Popular jobs for under-16s in the UK include ...
4 Anna2000 will be working ...
5 EdK's part-time work helped him to ...

4 Work in pairs. Ask and answer the questions.

1 At what age can you legally work in your country? Is there a national minimum wage?
2 Do many young people work where you live? If so, what kind of jobs can they do?
3 In your opinion, what are the advantages and disadvantages of working at weekends or in the holidays while you're a student?

Exercise 4
Students' own answers

VIDEO: CULTURE BYTE
Watch the video supplied by BBC.
WATCH

Social awareness

Part-time work

LESSON OBJECTIVES

In this lesson students will:

- read a text about part-time work
- discuss work opportunities for young people in their country

WARMER

Write the word *job* on the board. Put students into teams of three. Set a time limit of 2 minutes. Students write down as many different jobs as they can within the time limit. The team with the most words is the winner.

FACT!

Find out the current exchange rate of the UK pound to euro to calculate the equivalent rates in local currency.

BACKGROUND

In the UK 15–16 year-olds are not allowed to work during school hours, before 7 o'clock in the morning or after 7 o'clock in the evening. They are also not permitted to work for more than one hour before school, so this may affect doing a paper round, for example. They are also not allowed to work for more than 4 hours without taking a break of at least one hour. During school terms they can only work for a maximum of two hours on school days and Sundays, and eight hours on Saturdays.

1 25

- Students read the Fact box about the minimum wage in the UK.
- Ask students to read the text and elicit what they will need to write in their notebooks to fill gaps 1–3 (numbers).
- Play the audio. Students read and listen to the text and complete the task.
- Check answers as a class.

2 Words in context

- Ask students to read the definitions carefully first.
- Ask students to find these words in the text and then match them with the definitions.
- They compare answers in pairs.
- Check answers as a class.

3

- Students read the sentence beginnings carefully first.
- They work individually and complete the sentences using information from the text.
- They compare answers in pairs.
- Check answers as a class.

4

- Students work individually and note down their answers to the questions.
- They work in pairs and compare their answers.
- Listen to their ideas as a class.

VIDEO: CULTURE BYTE

This video is about the different options open to students when they finish school. For exploitation and comprehension practice based on this video, see the Culture byte video worksheets on the Resource Centre.

Grammar
Future continuous

LESSON OBJECTIVES
In this lesson students will:
- learn the future continuous
- ask and answer questions about the future
- read a conversation about a trip to England

WARMER
Write the question *What kind of job will you be doing?* on the board with the words in the wrong order. Students write the sentence in the correct order.

1 • Students read the examples and choose the correct words to complete the form and use of the future continuous.
- Check answers as a class.
- Highlight that the future continuous is used to talk about continuous actions that will be in progress at a specific time in the future.
- If you are using the TPK and your students need more work on the meaning of the words, do the Grammar basics exercise.

Grammar basics
Answer key: 1 I won't be living abroad in 20 years. **2** We will be prioritising waste reduction this year. **3** What will Sophia be doing in six months' time? **4** They will be preparing for their job interview this afternoon. **5** How will you be travelling to Spain in the summer? **6** This time next week Gerard will be taking his driving test.

2 • Do the first sentence with the whole class as an example and show how the prompts are used to form the future continuous (*On Friday Mo will be flying to England*).
- Students write the remaining sentences using the future continuous form of the verbs.
- Check answers as a class.

CULTURE NOTE
There are 356 airports in England and London has five airports. The largest is Heathrow, which is the second busiest international airport after Dubai in the United Arab Emirates. The second largest London airport in London is Gatwick, followed by Stansted, Luton and City airports.

3 • Students write the questions.
- Check the questions as a class.
- They then write answers to the questions that are true for them.

4 • Nominate two students to read aloud the example question and answer to the class.
- Students work in pairs and ask and answer the questions in exercise 3.

CLIL Grammar in context: Literature

5 • This activity practises all the different forms of the future covered in this unit. Ask students to read the whole conversation before they choose the correct words.

6 26
- Play the audio. Students listen and check their answers to exercise 5.

EXTRA ACTIVITY
Ask students to work in pairs and practise reading the conversation in exercise 5, each student taking one of the roles. They then swap roles.

LITERATURE TASK
Students use the internet to find out about an English writer. They choose one writer from the box, answer the questions and find out any other relevant, interesting information. Check answers.

Grammar reference > Workbook page 88

Grammar
Future continuous

Exercise 1
1 *-ing*
2 in progress

1 **Look at the table. Choose choose the correct words in rules a) and b).**

future continuous

Anna **will be working** four hours every Saturday.
She **won't be working** on school days.
What kind of job **will** she **be doing**?

a) We form the future continuous with *will* / *won't* + *be* + the ***-ing*** / **infinitive** form of the verb.
b) We use the future continuous for actions that will be **in progress** / **finished** at a specific time in the future.

Exercise 2
1 On Friday Mo will be flying to England.
2 The Smith family will be waiting for him at the airport.
3 On Monday morning Mo will be studying English.
4 On Monday evening he'll be having dinner with his host family.

2 **Mo is going to England next week. Write sentences about what he will be doing. Use the future continuous.**

1 On Friday / Mo / fly to England
2 The Smith family / wait for him / at the airport
3 On Monday morning / Mo / study English
4 On Monday evening / he / have dinner with his host family

Exercise 3
1 will you be doing
2 Will your teacher be working
3 will you be doing
4 Will your classmates be studying
5 will you be living

3 **Copy and complete the questions with the future continuous form of the verbs. Then write answers that are true for you.**

1 What ... (you / do) at three o'clock tomorrow afternoon?
2 ... (your teacher / work) on Sunday morning?
3 What ... (you / do) during the next holidays?
4 ... (your classmates / study) this time next year?
5 Where ... (you / live) in ten years' time?

Exercise 4
Students' own answers

4 **Work in pairs, and ask and answer the questions in exercise 3.**

What will you be doing at three o'clock tomorrow afternoon?

I'll be having lunch. What about you?

CLIL

Grammar in context: Literature

5 **Read the conversation and choose the correct words.**

Exercise 5
1 Are you going
2 'm going to
3 Are you going to
4 'll be
5 leaves
6 might
7 I'll lend
8 'll

England
by Rachel Bladon

Amy: Hi, Mo! What are you reading?
Mo: It's a book about England. I'm getting organized for my trip!
Amy: (1) **Will you go** / **Are you going** to England?
Mo: Yes! I (2) **might** / **'m going to** study English in London.
Amy: Fantastic! (3) **Are you going to** / **Do you** stay with a family?
Mo: Yes, they (4) **'re** / **'ll be** waiting for me at the airport when I arrive.
Amy: Great! When are you going?
Mo: My plane (5) **will leave** / **leaves** on Friday morning.
Amy: Are you going to visit any interesting places while you're there?
Mo: I'm not sure yet. We (6) **might** / **'ll** visit Stratford-upon-Avon, where Shakespeare was born.
Amy: Well, have a fantastic time. And enjoy the rest of the book!
Mo: Thanks. I (7) **'ll lend** / **'ll be lending** it to you when I've finished. It tells you all about life in England. It even tells you how to make a perfect cup of tea!
Amy: That (8) **'ll** / **might** definitely be useful!

6 **Listen and check your answers.** 26

LITERATURE TASK

Choose an English writer from the box. Then answer the questions.

George Eliot Emily Brontë
Thomas Hardy JRR Tolkien

1 When was the writer born?
2 Where did the writer live?
3 What are their most famous works?

Literature task

George Eliot
1 In 1819.
2 She lived most of her adult life in London. (George Eliot was the pen name of Mary Ann Evans.)
3 *The Mill on the Floss, Silas Marner, Middlemarch,*

Emily Brontë
1 In 1818.
2 In Yorkshire.
3 *Wuthering Heights.*

Thomas Hardy
1 In 1840.
2 He lived most of his life in Dorset.
3 *Far from the Madding Crowd, Tess of the d'Urbervilles.*

JRR Tolkein
1 In 1892.
2 He lived most of his adult life in Oxford.
3 *The Hobbit, The Lord of the Rings.*

Work experience opportunities

LEARNING OUTCOME

✔ Have a formal interview

In England, most students do work experience for one or two weeks at the age of 14 or 15. Do you do work experience in your country?

TASK Prepare for a formal interview

1. Read about work experience opportunities
2. Understand a formal interview
3. Write answers to interview questions
4. Have a formal interview

WORK EXPERIENCE

This is a reminder for all Year 10 students – it's time to apply for your work experience!

Don't put it off any longer – the deadline for applications is next Friday.

Three new local employers are now offering work placements.

If you're interested in any of these, please speak to Mrs Hammond in Room 12 on Monday at 4pm.

A GREENHILLS ACTIVITY CENTRE

On this placement you'll have the opportunity to learn about the organization of the activity centre, as well as trying your hand at various sports, including canoeing, rafting, climbing and orienteering.

B THE HIGHSTREET BANK

Interested in learning about the financial sector? At the Highstreet Bank you'll be able to get hands-on experience of different areas of banking, including commercial and retail banking.

C RADIO POP FM

If you do your work experience here, you'll find out how a radio station operates, and you'll meet the production and technical staff. You'll even be able to have a go at some live broadcasting!

1 Read

1 **Read the information about work experience opportunities. Which one do you think is the most interesting? When is the deadline for applications?**

2 **Find these expressions in the text. Then check the meaning of the phrases in your dictionary.**

- try your hand at ...
- get hands-on experience of ...
- have a go at ...

3 **Write a sentence about each work placement using the expressions in exercise 2.**

If you do your work experience at ..., you'll be able to ...

2 Listen

4 **Read and listen to the extracts from Emily's formal interview on page 37. When will Rachel call Emily?** 27

5 **Listen again and repeat. Practise your intonation.**

6 **Watch or listen to the complete interview. In which order do you hear these questions?** 28

a) What do you enjoy doing in your free time?
b) What are you studying at the moment?
c) What are you planning to do when you leave school?
d) What are you hoping to gain from your work experience?

7 **Listen again and make notes about Emily's answers to the questions in exercise 6. Then write full sentences.**

1 At the moment, Emily is studying ...

Exercise 1
Students' own answers
The deadline for applications is next Friday.

Exercise 3
If you do your work experience at the Greenhills Activity Centre, you'll be able to try your hand at various sports.
If you do your work experience at the Highstreet Bank, you'll be able to get hands-on experience of different areas of banking.
If you do your work experience at Radio Pop FM, you'll be able to have a go at some live broadcasting.

Exercise 4
by the end of the week

Exercise 6
1 b
2 a
3 c
4 d

Exercise 7
1 At the moment, Emily is studying for her GCSEs.
2 She volunteers as a DJ and she plays the guitar.
3 She's going to go to college.
4 She'll learn a lot about how the radio station works.

Integrated skills

Work experience opportunities

LESSON OBJECTIVES

In this lesson students will:

- work on all four skills
- read about work experience opportunities
- watch or listen to an interview
- write and present a personalized interview

WARMER

Write *work experience* on the board. Explain that in England, students aged 14 or 15 spend one or two weeks learning what it is like to do a particular job. Highlight Emily's speech bubble and elicit answers to the question. Ask students to think about what kind of job they would like to get work experience for.

1 Read

1
- Students read the two questions carefully.
- They read the text and find the answer to the second question. They decide which of the jobs is the most interesting.
- They compare their answers in pairs.
- Check answers as a class. Find out which placement is the most popular.

2
- Ask students to find the expressions in the text.
- Students check the meaning of the phrases.
- Elicit that if you *try your hand at something*, you do it for the first time in order to find out if you like it or if you are good at it.

3
- Students use the model sentence to write three sentences, one about each work placement.
- Point out that *will be able to* is the future form of *can*. Check answers.

2 Listen

Video with audio option

The dialogue is also available to play as an audio file. If you prefer to present it this way, play the audio and follow the teacher's notes as for the video.

4 27 REC

- Students watch, read and listen to the video extracts of Emily's interview. Elicit the answer to the question from the class (*by the end of the week*).

27 & 28 Audioscript, page 36, exercises 4, 6 and 7

Rachel: Hello! I'm Rachel. I work here at Radio Pop FM, and I'll be interviewing you today.
Emily: Hello! Pleased to meet you.
Rachel: Please take a seat.
Emily: Thank you!
Rachel: So, why are you interested in doing your work experience with us?
Emily: Well, I'm thinking about pursuing a career in the media eventually, so I think this will be a great experience.
Rachel: I see. So, what are you studying at the moment?
Emily: Well, at the moment I'm studying for my GCSEs. I'm in Year 11, so I'll be taking my exams in June.
Rachel: OK. And do you study anything that's related to this work experience?
Emily: Yes, I'm studying media studies and music.
Rachel: And what do you enjoy doing in your free time?
Emily: Well, I volunteer as a DJ at the Youth Club. I also play the guitar – I'm in a band with a couple of friends.
Rachel: That's interesting. So, what are you planning to do when you leave school?
Emily: Well, after my GCSEs I'm going to go to college. I'm going to do A Levels and after that, I'll probably go to university.
Rachel: I see. And what are you hoping to gain from your work experience?
Emily: Oh, I think I'll learn a lot about how the radio station works. That might help me to decide if I want to work in radio in the future, or in another sector of the media.
Rachel: Well, thanks for coming in today, Emily. We'll let you know our decision in a couple of days.
Emily: Great! I look forward to hearing from you.
Rachel: We'll call you by the end of the week.
Emily: Thank you! It's been a pleasure to meet you.

5
- Play the video again. Students watch and repeat to practise their intonation.

6 28

- Highlight the questions. Students listen and note down the order in which they hear questions a)–d).
- Check answers as a class.

CULTURE NOTE

GCSE stands for General Certificate of Secondary Education. In England, students normally take their GCSE exams at the age of 15 or 16, after four or five years of secondary education.

7
- Play the audio again. Students listen and make notes about Emily's answers to the questions in exercise 6. They then write full sentences.
- Monitor while they are writing and give help as necessary.
- They compare answers in pairs.
- Check answers as a class.

8
- Ask students to look at the Communication kit: Phrases for interviews.
- Ask how many of these typical interview phrases Rachel and Emily use in the work experience interview.
- Play the video again for students to check their answers.

3 Write

9
- Ask students to look at the three work experience placements again. They choose the one they are most interested in, explaining the reasons for their choice.
- They work individually and write notes about why they are interested in this particular work placement.
- Monitor while they are writing and give help if necessary.

10
- Students work individually and write their own answers to the questions in exercise 6 in preparation for the interview for the placement they have chosen.
- Monitor while they are writing and give help if necessary.

4 Communicate

11
- Students work in pairs and practise their interviews, taking it in turns to be the interviewer and the interviewee.

12
- Students act their interviews for the class. If possible, record the interviews. Ask students to watch the interviews to check that the participants look enthusiastic, calm and confident.

! COMMUNICATION TIP
INTERVIEW TECHNIQUE

Highlight the information in the Communication strategy box and emphasize the importance of a good interview technique.

Integrated skills > Resource centre

The beginning of the interview ...

Hello! I'm Rachel. I work here at Radio Pop FM, and I'll be interviewing you today.	Hello! Pleased to meet you.
Please take a seat.	Thank you!
So, why are you interested in doing your work experience with us?	Well, I'm thinking about pursuing a career in the media eventually, so I think this will be great experience.

The end of the interview ...

Well, thanks for coming in today, Emily. We'll let you know our decision in a couple of days.	Great! I look forward to hearing from you.
We'll call you by the end of the week.	Thank you! It's been a pleasure to meet you.

Communication kit

- Pleased to meet you.
- Please take a seat.
- Thanks for coming in today.
- We'll let you know our decision ...
- I look forward to hearing from you.
- It's been a pleasure to meet you.

Exercise 8
all of them

8 Look at the Communication kit. Which phrases do Rachel and Emily use in the Speaking sketch? Watch or listen again to check your answers.

3 Write

Exercise 9
Students' own answers

9 Choose one of the work experience placements from page 36. Explain the reasons for your choice and complete the notes.

I'm interested in this placement because ...

Exercise 10
Students' own answers

10 Write your own answers to the questions in exercise 6. Make sure they are about the placement you have chosen.

4 Communicate

11 In pairs, take turns to be the interviewer and practise your interviews.

Hello! I'm ...

Hello! Pleased to meet you.

12 Act your interview for the class. If possible, record your interviews and watch them. Do you look enthusiastic and confident?

COMMUNICATION TIP
INTERVIEW TECHNIQUE

Remember to always be polite in an interview situation. Use formal language and shake hands. Try to look enthusiastic, calm and confident.

INTEGRATED SKILLS

Writing

A CV

LEARNING OUTCOME

✔ Write a CV for a work experience position

Emily Jones

34 Market Street, Brentwood, CM5 9DL
+44 114 668120 emily.jones@email.com

Position applied for	Work experience at Radio Pop FM
Education and training	**September 2017–June 2019** Currently studying for 9 GCSEs
Work experience	**January 2019–present** Youth Monitor at Ultimate Fun Activity Camp
	January 2017–January 2019 Volunteer DJ at Sunnyside Youth Club
Personal skills	1 ... English, Spanish and French
	2 ... Excellent verbal and written skills
	3 ... Excellent skills gained as secretary of Youth Club committee
	4 ... Proficient with Microsoft and OS X
	5 ... First Aid certificate, Guitar Grade 5

Exercise 1
1 d
2 b
3 e
4 c
5 a

Exercise 2
Emily is applying for work experience at Radio Pop FM. All her personal skills might be useful.

Exercise 3
Because employers will probably spend less than one minute looking at your CV.

1 Focus on content Read the CV. Match headings a–e with sections 1–5 in 'Personal skills'.

a) Other skills
b) Communication skills
c) I.T. skills
d) Languages
e) Organizational skills

2 Read Emily's CV again. What position is she applying for? Which of her skills will be useful?

3 Focus on language Read the information. Why must you organize information clearly in a CV?

Writing a CV: being clear and concise

Employers will probably spend less than one minute looking at your CV, so you need to make a good impression quickly! Use headings and bullet points instead of full sentences.

I speak Spanish and French. ✘
Languages: Spanish and French ✔

4 Write your CV. Imagine you're applying for one of the work experience positions on page 36.

Exercise 4
Students' own answers

Writing kit

1 **Plan** your CV. Use Emily's CV to help you.

2 **Write** your CV. Adapt it specifically for the position you're applying for.

3 **Useful phrases**

Work experience at ... *Excellent ... skills gained as ...*
Currently studying for ... *Proficient with ...*

4 **Check** your writing.

☑ check your spelling
☑ check all dates and numbers
☑ check you've completed all the sections

Study guide > p101 | Collaborative project 1 > p108 | Writing hub > Workbook p116

Writing

A CV

LESSON OBJECTIVES
In this lesson students will:

- read a CV
- write a CV

WARMER

Write *CV* on the board. Ask students what these letters stand for and elicit that they stand for *curriculum vitae*, a document giving details of your education and work experience. Elicit what other information goes into a CV, eg *name*, *address*, *date of birth*, *nationality*, *skills*, *free-time interests*, etc.

1 Focus on content

- Students read the CV and match the headings to the sections.
- Check answers as a class.

2
- Ask students to read the questions first. They then read the information in the CV again and find the answers to the questions.
- Check the answers as a class.

3 Focus on language

- Make sure students understand the term *bullet points* and that they are used to making lists.
- Ask students to read the text. To emphasize the point, refer students back to the cv in exercise 1 and elicit more examples, eg *communication skills: excellent verbal and written communication skills*.

Writing kit

The aim of this activity is for students to write a CV to apply for one of the work experience positions on page 36. This will give them practice in checking their spelling, checking that all the dates and numbers are correct and checking that they have completed all the sections. Ask the students to follow the stages in the Student's Book. Encourage them to use Emily's CV for ideas. Monitor while they are writing and give help with vocabulary if necessary. At the Check stage, ask them to swap notebooks and check each other's writing.

4
- Ask students to follow the stages in the Writing kit.
- Encourage them to organize it in the same way as Emily's, with the same headings and using bullet points instead of full sentences.
- Monitor while they are writing and give help with vocabulary if necessary.
- At the Check stage, ask them to swap notebooks and check each other's writing.

Study guide > Student's Book page 101

Collaborative project 1 > Student's Book page 108

Writing hub > Workbook page 116

UNIT **4**

KEEP IN TOUCH

UNIT OBJECTIVES AND KEY COMPETENCES

In this unit the student will learn ...

- to understand, recognize and correctly use phrasal verbs related to family life and relationships and vocabulary related to non-verbal communication **CLC SCC CAE**
- to recognize, understand and correctly use different conditional forms, and use them in a short speaking activity **CLC L2L SIE**
- to recognize, understand and correctly use adverbs of possibility and probability **CLC L2L**
- about effective listening and how to put it into practice **CLC SCC CAE**
- about having a group debate by watching a short video **CLC DC SCC**

In this unit the student will learn how to ...

- take notes and summarize a text about a teenage rapper **CLC SCC CAE**
- look online for more information about rap music **CLC DC SCC CAE SIE**
- identify specific information in a text about the importance of active listening **CLC SCC CAE**
- read a quiz, listen to a group debate, prepare for and have a group debate **CLC SCC SIE**
- write instant messages **DC CLC**

LINGUISTIC CONTENTS

Main vocabulary

- Phrasal verbs: *look after*, *settle down with*, *fall out with*, etc
- Non-verbal communication: *kiss (somebody) on the cheek*, *shake hands*, *shrug your shoulders*, etc

Extra vocabulary

- Words in context: *jaw*, *live with*, *ambassador*, *go viral*; *tone*, *pitch*, *requirement*, *get distracted*, *multi-task*, etc
- Word builder: Separable and inseparable phrasal verbs; Idioms

Grammar

- The zero, first, second and third conditional
- Adverbs of possibility and probability

Functional language

- Using *so*, *neither* and *too*
- Presenting your opinion
- Phrases for talking about possible or hypothetical situations in an exam

Pronunciation

- Intonation in conditional sentences
- Diphthongs

SKILLS

Reading

- Read a profile of a rapper
- Read a text about effective listening
- Read a quiz about moral dilemmas
- Read an instant message conversation

Writing: Interaction and production

- Write notes for a discussion about a moral dilemma
- Write an instant message conversation in three steps
- Learn how to say and use informal expressions

Listening

- Listen to part of a radio phone-in about non-verbal communication
- Listen to two extracts from a group debate about moral dilemmas

Spoken interaction

- Ask and answer questions about friends and family

Spoken production

- Prepare and participate in a debate

LIFELONG LEARNING SKILLS

Self-study and self-evaluation

- Study guide: Student's Book page 102
- Progress check: Workbook page 38
- Extension: Workbook page 39
- Grammar reference and practice: Workbook pages 90–91
- Wordlist: Workbook pages 151–157

Learning strategies and thinking skills

- Taking notes and summarising
- Critical thinking: creating a verse for a rap song or poem

Life skills

- Active listening
- Practising active listening skills

Cross-curricular contents

- Reality TV shows featuring teenagers
- Literature: *A Midsummer Night's Dream* by William Shakespeare
- Literature task: searching the internet for further information about Shakespeare

EVALUATION

- Unit 4 End-of-unit test: Basic, Standard and Extra
- CEFR Skills Exam Generator

KEY COMPETENCES

CLC	Competence in linguistic communication
CMST	Competence in mathematics, science and technology
DC	Digital competence
SCC	Social and civic competence
CAE	Cultural awareness and expression
L2L	Learning to learn
SIE	Sense of initiative and entrepreneurship

DIGITAL MATERIAL

New Pulse Digital Course including:

- Interactive vocabulary presentation
- Grammar and Vocabulary basics exercises
- Getting started video
- Flipped classroom grammar video: conditional tenses
- Speaking sketch video: A formal interview

DIGITAL COMPETENCE

- Web quest: Find out about other songs by Isaiah Acosta and Trap House
- Digital competence worksheet: Online polls

REINFORCEMENT MATERIAL

- New Pulse Basics: Teacher's Resource Centre
- Vocabulary and grammar consolidation worksheets: Teacher's Resource Centre
- Grammar and Vocabulary basics exercises: Teacher's Presentation Kit

EXTENSION MATERIAL

- Vocabulary and grammar extension worksheets: Teacher's Resource Centre
- Advance your vocabulary: Workbook page 106
- The longer read: Teacher's Resource Centre
- Writing hub: Workbook page 118

TEACHER'S RESOURCE CENTRE

- Translation and dictation worksheets
- Evaluation rubrics
- Key competences worksheets
- Culture and CLIL worksheets
- Digital competence worksheets
- Macmillan Readers worksheets

Vocabulary
Phrasal verbs

LESSON OBJECTIVES
In this lesson students will:
- learn a set of phrasal verbs related to relationships
- learn rules for separable and inseparable phrasal verbs
- read a review
- learn which prepositions follow certain verbs

VIDEO: GETTING STARTED

In this video the speakers answer the question What different things do you use your mobile phone for?

- Focus the students on the unit title *Keep in touch*.
- Write these questions on the board: **1** Who uses the maps app on his / her mobile? **2** Who uses his / her phone to take photos? **3** Who uses the alarm on his / her phone to wake up in the morning?
- Students watch the video and write the answers in their notebooks.
- Students watch the video again and check their answers.
  At the end of the lesson, ask students to answer the question from the video: *What different things do you use your mobile phone for?*
- **Answer key: 1** Leo **2** Harry **3** Emily

WARMER

Introduce the topic. Write the phrasal verb *get on with* on the board. Ask students who they need to get on with.

1 29
- Students look at the image of the online dictionary and read the phrases in blue.
- Play the audio. Students listen and repeat the phrasal verbs in blue.
- Students work in pairs classifying the phrasal verbs. Point out that some can be in both categories.
- Check answers as a class.
- If you are using the TPK and your students need more work on the meaning of the words, do the Vocabulary basics exercise.

Vocabulary basics

Answer key: 1 bring up **2** fall out **3** hang out **4** tell off **5** settle down **6** get on

LANGUAGE NOTE

In phrasal verbs the main stress is not on the verb but on the adverbial particle, eg *look after*. In the case of three-word phrasal verbs, the main stress falls on the first particle, eg *get on with*.

2 Word builder
- Students read the Word builder box.
- Check students understand the difference between the two types of phrasal verbs.
- Students then work individually to answer the questions. Check answers as a class.

3
- Students read all the questions carefully first. Explain that they need to complete the phrasal verbs in each question by adding the correct particle.
- Students work individually to complete the task and compare their answers in pairs.
- Check answers as a class.

4
- Put students into pairs. They ask and answer the questions from exercise 3.
- Students report their partner's answers to the class.

EXTRA ACTIVITY

Write examples of separable phrasal verbs with noun prompts on the board: *take off / your coat, turn down / the radio, pick up / that rubbish, turn over / the page*. Students write each instruction in two ways, separated and not separated, eg *Take your coat off. Take off your coat.*

KEEP IN TOUCH

UNIT 4

LEARNING OUTCOMES IN THIS UNIT

- Take notes and summarize a text
- Listen for specific information in a radio phone-in
- Take part in a group debate
- Write an instant message conversation

Exercise 1
Family life – bring up, fall out with, get on with, hang out with, look after, make up with, meet up with, tell off
Relationships – ask out, go out with, settle down with, split up with

VIDEO: GETTING STARTED

WATCH Watch the teenagers talking about communication and answer the question.

Vocabulary
Phrasal verbs

1 Listen and repeat the phrasal verbs in blue. Which ones are related to family life? Which ones are only used to talk about relationships? 29

Dictionary

ask (someone) out
to invite someone to go with you to a cinema, restaurant, etc because you want to start a romantic relationship with them

bring (someone) up
to take care of a child until he / she becomes an adult

fall out (with someone)
to stop being friendly with someone because you have had an argument or disagreement

get on (with someone)
to have a friendly relationship with someone

go out (with someone)
to have a romantic relationship with someone and spend a lot of time with them

hang out (with someone)
to spend time in a particular place or with a particular person

look after (someone)
to take care of someone and make sure they are safe

make up (with someone)
to be friendly with someone again after having an argument

meet up (with someone)
to come together with someone, either by surprise or as planned

settle down (with someone)
to begin to live a quieter life by getting married or staying permanently in one place

split up (with someone)
to end a romantic relationship

tell (someone) off
to criticize someone angrily for doing something wrong

Dictionary History Favourites Settings

Exercise 2
ask out, bring up, tell off

2 Word builder Read the information. Which of the phrasal verbs in exercise 1 are separable? Use a dictionary to find example sentences.

SEPARABLE AND INSEPARABLE PHRASAL VERBS
A phrasal verb consists of a verb and a particle. You can separate the verb and the particle in some phrasal verbs, but in others you can't.
*Our teacher never ~~**tells off** us~~.* ✗
*She never **tells** us **off**.* ✓
*My brother's great! I **get on** ~~him **with**~~.* ✗
*I **get on with** him.* ✓

Exercise 3
1 on
2 off
3 after
4 out
5 out
6 down

3 Copy and complete the questions with the correct particles.

FAMILY, FRIENDS AND RELATIONSHIPS

1. Who do you get … best with in your family?
2. Do your parents ever tell you …? Why?
3. Do you ever have to look … your brothers or sisters?
4. Have you ever fallen … with a friend? Why?
5. Where do you usually hang … with your friends?
6. In your opinion, what is the best age to settle …?

Exercise 4
Students' own answers

4 Work in pairs. Ask and answer the questions in exercise 3.

Who do you get on best with in your family?
I get on really well with my sister. We're twins!

Exercise 1

Someone being helped by their friends through a difficult time.

Exercise 2

1 Phoenix / the USA
2 Trap House
3 *Oxygen to Fly*
4 instant messaging
5 music, fashion and hanging out with his friends

Exercise 3

a) go viral
b) ambassador
c) live with
d) jaw

Exercise 4

Students' own answers

Exercise 5

1 b
2 d
3 a
4 c

Possible summary: 17-year-old Isaiah Acosta can't speak, but he writes rap songs. He worked with the rapper Trap House and they produced the song *Oxygen to Fly* together. They also made a short film and a music video.

Other possible information to include:
e) why IA can't speak
f) IA is an ambassador for a charity
g) how IA and TH met.

Reading

A profile and song

LEARNING OUTCOME

✔ Take notes and summarize a text

1 **Look at the title. What do you think 'With a little help from his friends' refers to? Read and listen to the text and check your answer.** 30

2 **Copy and complete the sentences with information from the text.**

1 Isaiah Acosta is from ...
2 Isaiah collaborated with ...
3 Their first song was called ...
4 Isaiah communicates by ...
5 Isaiah loves ...

3 Words in context **Find these words in the text. Which one is a phrasal verb? Match them with definitions a–d.**

live with ambassador go viral jaw

a) to become very popular and spread quickly on the internet
b) someone who represents an organization
c) to accept something difficult that you can't change
d) the lower part of the face that includes the chin and teeth

4 **Read the information. When would you need to take notes from a text?**

TAKE NOTES AND SUMMARIZE

Decide which information in the text is more important. Think about what you'd want to include if you had to write a summary. Don't write full sentences in your notes. Use abbreviations for long words, and initials for names.

5 **Put notes a–d in order. Then write a summary. What other information could you include?**

Notes: Isaiah Acosta
a) produced song Oxygen to Fly together
b) IA (17) – can't speak but writes rap songs
c) also made short film and music video
d) worked with rapper TH

WITH A LITTLE HELP

18-year-old Isaiah Acosta was born with a condition called 'situs inversus', which has left him unable to speak. But that hasn't stopped him becoming a rap artist! With the collaboration of rapper Trap House, Isaiah released his first song, *Oxygen to Fly*, about the difficulties of living with his medical condition.

Writing is Isaiah's lifeline – his lyrics contain everything that he would say if he could speak. Over the years he has written a lot of poems, often about things that worry him. He usually composes poems on his mobile, and he communicates with others by instant messaging. Isaiah finds that rap music is the perfect way to express his feelings. It has given him a voice, and now – with the help of Trap House – he hopes to reach others whose voices are not heard.

The rapper Trap House, who was also brought up in Phoenix, agreed to be Isaiah's voice. He was very impressed by Isaiah's lyrics and creative ideas, and was delighted to work with him to transform his poem into a rap song.

So how did the rap duo get together? It probably wouldn't have happened if Isaiah hadn't been an ambassador for the Children's Miracle Network Hospitals (CMN Hospitals*). To cut

OXYGEN TO FLY

BY ISAIAH ACOSTA

I don't care what people think of me
Proud and honoured that they carry me
Jaw gone but I love myself, like a lion to my family
Heart big through a tragedy
I don't care what the people say
I don't ever say can't or won't
Had a dream to rap the other day
Just accept me for my differences
Everybody gonna hear my voice ...

You can download the song if you visit your favourite music streaming service

6 **Answer the questions.**

1 What is Isaiah's song about?
2 What does the writer mean by 'writing is Isaiah's lifeline'?
3 How do you think Isaiah's song might help others?
4 Do you think Isaiah and Trap House became friends?
5 What are the connections between Isaiah and the Children's Miracle Network Hospitals?
6 Give examples of Isaiah's ability to overcome adversity.

Exercise 6

1 The difficulties of living with his medical condition.
2 His lyrics say what he would say if he could speak.
3 Students' own answers
4 Students' own answers
5 He's their ambassador.
6 Students' own answers

Reading
A profile and song

LESSON OBJECTIVES
In this lesson students will:
- read the profile of a rapper
- take notes and summarize a text

WARMER
Ask students what rap singers they know. Ask if they like this type of music and to give their reasons why they do or don't like it.

1 30
- Students read the title and discuss with a partner what they think the text refers to.
- Do not check the answer to the question yet.
- Play the audio for students to read and listen the text.
- Check answers with the whole class.

READING STRATEGY

Scanning
If you scan a text, you read it to locate information that you are looking for, eg *facts and figures*. The key element of scanning is that you know what you are looking for and you do not need to understand the rest of the text to find it, eg *if you are in a restaurant and you want a burger, you look quickly through the menu until you find the word burger.*

2
- Students read all the sentence beginnings first. They read the text quickly to locate the answers.
- Check answers as a class.

3 **Words in Context**
- Remind students what a phrasal verb is (a verb + a particle). Read the instructions aloud to the class.
- Students find the words in the text and use the context to match the words with the definitions.
- Check answers as a class.

4
- Students read the information about note-taking and summarizing.
- Check students understand the basic strategies.

5
- Explain the task. Students read the notes and use the text to help them put them in the correct order.
- They work individually and write a summary using the information in the notes and any other information in the text they think is important.

6
- Ask students to read the questions carefully first.
- They read the text again and write the answers in their note-books.
- Students compare their answers in pairs.
- Check answers as a class.

7 Word Builder

- Students read the information about idioms and check they understand exactly what an idiom is. Point out that it may be a *false friend* (a word with a different meaning from a similar word in their language).
- Students find the example idioms in the text and discuss their meanings. They find the third idiom in the text (to help students locate it, you could point out that it is in the last paragraph of the main part of the text).
- Check answers as a class.

DID YOU KNOW?

Students read the information in the *Did you know?* box. Ask if they know any examples of freestyle rapping. Famous examples of freestyle rappers include Eminem, Big L, Lil Snupe and Kendrick Lamar.

8

- Put students into pairs and ask them to ask and answer the questions,
- Listen to their ideas as a class.

FINISHED?

Ask fast finishers to find the words in the text that mean the following: **1** *to understand something in a particular way* **2** *two people who perform together* **3** *a medical operation to improve someone's appearance* **4** *without a voice.* (**Answer key: 1** *interpret* **2** *duo* **3** *cosmetic surgery* **4** *voiceless*)

CRITICAL THINKING

- Students read the information in the box.
- Elicit an example of words that rhyme (eg *family* and *tragedy*) and point out that the stress on the words and the number of syllables in each line help to produce the rhythm.
- Students write their own verses and compare in pairs or small groups.
- They read their verses to the class.

WEB QUEST

Students go online and listen to Isaiah and Trap House's song. They find out if there are any other songs recorded by them.

1 **Think** Students open a search engine (eg *Google*) and decide which words to use to find Isaiah Acosta and Trap House's song online.
2 **Investigate** They search the internet for other songs or projects they have done together.
3 **Communicate** They discuss their findings as a class.

TIP! Remind students to look up the words they will use in their search to make sure they are using the correct spelling. Remind students to always be careful when they are writing words that their software doesn't recognize (such as names), as it might try to change this word.

It is really important that when students check through their work, they make sure that they have the correct spelling.

You could also explain that a lot of software and websites are defaulted to American spellings. This means that even though words might be spelled correctly in British English, spellchecks or auto correction tools are likely to change words for them! For example, *colour* might be changed to *color*.

VIDEO: FLIPPED CLASSROOM

You may want to ask students to watch the Flipped classroom video for unit 4 as homework in preparation for the following grammar lesson. The Flipped grammar presentation focuses on conditionals.

The longer read > Resource centre

FROM HIS FRIENDS ...

a long story short, when Isaiah expressed interest in becoming a rapper, CMN Hospitals put him in touch with Trap House. The pair got on really well when they met up and the result was not only the musical collaboration but also a short film (by director Torben Bernhard) about a music video that went viral on YouTube.

By sharing their experiences online, the rap duo has vshown the world the importance of supporting children's hospitals like CMN Hospitals.

If you watch the film, you'll soon see Isaiah's ability to overcome adversity. When doctors offered him cosmetic surgery, Isaiah turned it down – he said that he wouldn't need it unless it helped him to breathe or speak. All Isaiah wants is for others to accept him as he is – a teenager who loves music, fashion and hanging out with his friends – and to be able to give a voice to the voiceless. As they say, actions speak louder than words!

Children's Miracle Network Hospitals®

* CMNH is a non-profit organisation that raises funds for 170 children's hospitals across North America, including Phoenix Children's hospital where Isaiah still receives care.

Exercise 7
A dream come true = something that happens that you have always hoped for
To cut a long story short = to tell the main point of a story without giving any details
Actions speak louder than words = what you do is more important than what you say you will do

7 **Word builder** Read the information and answer the questions.

Idioms
An idiom is an expression whose meaning is different from the meaning of the individual words.
a dream come true
to cut a long story short

1 Find the example idioms in the text. What do they mean?
2 Find an idiom in the text that means 'what you do is more significant than what you say'. Do you have a similar expression in your language? Do you think it is true?

8 Work in pairs to ask and answer the questions.

Exercise 8
Students' own answers

1 Do you ...
a) listen to rap music?
b) write poems or songs?
2 Have you ever collaborated with friends on a creative project?
3 How have your friends and / or family helped you with challenges in your life?

CRITICAL THINKING

Critical Thinking
Students' own answers

Create
Discuss the lyrics to Isaiah Acosta's song. Think about:
- words that rhyme
- the sound of the words (the rhythm)
- the meaning of the words
- similes or metaphors

Create a verse for a new rap song or poem. Write about a subject that is important to you personally OR your reactions to Isaiah's song.

DID YOU KNOW?

'Freestyle' is when rappers improvise – they say things spontaneously and the lyrics aren't written down. In a 'freestyle battle', two or more rappers compete to create the best improvised lyrics.

WEB QUEST

Listen online to the song by Isaiah Acosta and Trap House and read the lyrics. Find out if they have recorded any other songs together.

1 **Think** Choose the search terms to find this song online.
2 **Investigate** Search online for the song and the lyrics. Find out whether Isaiah Acosta and Trap House have collaborated on other projects together.
3 **Communicate** Share your findings with the class. If possible, listen to the song together and discuss your reactions.

TIP! Be careful with spelling when you search for specific, unusual or foreign names. Don't let the autocorrect change the spelling for you!

Grammar

The zero, first, second and third conditional

VIDEO: FLIPPED CLASSROOM

WATCH

Watch the grammar presentation and do the task.

Exercise 1
a) third
b) second
c) first
d) zero

1 Look at the table. Then copy and complete rules a–d with *zero*, *first*, *second* or *third*.

zero conditional
If + present simple ↔ present simple
If you **visit** Spotify, you **can** download the song.
first conditional
If / Unless + present simple ↔ *will / won't* + infinitive
If you **watch** the film, you**'ll see** Isaiah's strength.
second conditional
If + past simple ↔ *would(n't)* + infinitive
If you **wrote** a song, what **would** it **be** about?
third conditional
If + past perfect ↔ *would(n't)* + *have* + past participle
If Isaiah **hadn't met** Trap House, he **wouldn't have recorded** a song.

a) We use the ... conditional when we imagine the consequences of a situation after it has happened.
b) We use the ... conditional for hypothetical situations in the future.
c) We use the ... conditional for possible or probable situations in the future.
d) We use the ... conditional for facts or things that are generally true.

Exercise 2
1 Unless I get home early, Mum will tell me off.
2 Unless I have to look after my sister, I'll meet you tonight.
3 Unless you help me, I won't finish this exercise.
4 Unless I study, I won't pass my exams.

2 Read the Look! box. Then rewrite the first conditional sentences replacing *if* with *unless*.

> **LOOK!**
> *unless* + affirmative verb = *if* + negative verb
> **If** I **don't do** my homework, I'll be in trouble.
> **Unless I do** my homework, I'll be in trouble.

1 Mum will tell me off if I don't get home early.
2 I'll meet you tonight if I don't have to look after my little sister.
3 I won't finish this exercise if you don't help.
4 I won't pass my exam if I don't study.

> **ANALYSE**
> We sometimes use the second conditional to give advice.
> *If I were you, I'd talk to him!*
> How do you say this in your language?

Exercise 3
1 If I fell out with my friends, I would talk to them.
2 You would make new friends if you moved home.
3 I would visit you if you were in hospital.
4 I would be happy if we were friends forever!

3 Decide which part is the situation and which is the consequence. Then write second conditional sentences.

my friends / have a problem ↔ I / help them
If my friends had a problem, I would help them.

1 I / fall out with my friends ↔ I / talk to them
2 you / make new friends ↔ you / move home
3 I / visit you ↔ you / be in hospital
4 I / be happy ↔ we / be friends forever!

Exercise 4
1 wouldn't have come
2 had come
3 wouldn't have used
4 would have learnt

4 Copy and complete the third conditional sentences with the correct form of the verbs in brackets.

1 If I'd felt ill today, I ... (not come) to school.
2 What would your parents have said if you ... (come) home at 4am this morning?
3 We ... (not use) mobile phones if we had been born in the 19th century.
4 If we had grown up in England, we ... (learn) perfect English!

Exercise 5
1 wouldn't be
2 had
3 wouldn't have met
4 'll love
5 won't know

5 Complete the text with the correct conditional form of the verbs in brackets.

> Do you want to help people with a disability to lead an active life? Then become a volunteer 'befriender'!
>
> Young volunteer Amy is paired with Zoe, who's autistic. If Zoe was alone, it (1) ... (not be) easy for her to communicate with others, but Amy helps her. 'It makes me more confident,' says Zoe. 'Amy would help me if I (2) ... (have) a problem. We have fun together!'
>
> Amy recommends the experience. 'If I hadn't become a befriender, I (3) ... (not meet) so many great people,' she says. If you enjoy going out and meeting new people, you (4) ... (love) it. You (5) ... (not know) unless you try!'

Exercise 6
1 Will you hang out
2 hadn't come
3 would you like

6 Copy and complete the conditional questions. Then, in pairs, ask and answer the questions.

1 ... (you / hang out) with your friends if you're free this weekend?
2 Would you have met any of your classmates if you ... (not come) to this school?
3 If you could go anywhere for your end-of-year trip, where ... (you / like) to go?

Grammar

The zero, first, second and third conditional

LESSON OBJECTIVES

In this lesson students will:

- Learn the zero, first, second and third conditional
- read a text about volunteering

WARMER

Write the sentence *If you watch the film you'll soon see Isaiah's resilience and determination* with the words in the wrong order. Students work in pairs and write the sentence in the correct order. Write the correct sentence on the board.

VIDEO: FLIPPED CLASSROOM

- If you set the video for homework, Students compare their Task time! answers and then check the answers as a class.
- If you didn't set it for homework, watch the video in class and answer the Task time! questions at the end of the presentation.
- **Answer key:** 1 his sister 2 French 3 he'll have a big party

1
- Students read the information in the table.
- They copy and complete the four rules.
- Check answers as a class.
- Point out that *will / won't* and *would / wouldn't* are never used in the if clause.
- If you are using the TPK and your students need more practice of the grammar, do the Grammar basics exercise.

Grammar basics

Answer key: 1 d 2 c 3 a 4 b

LANGUAGE NOTE

The *if* clause can be first or second in the sentence in affirmative and negative sentences, eg *They'll be in trouble if they don't follow the rules. If they don't follow the rules, they'll be in trouble.* A comma is necessary if the sentence begins with an *if* clause, but is not necessary if the main clause is first.

LOOK!

Write these examples on the board to help clarify the use of unless: *We'll go to the beach if it doesn't rain. We'll go to the beach unless it rains*. The meaning is the same but highlight the use of the affirmative verb after *unless*.

2
- Students complete the task individually.
- Check answers as a class.

ANALYSE

Read the example aloud to the class and highlight that the fixed expression *If I were you* followed by *would* + infinitive is often used to give advice. Students translate the sentence into their language.

3
- Read the example prompts aloud to the class and highlight that *help them* is the consequence.
- Encourage students to refer to the second conditional section of the rules in exercise 1.
- Students complete the exercise.
- Check answers as a class.

4
- Write this example sentence on the board: *If I had missed the bus this morning, I would have been late for school.* Emphasize that you didn't miss the bus and you weren't late for school.
- Encourage students to refer back to the third conditional rule in exercise 1.
- Students work individually and write sentences using the correct form of the verbs in brackets. Check answers.

5
- Explain the task. Point out that in each case the verb tense in the other clause should help students to choose the correct form of the verb in brackets. Students complete the task.
- Check answers as a class.

6
- Students complete the questions using the correct form of the verbs in brackets.
- Check the questions as a class.
- Students then ask and answer the questions in pairs.

Grammar reference > Workbook page 90

Pronunciation lab > Intonation in conditional sentences > Student's Book page 124

Vocabulary and Listening

Non-verbal communication

LESSON OBJECTIVES

In this lesson students will:

- learn a set of verbs and phrases related to body language
- listen for specific information

WARMER

Write *body language* on the board. Ask students not to speak but to perform the following actions: *shake your head*, *nod*, *wave*, *sigh* and *yawn*. Ask them what each example of body language means.

DIGITAL VOCABULARY FLASHCARDS

In this digital presentation, students match the vocabulary with definitions.

- Do the digital presentation with the class.
- Encourage students to repeat the words.

1 31

- Students read the information in the text. They work in pairs and compare the advice with customs in their country.
- Play the audio. Students listen and repeat.
- If you are using the TPK and your students need more work on the meaning of the words, do the Vocabulary basics exercise.

Vocabulary basics

Answer key: 1 smile **2** gesticulate **3** shake hands **4** frown **5** eye contact, the secret word is *stare*

2
- Students copy the diagram into their notebooks and write the words and expressions in the correct part of the Venn diagram.
- Check answers as a class.

3
- Point out that the situations are hypothetical so students should use the second conditional. They should write complete sentences.
- Students work individually and write complete sentences.
- They compare their sentences with a partner.
- Listen to students' sentences as a class.

4
- Read the questions aloud to the whole class. Students read the short piece of information about the radio programme and answer the questions.
- Check answers as a class.

5 32

- Students read the list of types of non-verbal communication carefully first.
- Point out that five of the eight types in the list are mentioned in the extract from the radio programme. They should note down which five are mentioned.
- Play the audio and check answers.

For audioscript, see page T44

6
- Students read the questions first.
- Play the audio again. Students take notes as they listen. Check answers. Make sure students understand *weird* (very strange).

LANGUAGE NOTE

Weird is now more widely used than *strange*. It can be used to describe anything that is very strange or unusual and difficult to explain, eg *a weird experience*, *a weird dream*, *a weird film*, etc.

Advance your vocabulary > Workbook page 106

Pronunciation lab > Diphthongs > Student's Book page 124

Vocabulary and Listening

Non-verbal communication

LEARNING OUTCOME

✔ Listen for specific information in a radio phone-in

DIGITAL VOCABULARY FLASHCARDS

Do the matching exercise to discover the new vocabulary.

frown gesticulate give (somebody) a hug hold hands kiss (somebody) on the cheek make eye contact raise your eyebrows roll your eyes shake hands shrug your shoulders smile stare

1 Read the 'How to ...' information. Is this advice also true in your country? Listen and repeat the words in blue. 31

Exercise 1
Student's own answers

How to ...
make new friends in the UK!

Do ...

✔ smile and be friendly.
✔ make eye contact, but don't stare.
✔ give people plenty of personal space.

Don't ...

✘ kiss people on the cheek if you've never met them.
✘ shake hands – it's too formal.
✘ give someone a hug or hold hands until you know them very well!
✘ frown or roll your eyes – it isn't very positive.
✘ gesticulate too much!

Remember! You can use other actions to help communicate what you mean – for example shrugging your shoulders (if you don't know something) or raising your eyebrows (if you're surprised).

2 Copy and complete the diagram with the words and expressions in blue in exercise 1.

positive	it depends ...	negative
give (someone) a hug	*gesticulate*	*frown*

Exercise 2
Positive – hold hands, kiss somebody on the cheek, make eye contact, smile
It depends – raise your eyebrows, shake hands, shrug your shoulders, stare
Negative – roll your eyes

3 What kind of non-verbal communication would you use in these situations? Write conditional sentences.

If I went for an interview, I'd smile and shake hands.

- you go for an interview
- you meet up with friends from your country
- you have an argument with someone
- you don't know the answer to a question in class

Exercise 3
Student's own answers

4 Look at the information about the radio programme and answer the questions.

1 When is the programme on?
2 What is it about?

Exercise 4
a) now
b) non-verbal communication around the world

5 Listen to part of the radio programme. Which five types of non-verbal communication do they mention? 32

1 smiling
2 frowning
3 kissing
4 shaking hands
5 holding hands
6 eye contact
7 posture
8 personal space

Exercise 5
1, 3, 4, 6, 8

6 Listen again and answer the questions.

1 Where did Sally go on holiday?
2 What did Sally find different about greeting people in that country?
3 Why was Dan in France?
4 What did Dan notice about shaking hands in France?
5 What is Mizuki doing in Britain?
6 According to Mizuki, what is impolite in Japan?
7 Where is Bethany from?
8 What has Bethany noticed about personal space when she has been travelling?

Exercise 6
1 Spain
2 Everyone kisses each other when they meet up and when they say goodbye.
3 He was on an exchange.
4 Boys always shake hands when they see their friends.
5 She's studying.
6 Making eye contact with older people.
7 the USA
8 There isn't enough personal space.

Vocabulary basics Advance your vocabulary > Workbook p106 Pronunciation > p124

Exercise 1

120 –150 = number of words we speak per minute
7 = the percentage of communication that involves the words we actually say
The number one = good communication skills, main requirement for employers
60—80 = the percentage you make eye contact for during a conversation

Life skills

Effective listening

FACT! We usually speak at about 120–150 words per minute, but we think at about 500 words per minute. That's why we often get distracted while listening!

1 Read the Fact box and the text. What do these numbers refer to?

- 120–150
- 7
- the number one
- 60–80

Exercise 2

Tone = the sound of someone's voice that shows what they are feeling
Pitch = high or low quality of a sound
Require-ment = something a rule, law or contract states that you must do
Get distracted = not be interested
Multi-task = do several things at the same time
Interrupt = to say or do something to stop someone who's speaking
Keep an open mind = to be willing to consider many different possibilities
Jump to conclusions = to make a decision too quickly

The truth about listening

Did you know that only 7% of communication involves the words you actually say? The rest consists of body language (55%) and the tone, pitch and speed of your voice (38%). So in order to be an effective communicator, you definitely need to put into practice all your non-verbal communication skills! As well as helping you to negotiate better in discussions with your parents, teachers and friends, these skills will probably also serve you well in the future – good communication skills are the number one requirement among employers.

1 Face the speaker

Show that you're listening by using positive facial expressions such as nodding and smiling. You definitely shouldn't frown or roll your eyes, as these expressions show hostility and signal a lack of interest.

2 Make eye contact

A comfortable amount of eye contact will probably put the speaker more at ease – but don't stare! You should aim to make eye contact about 60–80% of the time in Western countries, but this can differ in other parts of the world.

3 Don't get distracted

Focus on what the other person is saying, not on your planned reply. Don't try to multi-task while listening, or get distracted by your emotions. Oh, and maybe it's best to put your phone on silent, too!

4 Don't interrupt

Wait until the other person finishes expressing something before you speak. When it's your turn, don't just talk about yourself, and don't give advice unless it's asked for!

5 Interact

Summarize what you've heard, and ask questions to keep the conversation going. Perhaps you'll also want to ask for clarification to check anything that you didn't understand. Keep an open mind and don't jump to conclusions!

2 Words in context Find these words and phrases in the text. What do they mean?

tone pitch requirement get distracted multi-task interrupt keep an open mind jump to conclusions

3 Read the text again. Then copy and complete the sentences.

1 93% of communication consists of ...
2 Good communication skills are important because ...
3 Examples of positive non-verbal communication are ...
4 Examples of things you shouldn't do while listening are ...

4 Choose situation a or b. Prepare what you'd say to explain the situation to your friend.

a) You're in trouble with your English teacher because you haven't done your homework for two weeks.
b) You've had an argument with your parents because they won't let you go to a party.

Exercise 4

Student's own answers

5 Work in pairs and follow the instructions. Then swap roles. Who is the best listener?

Student A: Explain the situation (a or b in exercise 4) to your partner.
Student B: Listen to your partner. Follow the five steps in 'The truth behind listening'.

Exercise 5

Student's own answers

Exercise 3

1 body language and tone, pitch and speed of your voice
2 they will make you an effective communicator, which is the number one requirement for employers.
3 nodding and smiling
4 multi-tasking or getting distracted by your emotions

Life skills
Effective listening

LESSON OBJECTIVES
In this lesson students will:
- read a text about effective listening
- practise effective listening skills

WARMER
Write *listening* on the board. Ask the class what problems they have when they are listening (both to English and to someone speaking their own language). Elicit examples and write them on the board, eg *people speak too quickly, it's noisy in the room and you can't hear, different accents are sometimes difficult to understand, people speak too quietly, etc.*

FACT!
Ask students to read the fact box. Ask them to think about what other things can distract them while listening (eg not understanding a word, loud noises, ringtones on mobiles, something happening around them, etc ...)

1 31
- Read the instructions to the class. Students read the Fact box and the text to find what the numbers refer to.
- Students check their answers in pairs.
- Check answers as a class.
- Ask if they found the information surprising and, if so, why.

2 Words in context
- Students look in the text to find the words and use the context to help them decide on the meaning.
- They compare answers in pairs.
- Check answers as a class.
- Students give examples of *multi-tasking* (eg *cooking and talking on the telephone at the same time*). Ask them to translate the words and phrases into their language to check understanding.

3
- Students read the sentence beginnings carefully first. They copy them into their note-books.
- They work individually and read the text again, using the information in the text to complete the sentences.
- They compare answers in pairs.
- Check answers as a class.

4
- Students work individually to choose one of the situations and think about what they are going to say.
- Monitor while they are working and give help as necessary.

5 33
- Students work in pairs and take it in turns to state the problems and respond to them with effective listening techniques.
- Encourage them to say a bit more about each situation.

32 & 33 Audioscript page 43, exercises 1, 5 and 6

Presenter: Hello there and welcome to Your Call! Today we're talking about non-verbal communication around the world ... What would you do, for example, if you wanted to make friends abroad? Well, smiling is a kind of universal body language, but what should you avoid? Call us now ... the lines are open ... Right! We have our first caller ... Sally from London. Hello Sally?
Sally: Hi!
Presenter: Yes, what's your experience?
Sally: Well, we went on holiday to Spain in the summer, and over there everyone kisses each other on the cheek when they meet up! We were staying on this campsite, and I made friends with some Spanish people ... and every time we met up, it was, two kisses, and then again, every time we said goodbye. That's really different, because I don't kiss my friends all the time here at home!
Presenter: Yes, I bet! Thanks Sally. Our next caller is Dan in Manchester ...
Dan: Hi! Well, I went on a French exchange last year, with school, and I was quite surprised because the boys in France always shake hands when they see their friends. I mean, here you wouldn't shake hands if you went out with friends, would you? It'd feel a bit weird – I mean, you'd only shake hands if you went for an interview or something.
Presenter: Yes, that's right. Thanks Dan! Now, we have Mizuki. Where are you from, Mizuki?
Mizuki: I'm from Japan. I'm studying here in Britain.
Presenter: OK, and how are things different here, do you think?
Mizuki: What I notice, really, is that everyone makes eye contact a lot here. For Japanese people, this is strange, because in Japan we don't make eye contact with older people. I mean, if you made eye contact with a teacher in Japan, it would be impolite. But here, it's the opposite! Here it's impolite if you don't make eye contact!
Presenter: Hmm – that's interesting! Thanks Mizuki. Now ... Bethany is on the line. Hello?
Bethany: Hi! Yeah – I'm from the USA, and what I really notice when I travel is personal space. I mean, Americans have really strict boundaries, so if you stand too close, they'll be like 'that's weird' – it makes you feel uncomfortable ... but when I've travelled in Mediterranean countries, everyone's touching your arm when they're talking to you ...
Presenter: Thanks Bethany! Now, remember you can call us and tell us your experiences, or send us an email ... Let's go to some music now and then we'll take some more of your calls ...

Grammar
Adverbs of possibility and probability

LESSON OBJECTIVES
In this lesson students will:
- learn adverbs of possibility and probability
- read a text about a play

WARMER
Revise some of the body language expressions from the vocabulary lesson. Give instructions and ask the whole class to stand up and perform the actions in unison: *shrug your shoulders, roll your eyes, frown, smile, raise your eyebrows, gesticulate, stare.*

1
- Make sure students understand clause (part of a sentence with a verb in it).
- Students read the examples and match them with the three rules for the position in the sentence of adverbs of possibility and probability.
- They compare answers in pairs.
- Check answers as a class.
- If you are using the TPK and your students need more work on the meaning of the words, do the Grammar basics exercise.

Grammar basics
Answer key: a) beginning **b)** after **c)** before

2
- Rewrite the first sentence with the whole class as an example (*definitely isn't*). Remind students that *definitely* and *probably* go before negative auxiliaries and forms of *be*.
- Encourage students to refer back to the rules in exercise 1 to help them. They work individually to complete the exercise.
- They compare answers in pairs.
- Check answers as a class.

LANGUAGE NOTE
Definitely is sometimes used in a different place in a sentence, particularly with the first person of the verb be in negative sentences, eg *I'm definitely not going to the party.*

3
- Read the example question and answer aloud to the class. Highlight that the adverb in brackets (*definitely*) has to be used in the answer.
- Students work individually to write answers to the questions that are true for them using the adverb in brackets.
- Listen to some answers as a class.

EXTRA ACTIVITY
Students work in pairs and take it in turns to ask and answer the questions in exercise 3. Nominate different pairs to ask and answer different questions as a class.

CLIL Grammar in context: Literature

4
- This activity practises the different conditional forms and the position of adverbs of probability.
- Students read the whole text before they work individually to complete the exercise.
- They compare answers in pairs.

5 33
- Play the audio. Students listen and check their answers.
- Listen to their ideas as a class.

LITERATURE TASK
Students use the internet to find out about another Shakespeare play. They choose one of his plays and write a short summary of it.

CULTURE NOTE
William Shakespeare is probably Britain's best-known playwright. He was born in 1564 in Stratford-upon-Avon, a small town 160 km north-west of London. He was a prolific writer of plays and is believed to have written as many as 41 comedies, tragedies and histories. He died in Stratford in 1616.

Grammar reference > Workbook page 90

Grammar

Adverbs of possibility and probability

Exercise 1
a 2, 5
b 1, 3, 6
c 4

1 **Look at examples 1–6. Then match them with rules a–c.**

adverbs of possibility and probability

1 Eye contact will **probably** put the speaker at ease.
2 **Maybe** it's best to put your phone on silent.
3 These skills will **probably** also serve you well in the future.
4 You **definitely** shouldn't frown or roll your eyes.
5 **Perhaps** you'll also want to ask for clarification.
6 You'll **definitely** need to put it into practice!

a) *Maybe* and *perhaps* go at the beginning of the sentence or clause.
b) *Definitely* and *probably* go after affirmative auxiliaries (*will*, *would*, etc) and forms of *be*.
c) *Definitely* and *probably* go before negative auxiliaries (*won't*, *wouldn't*, etc) and forms of *be*.

Exercise 2
1 Active listening definitely isn't easy.
2 It's probably harder than you think.
3 Maybe we should learn to listen at school.
4 There probably wouldn't be so much conflict if everybody listened.
5 Perhaps the world would be a better place.

2 **Rewrite the sentences in your notebook putting the adverb in the correct place.**

My friends won't listen to me! (probably)
My friends probably won't listen to me

1 Active listening isn't easy. (definitely)
2 It's harder than you think. (probably)
3 We should learn to listen at school. (maybe)
4 There wouldn't be so much conflict if everybody listened. (probably)
5 The world would be a better place. (perhaps)

Exercise 3
Students' own answers

3 **Answer the questions so they are true for you. Use the adverb in brackets in your answer.**

What would you do if your family didn't approve of your friends? (definitely)
I'd definitely try to talk to them about it.

1 Who would you talk to if you had a problem? (probably)
2 Are your friends good listeners? (maybe)
3 Are you a romantic or a practical person? (definitely)
4 What's the most romantic film you've ever seen? (perhaps)
5 Would you prefer to go to the theatre or the cinema? (probably)

CLIL

Grammar in context: Literature

4 **Complete the text with the correct conditional form of the verbs in brackets.**

Exercise 4
1 will definitely laugh
2 would not be
3 fell
4 want
5 read
6 will help
7 wouldn't have understood
8 would have been

A Midsummer Night's Dream

by William Shakespeare

A Midsummer Night's Dream is a famous play by William Shakespeare. If you see it at the theatre, you (1) … (**definitely** / **laugh**) because it's a great comedy. It's about the themes of love, marriage and friendship.

There are two different worlds in this story: the real world and the world of fairies in the forest. Titania, the fairy queen, has fallen out with her husband Oberon. Another fairy, Puck, wants them to make up. Secretly, Puck gives Titania a magic potion so that she falls in love with the first person she sees when she wakes up. This (2) … (**not be**) a problem if the first person she saw was Oberon. But what would happen if she (3) … (**fall**) in love with the wrong person? You will have to read the story if you (4) … (**want**) to find out!

I'd definitely recommend this book – if you (5) … (**read**) it before you go to the theatre it (6) … (**help**) you to understand the play. If we hadn't studied it at school, I (7) … (**not understand**) the story because it's a bit complicated.

Oh, and did you know that if you'd been to see the play in Shakespeare's time, all the actors (8) … (**be**) men? Women weren't allowed to be actors then!

5 **Then listen and check your answers.** 33

LITERATURE TASK

Find out about other plays by Shakespeare. Write a short summary of one of his plays:

- a tragedy, eg *Romeo and Juliet*, *Macbeth*
- a history play, eg *Henry V*, *Richard III*

Literature task
Students' own answers

Grammar basics | Grammar reference > Workbook p90

INTEGRATED SKILLS

Moral dilemmas

LEARNING OUTCOME

✔ Take part in a group debate

Today we're going to discuss some moral dilemmas. What would you do in these situations?

TASK Talk about moral dilemmas

1	2	3	4
Read a quiz	Understand a group debate	Write sentences to present your opinion	Have a group debate

Quiz Moral dilemmas: What would YOU do?

1 You've fallen out with a friend because she posted photos of you on the internet. Now, you want to talk to her about it. How would you communicate?

a) I'd send a message – I'd rather not talk directly.
b) I'd probably give her a ring – it would be better to talk.
c) I'd definitely see her in person – it's hard to explain your feelings otherwise.

2 For your birthday, your boyfriend / girlfriend has given you an item of clothing which you really don't like. Would you …

a) make an excuse and say you lost it somewhere?
b) ask if you could change it for something else?
c) wear it anyway, so he / she doesn't feel bad?

3 Your best friend has got a new hairstyle which you think looks terrible. When he / she asks you what you think, what would you say?

a) I'd tell the truth. I couldn't lie to my best friend.
b) I'd say it looks great. I'd hate to hurt his / her feelings.
c) I'd probably keep quiet and try to change the subject.

4 Your brother has left his mobile phone in your room by accident. What would you do?

a) Read his messages of course! Who wouldn't?
b) Perhaps I'd use it to negotiate a favour.
c) I wouldn't want to feel guilty, so I'd give it straight back. That's what I hope he would do for me!

1 Read

Exercise 1
Students' own answers

1 **Read the quiz and look at Oliver's choices. Would you have chosen the same answers? Write a sentence for each question.**

1 I would / wouldn't have chosen the same answer as Oliver because …

Exercise 2
feel guilty, give somebody a ring, hurt somebody's feelings, keep quiet, make an excuse, tell the truth

2 **Match verbs from A with words from B to make expressions from the quiz. How do you say them in your language? Write example sentences.**

A
• feel • give • hurt • keep • make • tell

B
• an excuse • guilty • quiet • the truth
• somebody a ring • somebody's feelings

give somebody a ring
I'll give you a ring tonight at six o'clock.

2 Listen

Exercise 3
Oliver

3 **Read and listen to the extract from the group debate on page 47. Who changes their mind?** 34

Exercise 4
Students' own answers

4 **Listen again and repeat. Practise your intonation.**

Exercise 5
They are discussing the second moral dilemma.
1, 3, 4, 6

5 **Watch or listen to the next part of the group debate. Which moral dilemma are they discussing? Which four opinions do you hear?** 35

1 'I think it would be best to admit that you don't like it.'
2 'I don't think it's a good idea to fall out about it.'
3 'Personally, I don't think it really matters.'
4 'In my view, you have to be assertive.'
5 'If you ask me, it's a bad idea for a present!'
6 'I'd say that you should change it for something else.'

Integrated skills
Moral dilemmas

LESSON OBJECTIVES
In this lesson students will:
- work on all four skills
- read a quiz about moral dilemmas
- watch or listen to a debate about moral dilemmas
- prepare and participate in a group debate

WARMER
Books closed. Write *advice* on the board. Ask where we can often find advice for problems with relationships and similar problems. Ask students if they can remember a fixed phrase used to give advice that begins with *If I* ... and elicit the phrase *If I were you* ... .

1 Read

1 • Highlight Oliver's speech bubble and read the instructions aloud to the class.
• Students read the quiz and write a sentence saying whether they agree or disagree with each of Oliver's choices, giving reasons.
• Listen to some sentences as a class.

2 • Point out that these expressions are all in the text and that some are formed with a verb plus a noun or noun phrase and others by a verb plus an adjective. Remind students that words that go together in this way are called *collocations*.
• Students match the verbs from A with the words from B to make expressions from the text. Check answers. Elicit translations of the phrases into the students' language. Listen to some example sentences as a class.

2 Listen

Video with audio option
The dialogue is also available to watch as an audio file. If you prefer to present it this way, play the audio and follow the teacher's notes as for the video.

3 34 REC
• Students watch, read and listen and listen to the extract from the group debate.
• Elicit the answer to the question.

4 • Play the video again. Students watch and repeat to practise their intonation. Make sure they put the main stresses in the correct places as this will help with the intonation.

5 35
• Students will hear another moral dilemma and they should note down what it is.
• Students read the six opinions 1-6 and emphasize that they will hear four of these in the next part of the group debate.
• Play the audio. Students note down the four opinions they hear.
• Check answers as a class.

35 Audioscript, page 46, exercises 5 and 6

Teacher: OK. Now let's think about another dilemma ... For your birthday, your boyfriend or girlfriend gives you an item of clothing which you really don't like. What would you do? What do you reckon?
Emily: I think it would be best to admit that you don't like it.
Katy: Yes, it's better to be honest right from the beginning. I mean, you couldn't wear something that you really didn't like, could you?
Oliver: Why not? Personally, I don't think it really matters. It's only a piece of clothing! I mean, when I was younger I used to wear things all the time that I hadn't chosen ...
Jack: Yeah – my grandma used to knit these awful sweaters and give them to us as Christmas presents! We had to wear them so that we wouldn't hurt her feelings.
Katy: Yeah, but that's different. This is about your boyfriend or girlfriend, not your grandma! In my view, you have to be assertive. I mean, it's not a good precedent in the relationship, is it? If you just do what the other person wants you to!
Emily: I agree with Katy. I'd say that you should change it for something else. I mean, he should have the receipt so you can just go back to the shop together, and choose something you like.
Oliver: No ..., it's not worth the trouble. For me it wouldn't be a big deal.
Jack: Yeah, but I can see the point. Maybe you could just make an excuse – say you lost it or something, so then you wouldn't have to wear it ...

6
- Students look at the Communication kit: Presenting your opinion.
- Ask how many of these typical phrases for agreeing or disagreeing they can find in this part of the group debate. Students read the extract on page 47 again. Then play the audio of the next part from exercise 5 again for students to check their answers.

3 Write

7
- Students look at the third dilemma on page 46 again.
- Students think about the consequences of each action and write their own ideas.

8
- Highlight the two ways of giving opinions shown in the examples.
- Students work individually and write sentences to present their opinions.
- Monitor while they are writing and give help with ideas if necessary, eg *Personally, I think that if I lied it wouldn't help the situation because ...*

4 Communicate

9
- Students work in pairs and practise presenting their opinions, and agreeing or disagreeing with their partner. They give opinions using the phrases in the Communication kit and respond using *so*, *neither* and *too*.

LANGUAGE NOTE

Students will probably find it easier to use *me too* and *me neither* as these phrases remain constant. The phrases *so do I* and *neither do I* change depending on the tense the speaker uses, eg if the speaker says *I thought it was right*, the response would be *So did I*, and if the speaker says *I wouldn't say that*, the response would be *Neither would I*.

10
- Students discuss the third dilemma from page 46 as a class.
- Find out which solution is the most popular by taking a class vote.

11
- Students discuss the fourth dilemma from page 46 as a class.
- Then Students work in pairs or small groups and think of more moral dilemmas, eg 1 *You are invited for lunch at a friend's house. The food is awful. What would you do?* 2 *You go to see a friend perform in a play. The play is terrible. He / She asks you what you thought of it. What would you say?*
- Elicit ideas as a class. Ask students what they would do in each situation.

! COMMUNICATION TIP
QUESTION TAGS

Highlight that we use question tags to confirm information, check agreement, or just keep a discussion going.

! COMMUNICATION TIP
USING *SO*, *NEITHER* AND *TOO*

Highlight the information in the Communication tip box. Point out that we use *neither* when we agree with a negative opinion (eg *I don't think*) and *too* when we agree with a positive opinion (eg *I believe*). The expressions *so do I* and *neither do I* follow positive and negative verbs respectively in the present simple when you agree with the speaker.

Integrated skills > Resource centre

Teacher: OK. Today we're going to discuss some moral dilemmas. First of all, how would you choose to communicate with a friend if you had fallen out about something? Who would like to start?

Emily: No, neither do I. If I fell out with my friend, she would probably just misinterpret my messages.

Jack: So do I. In my opinion, you can't really understand someone properly if you can't see their body language.

Oliver: Personally, I'd say that it would be best to give them a ring. I don't think that text messages are a good idea when you've fallen out with someone.

Katy: I agree. But if you ask me, I think it would be even better to talk face to face.

Oliver: Yes, perhaps you're right. I think talking face-to-face would probably be better than speaking on the phone.

Communication kit

- Personally, I'd say that ...
- I think / don't think that ...
- If you ask me, ...
- In my opinion, ...
- In my view, ...
- For me, ...

Exercise 6
All of them

6 Look at the Communication kit. Which phrases are in the Speaking sketch? Watch or listen again to check your answers.

3 Write

Exercise 7
Students' own answers

7 Prepare for a group debate about the third dilemma in the quiz on page 46. Think about the consequences of each action. Write your ideas.

Exercise 8
Students' own answers

8 Write sentences to present your opinions. Use your ideas in exercise 7 and the phrases in the Communication kit.

For me, the best thing to do would be ...
I don't think it's a good idea to ...

4 Communicate

Exercise 9
Students' own answers

9 Before the debate, work in pairs. Practise presenting your opinions, and agreeing or disagreeing with your partner.

I think that it would be best to ...
Yes, so do I!

Exercise 10
Students' own answers

10 Have a group debate about the third dilemma. Do your classmates agree or disagree?

11 Now discuss the fourth dilemma in the quiz on page 46. Can you think of any more moral dilemmas?

! COMMUNICATION TIP
USING *SO, NEITHER* AND *TOO*

Use *so*, *neither* and *too* to agree with someone.
I think it's best to tell the truth. Yes, ***so*** *do I. / Me,* ***too****.*
I don't think it's a good idea to lie. No, ***neither*** *do I. / Me* ***neither****.*

Writing
Instant messages

LEARNING OUTCOME

✔ Write an instant message conversation

Exercise 1
Her mum won't allow her to get the bus home on her own from Sara's birthday party. Sara suggests asking if she could go home with another friend when their dad picks them up.

14:10

1 Hi Sara, how's it going? I've got a problem with your birthday party next Saturday. My mum won't let me get the night bus home on my own. It's so frustrating! I'm old enough to look after myself!!

2 Oh no! 😣 So what time will you have to leave? I don't want you to miss the end of the party!

3 Mum said she'd pick me up at ten. That's too early IMO …

4 Yeah, you won't be able to go to the disco with us unless you can leave later! Why don't you go back with Lou? Her dad's picking her up at 12. If I were you, I'd ask them. I'm sure they'd give you a lift if you asked.

5 Yes, I hadn't thought of that. Good idea, and my mum will definitely be happier with that plan. I'll message Lou and ask her if that's OK. Thanks, Sara! TTYL 🙂

6 Good luck! Bye for now!

1 Read the instant message conversation. What is Julia's problem? What solution does Sara suggest?

Exercise 2
1 b
2 d
3 a
4 f
5 c
6 e

2 Focus on content Read the conversation again and match messages 1–6 with a–f.

a) giving more details
b) sharing the problem
c) responding to the solution
d) asking for more details
e) saying goodbye
f) suggesting a solution

Exercise 3
Students' own answers

3 Focus on language Read the information. How do you say the informal expressions in your language?

Exclamations and personal questions
Oh no!
How's it going?

Phrasal verbs and colloquial expressions
She said she'd pick me up at ten.
I'm sure they'd give you a lift.

Abbreviations
IMO = in my opinion
TTYL = talk to you later

Exercise 4
Yeah!
TTYL
Bye for now!

4 How many other examples of informal language can you find in the instant message conversation?

5 Imagine you receive this message from a friend. Write an instant message conversation between you and your friend where you find a way to resolve the problem.

Exercise 5
Students' own answers

Hi! How's it going? I'm afraid I've got a problem with our plan to meet up on Saturday. I've got to look after my little sister until four o'clock …

Writing kit

1 **Plan** your instant message conversation. What solution will you suggest to resolve the problem?

2 **Write** the instant message conversation. Write five parts: three from you and two more from your friend.

3 **Useful phrases**

How's it going? *Oh no!* *Why don't you …?* *If I were you …* *Good luck!*

4 **Check** your writing.

- ☑ exclamations, abbreviations and personal questions
- ☑ phrasal verbs and colloquial expressions
- ☑ use the correct tenses in conditional sentences
- ☑ check you've suggested a solution to the problem

Study guide > p102 Writing hub > Workbook p118

Writing
Instant messages

LESSON OBJECTIVES
In this lesson students will:
- read an instant message conversation
- use examples of informal expressions
- write an instant message conversation

WARMER
Write *instant messaging* on the board. Elicit that it is online chat that enables real-time text transmission. Ask what other things instant messaging can do. Elicit examples and write them on the board.

1
- Students read the instant message conversation and find the answers.
- Check answers as a class.

CULTURE NOTE
The term *instant messaging* was first used in the 1990s. Early instant messaging consisted of real-time text, where the letters appeared on your screen as the other person typed.

2 Focus on content
- Students read a-f carefully before reading the text again.
- They work individually and match the messages with their functions.
- Students compare answers with a partner.
- Check answers as a class

3 Focus on language
- Students read the information in the Focus on language section.
- They translate the expressions into their language.

4
- Students read the instant message conversation again and find more examples of informal language.
- Students compare their answers in pairs.
- Check answers as a class.

5
- Ask students to follow the stages in the Writing kit.
- Encourage them to use exclamations and personal questions, phrasal verbs, colloquial expressions and abbreviations in their messages.
- Monitor while they are writing and give help with vocabulary if necessary.
- At the check stage, ask them to swap notebooks and check each other's writing.

Writing kit
The aim of this activity is for students to write an instant message conversation resolving a problem using examples of informal language and the correct tenses in conditional sentences. Ask the students to follow the stages in the Student's Book. Make sure they write five parts. Encourage them to use the instant message conversation in exercise 1 for ideas. Monitor while they are writing and give help with vocabulary if necessary. At the Check stage, Students swap notebooks and check each other's writing.

Study guide > Student's Book page 102

Writing hub > Workbook page 118

UNIT 5

TECHNOLOGY

UNIT OBJECTIVES AND KEY COMPETENCES

In this unit the student will learn ...

- to recognize, understand and correctly use vocabulary related to innovations and invention and revise adverbs of manner, degree and frequency **CLC CMST CAE**
- to recognize, understand and correctly use the different tenses in the passive **CLC L2L SIE**
- to recognize, understand and use the active and the passive voice and use them in a short speaking activity **CLC L2L**
- about virtual classrooms and other technologies used in the classroom **CLC SCC CAE**
- about giving a presentation by watching a short video **CLC DC SCC**

In this unit the student will learn how to ...

- scan for names, numbers and abbreviations in a text about young innovators and awards for young scientists and engineers **CLC CMST SCC CAE**
- look online for more information about the science fairs and their winners **CLC CMST DC CAE SIE**
- understand technical instructions **CLC SCC L2L**
- read timelines about new technology, listen to a presentation, prepare for and give a presentation **CLC CMST CAE SIE**
- write a formal letter **CLC**

LINGUISTIC CONTENTS

Main vocabulary

- Innovation and invention: *STEM / STEAM*, *NEC*, etc
- Adverb review (adverbs of manner, degree and frequency): *easily*, *extremely*, *rarely*, etc.

Extra vocabulary

- Words in context: *award*, *fair*, *stand*, *nanotechnology*, *pitch*, *pick up*, *up-to-date*, *headset*, *eye strain*, *replace*
- Word builder: Negative prefixes; Adverbs of manner

Grammar

- The passive
- Active and passive voice

Functional language

- Sequencing events

Pronunciation

- Linking words: Final consonant + vowel sound

SKILLS

Reading

- Read online information about young engineers and scientists
- Read an article about virtual classrooms
- Read timelines about the internet and mobile phones
- Read a formal letter

Writing: Interaction and production

- Write notes to prepare for a presentation about the history of the internet
- Write a formal letter in three steps
- Learn how to write a formal letter

Listening

- Listen to an extract from a TV technology show
- Listen to a presentation about the history of mobile phones

Spoken interaction

- Exchange information about innovations

Spoken production

- Prepare and give a presentation

LIFELONG LEARNING SKILLS

Self-study and self-evaluation

- Study guide: Student's Book page 103
- Progress check: Workbook page 46
- Extension: Workbook page 47
- Grammar reference and practice: Workbook pages 92–93
- Wordlist: Workbook pages 151–157

Learning strategies and thinking skills

- Scanning for names, numbers and abbreviations / acronyms
- Critical thinking: imagining a new design

Social awareness

- Virtual classrooms

Cross-curricular contents

- Innovations and inventions, the Google Science Fair and its winners
- Literature and history: *China* by Jennifer Gascoigne
- Literature task: searching the internet for information about the history of paper and printing

EVALUATION

- Unit 5 End of unit test: Basic, Standard and Extra
- CEFR Skills Exam Generator

KEY COMPETENCES

CLC	Competence in linguistic communication
CMST	Competence in mathematics, science and technology
DC	Digital competence
SCC	Social and civic competence
CAE	Cultural awareness and expression
L2L	Learning to learn
SIE	Sense of initiative and entrepreneurship

DIGITAL MATERIAL

New Pulse Digital Course including:

- Interactive vocabulary presentation
- Grammar and Vocabulary basics exercises
- Getting started video
- Flipped classroom grammar video: The passive
- Culture byte video: The perfect pitch
- Speaking sketch video: A presentation

DIGITAL COMPETENCE

- Web quest: Find out more about Science Fairs and their winners
- Digital competence worksheet: Web-based image-editing tools

REINFORCEMENT MATERIAL

- New Pulse Basics: Teacher's Resource Centre
- Vocabulary and Grammar consolidation worksheets: Teacher's Resource Centre
- Grammar and Vocabulary basics exercises: Teacher's Presentation Kit

EXTENSION MATERIAL

- Vocabulary and grammar extension worksheets: Teacher's Resource Centre
- Advance your vocabulary: Workbook page 107
- The longer read: Teacher's Resource Centre
- Writing hub: Workbook page 120

TEACHER'S RESOURCE CENTRE

- Translation and dictation worksheets
- Evaluation rubrics
- Key competences worksheets
- Culture and CLIL worksheets
- Culture byte worksheets
- Digital competence worksheets
- Macmillan Readers worksheets
- Integrated Skills

Vocabulary

Innovation and invention

LESSON OBJECTIVES
In this lesson students will:

- learn words related to innovations and inventions
- read and answer a quiz
- talk about their experience of innovations

VIDEO: GETTING STARTED

In this video the speakers answer the question *What great innovations do you think there will be during your lifetime?*

- Focus the students on the unit title *Technology*.
- Write the following sentences on the board:
  1 Who hopes a new product will be invented that is kinder to wildlife and the environment?
  2 Who wants a faster public transport system in his / her country?
  3 Who hopes people will travel to space in his / her lifetime?
- Students watch the video and decide whether the sentences are true or false.
- They watch the video again to check answers.
- At the end of the lesson, ask students to answer the question from the video: *What great innovations do you think there will be during your lifetime?*

Answer key: 1 Naomi **2** Emily **3** Josh

WARMER

Bring an everyday gadget to class, eg a digital watch, a camera, a memory stick. Do not show the object to the class but explain that you have an object with you and students should guess what it is by asking questions, eg *Can you use it to make telephone calls?* Explain that you can only answer *yes* or *no* to their questions. If students have not guessed what the object is after asking 20 questions, you are the winner.

1
- Students read the quiz and note down the meaning of the words in blue. Encourage them to use a dictionary if necessary.
- Check answers as a class.
- If you are using the TPK and your students need more work on the meaning of the words, do the Vocabulary basics exercise.

Vocabulary basics

Answer key: 1 driverless cars **2** smart materials **3** wearable gadgets **4** e-reader **5** bioplastics **6** satellite broadband **7** space station **8** desalinated water

2
- Explain that one of the statements in the quiz is not true. Students read the quiz carefully and find the untrue statement.
- They compare ideas in pairs.
- Check the answer as a class. Make sure students understand all the vocabulary in the text, eg *wearable* (that can be worn), *desalinated* (with the salt removed).

CULTURE NOTE

Forty-one US states have considered passing laws to allow driverless cars on public roads. Maglev trains already transport people to Shanghai airport at speeds of up to 430 km/hr. Apart from a test track at an International Transportation Exhibition in Hamburg, Germany in 1979, the first regularly used Maglev train in the world ran from Birmingham Airport terminal to Birmingham International railway station from 1984 to 1995. If you've got $250,000, you can put your name on the waiting list for a space trip with Virgin Galactic.

3 36
- Students work individually to write the words in blue in exercise 1 under the headings.
- They compare answers in pairs.
- Play the audio. Students listen and check their answers.
- Play the audio again for students to listen and repeat the words. Make sure they pronounce them correctly with the correct stress, especially *wearable* /'weərəbəl/ and *satellite* /'sætəlaɪt/.
- Check answers as a class.

4
- Read the example sentence aloud to the class. Explain that students should write sentences about their experience of the innovations. Encourage them to write at least six sentences.
- Students work individually and write their sentences. Monitor while they are writing and give help if necessary.
- They compare their sentences in pairs.
- Listen to their ideas as a class.

FINISHED?

Ask fast finishers to write a sentence about all twelve of the innovations in exercise 1.

TECHNOLOGY

UNIT 5

LEARNING OUTCOMES IN THIS UNIT

- Scan for names, numbers and abbreviations
- Understand technical instructions
- Give a presentation
- Write a formal letter of complaint

VIDEO: GETTING STARTED

WATCH Watch the teenagers talking about innovations and answer the question.

Vocabulary
Innovation and invention

Exercise 1
Students' own answers

1 Read the quiz and check the meaning of the words in blue. Have you seen or used any of these innovations?

Exercise 2
Statement 5 is not true.

2 Do the quiz. Which statements are not true?

Quiz: Fact or fiction?

1. In some parts of the USA, driverless cars already travel on public roads.
2. The future of high-speed trains is magnetic levitation! Maglev trains take people to Shanghai airport at speeds of up to 431 km/hr.
3. Smart materials are already used to make protective jackets which give attackers an electric shock.
4. 3D printing is now an affordable reality. You can buy a 3D printer for less than £200.
5. Wearable gadgets include a hat which scientists have developed to improve memory.
6. Millions of e-books have been sold since the first e-reader was designed in 2007.
7. Unlike traditional plastic, bioplastics are biodegradable. They can even be made from vegetables!
8. In desert countries such as Kuwait and Saudi Arabia people use desalinated water, which was originally sea water.
9. Flexible smartphones are much lighter, and they don't break if you drop them!
10. No wi-fi? Don't worry – now everyone can connect with satellite broadband.
11. China is building a space station in orbit, which it hopes to open by 2022.
12. How about space tourism for your next holiday? If you've got $250,000, you can sign up now!

Check your score!

3 Write the words in blue in exercise 1 under these headings. Then listen, check and repeat. 36

communication	entertainment	the environment	manufacturing	space travel	transport

4 What is your experience of these innovations? Write sentences. Compare with your partner.

I've got a wearable gadget – it tells me how many steps I walk every day!

Exercise 4
Students' own answers

Exercise 3
Communication – flexible smartphone, satellite broadband
Entertainment – e-reader, wearable gadgets
The environment – bioplastics, desalinated water
Manufacturing – smart materials, 3D printing
Space travel – space station, space tourism
Transport – driverless cars, high-speed trains

Reading

A science article

LEARNING OUTCOME

✔ Scan for names, numbers and abbreviations

Exercise 1

Suggested answers: STEM stars, 'The Big Bang', UK Young Engineer, more than 150 stands

It's about science, a fair with awards for young people

1 **Read the information and scan the text quickly. Find at least three names, numbers and abbreviations / acronyms. What clues do they give you about the content of the text?**

SCAN FOR NAMES, NUMBERS AND ABBREVIATIONS
Names, numbers and abbreviations stand out when you look at a text. If you scan them quickly, you can get some good clues to what the text is about.

Exercise 2

b

2 **Read and listen to the text. Choose the best summary, a or b.** 37

The article is about ...

a) science fairs for young people in the EU and USA, and how previous winners have developed their STEM / STEAM careers.

b) the annual 'Big Bang' STEM fair in Britain, including information about recent winners, the selection process, and the stands and events at last year's fair.

Exercise 3

1. The Big Bang Fair
2. Josh Mitchell and Emily Xu
3. More than 80,000
4. National Exhibition Centre in Birmingham
5. Dotography

3 **Copy and complete the sentences with names, numbers and abbreviations / acronyms from the text.**

1. Britain's biggest STEM fair for young people is called ...
2. The two top winners at the recent fair were ...
3. ... visitors attended the fair last year.
4. The fair was held at the ...
5. The name of the nanotechnology exhibition was ...

Exercise 4

a) nanotechnology
b) award
c) fair
d) pitch
e) stand

4 **Words in context** **Find these words in the text. Are they nouns or verbs? Match them with definitions a–e.**

award fair stand nanotechnology pitch

a) the construction and use of very small structures, using atoms and molecules
b) a prize that is given to someone who has achieved something
c) an event where people or companies bring their products for you to look at
d) to try to sell something by saying how good it is
e) a table at an exhibition where people show or sell information, products or services

STEM* stars at 'The Big Bang'

Emily Xu

Meet Josh Mitchell and Emily Xu, winners of this year's UK Young Engineer and GSK UK Young Scientist of the Year awards at The Big Bang Fair, the UK's biggest STEM fair for young people.

Young engineer Josh was awarded the top prize for his project to design an inexpensive 3D printer. The flat-pack machine, called 'The Plybot', fits into two 13-inch pizza boxes and can be assembled very easily. If Josh can market his product, it will be sold for just £49. Meanwhile, Emily won the top science prize for her project to create safer and more effective pharmaceutical drugs.

Josh Mitchell

The Big Bang UK Young Scientists & Engineers Fair is held every year to celebrate achievements and inspire young people in STEM. More than 80,000 visitors attended last year's fair, which was held at the National Exhibition Centre (NEC) in Birmingham. As well as interactive exhibitions and careers talks, there were also more than 150 stands about everything from bioplastics and satellite broadband

5 **Are the sentences true or false? Correct the false sentences.**

1. Josh Mitchell designed a flexible phone.
2. Emily Xu won the top prize for engineering.
3. The Big Bang fair is held every year.
4. 500 finalists are selected from around the world.
5. You can enter the competition if you are under 21.

Exercise 5

1. **False** – He designed an inexpensive 3D printer.
2. **False** – She won the top science prize.
3. **True**
4. **False** – They are selected from around the UK.
5. **False** – You must be under 18.

The longer read > Resource centre

Reading

An science article

LESSON OBJECTIVES
In this lesson students will:
- read a science article
- scan for names, numbers and abbreviations
- form negatives using prefixes

WARMER

Write these abbreviations on the board: *UAE, BBC, CIA, UN*. Elicit from the class what they stand for (*United Arab Emirates, British Broadcasting Corporation, Central Intelligence Agency, United Nations*).

DID YOU KNOW?

As STEM is central to this lesson, ask students to read the information in the *Did you know?* box on page 51 first. Check that they understand what STEM and STEAM stand for.

1
- Read the rubric with the whole class. Then ask students to read the information in the box.
- Students scan the text quickly to locate the answers and note them down. Remind students that the key element of scanning is that you know what you are looking for, eg *names, numbers and abbreviations*, and you do not need to understand the rest of the text to find it. Then, they answer the question.
- Students compare answers in pairs.
- Check answers as a class.

READING STRATEGY

Scanning for names, numbers and abbreviations

It is a useful strategy for readers to be able to have an initial idea of what the text is about.

2 37
- Students read the summaries carefully first.
- Play the audio. Students read and listen to the text and decide whether a) or b) is a summary of the text.
- Check the answer as a class.

3
- Students copy the sentences into their notebooks.
- They read the text again and fill the gaps in the sentences using abbreviations/acronyms, names and numbers.
- Check answers as a class.

LANGUAGE NOTE

Abbreviations and acronyms. These terms are very similar but the distinction is that an acronym is an abbreviation that is pronounced like a word, eg *UNESCO*. In this text, *STEM* would be pronounced as a word, /stem/, and is therefore an acronym.

4 Words in context
- Read the words aloud to the class.
- Students find the words in the text, read the definitions and try to match them in pairs. Note that *pitch* here is a verb and means to *try to sell an idea*.
- Check answers as a class.

5
- Students work individually to decide whether these statements are true or false.
- They compare their answers in pairs.
- Check answers as a class.

6 • Students read the text and write answers to the questions in their notebooks.
• They compare answers in pairs.
• Check answers as a class.

7 Word builder
• Highlight the fact that *il-* is used before adjectives beginning with *l*; *im-* before adjectives beginning with *m*, *b* or *p*, and *ir-* before adjectives beginning with *r*.
• Students write negative prefixes for *effective* and *visible* and check their answers in the text.
• They write negative prefixes for the adjectives in question 2 and use a dictionary to check.
• Check answers as a class.

FINISHED?

Write these adjectives on the board and ask students to write the negative forms: *probable*, *legal*, *mature*, *responsible*, *familiar*, *dependent*. (**Answer key:** improbable, illegal, immature, irresponsible, unfamiliar, independent).

8 • Put students into pairs. They read the questions and take turns asking and answering them.
• Nominate different pairs to say their questions and answers to the class.

CRITICAL THINKING

• Read the instructions with the class.
• Students work individually and think of a new design or invention. They compare their ideas in pairs.
• Listen to their ideas as a class.

WEB QUEST

Students find out more about the science fairs for young people and their winners.

1 **Think** Students work in groups of three and they choose one of the fairs each.

2 **Investigate** Students open a search engine (eg *Google*) and search for information about the fair they have chosen. Encourage them to find pictures and videos as well as textual information.

3 **Communicate** They share their findings with the group. Each group gives a summary of its findings to the whole class.

TIP! Remind students to bookmark the websites they accessed, so that they can find them again and exchange information with the members of the class who might want to read the same information.

VIDEO: FLIPPED CLASSROOM

You may want to ask Students to watch the Flipped classroom video for unit 5 as homework in preparation for the following grammar lesson. The Flipped grammar presentation focuses on the passive voice.

The longer read > Resource centre

DID YOU KNOW?

*STEM (science, technology, engineering and maths) and STEAM (science, technology, engineering, arts and maths) are ways of integrating different subjects. A designer, for example, would probably use all these subjects together in a real-world project.

to space exploration and wearable gadgets. Highlights included the 'rock music milkshake machine' which made milkshakes using sound waves from an amplified guitar, and a nanotechnology exhibition called 'Dotography,' consisting of photographs so small – a single pixel! – that they aren't visible without a special microscope attached to your phone.

Every year 500 young finalists of The Big Bang Competition are selected from around the UK to show their ideas at the fair. Ten of them are chosen to pitch their projects to a panel of judges, who award the top science and engineering prizes to their favourite projects. Emily and Josh have joined an impressive list of past winners, including young engineers David Bernstein and Sankha Kahagala-Gamage whose 'Medivest' jacket was designed to predict epileptic episodes using smart materials, and Stuart Chau, Ethan Dunbar Baker and Rogan McGilp whose 'Hot Rod' car was built for Rogan's 13-year-old brother David, who has a disability.

Organizer Mark Titterington believes that the future looks bright because the scientists, engineers and inventors of the future are already producing such exciting work. Hopefully more young people will be inspired to enter the competition by their achievements.

Who knows what exciting new projects will win next year's competition – maybe yours! If you're under 18 and love STEM, check out The Big Bang website to find out how to take part.

Exercise 6

1 Because it fits into two 13-inch pizza boxes and can be assembled very easily.
2 It was about creating safer and more effective pharmaceutical drugs.
3 bioplastics, satellite broadband, space exploration and wearable gadgets
4 a panel of judges
5 It's a jacket that was designed to predict epileptic episodes using smart materials.
6 It's a car that was designed for someone with a disability.

6 Answer the questions.

1 Why is Josh's 3D printer described as a 'flat-pack' machine?
2 What was Emily's winning project about?
3 What examples are given of things you can learn about on the stands?
4 Who do the finalists have to pitch their projects to?
5 What is the 'Medivest' jacket?
6 What is the 'Hot Rod' car?

7 **Word builder** Read the information and answer the questions.

Negative prefixes

We use negative prefixes such as *in-*, *un-*, *il-* / *ir-* / *im-* and *dis-* to make negative adjectives or nouns.

expensive > ***in**expensive*
ability > ***dis**ability*

1 How would you make the negative form of these adjectives from the text?

effective visible

2 Write the negative form of these words. Use a dictionary to help you.

advantage likely logical patient rational

Exercise 7

1 ineffective, invisible
2 disadvantage, unlikely, illogical, impatient, irrational

8 Work in pairs to ask and answer the questions.

1 What STEM / STEAM subjects do *you* study at school?
2 Have you ever designed, invented or discovered something?
3 Do you think you will have a job related to STEM / STEAM in the future?

Exercise 8

Students' own answers

CRITICAL THINKING

IMAGINE

Look at the article and find examples of winning designs or inventions. Write a list. Imagine you are going to enter a STEM / STEAM competition. Choose one of these categories and imagine a new design or invention.

- Science
- Engineering
- Art and Design

WEB QUEST

Work in groups of three. Find out about the winners of last year's science fairs for young people.

1 **Think** Each choose one of these science fairs:
- Intel International Science and Engineering Fair
- European Union Contest for Young Scientists
- The Big Bang STEM fair in the UK

2 **Investigate** Search online for information about last year's winners. Find out:
- their name, age and nationality
- what they invented / designed

3 **Communicate** Share your research with your group. Then present a summary to the class.

TIP! Remember to bookmark the websites you've used, so that it's easy to find them again.

Grammar

The passive

VIDEO: FLIPPED CLASSROOM

WATCH Watch the grammar presentation and do the task.

1 **Look at the table. Copy and complete the sentences with these words.**

• are • aren't • wasn't • were
• will be • won't be

present simple passive	
+	The competition **is held** every year.
-	Projects from non-students (1) ... **accepted**.
?	How (2) ... the finalists **selected**?
past simple passive	
+	The top prizes (3) ... **given** to Josh Mitchell and Emily Xu.
-	Unfortunately my project (4) ... **selected**!
?	Where **was** last year's fair **held**?
future passive	
+	Next year's finalists (5) ... **selected** soon.
-	Next year's winners (6) ... **announced** until March.
?	Where **will** next year's fair **be held**?

2 **Copy and complete the present simple passive sentences so they are true for you. Use the affirmative or negative.**

At my school ...

1 science ... (teach) three times a week.
2 students ... (encourage) to be innovative.
3 prizes ... (award) at the end of the year.
4 the computer room ... (use) every day.
5 students ... (give) laptops or tablets.

ANALYSE

We use the passive when the person who does the action isn't mentioned, or isn't important. Translate the sentences in exercise 2. Do you use the passive in your language?

3 **Write past simple passive sentences using the information in brackets. Write one negative and one affirmative sentence.**

3D printers / invent (last year / 1980s)
3D printers weren't invented last year.
They were invented in the 1980s.

1 The first cars / invent (in England / Germany)
2 iPads / design (by Amazon / Apple)
3 WhatsApp / introduce (in 2018 / 2009)
4 The World Wide Web / create (by an American scientist / a British scientist)

4 **Copy and complete the text with the correct form of the verbs in brackets. Use the passive.**

CARS: A HISTORY OF INNOVATION

The first car (1) ... (design) by the German inventor Carl Benz in 1886. Secretly, it (2) ... (test) on a 200 km journey by his wife Bertha, who suggested many improvements! Cheaper cars (3) ... (not produce) until 1908, when Henry Ford's first car factories (4) ... (open) in the USA. Since then, there have been many different types of cars. Although traditional fuels like petrol and diesel (5) ... (still / use) in most of them, greener fuels (6) ... (probably / use) more and more in future. Driverless cars are the latest innovation, though in most countries they (7) ... (not use) on public roads at the moment. What kind of vehicles (8) ... (invent) in the future, I wonder?

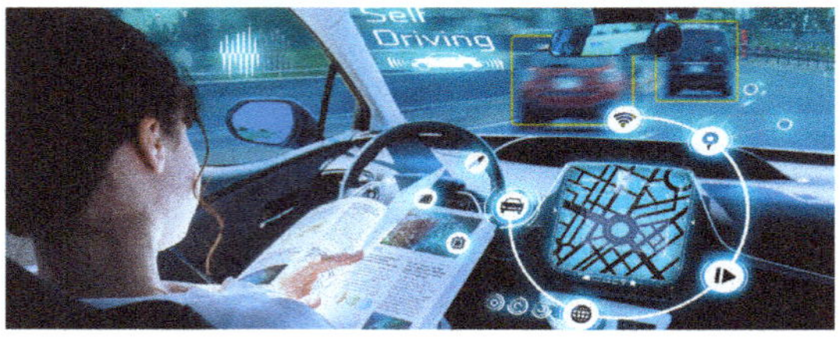

5 **Order the words to make passive questions. Then choose a gadget that you own, and write true answers to the questions.**

was / made / it / When ?
When was it made?
It was made about two years ago.

1 it / What / is / used / for ?
2 designed / it / by / Who / was ?
3 was / made / it / Where ?
4 Where / bought / was / it ?
5 the design / How / be / improved / will / in the future ?

6 **Work in pairs. Ask your partner about his / her chosen gadget. Use the questions in exercise 5.**

Exercise 1
1 aren't
2 are
3 were
4 wasn't
5 will be
6 won't be

Exercise 2
Students' own answers

Exercise 3
1 The first cars weren't invented in England. They were invented in Germany.
2 iPads weren't designed by Amazon. They were designed by Apple.
3 WhatsApp wasn't introduced in 2018. It was introduced in 2009.
4 The World Wide Web wasn't created by an American scientist. It was created by a British scientist.

Exercise 4
1 was designed
2 was tested
3 weren't produced
4 were opened
5 are still used
6 will probably be used
7 aren't used
8 will be invented

Exercise 5
1 What is it used for?
2 Who was it designed by?
3 Where was it made?
4 Where was it bought?
5 How will the design be improved in the future?

Exercise 6
Students' own answers

Grammar basics | Grammar reference > Workbook p92 | Pronunciation > p124

Grammar
The passive

LESSON OBJECTIVES
In this lesson students will:
- learn the passive voice in the present simple, the past simple and the future with *will*
- read a text about the history of books

WARMER
Write these verbs on the board: *write, teach, give, make, choose, sell, read, break, drive, take*. Students work in pairs and write down the past participle of each verb. The first pair to write down all ten past participles correctly wins. (Answers: *written, taught, given, made, chosen, sold, read, broken, driven, taken*)

VIDEO: FLIPPED CLASSROOM
- If you set the video for homework, ask students to compare their Task time! answers and then check the answers as a class.
- If you didn't set it for homework, watch the video in class and answer the Task time! questions at the end of the presentation.

Answer key: 1 false **2** false **3** true

1
- Students read the six auxiliary verbs.
- They read the sentences in the table and copy and complete the sentences in their notebooks using the auxiliary verbs given.
- Check answers. Highlight the use of *be* after *will* / *won't* and before the past participle.
- If you are using the TPK and your students need more practice of the grammar, do the Grammar basics exercise.

Grammar basics
Answer key: 1 was **2** is **3** won't be **4** will be **5** are **6** were

2
- Complete the first sentence with the whole class to illustrate the activity. Point out that either the affirmative or negative can be used depending on the situation in their school.
- Students complete the task.
- Check answers as a class. If question 1 is negative in their school, ask them to rewrite the sentence in the affirmative, changing the time expression to make it true, eg *Science is taught five times a week.*

ANALYSE
Highlight the fact that we use the passive when we want to focus more on the recipient of an action in a sentence. The person who does the action isn't mentioned, or isn't important. Students translate the sentences in exercise 2 into their language and elicit whether they would also use the passive form in their language.

3
- Show how the two example sentences are formed from the prompts.
- Highlight the use of the pronouns *it* or *they* in the second sentence in each case.
- Check answers as a class.

4
- Encourage students to read the whole text first to get the gist before they begin the exercise.
- They complete the text with the correct passive form of the verbs in brackets.
- Check answers. Ask students if they prefer 'real' cars or driverless cars.

5
- Show how the example passive question is made from the prompts. Point out that the *wh-* word in capitals is the first word each time.
- Students write the questions. Check that they have written the questions correctly.
- Then Students think of a gadget, eg mobile phone, digital camera, iPad, etc.
- They write answers that are true for the gadget they have chosen.

6
- Students work in pairs and ask and answer the questions in exercise 5.

LANGUAGE NOTE
The passive voice can also be used in constructions with modal verbs. These are formed in the same way as the examples of the future passive in the table in exercise 1, with the appropriate modal verb + *be* and the past participle, eg *The problem could be solved immediately.*

Grammar reference > Workbook page 92

Pronunciation lab > Linking words: final consonant + vowel sound > Student's Book page 124

Vocabulary and Listening

Adverb review

LESSON OBJECTIVES

In this lesson students will:

- learn a set of adverbs
- learn to understand technical instructions

WARMER

Write these questions on the board: *What is it famous for?*; *What food is typically eaten there?*; *Which famous people come from there?*; *What language is spoken there?* Think of a country (eg Spain) and answer the questions (eg it's famous for flamenco, bullfighting and Don Quijote; Paella, ham and gazpacho is typically eaten there; etc...) Now tell students to think of a country and prepare the answers. In pairs, students take it in turns to describe their countries. Make sure they are using full sentences.

DIGITAL VOCABULARY FLASHCARDS

In this digital presentation, students match the vocabulary with definitions.

- Do the digital presentation with the class.
- Encourage students to repeat the words.

1 38

- Students read the text and answer the question.
- Play the audio. Students listen and repeat the words in blue.
- If you are using the TPK and your students need more work on the meaning of the words, do the Vocabulary basics exercise.

Vocabulary basics

Answer key: absolutely, easily, rarely, fast, quickly, safely, usually, extremely

2
- Explain that students should categorize the adverbs according to their function.
- Students copy the table into their notebooks and write the adverbs in the correct column.
- Check answers as a class.

3 Word builder

- Students read the rules in the Word builder box. They find an example for each rule in the word box in exercise 1.
- Check answers. Point out that *often*, *always*, *very* and *quite* are only adverbs and have no adjectival equivalents.

4
- Students read the rules about adverbs of manner, degree and frequency.
- Highlight that we never use adverbs after the verbs *look*, *seem* or *feel*, *eg It feels good* (not *It feels well*).
- They use the information in the rules to correct the errors in sentences 1–4.
- Check answers as a class.

LANGUAGE NOTE

The main irregular adverbs are *well*, *fast*, *late* and *hard*. The adverb *hard*, as in *She works hard* should not be confused with the adverb *hardly*, which means 'very little', as in *She hardly works*. Note the position of *hardly* before the verb for this meaning.

5
- Students look at the information and the picture. Elicit the answer to the question (*3D printing*).
- Pre-teach *power cable*, *spool*, *nozzle* and *printing platform*.

6 39

- Students read all the instructions first.
- Play the audio. Students write the instructions in the correct order.
- Check answers as a class.

For audioscript, see page T54

7
- Play the audio again. Students choose the correct answers.
- Check answers as a class.

Advance your vocabulary > Workbook page 107

Vocabulary and Listening

Adverb review

LEARNING OUTCOME

✔ Understand technical instructions

DIGITAL VOCABULARY FLASHCARDS

Do the matching exercise to discover the new vocabulary.

absolutely always comfortably easily extremely fast often quickly quite rarely safely usually very well

1 Read the text. Are you a digital native? Listen and repeat the words in blue. 38

Exercise 1
Students' own answers

AM I A DIGITAL NATIVE?

You can be absolutely sure that you are a digital native when you can discover comfortably and easily how new technology works. You always want the latest software and you are usually one of the first to install updates on your phone. You are rarely tricked by internet hoaxes and you delete suspicious emails so you can navigate quickly and safely. You are quite fast at texting and you often use social media to organize your life. On the downside, you get extremely annoyed when devices don't work very well!

2 Copy and complete the table with the adverbs in exercise 1.

adverbs of manner	adverbs of degree	adverbs of frequency

Exercise 2
Adverbs of manner: comfortably, easily, fast, quickly, safely, well
Adverbs of degree: absolutely, extremely, quite, very
Adverbs of frequency: always, often, rarely, usually

3 Word builder Read the information. Find adverbs in exercise 1 that match rules 1–5. Then write an example sentence for each rule.

ADVERBS OF MANNER
1 Most adverbs of manner are formed by adding *-ly* to the adjective.
2 Adjectives that end in *-y* change the *-y* to *-i*.
3 Some adjectives that end in *-e* drop the *-e* in the adverb.
4 Some adverbs have the same form as the adjectives.
5 Some adverbs are irregular.

Exercise 3
1 absolutely, extremely, quickly, rarely, safely, usually
2 easily
3 comfortably
4 fast
5 well
Students' own answers

4 Read rules a–d about adverbs of manner, degree and frequency. Then correct sentences 1–4.

a) The adverbs *hard*, *fast* and *late* all have the same form as the adjective.
b) We don't use adverbs of manner after *look*, *seem* or *feel*.
c) We don't use *very* with extreme adjectives.
d) Adverbs of frequency go after *be*, but before other verbs.

1 Inventors worked hardly to develop computers. ✗
2 Your new tablet looks well! ✗
3 The first computer was very enormous. ✗
4 Nowadays, computers often are tiny. ✗

Exercise 4
1 hard
2 good
3 was enormous
4 are often

5 Look at the information and the picture. What do you think the TV show will be about?

TV Review:
Technology Matters!
(Channel 6, 8pm)
In tonight's show we'll learn all about 3D printing, and watch a demonstration.

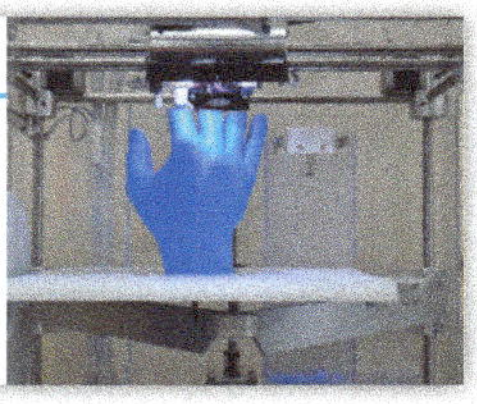

Exercise 5
3D printing

6 Listen to part of the TV show. Write the instructions in the correct order. 39

1 – c The power cable should be connected.

a) Click on 'Print'.
b) The plastic should be put on the spool.
c) The power cable should be connected.
d) The printing platform must be levelled.
e) The nozzle height should be selected.
f) The printer should be turned on.

Exercise 6
2 f
3 b
4 e
5 d
6 a

7 Listen again and choose the correct answers.

1 During the programme, they make ...
a) a children's toy. **b)** a smartphone case. **c)** a wearable gadget.
2 The material used for the demonstration is ...
a) aluminium. **b)** paper. **c)** plastic.
3 This 3D printer costs ...
a) £300. **b)** £399. **c)** £1,369.

Exercise 7
1 b
2 c
3 b

Vocabulary basics | Advance your vocabulary > Workbook p107

Social awareness

Virtual classrooms

Exercise 1
Virtual reality, wearable gadgets, robot teachers

1 **Look at the headline and photo. Which topics do you think you will read about? Then read, listen and check.** 40

- virtual reality
- vocational education
- wearable gadgets
- health and safety
- gaming
- robot teachers

FACT! In 2018, virtual newsreaders were presented by a Chinese news agency. These were created using artificial intelligence (AI) and were built using the voice and facial expressions of real presenters.

Home | Technology | Business | Health | Entertainment | Family | About us

Towards a 'virtual' classroom?

New educational technology is developing constantly, and VR (virtual reality) is already a reality in some classrooms.

In China, so far VR software has been installed in some institutions for vocational courses such as tourism and vehicle mechanics. Soon, new VR software will be developed for teaching English, too.

Some of the students had never heard of virtual reality before using the technology in their classes, but they really enjoyed it. One teacher said that students were picking up the new technology very quickly. When schools are in a rural location, VR technology enables students to learn up-to-date skills without needing to study in the city.

Of course virtual reality has been widely used by gamers for years, but it was rarely used in schools because the special headsets were still quite expensive. Now, with cheaper headsets made from cardboard (which are sold for about $10), VR technology is expected to reach a much wider audience over the next decade. Imagine taking a virtual tour down the Nile from the comfort of your geography classroom, or travelling through space before lunch in your science class!

However, despite the potential for fun-filled interactive learning, virtual reality also comes with health warnings. Users are advised to take regular breaks to avoid eye strain, headaches and hearing damage, and the technology isn't recommended for under-13s. In addition, VR is no substitute for interpersonal communication, so it will probably never replace your real teachers!

Exercise 2
1 **replace** (verb)
2 **pick up** (verb)
3 **headset** (noun)
4 **up-to-update** (adjective)
5 **eye strain** (noun)

2 Words in context **Find these words in the text. Are they nouns, verbs or adjectives? Match them with definitions 1–5.**

pick up | up-to-date | headset | eye strain | replace

1 to substitute for a new person or thing
2 to learn a new skill (phrasal verb)
3 VR equipment that you wear over your eyes
4 modern and using the latest ideas
5 a pain in your eyes, for example after reading a lot

3 **Copy and complete the sentences with information from the text.**

1 In China, some schools have installed …
2 Gamers have used …
3 VR was rarely used in schools because …
4 … probably won't be replaced by VR!

4 **Work in pairs. Ask and answer the questions about your country.**

1 What kinds of technology are used in your school at the moment?
2 Have you ever used Virtual Reality (VR)? If so, what for? If not, would you like to?
3 In your opinion, what new technology will be used in schools in the future?

Exercise 4
Students' own answers

VIDEO: CULTURE BYTE
Watch the video supplied by BBC.
WATCH

Exercise 3
1 VR software for vocational courses such as tourism and vehicle mechanics.
2 virtual reality for years.
3 the headsets were very expensive.
4 Real teachers

Social awareness

Virtual classrooms

LESSON OBJECTIVES

In this lesson students will:

- read a text about virtual classrooms
- discuss Virtual Reality and the technology used in their schools

WARMER

Write *Virtual Reality* on the board followed by this gapped definition: *Images and _____ that are produced by a _____ and connected equipment to make the user _____ as if they are in real _____-dimensional space.* Elicit which words could go in the gaps. (**Answer key:** sounds, computer, feel, three).

FACT!

- Students read the information in the Fact box.
- Ask if they are surprised by this information and why or why not.
- Ask if they think AI could replace humans in other jobs. Which?

1 40

- Students read the article headline and look at the photo. They decide which of the topics they think the article will be about.
- Listen to their suggestions but do not correct them at this point.
- Play the audio. Students read and listen to the text. They check their answers.

2 Words in context

- Students find the words in the text. Encourage them to use the context to decide whether the words are nouns, verbs or adjectives.
- Students complete the task individually.
- Check answers as a class.

3

- Students copy the gapped sentences into their notebooks.
- They read the text again and use the information in the text to complete the sentences.
- Check answers as a class.

4

- Put students in pairs to compare their ideas.
- Listen to their ideas a class.

VIDEO: CULTURE BYTE

This video is about some young inventors. For exploitation and comprehension practice based on this video, see the Culture byte video worksheets on the Resource Centre.

39 Audioscript, page 53, exercises 6 and 7

Julie: Hello and welcome to Technology Matters! Well, as you know, we're always excited about new gadgets here, and tonight is no exception … Tonight's show is all about 3D printing. Everyone's talking about it, but what is it exactly? Well, here we'll fill you in, and we'll also be giving you a demonstration of how it works!

So, what is a 3D printer? Well, it's a machine that can make … pretty much anything you want! From plastic toys to musical instruments, from wearable gadgets to new parts for spacecraft! All these things can be made quickly, easily and relatively cheaply on a 3D printer!

So, so that you can see how simple it really is, we're going to make something here in the studio … Let's go over to Ben to see how it works …

Ben: Hi there! Well, here we are: the 3D printer is ready to go. The software has already been installed on the PC, and I've selected the design for what we're going to print. So, we're going to make a plastic smartphone case, OK? Just like this one here, see? We're going to make a nice blue one … So! Let's get started! Here's the instruction leaflet …

Right! So, what do we do first? 'The power cable should be connected.' OK, here's the cable, so I'm just going to plug that in now … All right, what's next? Let's see … Then … 'The printer should be turned on.' So, here's the on / off button …

Next … 'The plastic should be put on the spool.' OK … this is the spool, see? It's where you put the material you're going to print with … OK, that's that! What's next?

So … after that … 'The nozzle height should be selected.' … Right, this is the nozzle, see? It's where the liquid plastic comes out … OK … so, select the correct nozzle height …

Right, then … 'The printing platform must be levelled.' So, apparently there's a reset button here that we need to press … ah, yes, here it is. That makes the platform absolutely level before we start printing.

Then, finally … 'Click on "Print".' Right! That's it then! We're ready to start printing … This will take a few minutes, so let's go back to Julie while we're waiting …

Julie: Thanks Ben! Well, that was quite easy, wasn't it? In a moment we'll go back to Ben and have a look at the final printed product. But while we're waiting, let's have a quick look at the specifications of this 3D printer, in case you're tempted to buy one … So, this printer costs £399, and can be ordered online … It is still quite expensive, but prices are coming down all the time …

Grammar

Active and passive voice

LESSON OBJECTIVES

In this lesson students will:

- learn the use of the active and passive voice
- complete a quiz about China

WARMER

Write these languages on the board: *English*, *Portuguese*, *Mandarin Chinese*, *Hindi*, *Arabic*, *Spanish*. Tell students these are the six languages with the largest number of native speakers in the world. Students work in pairs and order the languages from 1 (most number of native speakers) to 6. (**Answer key: 1** Mandarin Chinese **2** Spanish **3** English **4** Hindi **5** Arabic 6 Portuguese)

1
- Students read the examples and answer the question.
- Check the answer as a class. Highlight the fact that we sometimes do not need to use *by* and the agent, eg *Portuguese is spoken in Brazil*.
- Highlight the different word order in active and passive sentences and the fact that the object in an active sentence becomes the subject in a passive sentence.
- If you are using the TPK and your students need more work on the meaning of the words, do the Grammar basics exercise.

Grammar basics

Answer key:

1 a	English is spoken all over the world	P
b	People speak English all over the world	A
2 a	Someone gave him a tablet for his birthday.	A
b	He was given a tablet for his birthday.	P
3 a	We will be sent an email next week.	P
b	They will send us an email next week.	A
4 a	You can find an application form online.	A
b	An application form can be found online.	P

LANGUAGE NOTE

If the person who does the action is very general, irrelevant or unknown, we often do not include this information. For example, *by people*, *by someone*, *by everyone*, *by an unknown person*, *etc.* If the agent is relevant, we need to use *by* and the agent, eg *by the police*, *by* Joe Smith, *by one million people*.

2
- Students complete the exercise individually.
- Check answers as a class.

3 41
- Explain the task. Encourage students to read the whole text before choosing the correct words.
- Play the audio. Students listen and check their answers.

CLIL

Grammar in context: Literature

4
- Point out that some statements and questions in the quiz are in the present tense while others are in the past or future tenses.
- Students read the quiz carefully and fill the gaps with the active or passive form of the verb in brackets in each question.

5 42
- Students work in pairs and answer the quiz.
- Play the audio. Students listen and check their answers.

CULTURE NOTE

Four per-cent of the world's population is American. Cantonese is the second most widely spoken language in China. It is spoken in the south of China, particularly in the Guangdong Province and in Hong Kong. A US-based Chinese astronaut went into space with NASA in 1985, but Yang Liwei was the first sent by China.

LITERATURE TASK

Students use the internet to find out about one of the three important innovations related to the history of books that were developed in China.

Grammar reference > Workbook page 92

Grammar
Active and passive voice

Exercise 1
Passive

1 **Look at the table. Do we use *by* in the active or passive voice?**

active voice
In the **active** voice, the subject of a sentence is active: it does something.
Chinese students use Virtual Reality.
Virtual Reality is used by Chinese students.
passive voice
In the **passive** voice, the subject is passive: something is done to it.

Exercise 2
1 Virtual reality is used by gamers.
2 Chinese is spoken by more than a billion people.
3 Mandarin is not taught at my school.
4 Chinese will probably be studied by more people in the future.
5 Chinese is used by a lot of business people.

2 **Transform the sentences from active to passive. Only include *by* if necessary.**

They sell thousands of VR headsets every year.
Thousands of VR headsets are sold every year.

1 Gamers use virtual reality.
2 More than a billion people speak Chinese.
3 They don't teach Mandarin at my school.
4 People will probably study Chinese more in the future.
5 A lot of businesspeople use Chinese.

Exercise 3
1 is used
2 wasn't invented
3 contributed
4 was conceived
5 were designed
6 encourages
7 be bought
8 be used

3 **Choose the correct words. Then listen and check.** 41

FACTS ABOUT VR

- When we think of virtual reality, we often think of gaming, but in fact VR (1) **uses** / **is used** in many situations that aren't related to gaming, such as medicine, tourism and space travel.
- VR (2) **didn't invent** / **wasn't invented** by one person – many people (3) **contributed** / **were contributed** to its development. But the term 'virtual reality' (4) **conceived** / **was conceived** in the 1980s by the American computer scientist, artist and composer Jaron Lanier.
- The first cardboard headsets (5) **designed** / **were designed** by engineers David Coz and Damien Henry during Google's 'innovation time' – a programme that (6) **is encouraged** / **encourages** engineers to spend 20% of their working time on projects of their choice.
- Now that VR headsets can (7) **buy** / **be bought** very cheaply, they will probably become more and more popular. Who knows how VR will (8) **use** / **be used** in the future?

CLIL

Grammar in context: Literature

4 **Complete the quiz with the correct active or passive form of the verbs in brackets.**

Exercise 4
1 is
2 are spoken
3 leads
4 was built
5 did the Olympic Games take place
6 invented
7 was she sent
8 will it be completed

China
by Jennifer Gascoigne

Quiz: How much do you know about China?

1 What percentage of the world population ... (be) Chinese?
a) 4% b) 20%
2 Several languages ... (speak) in China. Which is the most common?
a) Cantonese b) Mandarin
3 For centuries, China was ruled by emperors. Who ... (lead) the country now?
a) the Communist Party b) an emperor
4 China's tallest building ... (build) in the country's largest city. Where is it?
a) Beijing b) Shanghai
5 In which year ... (the Olympic Games / take place) in Beijing?
a) 2008 b) 2018
6 The Chinese ... (invent) paper, printing and gunpowder. What else was a Chinese invention?
a) the computer b) the compass
7 Liu Yang was the first female Chinese astronaut. When ... (she / send) into space?
a) 2012 b) 2017
8 China is in the process of building a space station in orbit. When ... (it / complete)?
a) 2022 b) 2050

5 **Answer the quiz questions in exercise 4. Then listen and check your answers.** 42

Exercise 5
1 20%
2 Mandarin
3 the Communist Party
4 Shanghai
5 2008
6 the compass
7 2012
8 2022

LITERATURE TASK

Some important innovations related to the history of books were developed in China. Find out about one of these:

- the invention of paper
- woodblock printing
- moveable type printing

Grammar basics
Grammar reference > Workbook p92

INTEGRATED SKILLS

Great innovations

LEARNING OUTCOME

✔ Give a presentation

Today we're going to give presentations about different inventions. I'm going to talk about mobile phones. Did you know that the first mobiles weighed nearly 1 kg?

TASK Prepare a presentation

1 Read timelines about new technology

2 Understand a factual presentation

3 Write a presentation

4 Give a presentation

NEW TECHNOLOGY

THE INTERNET

1969
four American universities were connected by the ARPA network

a 

1971
the first email was sent by American programmer Ray Tomlinson

1982
the word 'internet' was used for the first time

1989
the World Wide Web was invented by British scientist Tim Berners-Lee

b 

1998
the search engine Google was founded

1999
the internet became available on mobile phones in Japan

c 

2005
the video-sharing website YouTube was founded

2020
it's estimated that the internet will be used by more than 4 billion people worldwide

MOBILE PHONES

1973
the first mobile phone call was made by Motorola in New York

d 

1 ...
the first mobile phone call in Britain was made by Vodafone on 1st January

2 ...
Nokia's 'Cityman' mobile phone was produced

3 ...
SMS text messaging was introduced in Finland

e 

4 ...
the first mobile ringtone was downloaded

5 ...
the first camera phones were sold in Japan

6 ...
the first iPhone was produced by Apple

2025
it's estimated that there will be more mobile phones than people on the planet

f 

Exercise 1

b) The World Wide Web was invented in 1989.
c) YouTube was founded in 2005.
d) The first mobile phone call was made in 1973.
e) The first mobile ringtone was downloaded in 1998.
f) It's estimated that there will be more mobile phones than people on the planet by 2025.

1 Read

1 Read the timelines about the internet and mobile phones. What do pictures a–f refer to? Match them with information from the text.

a) = the first email was sent in 1971

2 Read the internet timeline again. Copy and complete the sentences in your own words.

1 The ARPA network ...
2 In 1982, ...
3 Tim Berners-Lee ...
4 Google was ...
5 Mobile phone internet ...
6 By 2020, ...

Exercise 2

Possible answers:

1 The ARPA network connected four American universities.
2 In 1982, people used the word 'internet' for the first time.
3 Tim Berners-Lee invented the World Wide Web in 1989.
4 Google was founded in 1998.
5 Mobile phone internet became available in 1999.
6 By 2020, the internet will probably be used by more than 4 billion people worldwide.

2 Listen

3 Read and listen to the extract from Jack's presentation on page 57. Where was the first mobile phone call made? 43

4 Listen again and repeat. Practise your intonation.

5 Watch or listen to the complete presentation. Complete dates 1–6 in the timeline about mobile phones. 44

Exercise 3
New York

Exercise 4
Students' own answers

Exercise 5
1 1985
2 1987
3 1994
4 1998
5 2000
6 2007

Integrated skills

Great innovations

LESSON OBJECTIVES

In this lesson students will:

- work on all four skills
- read timelines about the internet and mobile phones
- watch or listen to a presentation
- write and give a presentation

WARMER

Draw three columns on the board. In the left-hand column, write these compound nouns: *phone call*, *cash machine*, *radio signal*. In the middle column, write these countries: *the UK*, *Italy*, *Canada*. In the right-hand column, write these years: *1967*, *1895*, *1876*. Students match the innovations with the countries they were introduced in and the years they were introduced. (**Answer key:** phone call, Canada, 1876; cash machine, the UK, 1967; radio signal, Italy, 1895)

1 Read

1
- Students look at pictures a–f. Read the example sentence aloud.
- Students match the pictures with the information in the timelines.
- They compare their answers in pairs.
- Check answers as a class.

2
- Point out that either the active or passive voice can be used in this exercise.
- Students complete the sentences in their own words using the information in the internet timeline.
- Check answers as a class. Make sure their sentences are accurate.

2 Listen

Video with audio option

The dialogue is also available to play as an audio file. If you prefer to present it this way, play the audio and follow the teacher's notes as for the video.

3 43 REC
- Students watch, read and listen to the extract from Jack's presentation. Elicit the answer to the question from the class.

4
- Play the video again. Students watch and repeat and practise their intonation.

5 44
- Students copy the mobile phones timeline into their notebooks, read and listen to the presentation and complete the timeline with the correct dates.
- Play the audio. Check progress and if necessary, play the audio again.
- Check answers as a class.

43 & 44 Audioscript, exercises 5, 6 and 7

Jack: Hello! Today I'm going to talk about the invention and development of mobile phones. Look at my mobile – it's really light, and can probably do everything that can be done on a computer! But early mobile technology was very different, so let's start at the beginning.

Mobile technology was first developed in the early 1970s, so I'm going to talk about the 70s, 80s and 90s, and then the innovations since the year 2000. I'd be happy to answer any questions at the end of the presentation.

OK, so our story begins in 1973, when the first mobile call was made by Motorola in New York. But it wasn't until January 1985 that the first mobile call was made in Britain, by Vodafone. After that mobile technology really started to develop.

In 1987, Nokia produced a mobile phone called the 'Cityman'. It was huge! It weighed about 800 grams, and it cost the equivalent of about €4,000, but it was still really successful. So, over the next few years, phones started getting smaller and cheaper. And by the mid-90s, mobile phones had become quite common.

Then came text messaging! Text messaging was first introduced in Finland in 1994. It was called SMS – which stands for 'short message service'. At first, you could only send texts to people on the same network, but after a few years you could send texts to anyone.

Later, in 1998, the first ringtone was downloaded – this was in Finland too. Before that, you couldn't customize your ringtone – you just had the standard ones on your phone.

Camera phones were the next big thing. The first camera phones were sold in Japan in the year 2000, and they were a huge success. Six years later, 50% of all mobile phones had cameras built in. And of course it wasn't long then till the arrival of Apple's iPhone. The first generation iPhone was produced in 2007 (and a year later in most European countries). They sold almost 1.4 million iPhones in the first year!

So, after the first generation iPhone ...

6 • Students read the statements and the different answers carefully first.
- Play the audio again.
- Students compare their answers in pairs.
- Check the answers as a class.

7 • Students look at the sequencing phrases in the Communication kit on page 57.
- Ask how many of these sequencing phrases they can find in Jack's presentation.
- Play the audio again for students to check their answers.

3 Write

8 • Students read the timeline about the internet again and add these three facts to the timeline in the correct places.
- Encourage them to add their own ideas to the timeline, eg *Facebook*, *Instagram*, *WhatsApp*, *mobile phone apps*, *etc*.
- They research the dates when these items were introduced and add them to the timeline.

9 • Students work individually and write notes to include in their presentation.
- Monitor while they are writing and give help if necessary.

4 Communicate

10 • Point out that a presentation should not be too long. Jack's presentation takes less than three minutes, so they should aim for a presentation of between two and a half to three minutes.
- Students work in pairs and practise giving their presentation.
- Encourage them to time their partner's presentation using a stopwatch or a clock facility on their phone.

11 • Students make adjustments to their presentations, adding extra information or removing parts if their presentations are too long.
- If possible, record the presentations.
- Alternatively, nominate students to give their presentations to the whole class.

! COMMUNICATION TIP
GIVING A PRESENTATION

Highlight the Communication tip. Point out that reading a presentation from a script is not a good idea, as it can sound boring. It is much better to use key words to remind you what to say, eg *YouTube – 2005*.

Integrated skills > Resource centre

Hello! Today I'm going to talk about the invention and development of mobile phones. Look at my mobile – it's really light, and can probably do everything that can be done on a computer! But early mobile technology was very different, so let's start at the beginning.
Mobile technology was first developed in the early 1970s, so I'm going to talk about the 70s, 80s and 90s, and then the innovations since the year 2000. I'd be happy to answer any questions at the end of the presentation.
OK, so our story begins in 1973, when the first mobile call was made by Motorola in New York. But it wasn't until January 1985 that the first mobile call was made in Britain, by Vodafone. After that mobile technology really started to develop.

Communication kit

- In the early / mid- / late (1970s), ...
- Then / Next / After that, ...
- The following year, ...
- It wasn't until (1985) that ...
- By (the mid-1990s), ...
- Later / (A few) years later, ...

Exercise 6
1 c
2 a
3 b
4 b

6 **Listen again and choose the correct answers.**

1 The 'Cityman' mobile cost about ...
a) €400 **b)** €1,000 **c)** €4,000
2 'SMS' means '... message service'.
a) short **b)** standard **c)** Scandinavian
3 By 2006, ... % of mobiles had cameras.
a) 10% **b)** 50% **c)** 90%
4 About ... iPhones were sold in the first year.
a) 400,000 **b)** 1.4 million **c)** 4.1 million

Exercise 7
All of them except for *The following year*

7 **Look at the Communication kit. Which expressions does Jack use? Watch or listen again to check your answers.**

3 Write

Exercise 8
Students' own answers

8 **Prepare a presentation about the history of the internet. Add this information to the timeline on page 56. Then add your own ideas.**

1994 the White House website was launched
1997 the term weblog (*blog*) was introduced
2003 iTunes was launched

Exercise 9
Students' own answers

9 **Choose the key information that you want to include in your presentation. Write notes.**

4 Communicate

Exercise 10
Students' own answers

10 **Work in pairs. Practise your presentation. Use a stopwatch to time your partner's presentation. Is it too long or too short?**

Exercise 11
Students' own answers

11 **Try to improve your presentation. If possible, record it or present it to the class.**

! COMMUNICATION TIP
GIVING A PRESENTATION

Don't read directly from your notes. Make your presentation interesting by using your own words and varying your tone of voice. Pause from time to time, and don't speak too quickly!

Exercise 1
1 A mobile phone from a website
2 He hasn't received the phone that he ordered even though the money has been taken. It will be resolved either by sending a new phone or refunding his money.

Writing
A formal letter

LEARNING OUTCOME
✔ Write a formal letter of complaint

1 **Read Tom's letter and answer the questions.**

1 What is the product and where was it bought?
2 What is the problem and how will it be resolved?

A 45 Grove Street
Sheffield
S6 7LP

B 25th April

C The Manager
Mobiles-To-Go
123 Long Street
London NW 8ED

D Dear Sir / Madam,

On 2nd April, I ordered a mobile phone (a Flex400s at £149.99) on your website. My order was placed at 5.40pm, and I received a confirmation email. The money was taken from my account the following day.

Unfortunately, the phone has not arrived. When I called your Customer Help Line, I was told that the phone was sent on 4th April. That is now three weeks ago, and I still haven't received it.

To resolve the situation, I would appreciate it if you could send a new phone or refund my money as quickly as possible. I look forward to your reply and a solution to this problem.

E Yours faithfully,

Tom Sherwood

F Tom Sherwood

LOOK!
We often use passive forms when we write in a formal style.

2 **Focus on language** **Read the information. Match 1–6 with A–F in the letter.**

Writing a formal letter
When you don't know the person's name:
1 start with *Dear Sir / Madam*
2 finish with *Yours faithfully*
Include both your address and their address:
3 put your address top right
4 put their address on the left
Don't forget:
5 to sign and print your name
6 to date the letter

3 **Read the letter again and find phrases 1–4. Then copy and complete the sentences with Tom's words.**

1 On 2nd April ...
2 Unfortunately, ...
3 To resolve the situation, ...
4 I look forward to ...

4 **Focus on content** **Read the letter again. Which paragraph ...**

a) suggests possible solutions?
b) describes the product and when it was bought?
c) explains the problem?

5 **Imagine you've bought one of these products and it doesn't work. Write a letter of complaint.**

• a tablet • a laptop • a games console

Writing kit

1 **Plan** your letter. Answer the questions in exercise 1 about your product.
2 **Write** three paragraphs:
 1 describe the product that you bought
 2 explain the problem
 3 suggest possible solutions
3 **Useful phrases**
 I ordered / bought ...
 Unfortunately, ...
 To resolve the situation, ...
 I look forward to your reply.
4 **Check** your writing.

☑ layout for a formal letter
☑ formal greetings and phrases
☑ check that you've used the correct passive forms
☑ three paragraphs

Exercise 2
1 D
2 E
3 A
4 C
5 F
6 B

Exercise 3
1 ... I ordered a mobile phone (a Flex400s at £149.99) on your website.
2 ...the phone has not arrived.
3 ... I would appreciate it if you could send a new phone or refund my money as quickly as possible.
4 ... your reply and a solution to this problem.

Exercise 4
a the last paragraph ('To resolve the situation')
2 the first paragraph ('On 2nd April')
c the middle paragraph ('Unfortunately')

Exercise 5
Students' own answers

Study guide > p103 Writing hub > Workbook p120

Writing
A formal letter

LESSON OBJECTIVES
In this lesson students will:
- read a formal letter of complaint
- learn how to use a formal style and layout
- write a formal letter

WARMER
Ask students if they ever have problems with their mobile phones. Elicit typical problems and make a list on the board, eg *the battery doesn't last long*, *there is no phone signal*, *I can't connect to the internet*, *an app sometimes doesn't work*.

1
- Students read the questions first. Students read Tom's letter of complaint and find the answers.
- Check answers as a class.

LOOK!
Highlight that we often use passive forms when we write in a formal style.

2 Focus on language
- Students read the information in the Focus on writing and match the instructions for writing a formal letter with sections A–F in the letter.
- Check answers as a class.

3
- Students read the letter again and find phrases 1-4.
- They copy the phrases into their notebooks and complete the sentences using the information in the text.
- They check their answers in pairs.
- Check answers as a class.

4 Focus on content
- Students read the three summaries carefully first.
- They read the text again and match the paragraphs to the summaries.
- Check answers as a class.

5
- Explain the task.
- Students choose one of the products and write a letter following the procedure in the Writing kit.
- Monitor while they are writing and give help with vocabulary if necessary.
- At the check stage, ask them to swap notebooks and check each other's writing.

Writing kit
The aim of this activity is for students to write a formal letter of complaint about a product that doesn't work using the correct layout for a formal letter, the correct formal greetings and phrases, and the correct passive forms. Ask the students to follow the stages in the Student's Book. Encourage them to use Tom's letter of complaint for ideas. Make sure they answer the questions in exercise 1 and use the answers as part of their letter. Monitor while they are writing and give help with vocabulary if necessary. At the Check stage, ask them to swap notebooks and check each other's writing.

Study guide > Student's Book page 103

Writing hub > Workbook page 120

UNIT 6

YOUR IDENTITY

UNIT OBJECTIVES AND KEY COMPETENCES

In this unit the student will learn …

- to recognize, understand and correctly use vocabulary related to identity theft and personal identity CLC SCC CAE
- to recognize, understand and correctly use modals of ability and possibility, obligation and prohibition and use them in a short speaking activity CLC L2L SIE
- to recognize, understand and correctly use modals of deduction CLC L2L SIE
- about the importance of managing their digital footprint CLC CMST SCC DC SIE
- about having a pairwork debate by watching a short video CLC CMST DC SCC

In this unit the student will learn how to …

- identify text purpose in a text about identity theft CLC CMST SCC CAE
- look online for more information about protecting their personal identities CLC CMST DC SCC SIE
- identify specific information in a radio discussion CLC CMST DC SCC
- read about online identity, listen to a pairwork debate, prepare for and have a pairwork debate CLC CMST DC SCC SIE
- write a personal profile of someone they admire CLC

LINGUISTIC CONTENTS

Main vocabulary

- Identity theft: *bank account*, *junk mail*, *spending spree*, etc
- Personal identity: *nationality*, *personality*, *ethnicity*, etc

Extra vocabulary

- Words in context: *pretend*, *inappropriate*, *lock*, *asset*, *throw away*, *strangers*, *harmful*, *reputation*, *rumours*, *fake news*, *regret*, *screen-grab*
- Word builder: Uses of *get*; Noun suffixes

Grammar

- Modals of ability and possibility, obligation and prohibition
- Modals of deduction

Functional language

- Giving counter-arguments

Pronunciation

- /ə/ in *have to* / *had to*
- Silent letters

SKILLS

Reading

- Read a quiz about identity theft
- Read a text about digital footprints
- Read a text about online identity
- Read a personal profile

Writing: Interaction and production

- Write notes to prepare for a class debate about online identity
- Write a profile in three steps
- Learn how to use connectors of cause and effect

Listening

- Listen to part of a radio discussion about ID cards
- Listen to a pairwork debate about online identity

Spoken interaction

- Ask and answer questions about abilities and obligations in the past and present

Spoken production

- Prepare and participate in a pairwork debate

LIFELONG LEARNING SKILLS

Self-study and self-evaluation

- Study guide: Student's Book page 104
- Progress check: Workbook page 54
- Extension: Workbook page 55
- Grammar reference and practice: Workbook pages 94–95
- Wordlist: Workbook pages 151–157

Learning strategies and thinking skills

- Learning to Identify text purpose
- Critical thinking: comparing and evaluating crimes and antisocial behaviour

Life skills

- Digital competence

Cross-curricular contents

- Protecting your personal identity
- Literature: *The Invisible Man* by H G Wells
- Literature task: searching the internet for information about other books by H G Wells

EVALUATION

- Unit 6 End-of-unit test: Basic, Standard and Extra
- End-of-term test, Units 4–6: Basic, Standard and Extra
- CEFR Skills Exam Generator

KEY COMPETENCES

CLC	Competence in linguistic communication
CMST	Competence in mathematics, science and technology
DC	Digital competence
SCC	Social and civic competences
CAE	Cultural awareness and expression
L2L	Learning to learn
SIE	Sense of initiative and entrepreneurship

DIGITAL MATERIAL

New Pulse Digital Course including:

- Interactive vocabulary presentation
- Grammar and Vocabulary basics exercises
- Getting started video
- Flipped classroom grammar video: Modals of ability and possibility, obligation and prohibition
- Speaking sketch video: A pairwork debate

DIGITAL COMPETENCE

- Web quest: Find out more about how your and your family can protect your personal identities
- Digital competence worksheet: Infographics

REINFORCEMENT MATERIAL

- New Pulse Basics: Teacher's Resource Centre
- Vocabulary and grammar consolidation worksheets: Teacher's Resource Centre
- Grammar and Vocabulary basics exercises: Teacher's Presentation Kit

EXTENSION MATERIAL

- Vocabulary and grammar extension worksheets: Teacher's Resource Centre
- Advance your vocabulary: Workbook page 108
- The longer read: Teacher's Resource Centre
- Writing hub: Workbook page 122

TEACHER'S RESOURCE CENTRE

- Translation and dictation worksheets
- Evaluation rubrics
- Key competences worksheets
- Culture and CLIL worksheets
- Digital competence worksheets
- Macmillan Readers worksheets
- Integrated Skills

Vocabulary
Identity theft

LESSON OBJECTIVES
In this lesson students will:
- learn words related to personal identity and identity theft
- discuss ways of avoiding identity theft

VIDEO: GETTING STARTED

In this video the speakers answer the question *What steps can we take to protect our digital identity?*

- Focus the students on the unit title *Your identity.*
- Write these gapped sentences on the board:
  1 Who discusses the importance of secure passwords?
  2 Who thinks we need to be careful with who we trust?
  3 Whose dad was the victim of an online scam?
- Students watch the video and write the missing words in their notebooks.
- They watch the video again to check answers.

At the end of the lesson, ask students to answer the question from the video: *What steps can we take to protect our digital identity?*

Answer key: 1 Harry **2** Josh **3** Emily

WARMER

Introduce the topic. Write *online shopping* on the board. Ask students if they ever buy things online and, if so, what they buy. Ask why some people think it is dangerous to buy things online.

1 45
- Students read the quiz, think about the meaning of the words highlighted in blue and decide which of them are related to identity theft.
- Check answers as a class.
- Play the audio. Students listen and repeat.
- Make sure students pronounce the word *phishing* /ˈfɪʃɪŋ/ correctly.
- If you are using the TPK and your students need more work on the meaning of the words, do the Vocabulary basics exercise.

Vocabulary basics

Answer Key: Crime and security: scam, fraudster, shred documents, phishing.

Technology and communication: wi-fi hotspot, log on, junk mail, social networking site

Money: credit card, bank account, loan, credit rating, spending spree, debt

LANGUAGE NOTE

In two-word noun phrases like *<u>bank</u> account, <u>credit</u> card, <u>junk</u> mail* and *<u>spending</u> spree,* the first noun carries the main stress.

2
- Students work individually to complete the quiz and answer the question.
- They compare their answers with a partner.
- Listen to their answers as a class.

3
- Make sure students understand all the words in blue. If necessary, ask them to translate them into their language to check. Note that phishing is the practice of sending fraudulent emails that look like genuine emails from banks, online shops, etc, asking for your bank details and passwords.
- Students read the questions carefully first. Clarify the categories they have to look for.
- They answer the questions in pairs.
- Listen to their answers as a class.

4
- Students copy the gapped questions into their notebooks.
- They use the words in blue in the quiz to complete the questions.
- Students work in pairs to ask and answer the questions.
- Get feedback as a class.

YOUR IDENTITY

UNIT 6

LEARNING OUTCOMES IN THIS UNIT

- Identify text purpose
- Listen for specific information in a radio discussion
- Have a pairwork debate
- Write a profile of someone you admire

VIDEO: GETTING STARTED

WATCH Watch the teenagers talking about identity theft and answer the question.

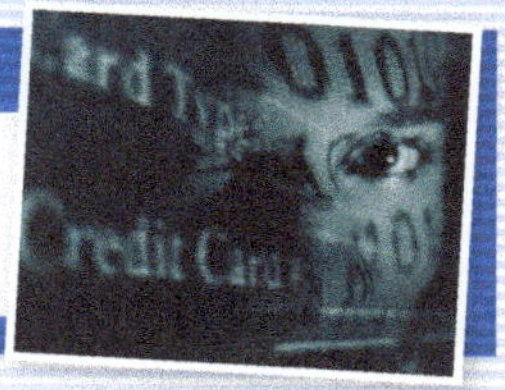

Exercise 1
scam, shred documents, fraudster, phishing

Vocabulary

Identity theft

1 Read the quiz and check the meaning of the words in blue. Which ones are related to identity theft? Listen and repeat. 45

2 Do the quiz and check your answers. Do you agree with your result?

Exercise 2
Students' own answers

HOW SAVVY ARE YOU?

1 How can you avoid being the victim of a scam when buying concert tickets?
a) You can't.
b) You only buy tickets from links on the official website.
c) You pay by credit card, not debit card.

2 Which of these websites makes it more difficult for a fraudster to steal your information?
a) ones that begin https://
b) ones that begin http://
c) both of the above

3 If a wi-fi hotspot requires a password, then it is safe to …
a) log on to your bank account.
b) apply for a loan or check your credit rating.
c) neither of the above.

4 Imagine your uncle goes on a €1,000 spending spree. The interest rate on his credit card is 20%. How much debt must he repay after one year?
a) €1,000 b) €1,020 c) €1,200

5 To avoid identity theft, you should …
a) shred documents that contain personal information.
b) avoid opening junk mail.
c) both of the above.

6 Which of the following are examples of phishing attacks?
a) creating a fake website to trick users into giving personal information
b) sending someone a message on a social networking site with a malicious link
c) both of the above

YOUR SCORE
If you get:
5+ You are very savvy.
3–4 You need to be more aware of finance scams.
0–2 Your digital identity is in danger – take action now!

3 Look at the words in blue in exercise 1 again and answer the questions.

1 Which ones are verbs?
2 Which two can be a noun or a verb?
3 Which ones are compound nouns?
4 What do you think is the origin of the word 'phishing'?

Exercise 3
1 loan, log on, (scam), shred
2 loan, scam – more common as noun but can be verb
3 credit card, wi-fi hotspot, bank account, credit rating, spending spree
4 Students' own answers

4 Copy and complete the questions with the correct words. In pairs, ask and answer.

1 Have you got a … account?
2 Do you use a social … site? Which one(s)?
3 Where are the wi-fi … in your town? Do you ever use them?
4 Do you know anyone who has been the victim of a scam or identity …?

Exercise 4
1 bank
2 networking
3 hotspots
4 theft

Vocabulary basics

Exercise 1

Abby Brown – had her mobile phone stolen as well as her identity
Debra – Abby's mum
Mike Haley – member of Cifas, gave advice to remember to protect our possessions

Reading

An article and advice

LEARNING OUTCOME

✔ Identify text purpose

1 **Read and listen to the text. Who are these people and why does the writer mention them?** 46

- Abby Brown
- Debra
- Mike Haley

Exercise 2

c

2 **Read the information. What is the purpose of this text: a, b or c?**

IDENTIFY TEXT PURPOSE
The purpose of the text is the author's reason for writing. The three main purposes are to inform, entertain or persuade.

a) to persuade people to buy a product
b) to entertain or amuse readers
c) to inform readers about the dangers of identity theft

Exercise 3

1 b
2 c
3 a
4 c

3 **Read the text again and choose the correct answers.**

1 Abby Brown ...
a) lost her mobile.
b) left her mobile unattended.
c) stole a mobile.

2 In 2016, more than 325,000 frauds ...
a) were committed online.
b) affected teenagers.
c) were reported.

3 Social networking sites ...
a) can provide personal details for fraudsters.
b) are safer than email.
c) are often hacked.

4 You mustn't ...
a) shred personal documents.
b) prevent identity theft.
c) choose passwords that are easy to guess.

4 **Are the sentences true or false? Find evidence in the text to support your answers.**

1 Thieves stole Abby's phone in a restaurant.
2 Abby's mum told their story to a newspaper.
3 A large number of identity crimes in the UK affect young people.
4 Fraudsters sometimes acquire huge debts.
5 You should always open phishing emails.

Stolen phone,

Abby Brown was angry when thieves stole her mobile, but she was devastated the moment she discovered that they had stolen her identity, too. The fraudsters changed Abby's passwords so she couldn't get online, while pretending to be her and sending inappropriate messages to her friends. Abby had left her bag at the beach when she and her friends visited South Harbour in Northumberland.

Fortunately, Abby's mum Debra was able to inform her daughter's friends that Abby's mobile had been hacked. 'Once someone gets their hands on your phone, they get your whole life and you can't stop it,' she told the *Daily Mirror* newspaper. 'My daughter is afraid to go out now because she's scared she will run into these people. They know so much about her!'

Unfortunately, identity theft is getting more and more common. According to the fraud prevention organization Cifas, more than 325,000 frauds were recorded in the UK in 2016, with many of these affecting under-21-year-olds. In the USA, young people are even more at risk due to the fact that they are given social security numbers at birth. If a criminal stole a child's identity, they probably wouldn't realize there was a problem until they tried to open a bank account or apply for a credit card at the age of 18.

5 **Words in context** **Find these words in the text. Are they nouns, verbs or adjectives? Match them with definitions a–e.**

pretend inappropriate lock asset throw away

a) get rid of something that you don't want
b) property or money that a person owns
c) to close something with a key so that other people can't open it
d) wrong, unacceptable
e) to behave in a particular way because you want someone to believe that something is true when it is not

Exercise 5

a) throw away (verb)
b) asset (noun)
c) lock (verb)
d) inappropriate (adjective)
e) pretend (verb)

Exercise 4

1 **False** – 'Abby had left her bag at the beach'
2 **True** – 'she told the *Daily Mirror* newspaper'
3 **True** – 'more than 325,000 frauds were recorded in the UK in 2016, with many of these affecting under-21-year-olds'
4 **True** – 'or going on a spending spree and acquiring massive debts'
5 **False** – 'Some also obtain sensitive information through phishing scams'

The longer read > Resource centre

Reading
An article and advice

LESSON OBJECTIVES
In this lesson students will:
- read an article giving advice
- identify text purpose
- use different expressions with *get*

WARMER
Briefly revise some of the vocabulary from the previous lesson. Write these words followed by gaps on the board: *bank _____, spending _____, wi-fi _____, junk _____.* Students tell you which words follow these words to make collocations (**Answer key**: account, spree, hotspot, mail).

1 46
- Students read the names first.
- Play the audio. Students read and listen to the text and note down their answers.
- Check answers as a class.

READING STRATEGY
Identify Text Purpose
Being able to identify whether the purpose of a text is persuading, entertaining or informing is a key sill for readers. A text whose purpose is to inform will generally give factual, verifiable information. Texts whose purpose is to persuade or to entertain need not be so trustworthy.

2
- Read the information about text purpose aloud to the class and highlight the three main purposes.
- Students choose the correct purpose for this text.

3
- Students read the sentence beginnings and the possible endings carefully first.
- They read the text again and choose the correct endings.
- Students compare their answers in pairs.
- Check answers as a class.

4
- Students read the sentences, decide whether they are true or false and note down words or phrases in the text that support their answers.
- Students compare their answers in pairs.
- Check answers as a class.

5 Words in context
- Students find the words in the box in the text. Encourage them to use the context to help them determine the meaning.
- They match the words with the definitions and compare answers in pairs.
- Check answers as a class.

6 Word builder

- Write the word *get* on the board. Explain that it has several different meanings depending of the context.
- Students read the information in the box and answer questions 1 and 2.
- Check answers as a class.

7
- Students work individually to answer the questions using the information in the text.
- They compare their answers in pairs.
- Check answers as a class.

8
- Students read the information in the Did you know? box. Ask whether they are surprised by this information.
- Students read the questions and note down their answers.
- Put them into pairs to ask and answer the questions.
- Listen to their ideas as a class.

DID YOU KNOW?

Highlight the *Did you know?* box. Students read about victims of identity theft in the USA and France.

CULTURE NOTE

According to a research conducted by SplashData, the most common password for users in North America and Western Europe in 2018 was 123456. Unsurprisingly, this is quite easy for fraudsters to guess! In second place was the word *password* itself and in third place 123456789. The ninth most common was *qwerty*, the first six letters on a computer keyboard and in tenth place *iloveyou*. 10% of the people in this survey are estimated to have used at least one of the 25 most common passwords on this year's list, and nearly 3% of people have used the password, 123456!

FINISHED?

Ask fast finishers to find the words in the text that match these definitions: **1** *someone who commits the crime of fraud* **2** *in danger* **3** *money you borrow from a bank* **4** *enormous*. (**Answer key: 1** fraudster **2** at risk **3** loan **4** massive)

CRITICAL THINKING

- Explain the task. Students should decide which of the four actions are the worst and decide on a punishment for each.
- They work in pairs and discuss their answers.
- Listen to their ideas as a class.

WEB QUEST

Students find out more about how they and their family can protect their personal identities.

1. Investigate Students open a search engine (eg *Google*) and type in *protect your identity* or prevent identity theft. They find as much information as they can and make notes.
2. Create They use the information to make a list of ten top tips for preventing identity theft in their own words. Monitor while they are working and give help with vocabulary if necessary.
3. Communicate They present their list to the rest of the class.

TIP! Explain that copying a text directly from internet and using it makes them liable of plagiarism. That is why they should get used to rewriting the information they get in their own words.

VIDEO: FLIPPED CLASSROOM

You may want to ask students to watch the Flipped classroom video for unit 6 as homework in preparation for the following grammar lesson. The Flipped grammar presentation focuses on modals of ability and possibility, obligation and prohibition.

The longer read > Resource centre

stolen life ...

How do fraudsters get access to your identity? They don't have to steal your phone or hack your computer – they often just exploit personal information from social networking sites. Some also obtain sensitive information through phishing scams (fraudulent emails that appear to be from official organizations). Once they've got the information they need, nothing will stop the criminals from taking out loans in your name, or going on a spending spree and acquiring massive debts.

'We all remember to protect our possessions by locking our house,' Mike Haley of Cifas told the BBC. 'But we don't take the same care to protect our most important asset – our identity.'

What can you do to prevent identity theft?

- You shouldn't share personal information online.
- If you get suspicious junk mail, you mustn't open it – it might be a phishing scam.
- Don't allow others to know your passwords and PIN.
- When you have to choose a new password, don't use something obvious, like your date of birth.
- You should shred all sensitive documents – don't throw them away.

DID YOU KNOW?

Americans are more likely to be victims of identity theft than anyone else – over 791 million identities were stolen in the US in 2016. France was in second place with 85 million identities stolen.

7 Answer the questions.

1 How did the thieves contact Abby's friends?
2 Why do you think Abby's mum spoke to a reporter?
3 How do criminals sometimes steal identities in the USA?
4 How do you think thieves could exploit information from social media sites?
5 What are strong and weak passwords?

Exercise 7

1 They managed to get access via her mobile phone.
2 To raise awareness amongst other young people.
3 By obtaining someone's social security number.
4 They find out personal information like pet names etc.
5 A weak password is something obvious, like your date of birth, whereas a strong password is something someone can't easily guess.

8 Work in pairs to ask and answer the questions.

1 Have you or people in your family ever been the victim of ...
- phone theft?
- identity theft?
- social media hacking?

2 What measures do you take to protect your identity and online identity?
3 Do you follow all the steps in 'What can you do to prevent identity theft?'

Exercise 8

Students' own answers

CRITICAL THINKING

JUDGE

Look at the text again. Find examples of crimes and antisocial behaviour. In your opinion, which ones are the worst? Compare and judge these activities. In your opinion, what should the punishments be?

- phone theft • identity theft
- uploading photos without permission
- hacking of social media accounts

6 Word builder Read the information and answer the questions.

USES OF *GET*

The verb *get* has many different meanings, such as *obtain*, *become*, *receive*, *buy*, *arrive* or *bring*.

Identity theft ***is getting*** *more common.*
How do fraudsters ***get*** *access to your information?*
If you ***get*** *suspicious junk mail, don't open it.*

1 Find the examples in the text. Does *get* mean *obtain*, *become* or *receive*?
2 We often use *get* in expressions. What do the expressions 'get online' and 'get your hands on something' mean?

Exercise 6

1 Students' own answers
2 **get online** = surf the web, go to a website; **get your hands on something** = obtain, access

WEB QUEST

Find out more about how you and your family can protect your personal identities.

1 **Investigate** Search online for 'protect your identity' or 'prevent identity theft'. Take notes about the information and tips you find.
2 **Create** In your own words, make a list of ten top tips to protect your identity.
3 **Communicate** Share your tips with the class.

TIP! You mustn't copy text directly from the internet. Make notes, then rewrite the information in your own words.

Grammar

Modals of ability and possibility, obligation and prohibition

VIDEO: FLIPPED CLASSROOM

WATCH

Watch the grammar presentation and do the task.

Exercise 1
a) can, can't
b) could, couldn't
c) must, have to
d) had to
e) mustn't
f) don't have to, didn't have to

1 Look at the table. Then use the words in blue to complete rules a–f.

	present	past
ability and possibility		
+	Criminals **can** steal your identity.	I **could** start using social media when I was 13.
-	You **can't** get a credit card until you're 18.	She **couldn't** get online.
obligation and prohibition		
+	You **must** / **have to** shred all personal documents.	Abby **had to** get a new phone.
-	You **mustn't** open suspicious emails.	
no obligation		
-	The fraudsters **don't have to** hack your computer.	They **didn't have to** go to prison.

a) We use … and … to talk about ability or possibility in the present.
b) We use … and … to talk about ability or possibility in the past.
c) We use … or … for obligation in the present.
d) We use … for obligation in the past.
e) We use … for prohibition.
f) We use … when there is no obligation in the present and … when there is no obligation in the past.

LOOK!
We don't use **must** / **mustn't** in the past.

2 Copy and complete the sentences with these words. Then match them with rules a–f in exercise 1.

- can
- couldn't
- don't have to
- had to
- has to
- mustn't

1 My sister … wear braces on her teeth now.
2 The dentist says that she … take them off until she is 16.
3 Fortunately, I … wear braces.
4 When I was young, I … go to piano lessons.
5 I … play the piano very well when I was little.
6 Now I … play songs by Ariana Grande!

Exercise 2
1 has to, c
2 mustn't, e
3 don't have to, f
4 had to, d
5 could, b
6 can, a

3 Read the text and choose the correct words.

Exercise 3
1 had to
2 couldn't
3 don't have to
4 have to
5 didn't have to
6 could

CHANGING APPEARANCE

I think I look quite different now from when I was little. When I was a child I (1) **have to** / **had to** / **must** wear glasses because I (2) **can** / **could** / **couldn't** see very well. Now I (3) **mustn't** / **don't have to** / **didn't have to** wear glasses because I've got contact lenses. Now, I (4) **have to** / **had to** / **can't** wear a school uniform. When I was younger, I (5) **can't** / **don't have to** / **didn't have to** wear a school uniform. I (6) **could** / **must** / **can't** wear my own clothes. But my mum used to choose them for me!

4 Copy and complete the sentences so they are true for you.

When I was five,
1 I had to …
2 I didn't have to …
3 I could …
4 I couldn't …

Now,
5 I have to …
6 I don't have to …
7 I can …
8 I can't …

Exercise 4
Students' own answers

5 Work in pairs. Ask and answer questions about your ideas in exercise 4.

What did you have to do when you were five?
I had to go to swimming lessons. What about you?

Exercise 5
Students' own answers

Grammar

Modals of ability and possibility, obligation and prohibition

LESSON OBJECTIVES
In this lesson students will:
- learn modals of ability and possibility, obligation and prohibition
- read a text about changing appearance

WARMER

Books closed. Write these words from the previous lesson on the board with lines to represent each letter: _ _ _ _ _ _ _ _ (*phishing*), _ _ _ _ _ _ _ _ (*junk mail*) and _ _ _ _ _ _ _ _ (*identity*). Students call out different letters of the alphabet until they have guessed all three.

VIDEO: FLIPPED CLASSROOM

- If you set the video for homework, ask students to compare their Task time! answers and then check the answers as a class.
- If you didn't set it for homework, watch the video in class and answer the Task time! questions at the end of the presentation.

Answer key: 1 password **2** mustn't **3** ten

1
- Students read the examples in the table and use the words in bold to complete rules a–f.
- They compare answers in pairs.
- Check answers as a class.
- If you are using the TPK and your students need more practice of the grammar, do the Grammar basics exercise.

Grammar basics

Answer key: 1 e **2** g **3** c **4** f **5** d **6** b **7** a

LANGUAGE NOTE

For obligation in the present, we can use either *must* or *have to*, but there is a difference of emphasis between them. *I must clean my room* suggests that you personally feel the obligation to do it. *I have to clean my room* suggests that someone else (your mother or father, for example) has asked you to do it.

LOOK!

Point out that while there is a subtle difference in meaning in the present, in the past, both *have to* and *must* become *had to.*

2
- Do the first sentence with the whole class as an example (*has to*, *c*).
- Students work individually to complete the task.
- They compare answers in pairs.
- Check answers as a class. Point out that *must* is not possible in sentence 1 because the obligation is external not internal.

3
- This activity practises the difference between obligation and ability in the past and the present.
- Students read the whole text before they choose the correct answers.
- Students work individually to complete the exercise.
- They compare answers in pairs.
- Check answers as a class.

4
- Explain the task.
- Students complete the sentences with endings that are true for them.
- Encourage them to refer back to the table in exercise 1 to help them with modals of ability and obligation.
- Highlight that in English we use *have* to or *must* to talk about obligation.

5
- Highlight the question form in the example.
- Elicit the other question forms needed to talk about the ideas in exercise 4: *What could you do when you were five? What couldn't you do when you were five?*, etc.
- Students work in pairs and ask and answer the questions.
- Listen to some pairs as a class.

Grammar reference > Workbook page 94

Pronunciation lab > /ə/ in have to / had to > Student's Book page 125

Vocabulary and Listening

Personal identity

LESSON OBJECTIVES

In this lesson students will:

- learn words related to personal identity
- listen to identify opinions

WARMER

Play a guessing game to introduce the topic. Describe one of the students in the class but do not say who he or she is. Begin with general appearance and characteristics and, if students cannot guess who you are talking about, say what he or she is wearing today.

DIGITAL VOCABULARY FLASHCARDS

In this digital presentation, students match the vocabulary with definitions.

- Do the digital presentation with the class.
- Encourage students to repeat the words.

1 47

- Students match definitions 1–4 with circles a–d. Check answers.
- Play the audio, pausing after each word. Students listen and repeat the words.
- If you are using the TPK and your students need more work on the meaning of the words, do the Vocabulary basics exercise.

Vocabulary basics

Answer key:
appearance, nationality, possessions, personality, ethnicity, friendships, beliefs, relationships

2
- Students copy the diagram into their notebooks.
- Students add another idea to each group and answer the question.
- Listen to their ideas as a class.

3 Word builder
- Students read the information in the Word builder box.
- Elicit the answer to the question

4
- Students copy the table into their notebooks. They then complete the table with the root words. Check answers.

5 48
- Point out that both Sophie and Miguel could be for or against ID cards or one could be for and the other against.
- Play the audio. Check the answer as a class.

For audioscript, see page T68.

6
- Students read the arguments carefully and decide which ones are for ID cards and which are against them.
- Explain the listening task. Students listen and note which arguments are made by Sophie and which by Miguel.
- Play the audio again and check answers.

7
- Students read the questions first.
- Play the audio again. Students answer the questions. Check answers.

Advance your vocabulary > Workbook page 108

Pronunciation lab > Silent letters > Student's book page 125

Vocabulary and Listening

Personal identity

LEARNING OUTCOME

✔ Listen for specific information in a radio discussion

DIGITAL VOCABULARY FLASHCARDS

Do the matching exercise to discover the new vocabulary.

appearance beliefs ethnicity friendship gender nationality peer group personality possession relationship style values

Exercise 1
1 c
2 b
3 d
4 a

1 Look at the diagram and match 1–4 with a–d. Listen and repeat the words in blue. 47

1 characteristics that you're born with
2 other people in your life
3 physical things that you can see
4 abstract things about you that you choose

Exercise 2
Students' own answers

2 Copy the diagram into your notebook. Add one more idea to each group. In your opinion, which things are most important to your personal identity?

Exercise 3
The end of the word

3 Word builder Read the information. Does the suffix go at the beginning or the end of a word?

NOUN SUFFIXES
Many nouns are formed by adding a suffix to the root word (a verb, adjective or other noun), such as *-ity*, *-ness*, *-ment*, *-ship* and *-ance*.
happy (adj) – happiness
improve (v) – improvement
citizen (n) – citizenship

4 Copy and complete the table with the root words.

root word	noun with suffix
relation (n)	relationship
1 ... (n)	friendship
2 ... (v)	appearance
3 ... (adj)	ethnicity
4 ... (adj)	nationality
5 ... (adj)	personality
6 ... (v)	possession

Exercise 4
1 friend
2 appear
3 ethnic
4 national
5 personal
6 possess

5 Listen to a radio discussion about ID cards. Are Sophie and Miguel for or against? 48

Exercise 5
Sophie is against ID cards, Miguel is for them.

THE BIG DEBATE
ID CARDS: for or against?
Tell us what you think!

6 Read arguments a–f. Which are for ID cards, and which are against? Then listen again. Which arguments do Sophie and Miguel use?

a) Having an ID card makes life easier.
b) It would be very expensive to introduce obligatory ID cards.
c) ID cards help to reduce fraud and fight crime.
d) Your information could fall into the wrong hands.
e) Keeping personal information on a national database goes against civil liberty.
f) You don't have to buy a passport because you can use your ID card to travel in the EU.

Exercise 6
For: a, c, f
Against: b, d, e
Sophie: b, e
Miguel: a, c

7 Listen again and answer the questions.

1 Are ID cards obligatory in the UK?
2 How many countries have obligatory ID cards?
3 What other kind of cards does Sophie mention?
4 When did Miguel get his identity card?
5 Which six pieces of personal information are on Miguel's identity card?
6 Which three examples does Miguel give of bureaucratic procedures where you need to use your ID card?

Exercise 7
1 No
2 about 100 around the world
3 a student card and a proof of age card.
4 when he was 14
5 name, nationality, gender, date of birth, identity number, photo.
6 getting a mobile phone, opening a bank account, getting a credit card

Life skills
Digital competence

Exercise 1
All of them

Exercise 2
1 b 2 a
3 e 4 d 5 c

Exercise 3
strangers = people who don't know you at all
harmful = could hurt you in some way later down the line
reputation = what people think about you in future
rumours = information about you that is told or passed around but is not true
fake news = stories that seem to be genuine but are not true
regret = to feel bad for something has happened
screen-grab = a screen shot which shows an image from a video or any kind of screen that is stored as a still image

1 What is your digital footprint? Which of these things are part of your digital footprint?

- websites you visit
- emails and attachments
- forum registrations and comments
- profile posts without privacy settings
- images and videos you share or download

2 Check the meaning of a–e. Then read the text and match steps 1–5 with headings a–e.

a) Un-tag yourself
b) Search yourself online
c) Delete the cookies
d) Unsubscribe
e) Check your privacy settings

3 Words in context Find these words in the text. What do they mean?

strangers harmful reputation
rumours fake news regret
screen-grab

4 Read the text again and answer the questions.

1 Why is a digital footprint 'like walking through wet concrete'?
2 What should you do if you find something you don't like when you search yourself online?
3 What personal qualities should a positive digital footprint reflect?
4 Are people legally responsible for anonymous online posts?

5 Work in pairs. Choose activity a or b.

a) Search for each other online. Share your findings and make suggestions for improving your digital presence.
b) Make real digital 'footprints' – draw round your partner's shoe and write the names of all the digital sites that he / she uses.

Exercise 4
1 Everyone can see clearly what you've left behind and it stays forever.
2 Contact the site administor and ask for it to be removed.
3 Your beliefs, values and personality
4 Yes

FACT! 43% of employers said online postings disqualified candidates.

MANAGING YOUR
DIGITAL FOOTPRINT

Your digital footprint is like walking through wet concrete! Complete strangers can see where you've been and what you've done – including that funny picture or comment you uploaded – both now and in the future. Even when you delete a post, it's still stored digitally. Everything you do online contributes to your digital footprint, and all your choices could be harmful to your reputation or future opportunities. So take the time to clean up your digital identity and put your best foot forward …

5 STEPS TO CLEANING YOUR DIGITAL FOOTPRINT

1 …
Check what comes up for yourself online, in both text and images. If you find anything you don't like, ask the site administrator to take it down.

2 …
If you've been tagged in inappropriate photos or videos, ask the person to delete it. To protect your friendships, never tag others without permission.

3 …
Restrict access on social networking sites to people you know. 'Unfriend' anyone you don't know.

4 …
Delete any unused accounts or apps, and unsubscribe from any unwanted email subscriptions.

5 …
Disable cookies or set your browser to delete them when you log out.

CREATING A POSITIVE DIGITAL PRESENCE

- Build your own 'digital identity': if you don't, someone else might!
- Be positive and true – your digital footprint should reflect your beliefs, values and personality. Share your talents, blog about useful things, inspire others! Avoid focusing on your appearance, relationship status, etc.
- *'If I'm anonymous I can't be traced.'* FALSE! You're still legally responsible for your actions.
- *'If it's on the internet it must be true!'* FALSE! Don't spread rumours or fake news.
- Think long-term: don't post today what you might regret tomorrow (or in five years).
- Remember – anyone can take a screen grab of what you post, so *'if you wouldn't say it face to face, don't say it in the social space!'*

Exercise 5
Students' own answers

Life skills

Digital competence

LESSON OBJECTIVES
In this lesson students will:
- read a text about managing their digital footprint
- discuss their digital footprint and how to keep it clean

WARMER

Write *smartphone* on the board. Elicit from the class what they use smartphones for, eg *making phone calls, surfing the internet, sending texts, taking photos*. Ask students what kind of photos they take with their smartphones, eg *pictures of friends, family, pets, places they visit.*

FACT!
- Find out whether they are surprised at this fact.
- Ask students if they regularly post things on social media. What kinds of things do they / their friends / their family post?

1
- Students read the information in the Fact! box about online postings and ask students what they understand by this (*candidates for jobs would not be accepted if they posted unacceptable comments online*).
- Check students understand the term *digital footprint* (*the amount of information about you that exists on the Internet because of your activity online*).
- Students read the questions and note down their answers. Check answers as a class.

2
- Students read headings a-e carefully first and make sure they understand them. If necessary, ask them to translate the terms into their language.
- Students reads the text and match steps 1-5 with the headings.
- They compare answers in pairs.
- Check answers as a class.

3 Words in context
- Students look in the text and find the words in the box. Encourage them to use the context to help them with the meaning.
- Check answers as a class.

EXTRA ACTIVITY

Focus on some of the other vocabulary in the text. On the left of the board, write: **1** *clean up* **2** *put your best foot forward* **3** *restrict* **4** *disable. On the right of the board, write these definitions:* **a)** *stop something working* **b)** *limit* **c)** *start trying hard to behave as best you can* **d)** *make something tidy.* Students work in pairs and match the words and their meanings. (**Answer key: 1** d, **2** c, **3** b, **4** a)

4
- Students read the questions carefully first.
- They work individually and make notes about each question.
- They work in pairs and compare their ideas.
- Listen to their ideas as a class.

5
- Explain the choice of tasks. Students work in pairs and choose which activity they want to work on.
- If they choose a), they should use Google or a similar search engine to enter their partner's name and find out where he or she is mentioned on line and then suggest how they could reduce their digital presence.
- If they choose b), they should take a large sheet of paper, ask their partner to place their foot on it, draw around the outline of their partner's shoe and write inside the drawing all the digital sites that he or she uses.
- Get feedback from each pair by asking them to share their findings with the class.

EXTRA ACTIVITY

As a homework task, ask students to reflect on their own digital footprint by keeping a record of all the sites they visit and everything they upload and download for a whole week. Ask them to record the information in a footprint-shaped diagram like the one in exercise 5. At the beginning of the next lesson, ask them to work in small groups and compare their diagrams.

Grammar

Modals of deduction

LESSON OBJECTIVES

In this lesson students will:

- revise / learn modals of deduction
- read a text about a science fiction novel

WARMER

Books closed. Bring a small object (eg a pen, a chocolate bar, a key, a memory stick) and conceal it inside a bag or similar. Tell the class there is an object inside the bag and that they have to guess what it is by asking questions which elicit only a yes or no answer, eg *Is it made of plastic?*

1
- Students read the sentences.
- They work individually and complete the two rules using the modal verbs.
- Check answers as a class.
- If you are using the TPK and your students need more work on the meaning of the words, do the Grammar basics exercise.

Grammar basics

Answer key: 1 S **2** U **3** S **4** U **5** S **6** U

LANGUAGE NOTE

Sometimes the negative form of modal verbs does not have the opposite meaning, eg we can say *The house must be empty* to express certainty, but if we say *The house mustn't be empty*, this expresses prohibition and not certainty, ie *You must not leave the house empty.* The opposite of *The house must be empty* is *The house can't be empty.*

The modal verb *may* can also be used to express possibility, eg *We may go to the beach on Saturday*, but it is much less common than *might*. The negative form *may not*, which cannot be contracted, is rare.

2
- Complete the first sentence as an example (*Louise must be in a restaurant*).
- Students copy and complete the sentences using the pictures and the rules in the table in exercise 1 to help them.

3
- Explain the task. Show how the prompts in A, B and C are used to make the example sentence.
- Students complete the exercise.
- Listen to their examples sentences as a class. Students translate each example sentence into their language and say if it is certain or not.

FINISHED?

Ask fast finishers to write sentences using modal verbs of certainty and possibility using these prompts: *Running a marathon …, Living in the country …, Having a credit card … .*

CLIL

Grammar in context: Literature

4 49
- This activity practises the modal verbs from this lesson and the previous grammar lesson.
- Students read the whole text before they choose the correct verbs.
- Play the audio. Students listen and check their answers.

5
- Students read the text again and find which modal verbs are in the past tense. Check answers.

CULTURE NOTE

H. G. Wells (1866–1946) was an English writer who became most famous for his science fiction novels, *The Time Machine*, *The Island of Doctor Moreau*, *The Invisible Man*, *The War of the Worlds*. In 1938 a radio broadcast of *The War of the Worlds*, directed and narrated by Orson Welles, created panic in the USA because many listeners believed it was real and that a Martian invasion was taking place.

LITERATURE TASK

Students use the internet to find out about the story of either *The War of the Worlds or The Time Machine* by H G Wells. They write a brief summary of what happens in the book. Encourage students to use their own words and not simply copy from the internet.

Grammar reference > Workbook page 94

Grammar
Modals of deduction

Exercise 1
1 might not, could, might
2 can't, must

1 Look at the table. Then copy and complete rules a) and b) with *can't*, *must*, *might not*, *could* and *might*.

modals of deduction
1 It **must be** true – I saw it on the national news!
2 It **might not be** true – I read it online.
3 It **could** / **might be** true – I'm not sure.
4 That **can't be** true – it's completely impossible!

a) We use ..., ... or ... when we aren't sure about something.
b) We use ... or ... when we are sure about something.

Exercise 2
1 must
2 can't
3 might
4 can't
5 must
6 might

2 Copy and complete the sentences with *might*, *must* or *can't*.

Louise

Okan

1 Louise ... be in a restaurant.
2 She ... be at school.
3 She ... be with her brother.
4 Okan ... be in Turkey.
5 He ... be in England.
6 He ... be at the British Museum.

Exercise 3
Students' own answers

3 Write sentences using the ideas in A, B and C. Then translate them into your language. Which ones are certain?

Living in England could be fun.

A

Living in England Being famous Learning Chinese	Opening junk mail Being an astronaut Tagging people in photos

B	C
must be could / might be can't be might not be	risky difficult fun easy boring a good / bad idea

CLIL

Grammar in context: Literature

4 Read the text and choose the correct answers. Then listen and check. 49

Exercise 4
1 see
2 must
3 can't
4 Might
5 had to
6 couldn't
7 didn't have
8 must

The Invisible Man
by H. G. Wells

HIDDEN IDENTITY

This story is about a man called Griffin who arrives in an English village. He's wearing a big coat, and people can't (1) **seen** / **to see** / **see** his face because it's completely hidden. Griffin's identity is a mystery, and the people in the village think that there (2) **must** / **has to** / **can't** be something strange about their new neighbour. Why (3) **can** / **can't** / **must** they see his face? (4) **Had to** / **Might** / **Can't** he really be invisible?

This book is a great mystery story and I enjoyed it very much. I (5) **have to** / **had to** / **must** read it last year in my literature class because we were studying science fiction. I (6) **can** / **must** / **couldn't** believe that the story was originally written in 1897, because some of its themes are quite modern.

Although we (7) **have to** / **mustn't** / **didn't have** to read any other books by H.G. Wells in class, I'm planning to borrow *The War of the Worlds* from the school library as well. I think that (8) **must** / **has to** / **can** be a really exciting story too!

5 Read the text again. Which modals are in the past tense?

Exercise 5
had to, didn't have to

LITERATURE TASK

Choose one of these other books by H. G. Wells. Find out what the story is about and write a short synopsis.

The War of the Worlds *The Time Machine*

Literature task
Students' own answer

INTEGRATED SKILLS

Your online identity

LEARNING OUTCOME

✔ Have a pairwork debate

Today we're going to have a debate about social networking. Does using social media improve our life?

TASK Argue for and against something

1 Read a text about you and your online identity

2 Understand a pairwork debate

3 Prepare your arguments

4 Have a pairwork debate

You and your online identity ...

For most of us, social networking has become an integral part of life. According to the Global Digital Report 2018, over three billion people use social media around the world. But does our cyber-identity reflect our real life, or do we create a parallel universe online?

Many of us choose to share only the 'good bits' of our life online, such as pictures of parties and holidays. We can literally 'airbrush' the image of our life – especially with photo-manipulation apps like Instagram. There's even an app which helps people to create a completely fake social life, just to impress others.

All this can lead to 'social media envy', where you think that all your friends must lead really exciting lives. In reality, this is far from the truth. According to a survey by the Future Foundation, 44% of people wish they could be more like the person they describe themselves as on social media.

Perhaps one advantage is that social media can inspire us to enjoy more new experiences in real life – just so that we can share them online!

1 Read

1 Read the text and find words 1–5. Are they nouns, verbs or adjectives? Match them with definitions a–e.

1 share
2 airbrush
3 app
4 fake
5 envy

a) improve an image by hiding defects
b) show or tell other people
c) feeling of discontent when you want what someone else has got
d) software designed to do a particular thing
e) artificial, not genuine

Exercise 1
1 b) (verb)
2 a) (verb)
3 d) (noun)
4 e) (adjective)
5 c) (noun)

2 Read the text again and answer the questions.

1 How many people use social media?
2 What examples does the author give of the 'good bits' of our online life?
3 How can people 'airbrush' their life?
4 What is 'social media envy'?
5 According to the author, what could be an advantage of social media?

Exercise 2
1 over three billion
2 pictures of parties and holidays
3 with photo-manipulation apps like Instagram
4 thinking that all your friends must lead really exciting lives
5 They can inspire us to enjoy more new experiences in real life.

2 Listen

3 Read and listen to the extract from a pairwork debate about social media on page 67. Who is in favour, Oliver or Katy? 50

Exercise 3
Katy

4 Listen again and repeat. Practise your intonation.

Exercise 4
Students' own answers

5 Watch or listen to the complete pairwork debate. Which three of these counter-arguments does Oliver use? 51

1 All your experiences are fake if you only have them to share online.
2 You could have lots of friends on social networking sites, though that doesn't mean you actually see them.
3 Using social media can make people envious and unhappy.
4 You could have no idea about your friends' real lives – they might just share the good bits.

Exercise 5
1, 2, 4

Integrated skills

Your online identity

LESSON OBJECTIVES
In this lesson students will:

- work on all four skills
- read an text about online identity
- watch or listen to a pairwork debate
- participate in a pairwork debate

WARMER

Do a class survey. Ask the class if they use sites and, if so, which sites they use. Elicit examples (eg *Instagram*) and write them on the board. When the list is complete, find out how many students use each site and which one is the most popular.

1 Read

1
- Students read the words carefully.
- They read the text and note down what part of speech each word is.
- They match the words to the definitions, using the context in the text to help them.
- They compare their answers in pairs.
- Check answers as a class. Note that *envy* is a noun in this context but it can also be a verb, eg *I envy her knowledge of computers*.

2
- Students read the questions carefully first.
- They read the text again and find the answers.
- They compare answers in pairs.
- Check answers as a class.

2 Listen

3 50 REC
- Students watch, read and listen to the extract from a pairwork debate. Elicit the answer to the question from the class.

4
- Play the video again. Students listen and repeat and practise their intonation.

Video with audio option

The dialogue is also available to play as an audio file. If you prefer to present it this way, play the audio and follow the teacher's notes as for the video.

50 audioscript, exercises 3 and 4

Katy: In my opinion, social media motivates you to have more interesting real-life experiences.
Oliver: I'm sorry, but I completely disagree. The way I see it, all your experiences are fake if you only have them to share online! That isn't real life at all!
Katy: Also, I think that you can keep in touch with more friends online than in real life so it makes communication much easier.
Oliver: I don't see it like that at all. I mean, you could have hundreds of friends on social networking sites, but that doesn't mean you actually see them. That isn't real communication at all.
Katy: Well, with social media, you always know what's going on in your friends' lives.
Oliver: That's not how I see it. In my view, you could have no idea about your friends' real lives – they might just share the good bits.

5 51
- Students read the counter-arguments carefully first.
- Point out that Oliver only uses three of the four counter-arguments.
- Play the audio. Students note down Oliver's three counter-arguments.
- Students compare answers in pairs.
- Check answers as a class.

51 Audioscript, exercise 5

Katy: I'm afraid I don't agree. You do have an idea of about what's going on in your friends' lives. You can see your friends' photos and read updates about everything they're doing.
Oliver: Well, you've made some interesting points, but I see things differently. It's much better to meet up with friends to talk about news and see photos, I think.
Katy: And you've made some interesting points too ... There are obviously arguments for and against social media!
Oliver: Yes, exactly ... OK, now let's talk about ...

6 • Students look at the Communication kit on page 67 and read through the expressions.
• Ask which counter-arguments are used in the complete debate.
• Play the audio again for students to check their answers.

3 Write

7 • Students copy the table and complete it with Katy's arguments in the extract and counter-arguments from Katy and Oliver's pairwork debate from exercise 5.
• They compare answers in pairs.
• Check answers as a class.

8 • Students add two more counter-arguments of their own.
• Listen to some ideas as a class.

4 Communicate

9 • Show how the two example expressions can be used in the debate, eg *In my opinion, social media motivates you to have more interesting real-life experiences and That's not how I see it.* and *I think all your experiences are fake if you only have them to put on social networking sites.*
• Students work in pairs and practise saying their arguments for and against using the expressions for giving counter-arguments in the Communication kit.

10 • The purpose of this activity is for students to have a debate about the topic *Using social media improves our life.*
• Divide the class into two halves. In each half, nominate one student to start the debate with a point in favour and a point against respectively.
• Encourage other students to contribute with points in favour followed by points against.
• At the end of the debate, take a class vote and decide which side has won the debate.

! COMMUNICATION TIP
TAKING ROLES IN A DEBATE

Students read the information in the Communication tip box. Emphasize the importance of trying to be convincing in a debate, even if the role you have to take is different from your real opinion.

Integrated skills > Resource centre

In my opinion, social media motivates you to have more interesting real-life experiences.	I'm sorry, but I completely disagree. The way I see it ...
Also, I think that you can keep in touch with more friends online than in real life so it makes communication much easier.	I don't see it like that at all. I mean ...
Well, with social media, you always know what's going on in your friends' lives.	That's not how I see it. In my view ...

Exercise 6
All the counter-arguments

Exercise 7
For
You can keep in touch with more friends online than in real life. With social media, you always know what's going on in your friends' lives.
Against
You could have hundreds of friends on social networking sites, but that doesn't mean you actually see them. You could have no idea about your friends' lives. They might just share the good bits.

Communication kit

- I'm sorry, but I completely disagree.
- I don't see it like that at all.
- That's not how I see it.
- I'm afraid I don't agree.
- You've made some interesting points, but I see things differently.

6 Look at the Communication kit. Which counter-arguments are used in the Speaking sketch? Watch or listen again to check your answers.

3 Write

7 Prepare for your debate about social media. Copy and complete the table with Katy's arguments in the extract on page 66 and counter-arguments from exercise 5.

Using social media improves our life.	
For	**Against**
Social media motivates you to have more interesting real-life experiences.	*All your experiences are fake if you only have them to share them online.*

8 Add two more counter-arguments of your own.

Exercise 8
Possible answers: You don't learn anything on social media – it's just gossip! Using social media can make people envious and unhappy.

4 Communicate

9 In pairs, prepare for your debate. Practise saying your arguments for and against. Use the expressions for giving counter-arguments in the Communication kit.

In my opinion, ...
That's not how I see it. ...

Exercise 9
Students' own answers

10 Have a class debate. Half of you are for and half are against. Which side is more convincing?

Exercise 10
Students' own answers

! COMMUNICATION TIP
TAKING ROLES IN A DEBATE

Be prepared to take a role which is different from your real opinion. Always write a list of arguments that support your role before the debate, and then try to be convincing!

Writing

A personal profile

LEARNING OUTCOME

✔ Write a profile of someone you admire

Personal details	
Born	2003
Nationality	Canadian
Residence	Ontario, Canada
Occupation	Blogger, activist, motivational speaker

Exercise 1
1 d
2 b
3 a
4 c

1 Focus on content Read the profile and match paragraphs 1–4 with a–d.

a) Alper's values and achievements
b) The development of Alper's interests
c) Concluding paragraph
d) Who is Hannah Alper?

Hannah Alper

1 **Hannah Alper** is a Canadian blogger, activist and motivational speaker. You might recognize her name <u>because</u> she's already given a TED talk, met inspirational leaders and published a book – all before the age of 15!

2 <u>As</u> she launched her blog at the age of nine, Alper is already used to networking. Since then, she has worked with lots of non-profit organizations, such as 'ME to WE' and the World Wide Fund for Nature (WWF). Alper wanted to show that young people could change the world, <u>so</u> she interviewed 19 young role models for her book, *Momentus: Small Acts, Big Change*.

3 Alper's key values include a commitment to young people's rights and social justice and. <u>As a result</u> of this, she has helped to raise awareness and funds for campaigns including anti-bullying, educational equality and environmental issues.

4 <u>Due to</u> her excellent communication skills, Alper has already become a successful public speaker. It can't be easy speaking with confidence in front of so many people! <u>Because of</u> her passionate belief that young people can make a difference, Alper is a role model to many people around the world.

Exercise 2
cause = because, due to, because of
effect = as a result

2 Focus on language Read the information. Copy and complete the table with the <u>underlined</u> words from the text.

Connectors of cause and effect

cause	effect
as	*so*

Exercise 3
1 because
2 As a result
3 as
4 so
5 Due to

3 Choose the correct connectors.

Malala Yousafzai is a passionate activist for educational equality. In her homeland, Pakistan, Malala was targeted by extremists (1) **therefore** / **because** / **so** she had written a blog about girls' education. (2) **Due to** / **Because of** / **As a result**, Malala and her family moved to Britain. When she turned 16, Malala gave a speech about education at the United Nations. The UN declared 12th July 'Malala Day' (3) **as** / **so** / **therefore** it is her birthday. Malala wanted to continue campaigning for educational equality (4) **because** / **so** / **as a result** she set up the 'Malala Fund' soon after. (5) **Therefore** / **Due to** / **So** her campaigning, people around the world are now more aware of these issues.

4 Write a profile of someone you admire.

Exercise 4
Students' own answers

Writing kit

1 Plan your profile. Answer these questions.

- Who is the person? Is he / she well known?
- How did his / her interests develop?
- What are his / her values and achievements?
- Why do you admire him / her?

2 Write your profile. Use the model and the answers from your plan. Write four paragraphs.

1 introduction
2 development of interests
3 values and achievements
4 conclusion

3 Useful phrases

You might recognize him / her ...
as / because
as a result (of) / due to / because of / so

4 Check your writing.

- ☑ past and present modals
- ☑ modals of deduction
- ☑ connectors of cause and effect
- ☑ four paragraphs

Study guide > p104 | Collaborative project 2 > p110 | Writing hub > Workbook p122

Writing
A personal profile

LESSON OBJECTIVES
In this lesson students will
- use connectors of cause and effect
- write a profile of a person they admire

WARMER
Describe a person you admire. Give his/her age, describe his/her appearance and what he/she likes doing, etc until the students guess who you are describing.

1 • Students read the text and do the matching exercise. Check answers as a class.

2 Focus on language
- Students look at the language focus.
- Students complete the table with the underlined words from the text. Check answers.

3 • Students read the short text and choose the correct connectors. Check answers.

Writing kit
The aim of this activity is for students to write a profile of someone they admire and include the correct use of past and present modals, modals of deduction, and connectors of cause and effect.

4 • Ask students to follow the stages in the Student's Book.
- Monitor while they are writing and give help with vocabulary if necessary.
- At the Check stage, ask them to swap notebooks and check each other's writing.

48 Audioscript, page 63, exercises 5, 6 and 7

Presenter: Hello and welcome to today's debate about ID cards! Should we have them here in the UK? It's a controversial subject! ID cards are obligatory in about 100 countries around the world ... But here, for the moment, we don't have to carry ID of any kind. Is that a good idea? What do you think? Well, to start our debate, we've got Sophie and Miguel here with us, so let's see what they think ... Hello there!
Sophie: Hi.
Miguel: Hello.
Presenter: Now, Sophie, should we introduce ID cards? What do you think?
Sophie: No, definitely not! For me, there are two main arguments against ID cards. Firstly, I'm really against the idea of having all our personal information on a central database. I think this goes completely against our personal freedom. I mean, they could do what they want with all that information ... Then, secondly, we mustn't forget the enormous cost of introducing ID cards. I mean, it'd be a huge amount of money, and who would have to pay for it? We would!
Presenter: Yes, I see your point, but what about when we need to show ID? Wouldn't an ID card make that easier?
Sophie: Well, yeah, but it doesn't have to be an obligatory ID card, does it? I mean, there are alternatives. I've got a student card, for example, with my photo on it ... and then when you're 18 you can get a 'proof of age' card, that you have to show, for example, when you go to a club or whatever ...
Presenter: But isn't that the same as having an ID card?
Sophie: No, not at all! That's the whole point – it's different because it's not obligatory. And because it's just the card – that's not the same as having all your personal information on a database!
Presenter: I see. OK – thanks Sophie. Now, Miguel, you're studying in Britain at the moment, but you're from Spain, is that right?
Miguel: Yes – and in Spain we all have an ID card ... the National Document of Identity. See? This is my card – I had to get it when I was 14 years old.
Presenter: OK! And what sort of information is there on the card?
Miguel: Well, it gives your name, nationality, gender, date of birth ... and of course your identity number. And your photo!
Presenter: I see. And do you have to carry it with you all the time?
Miguel: Yes, in Spain you must always have it – you must show it to the police, for example, if they stop you.
Presenter: OK, and how do you feel about that?
Miguel: Well, I'm fine with this ID card. I mean, we're just used to it – we don't really think about it much. I guess there are two main reasons why I think it's a good idea ... First of all, it just makes everything so ... so easy ... you can do all the official things with just this one little card... you can get a mobile phone ... you can open a bank account ... you can get a credit card, everything really! And then secondly, I think it must improve security to have ID cards, as well. It must reduce fraud, I'm sure, and make it easier to catch criminals, because the police could just check people's identity straight away ...
Presenter: OK! Thanks Miguel! So, we've heard some different arguments. Now, what do you think? Get in touch to let us know your views ...

Study guide > Student's book page 104

Collaborative project 2 > Student's book page 110

Writing hub > Workbook page 122

UNIT 7

THAT'S ENTERTAINMENT

UNIT OBJECTIVES AND KEY COMPETENCES

In this unit the student will learn ...

- to recognize, understand and correctly use vocabulary related to film-making and a set of reporting verbs **CLC CAE**
- to recognize, understand and correctly use reported speech and use it in a short speaking activity **CLC L2L SIE**
- to recognize, understand and correctly use reported questions **CLC L2L**
- about 'entertechment' (entertainment and technology) **CLC CMST SCC SIE**
- about informing the results of a survey by watching a short video **CLC DC SCC**

In this unit the student will learn how to ...

- recognizing informal language in a text about film-making courses **CLC SCC CAE**
- look online for more information about 'netiquette' **CLC DC CAE SIE**
- understand phone calls and messages **CLC CMST SCC SIE**
- read, listen to, prepare for, carry out and inform the class about a survey **CLC CMST SCC SIE**
- write a report **CLC CMST**

LINGUISTIC CONTENTS

Main vocabulary

- Film-making: *cast*, *crew*, *costume designer*, etc
- Reporting verbs: *admit*, *complain*, *refuse*, etc

Extra vocabulary

- Words in context: *buff*, *hands-on*, *subsidized*, *residential*, *props*; *inseparable*, *overwhelming*, *viewers*, *streaming*, *e-sports*
- Word builder: adjective + preposition: *interested in*, *well-known for*, *happy with*; verb patterns: *agree to*, *invite someone to*, *complain that*

Grammar

- Reported speech
- Reported questions

Functional language

- Phrases for surveys

Pronunciation

- Intonation in reported speech

SKILLS

Reading

- Read an online forum about film-making courses
- Read a text about 'entertechment'
- Read an entertainment survey
- Read a report about entertainment facilities

Writing: Interaction and production

- Write notes to prepare questions and answers for an entertainment survey
- Write a report in three steps

Listening

- Listen to phone calls and messages
- Listen to a survey

Spoken interaction

- Ask and answer questions about online forums and film courses

Spoken production

- Prepare and participate in a survey

LIFELONG LEARNING SKILLS

Self-study and self-evaluation

- Study guide: Student's Book page 105
- Progress check: Workbook page 62
- Extension: Workbook page 63
- Grammar reference and practice: Workbook pages 96–97
- Wordlist: Workbook pages 151–157

Learning strategies and thinking skills

- Recognizing informal language
- Critical thinking: proving information and suggesting rules about 'netiquette'

Social awareness

- Entertainment and technology

Cross-curricular contents

- Making a film in five steps
- Literature: *Casino Royale* by Ian Fleming
- Literature task: searching the internet for information about Ian Fleming and James Bond stories

EVALUATION

- Unit 7 End-of-unit test: Basic, Standard and Extra
- CEFR Skills Exam Generator

KEY COMPETENCES

CLC	Competence in linguistic communication
CMST	Competence in mathematics, science and technology
DC	Digital competence
SCC	Social and civic competence
CAE	Cultural awareness and expression
L2L	Learning to learn
SIE	Sense of initiative and entrepreneurship

DIGITAL MATERIAL

New Pulse Digital Course including:

- Interactive vocabulary presentation
- Grammar and Vocabulary basics exercises
- Getting started video
- Flipped classroom grammar video: reported speech
- Culture byte video: Computers and emotions
- Speaking sketch video: An entertainment survey

DIGITAL COMPETENCE

- Web quest: Find out about 'netiquette'
- Digital competence worksheet: Storyboards

REINFORCEMENT MATERIAL

- New Pulse Basics: Teacher's Resource Centre
- Vocabulary and grammar consolidation worksheets: Teacher's Resource Centre
- Grammar and Vocabulary basics exercises: Teacher's Presentation Kit

EXTENSION MATERIAL

- Vocabulary and grammar extension worksheets: Teacher's Resource Centre
- Advance your vocabulary: Workbook page 109
- The longer read: Teacher's Resource Centre
- Writing hub: Workbook page 124

TEACHER'S RESOURCE CENTRE

- Translation and dictation
- Evaluation rubrics
- Key competences worksheets
- Culture and CLIL worksheets
- Culture byte video worksheets
- Digital competence worksheets
- Macmillan Readers worksheets
- Integrated Skills

Vocabulary
Film-making

LESSON OBJECTIVES
In this lesson students will:
- learn words related to films and film-making
- discuss whether they would like to make a film

VIDEO: GETTING STARTED

In this video the speakers answer the question *Tell us about some kinds of entertainment you enjoy*.
- Focus the students on the unit title *That's Entertainment*.
- Write the following questions on the board:
  1 Who loves crime books?
  2 Who loves watching and playing sport?
  3 Who loves watching programmes online and on TV?
- Students watch the video and answer the questions on the board.
  They watch the video again to check answers.
- At the end of the lesson ask students to answer the question from the video: *Tell us about some kinds of entertainment you enjoy.*

Answer key: 1 Emily 2 Naomi 3 Josh

WARMER

Introduce the topic. Write *film* on the board. Students suggest films they have enjoyed watching. On the basis of the films mentioned, make a list of types of film on the board, eg *action*, *adventure*, *crime*, *science fiction*, *horror*, etc. Which is the most popular film type?

1 52
- Check students understand the meaning of all the words in blue in the text. Ask them to translate the words or phrases into their language if necessary.
- Play the audio. Students listen and repeat.
- Make sure students pronounce *crew* /kru:/ correctly.
- Ask them which of the jobs they would prefer.
- If you are using the TPK and your students need more work on the meaning of the words, do the Vocabulary basics exercise.

Vocabulary basics

Answer key: **1** soundtrack is **2** credits **3** script **4** cast **5** subtitles **6** location

LANGUAGE NOTE

In two-word noun phrases, the first noun carries the main stress, eg *camera operator, costume designer, make-up artist, set designer*.

2
- Students read the definitions carefully first.
- They read the text and find the words that match the definitions.
- They compare answers in pairs.
- Check answers with the whole class.

3
- Students copy the short text into their notebooks.
- They work individually to complete the task.
- Check answers with the whole class.

4
- Read the three questions aloud to the class.
- Students discuss the answers in pairs.
- Listen to their ideas as a class.

THAT'S ENTERTAINMENT!

UNIT 7

LEARNING OUTCOMES IN THIS UNIT

- Recognize informal language
- Understand phone calls and messages
- Inform your class about survey results
- Write a report

VIDEO: GETTING STARTED

WATCH Watch the teenagers talking about entertainment and answer the question.

Vocabulary
Film-making

Exercise 1
Students' own answers

1 Read the Careers guide and check the meaning of the words in blue. Which job would you prefer? Listen and repeat. 52

Exercise 2
1 soundtrack
2 cast
3 script
4 location
5 credits

2 Find words in the Careers guide that mean ...

1 all the songs or music played during a film
2 all the people who act in a play or film
3 the written words of a film, play or TV programme
4 a place where a film is made away from a studio
5 a list of all the people that have worked in a film, shown at the beginning or the end

Exercise 3
a) storyboard
b) crew
c) cast
d) set
e) soundtrack
f) subtitles

3 Copy and complete the text with these words.

- cast • crew • set • soundtrack • storyboard
- subtitles

Make a film in five easy steps!

1. Write a script based on your idea and draw a (a) … for each of the scenes.
2. Find the (b) … (director, camera operator, costume designer and make-up artist) and the (c) … (stars and supporting actors).
3. Look for a location, or design the (d) … if you're filming indoors.
4. Shoot your film!
5. Afterwards, edit the film. Add sound effects or a (e) … .

(Don't forget to add the credits, and (f) … if it's in a foreign language!)

Exercise 4
Students' own answers

4 In pairs, ask and answer the questions.

1 Would you like to make a film? Why (not)?
2 What do you think the most difficult parts of making a film would be?
3 Which parts do you think would be the most interesting?

Home | About | Careers | Education | Advice

Careers guide
So you want to work in **the movies?**

There are plenty of opportunities if you want to be part of a film crew. Here are some of the different roles …

Camera operator
This person records film scenes either in the studio or on location.

Costume designer
This job involves designing clothes, shoes and accessories for all members of the cast.

Set designer
This person plans and creates the scenery for a film, play or TV show.

Lighting technician
This job involves setting up and operating the lights on a film set or at a concert.

Make-up artist
This person works with hair, make-up and special effects to prepare actors for their roles.

Words and music
There are also lots of jobs for writers and musicians. You could write the script or storyboard, plan the sound effects or compose the soundtrack. Specialist translators write the subtitles for foreign films, and the credits are usually written by the producer.

more jobs

Vocabulary basics

Reading

A forum

LEARNING OUTCOME

✔ Recognize informal language

Exercise 1
Film-making
Yes

1 Read and listen to the text. What does Jack want to find out about? Does he find all the information he's looking for? 53

Exercise 2
a) What a great idea!
b) they're, I'm, she's
c) The courses aren't expensive, are they?
d) Yes – me too!

2 Read the information. Find at least one example for each of a–d in the text.

RECOGNIZE INFORMAL LANGUAGE
In informal language we often use:
a) exclamations
b) contractions
c) question tags
d) agreements with *too* / *so* / *neither*

Exercise 3
1 b
2 d
3 a
4 e
5 c

3 Match the sentence beginnings and endings.

1 Jack asked if anyone on the web forum
2 Suki told Jack
3 Jack asked whether
4 Ahmed said that
5 Jack thanked everyone

a) the courses were expensive.
b) could help him.
c) for all the useful information.
d) about the BFI Film Academy courses.
e) his sister was doing a residential course.

Exercise 4
a) props
b) buff
c) residential
d) hands-on
e) subsidized

4 Words in context Find these words in the text. Match them with definitions a–e.

buff hands-on subsidized residential props

a) objects used in a film or theatre play
b) someone who is very interested in a particular subject
c) involves living at the place where you are studying
d) practical, rather than theoretical
e) paid for in part by the government so that you pay less

5 Answer the questions.

1 Which areas of film-making is Jack particularly interested in?
2 According to Suki, what kinds of hands-on experience can you get on the film course?
3 What did Suki find on the BFI website?
4 What is Ahmed's sister doing on her course?
5 How is Jack going to find out more information?

6 Word builder Read the information and answer the questions.

Exercise 6
1 Students' own answers
2 involved in, committed to, excited about

ADJECTIVE + PREPOSITION
Some adjectives go with certain prepositions. There aren't any rules, so make a list of them in your notebook.

interested in well known for happy with

1 Read the examples. Do you use prepositions with these adjectives in your language?
2 Find these adjectives in the text. Which preposition are they used with?

involved committed excited

7 Work in pairs to ask and answer the questions.

Exercise 7
Students' own answers

1 Have you ever used an online forum to ask for information or to answer a question?
2 Would you like to do a BFI film course?
3 Do you know about any film courses in your country?

CRITICAL THINKING

DECIDE
Look at the text again. What specific questions does Jack ask? Who answers his questions? Imagine Jack is asking about film courses in your country. Decide on a response.
a) If you know the answer, give information.
b) If you don't know, suggest ways that he could find out more information.

WEB QUEST

Work in pairs. Find out more about 'netiquette' and write instructions for participating in online forums.

1 Think Consider these things and any others that you think are relevant:
- appropriate language
- how to identify yourself
- length of posts
- use of emoticons
- respect for diversity
- how to present your opinions / express your feelings

2 Investigate Search for information and take notes. Share your research with your partner.
3 Create Prepare instructions for participating in online forums and share with the class.

TIP! Adding 'education' to a web search will often help to return results which are suitable for schoolwork.

Exercise 5
1 Script writing and set design/visual effects.
2 You can get involved in all areas of film-making.
3 Prices for the course and video clips from people who have done the course already.
4 Working with cast and organizing the costumes and props.
5 By looking at the BFI's website.

Reading

A forum

LESSON OBJECTIVES
In this lesson students will:
- read an online forum
- recognize examples of informal language

WARMER
Put students into pairs and ask them to think of different genres of film. Set a time limit of two minutes. The pair with the most genres is the winner. Make a list on the board, e.g. *horror*, *romantic*, *thriller*, *sci-fi* etc.

1 53
- Read the rubric with the class.
- Play the audio. Students listen and follow the text in their books.
- They note down the answers to the questions.
- Check answers as a class.

READING STRATEGY

Recognize informal language
Being able to identify whether the language used in a text is formal or informal is a key sill for readers. In internet forums, emails, SMS exchanges, etc, people use informal language.

2
- Go through the information in the box with the class and make sure they understand the task.
- Students find examples of informal language in the text and write them in their note-books.
- Check answers as a class.

3
- Explain the task. Students read the half-sentences carefully.
- They match the sentence beginnings with the endings using the text to help them.
- Check answers as a class.

4 Words in context
- Students find the words in the box in the text. Encourage them to use the context to help them determine the meaning.
- They match the words with the definitions and compare answers in pairs.
- Check answers as a class.

5
- Students read the questions carefully first.
- They read the text again and note down the answers.
- Check answers as a class.

6 Word builder
- Write the sentence beginning *I'm interested in ...* on the board and give a true sentence about yourself, eg. *I'm interested in history*. Invite students to say what they are interested in.
- Point out that some adjectives are followed by prepositions and highlight the examples in the box. Elicit how these adjectives are used in their language.
- Students find the three adjectives in question 2 in the text and write them in their notebooks together with the prepositions that follow them.

7
- Read the three questions aloud to the class.
- Put students into pairs to ask and answer the questions.
- Listen to their ideas as a class.

CRITICAL THINKING
- Students read the task carefully.
- They work individually and respond following either a) or b).
- Listen to their ideas as a class.

WEB QUEST

Students find out about 'netiquette' in online forums.

1. **Think** Put students into pairs. They consider the eight factors and add any others they think are relevant.
2. **Investigate** They open a search engine (eg *Google*) and type in 'netiquette in online forums'. They find information that relates to the factors in stage 1 and any other factors they added. They note down important information they find.
3. **Create** They write a list of ten instructions on how to behave when taking part in online forums. Each pair shares their instructions with the class.

TIP! Explain to students that 'netiquette' is the correct way to interact online. This code of conduct is different from normal social interaction because it is used for text-based communication only. Because we cannot rely on body language, intonation, facial expressions etc, we need guidelines to help us avoid misunderstandings.

DID YOU KNOW?

Highlight the *Did you know?* box. Students read the meaning of 'netiquette' and think about possible rules of 'netiquette'.

FINISHED?

Netiquette is a so-called blend – a word made by combining two other words. Ask students what these blends mean and which words were used to form them: **1** brunch **2** motel **3** flexitarian **4** malware (**Answer key: 1** breakfast + lunch **2** motor + hotel **3** flexible + vegetarian **4** malicious + software).

Video: Flipped classroom

You may want Students to watch the Flipped classroom video for unit 7 as homework in preparation for the following grammar lesson. The Flipped grammar presentation focuses on reported speech.

The longer read > Resource centre

Virtual Teen Forum

Home | Web forum | Register | News | Archive

This conversation: Information about film-making courses

Jack Tuesday 5th May 19.08
Hi all! Can anyone help me? I'm a total film buff and I want to learn more about film-making. A friend told me that she'd heard about some great film courses all around the UK, but she couldn't remember the name of the organization. Has anyone done one of these courses? I'm particularly interested in writing scripts and also set design / visual effects. Thanks for your help!

Suki Tuesday 5th May 19.42
Hi, Jack. I think your friend might mean the BFI – they're well known for their film courses. There are more than 40 courses all over the UK, so there must be one near where you live. I did one and I was really happy with it. They're very hands-on and you can get involved in all areas of film-making, from writing storyboards to doing the lighting or being the camera operator – you really feel like part of a professional film crew. Plus, the teachers are really committed to film and they gave us loads of support and advice. They told us that we were the future of the British film industry!

Jack Tuesday 5th May 19.50
Thanks, Suki. How amazing is that? The courses aren't expensive, are they?

Suki Tuesday 5th May 20.14
No – they're subsidized so you don't have to pay very much. Check out the website for the up-to-date prices. They also have some great video clips by people who've done the course. Everyone was really excited about it and said that you wouldn't regret it! Oh, the only other thing is that you have to be over 16, so you could apply for next year.

Ahmed Tuesday 5th May 20.36
What a great idea! My sister's doing one of the two-week BFI residential courses right now and she loves it there – she told me she was learning loads. She said they'd spent two days filming on location in Oxford, then two days editing in the studio. She's enjoying working with the cast and organizing the costumes and the props. She said they were going on a trip to the BFI cinema in London to watch all the short films they're making. It must be great to see your name in the credits – I think I might go next year!

Jack Tuesday 5th May 20.57
Yes – me too! Thanks, everyone, for all the info. That's really useful! I'm going to have a look at the website now for more information.

DID YOU KNOW?

'Netiquette' = net + etiquette
Netiquette means being polite and respecting other people's views when using online discussion forums.

Grammar

Reported speech

VIDEO: FLIPPED CLASSROOM

WATCH Watch the grammar presentation and do the task.

Exercise 1
a) Direct
b) different from

1 Look at the table. Choose the correct words to complete rules a) and b).

direct speech
'I **want** to do a course,' said Jack.
reported speech
Jack said (that) he **wanted** to do a course.

a) Direct / **Reported** speech contains the speaker's exact words.
b) In reported speech, the tense is **the same as** / **different from** the direct speech.

Exercise 2
1 could
2 was
3 would
4 had done
5 wanted
6 was hoping

2 Look at the table. Then copy and complete the reported speech in sentences 1–7.

tense changes		
direct speech		**reported speech**
am / is / are	→	*was / were*
present simple	→	past simple
present continuous	→	past continuous
past simple	→	past perfect
present perfect	→	past perfect
will or *would*	→	*would*
must or *have to*	→	*had to*
can or *could*	→	*could*

'You must find out about the BFI.'
Suki said that I *had to* find out about the BFI.

1 'You can try all areas of film-making.' She said that I ... try all areas of film-making.
2 'I'm interested in visual effects.' Jack said that he ... interested in visual effects.
3 'I will look on the website.' He said that he ... look on the website.
4 'My sister has done a film course.' Ahmed said that his sister ... a film course.
5 'I want to go, too.' He said that he ... to go.
6 'I'm hoping to apply with a friend.' He said that he ... to apply with a friend.

Exercise 3
1 Suki said (that) she had really enjoyed it.
2 Suki said (that) the teachers were very good.
3 Suki said (that) she hadn't done a residential course yet.
4 Suki said (that) she would apply the following year.
5 Suki said (that) she was going to work in the film industry.

ANALYSE

Can you omit *that* when you use reported speech in your language?

3 Rewrite Suki's sentences using reported speech.

'I did a film course.'
Suki said (that) she had done a film course.

1 'I really enjoyed it.'
2 'The teachers are very good.'
3 'I haven't done a residential course yet.'
4 'I'll apply next year.'
5 'I'm going to work in the film industry.'

4 Read the information in the table. Then rewrite Kate's post in reported speech, making any necessary changes.

changes to time expressions
direct speech → reported speech
today → that day tomorrow → the following day / the day after next week → the following week / the week after yesterday → the previous day / the day before last week → the previous week / the week before four years ago → four years before
changes to other words
here → there this → that these → those

I'm camping at the Blueberry Rock Festival. I arrived two days ago. It's amazing here! I'm going to see my favourite band this evening. They're going to play again tomorrow. I hope it won't rain!

Kate said (that) she was camping at ...

Exercise 4
Kate said (that) she was camping at the Blueberry Rock Festival. She had arrived two days before. She said (that) it was amazing there. She said (that) she was going to see her favourite band that evening. She said (that) they were going to play again the following day. She said (that) she hoped that it wouldn't rain.

5 In pairs, ask and answer the questions. Then report your partner's answers to the class.

Mo said that he'd never been to a music festival.

1 Have you ever been to a music festival?
2 Do you download music?
3 Did you listen to music on your way to school today?
4 Will you work in the music industry?

Exercise 5
Students' own answers

Grammar
Reported speech

LESSON OBJECTIVES
In this lesson students will:
- learn the rules for reported speech
- report a social media message

WARMER
Write the sentence *She said they had spent two days filming on location* on the board with the words in the wrong order: *scene / been / a / said / had / crowd / in / Jack / he / that*. Students work in pairs and write the sentence in the correct order.

VIDEO: FLIPPED CLASSROOM
- If you set the video for homework, ask students to compare their Task time! answers and then check the answers as a class.
- If you didn't set it for homework, watch the video in class and answer the Task time! questions at the end of the presentation.

Answer key: 1 A Hollywood director.
2 She said they had used about 500 extras.
3 Another musical (but for a younger teenage audience).

1 • Students read the examples and complete the rules.
- Highlight the fact that we only use quotation marks for direct speech.
- Check answers as a class.
- If you are using the TPK and your students need more practice of the grammar, do the Grammar basics exercise.

Grammar basics
Answer key: 1 e **2** f **3** a/g **4** g/a **5** c **6** b **7** d

LANGUAGE NOTE
The example uses the verb *say* but if an indirect object is mentioned, the verb *tell* is used, eg *Jack told me (that) he wanted to do a course*. Note that we never use an indirect object after the verb *say* in reported speech.

2 • Point out that the tense in direct speech moves back into the past or further back into the past in reported speech.
- Students study the information about tense changes in the table.
- Point out that *would* and *could* do not change and that *must* becomes *had to* in reported speech.
- Students complete the exercise individually.
- They compare answers in pairs.
- Check answers as a class.

ANALYSE
That can be omitted when reporting direct speech, particularly in spoken English. Ask students if it can be omitted in their language. Ask them to translate the sentence *She said (that) we could omit 'that'* into their language to check.

3 • Read the example sentences aloud to the class.
- Ask them to rewrite the direct speech sentences in the same way beginning each one with *Suki said (that) …*
- Students work individually to rewrite the sentences.
- They compare answers in pairs. Check answers.

FINISHED?
Ask fast finishers to close their books and rewrite their five answers in exercise 3 using direct speech without looking at Suki's original sentences. They then open their books and look at exercise 3 to check their answers.

4 • Students look at the examples in the table.
- Highlight the changes to time expressions in direct and reported speech.
- Point out that when they report the text, *I* will change to *she*.
- Students work individually and report Kate's post.
- Check answers as a class. Point out that it isn't necessary to write *She said …* before every sentence, as it is understood that it is Kate's post that is being reported.

5 • Highlight the example and show how the first question is reported when Mo answers it.
- Students work in pairs and ask and answer the questions.
- They report their partner's answers to the class.

Grammar reference > Workbook page 96

Pronunciation lab > Intonation in reported speech > Student's book page 125

Vocabulary and Listening
Reporting verbs

LESSON OBJECTIVES
In this lesson students will:
- learn a set of reporting verbs
- listen to and understand phone calls and messages

WARMER
Write *rock festival* on the board. Ask students if they know any famous rock festivals in their country or in other countries around the world (eg *Glastonbury in the UK, EXIT in Serbia*). Elicit what possible problems there can be at rock festivals.

DIGITAL VOCABULARY FLASHCARDS
In this digital presentation, students match the vocabulary with definitions.
- Do the digital presentation with the class.
- Encourage students to repeat the words.

1 54
- Read the question to the class. Students read the text and find the answer.
- Play the audio. Students listen and repeat the words in blue.
- If you are using the TPK and your students need more work on the meaning of the words, do the Vocabulary basics exercise.

Vocabulary basics
Answer key: 1 ask **2** promise **3** refuse
4 convince **5** admit **6** complain

2 Word builder
- Students read the Word builder box.
- Highlight the three different patterns that reporting verbs can follow.
- Students copy the table into their notebooks and complete it with the verbs in blue in exercise 1. Encourage them to write the infinitive of the verbs in the table.
- They compare answers in pairs.

LANGUAGE NOTE
Promise and *agree* can also be followed by *that*, eg They *promised that* they would give compensation. They *agreed that* they would refund half the ticket price.

3
- Do the first sentence with the whole class as an example. Elicit the answer from the class (*We agreed to go to the extra concert*).
- Students work individually and write the remaining sentences in reported speech using the words in brackets.
- Check answers as a class.

4
- Students read the information and note down their answers to the questions.
- Check answers as a class.

5 55
- Explain the task. Students should match the five phone calls or messages with the type of phone call or message.
- Encourage them to read a–e carefully first. Check that they understand all the vocabulary, especially *landline* (the fixed telephone that people have in their houses).
- Play the audio. Check progress.
- Students compare answers in pairs.
- Check answers as a class.

6
- Students read the five statements carefully first. Point out that they should also correct any false statements. Encourage them to take notes.
- Play the audio. Students do the task.
- Students compare answers in pairs

7
- You may need to play the audio again. Students choose the correct answers.
- Check answers as a class.

55 Audioscript, page 73, exercises 5 and 6
Narrator: 1
Emily: Hi, Jack! How're you doing?
Jack: Hi, Emily! Yeah, good, thanks ...
Emily: Listen – I was just ringing to see if you want to go to a concert with me and Katy and Oliver on Saturday?
Jack: Yeah? Who's playing?
Emily: Err, there's a few people, I think. It's the extra concert for the Blueberry Rock Festival – you know, the one that was cancelled in the storms.
Jack: Oh, yeah, definitely. Someone told me that The Rage had promised to play again ...
Emily: Yeah, that's what I heard, too. So I'll get four tickets, then.
Jack: Yeah, great!
Emily: I've agreed to meet Katy and Oliver at the bus station at seven o'clock, OK?
Jack: Yeah, cool. I'll be there.

55 Audioscript continued on page T74

Advance your vocabulary > Workbook p109

Vocabulary and Listening

Reporting verbs

LEARNING OUTCOME

✔ Understand phone calls and messages

DIGITAL VOCABULARY FLASHCARDS

Do the matching exercise to discover the new vocabulary.

admit agree ask complain convince invite offer promise refuse say suggest tell

1 Read the magazine article. Why was the festival stopped? Listen and repeat the words in blue. 54

Exercise 1
Because of torrential rain and storms making the festival unsafe

STORM CHAOS at rock festival

Torrential rain caused chaos at Blueberry Rock Festival, where organizers admitted that they weren't prepared for the storms. After some bands complained that it wasn't safe to perform, the organizers asked everyone to leave the festival early on Sunday morning.

Rock group Red Box refused to finish their performance on Saturday night. Lead singer Harry said that the organizers had convinced them to play, but then lightning struck the electrical equipment. They told people not to panic as they abandoned the stage.

Festival organizers offered to organize an extra concert in August and they invited all the bands to return. They also promised to give compensation. They agreed to refund half the ticket price, and suggested that people should check their website for more information.

2 **Word builder** Read the information. Then copy and complete the table with the infinitive of the verbs in blue in exercise 1.

LEARNING VERB PATTERNS

Reporting verbs can follow three patterns: it's important to learn how they are used.
verb + infinitive with *to*
verb + object + infinitive with *to*
verb + *that*

verb + infinitive with *to*	verb + object + infinitive with *to*	verb + *that*
agree to …	*invite someone to …*	*complain that …*

Exercise 2
verb + infinitive with to: agree to, offer to, promise to, refuse to
verb + object + infinitive with to: invite someone to, convince someone to, tell someone to, ask someone to
verb + that: complain that, say that, suggest that, admit that

3 Rewrite the sentences in reported speech. Make any necessary changes.

1 'Let's go to the extra concert.' (we / agree)
2 'I'll get the tickets!' (I / offer)
3 'Will you bring your sister?' (he / ask)
4 'Get four tickets!' (he / tell)
5 'My cousin is going to come, too.' (he / say)

Exercise 3
1 We agreed to go to the extra concert.
2 I offered to get the tickets.
3 He asked me to bring my sister.
4 He told me to get four tickets.
5 He said (that) his cousin was going to come too.

4 Look at the information. Who can get free tickets? How?

BLUEBERRY ROCK FESTIVAL

Did you have to leave the festival due to the bad weather?

Call our Ticket Line on 0801 776332 to reserve tickets for the FREE extra concert on Saturday 19th August!

Exercise 4
People who had to leave the festival due to the bad weather. By calling the Blueberry Rock Festival Ticket Line.

5 Listen to five short phone calls or messages. Match 1–5 with a–e. 55

a) an informal voicemail message
b) a pre-recorded message
c) a conversation on a landline
d) an informal mobile conversation
e) a call to the Ticket Line

Exercise 5
1 d
2 b
3 e
4 a
5 c

6 Listen again. Are the sentences true or false? Correct the false sentences.

1 Emily and Jack agreed to meet at 7.30.
2 The Ticket Line was very busy.
3 Emily asked if she could reserve two tickets.
4 Jack rang to say that he would be late.
5 Jack's mum told Emily that he hadn't left yet.

Exercise 6
1 **False** – They agreed to meet at 7 o'clock.
2 **True**
3 **False** – She asked if she could reserve four tickets.
4 **False** – Jack didn't ring to say that he would be late.
5 **False** – Jack's mum said that he had left the house about twenty minutes earlier/ before.

7 Choose the correct answers.

1 Emily and her friends are going to the concert by **bus** / **train**.
2 Emily can't get through to the Ticket Line because it's **closed** / **busy**.
3 Emily must **pay by credit card** / **show ID** before collecting the tickets.
4 Jack was late because his mum asked him to return a **DVD** / **library book** on the way.

Vocabulary basics | Advance your vocabulary > Workbook p109

Exercise 7
1 bus
2 busy
3 show ID
4 DVD

Exercise 1

Entertainment + Technology

Exercise 2

750,000 = number of tracks streamed on Spotify every minute
292 = how many millions of people worldwide view and play e-sports
one billion = the number of hours per week Netflix users worldwide view content
27 = the number of apps an average user has
2,200,000 = the approximate number of new books published worldwide every year

Social awareness

Entertainment and technology

> **FACT!** Around the world, almost 2.4 billion people use a smartphone.

1 Look at the infographic. What is 'entertechment'?

2 Read and listen to the text. What do these numbers refer to? 56

- 750,000
- 292
- one billion
- 27
- 2,200,000

3 Words in context Find these words in the text. What do they mean? Are they nouns, verbs or adjectives?

inseparable overwhelming viewers streaming e-sports

4 Are the sentences true or false? Find evidence in the text to support your answers.

1 Music streaming sites have more than 100 million subscribers.
2 Worldwide, more gamers use consoles than PCs.
3 More than 70% of cinema tickets are bought by over-25s.
4 The average user makes 44 website visits each month.
5 17% of books sold are e-books.

5 Work in pairs. Ask and answer the questions about your country.

1 How do you and your friends usually watch films, read books and listen to music?
2 Is gaming popular in your country? And e-sports?
3 Which websites and apps do you and your friends use most?

VIDEO: CULTURE BYTE

WATCH Watch the video supplied by BBC.

Exercise 4

1 **True** – more than 112 million people subscribe worldwide
2 **False** – 62% use a PC and 56% a console
3 **True** – 29% of cinema tickets were bought by 12–24-year-olds
4 **False** – the average user makes 96 website visits per month (but spends 44% of the time on just five websites)
5 **False** – real books up 5% and e-books down 17% last year

Exercise 5

Students' own answers

ENTERTAINMENT + TECHNOLOGY = 'ENTERTECHMENT'!

MUSIC

More than 112 million people subscribe to music streaming sites worldwide.

Worldwide, more than 750,000 tracks are streamed on Spotify every minute.

GAMING

There are about 1.8 billion gamers in the world (62% use a PC and 56% a console).

48% of gamers play social games

More than 292 million people worldwide view and play e-sports.

CINEMA, TV AND STREAMING

In 2016, only 29% of cinema tickets were bought by 12–24-year-olds.

Worldwide, Netflix users collectively view more than one billion hours per week.

Out of 194 available channels, the average viewer watches no more than 19 channels.

INTERNET AND APPS

The average user makes 96 website visits per month (but spends 44% of the time on just five websites).

The average user has 27 apps (but spends 79% of the time on just five apps).

300 hours of video are uploaded to YouTube every minute.

BOOKS AND E-BOOKS

Sales of real books up 5% and sales of e-books down 17% last year.

Approximately 2,200,000 new books are published worldwide every year.

If someone asked you how much of your entertainment involved technology, what would you say? Most of us would probably agree that due to smartphones and tablets, technology and entertainment are often inseparable. Nowadays, nearly everyone carries a portable 'entertechment hub', which is full of promises to entertain us constantly. But the huge choice offered by technology can be overwhelming. For example, when asked whether they used all 194 TV channels in one country, viewers admitted that they'd never watched more than 19. In addition, technology has made us all potential entertainers: uploading videos, sharing photos and suggesting playlists.

Exercise 3

inseparable = go hand-in-hand, usually go together (adjective)
overwhelming = way more than is needed for that situation (adjective)
viewers = someone who watches TV (noun)
streaming = technology that allows the user to view something as a continuous stream (noun)
e-sports = organized event where people play video games in front of an audience (noun)

Social awareness

Entertainment and technology

LESSON OBJECTIVES
In this lesson students will:
- read about entertainment and technology
- discuss their country in relation to the topic

WARMER

Write these ways of listening to music on the board: *music streaming*, *vinyl records*, *CDs*, *cassette tapes*. Students put them in order from the oldest form to the newest (**Answer key:** vinyl records, cassette tapes, CDs, music streaming).

FACT!

Students read the information in the Fact! box. Ask them if they are surprised by this piece of information. Ask them if they know anyone who doesn't have a smartphone.

1 • Highlight the term *entertechment*. Students find its meaning by looking at the infographic.

2 56
- Students read and listen to the text. They find the correct answers.
- Check answers as a class.

3 Words in context
- Students find the words in the box in the text. Encourage them to use the context to help them decide on the part of speech and the meaning of each word.
- They compare answers in pairs.

4 • Explain the task. Students read the statements and decide if they are true or false.
- They note down where in the text they found the evidence to support their choice.
- Check answers as a class.

5 • Students work in pairs and ask and answer the questions.

VIDEO: CULTURE BYTE

This video is about the link between violence and video games. For exploitation and comprehension practice based on this video, see the Culture byte video worksheets on the Resource Centre.

55 Audioscript, exercises 5 and 6 (continued from page T73)

Emily: OK. See you soon!
Jack: Bye!
Narrator: 2
Woman: Hello! You're through to the Ticket Line for the Blueberry Rock Festival. I'm afraid we're experiencing exceptionally high call volumes at the moment, and all our sales staff are busy right now. We suggest you try ringing back later or, alternatively, why not visit our website at www.blueberryrockfestival.uk? Otherwise, please hold the line.
Narrator: 3
Man: Hello, Ticket Line at Blueberry Rock Festival. How can I help you?
Emily: Oh, hi! I'd like to book four tickets for the extra concert on Saturday 19th August? Err … I went to the festival and they said that we could get free tickets.
Man: Yes, that's right. What's your name, please?
Emily: Emily Jones.
Man: OK, four tickets – is that right?
Emily: Yes, please.
Man: Hold on a minute! OK, I've reserved those for you.
Emily: Great, thanks. Shall I just collect them there?
Man: Yes, you can pick them up on the night. Remember to bring ID.
Emily: OK! Thanks. Bye.
Man: Bye. Thanks for calling!
Narrator: 4
Jack's voice: Hi! Sorry I can't get to the phone right now. Please leave a message and I'll get back to you as soon as I can!
Emily: Jack … where are you? We're all here at the bus station where we agreed to meet. It's um … 7.15 … we agreed to meet at seven o'clock? Call me as soon as you can, right? The bus leaves in … five minutes! Anyway, I'll give you a ring at home and see if you're still there … See you later!
Narrator: 5
Jack's mum: Hello?
Emily: Oh, hi, Mrs Smith. It's Emily here … Jack's friend from school?
Jack's mum: Oh, hi there!
Emily: Err … I was just wondering if Jack was there?
Jack's mum: No, I'm afraid he's already left …
Emily: Oh, it's just I've tried his mobile, but there's no answer. Do you know when he left?
Jack's mum: Errm, about 20 minutes ago, I think. But I asked him to return a DVD, so he offered to drop it off on the way. He said it wouldn't take long …
Emily: Oh, OK. Anyway, sorry to bother you … Ah! Here he is! He's just coming round the corner now …
Jack's mum: Oh, good. Well, have a nice time, won't you?
Emily: Thanks! I'm sure we will. Bye!
Jack's mum: Bye now.

Grammar
Reported questions

LESSON OBJECTIVES
In this lesson students will:
- learn to report questions
- read a text about a James Bond story

WARMER
Write *What are they doing?* on the board. Elicit from the class how we report this question, beginning with *She asked ...* . Write the correct version (*She asked what they were doing*) on the board. Highlight the word order (*the subject they comes before the verb*) and the change in tense from present to past.

1
- Students read the examples.
- They work individually and answer questions 1–3 using the information in the table.
- They compare answers in pairs.
- Check answers as a class. Highlight the fact that in reported questions, we do not invert the subject and the verb as we do in direct questions.
- If you are using the TPK and your students need more work on the meaning of the words, do the Grammar basics exercise.

Grammar basics
Answer key: 2 √ **4** √ **6** √

LANGUAGE NOTE
The auxiliary verb *do* / *does* / *did* is not used in reported questions. For example, the direct question *'What does she want?'* becomes *He asked what she wanted* when reported and the direct *Yes* / *No* question *'Do you play tennis?'* becomes *She asked me if I played tennis.*

2
- Do the first sentence with the whole class as an example.
- Students work individually and choose the correct words using the table in exercise 1 to help them.
- They compare answers in pairs.
- Check answers as a class.

3
- Explain the task. Remind students that the past forms of the verbs go back to present forms in direct questions (eg *had* → *have*, *would* → *will*).
- Students complete the task individually.
- They compare ideas in pairs.
- Check answers as a class.

FINISHED?
Ask fast finishers to write two more direct questions for the famous actor, eg *What are your hobbies? Do you like sport?* and then report the direct questions using *We asked him ...* .

CLIL Grammar in context: Literature

4 57
- This activity practises reported questions from this lesson and reported speech from the previous grammar lesson.
- Students read the whole text before they choose the correct answers.
- Students work individually to complete the exercise.
- They compare answers in pairs.
- Play the audio so students can check their answers. Point out that told is the answer in question 3 because it is followed by *him*, an indirect object.

CULTURE NOTE
The first James Bond film was *Dr No* in 1962, with Sean Connery as James Bond. Several other actors have played the role of James Bond, including Daniel Craig, Pierce Brosnan and Roger Moore. The James Bond films were the first to earn over £1 billion at the box office.

LITERATURE TASK
Students use the internet to find out more about the James Bond stories and answer the questions. Check answers.

Grammar reference > Workbook page 96

Grammar
Reported questions

Exercise 1
1 No
2 Yes
3 With yes / no questions

1 Look at reported questions a–d in the table. Then answer the questions.

reported questions
wh- / *how* questions
'How many channels **do** people **watch**?'
a) They asked how many channels people **watched**.
'Which apps **have** you **used**?'
b) They asked which apps I **had used**.
yes / *no* questions
'**Do** you **buy** music?'
c) They asked if / whether I **bought** music.
'Have you **played** e-sports?'
d) They asked if / whether I **had played** e-sports.

1 Do we use question marks in reported questions?
2 Are the tense changes the same as in reported statements?
3 When do we use *if* / *whether*?

Exercise 2
1 if he liked
2 he had made
3 his next film would be
4 he lived
5 if he would

2 Choose the correct words.

Guess what! A famous actor came to our school yesterday, and we asked him …
1 **if he liked** / **does he like** the James Bond films.
2 how many films **had he made** / **he had made**.
3 what **will be his next film** / **his next film would be**.
4 where **he lived** / **did he live**.
5 **would he** / **if he would** give us his autograph.

Exercise 3
2 How many films have you made?
3 What will your next film be?
4 Where do you live?
5 Will you give us your autograph?

3 Read the reported questions in exercise 2 again. Then write them in direct speech.

1 'Do you like the James Bond films?'

CLIL
Grammar in context: Literature

4 Read the text and choose the correct answers. Then listen and check. 57

Exercise 4
1 that I should
2 to go
3 had to
4 told
5 would
6 would be
7 what
8 me to

Casino Royale
by Ian Fleming

THE FIRST JAMES BOND STORY

At the moment I'm reading *Casino Royale*, which is the first James Bond story. It's full of intrigue, crime and deception. A friend of mine (1) suggested **that I should** / **to** / **me to** read it because I'm a big fan of the James Bond films.

At the start of this story, Secret Agent 007 was sent to France. His boss told him (2) **go** / **to go** / **going** to a casino and play against the Russian agent, Le Chiffre. He explained that Bond (3) **has to** / **must** / **had to** beat Le Chiffre and win all his money. He (4) **told** / **said** / **explained** him that his assistant (5) **will** / **would** / **is going to** be the beautiful spy, Vesper Lynd.

I'm only about half-way through the book so I don't know the end of the story yet. My friend said that I (6) **will be** / **would be** / **am** surprised, but when I asked her (7) **if** / **what** / **whether** happened, she told (8) **me** / **to me** / **me to** wait and see!

LITERATURE TASK

Find out more about the James Bond stories.
- Where was Ian Fleming born?
- Where did he write *Casino Royale*?
- How many James Bond books did he write?
- What other jobs did Ian Fleming do?

Literature Task
Students' own answers

An entertainment survey

LEARNING OUTCOME

✔ Inform your class about survey results

Today we're going to carry out a class survey about entertainment. How often do you go out with your friends?

TASK Do a survey

1 Read an entertainment survey | 2 Understand a survey | 3 Practise a survey | 4 Inform your class about survey results

Entertainment survey

Name: Katy Smith
Age: 15

1 How often do you usually go out with your friends?
a) once or twice a week ◯
b) three or four times a week ✓
c) more than four times a week ◯

Comments: I usually go out on Fridays and Saturdays, and once or twice in the week.

2 Do you ever go to the cinema?
a) No, there isn't a cinema where I live. ◯
b) Yes, once or twice a month. ✓
c) Yes, more than twice a month. ◯

Comments: I also watch films at my friends' houses.

3 Have you ever been to the theatre?
a) Yes, to see a play. ✓
b) Yes, to see a concert or performance. ◯
c) No, I haven't. ◯

Comments: I've seen a few plays and a ballet at the theatre – with my parents!

4 Are you interested in computer games?
a) No, I never play computer games. ◯
b) Yes, I play occasionally. ◯
c) Yes, I'm a frequent gamer. ✓

Comments: I've got a PlayStation 4.

5 How many hours do you spend in front of a screen?
a) Less than 7 hours per week. ◯
b) 7–15 hours per week. ✓
c) More than 15 hours per week. ◯

Comments: I also do sports, so I don't spend all my time in front of a screen!

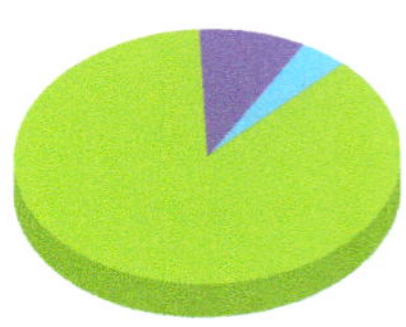

If you have any additional comments, please write them here:
I'd love to go to more concerts, but there isn't a concert venue in my town.

Exercise 1
7–15 hours per week
Students' own answers

Exercise 2
1 three or four times
2 once or twice
3 had seen a few plays and ballet
4 had got
5 concert venue

1 Read

1 Read the survey. How many hours does Katy spend in front of a screen? Do you spend more or less time than this?

2 Read the survey again. Then copy and complete the sentences.

1 Katy said she went out ... a week.
2 She said she went to the cinema ... a month.
3 She told Jack that she ... at the theatre.
4 She said that she ... a PlayStation.
5 She said there wasn't a ... in her town.

2 Listen

3 Read and listen to the extract from a survey on page 77. When does Emily go out? 58

Exercise 3
Once or twice a week

4 Listen again and repeat. Practise your intonation.

5 Watch or listen to the complete survey. Are the sentences true or false? Correct the false sentences. 59

1 Jack said the survey would take twenty minutes.
2 Emily said she often watched films online.
3 Emily said she had never been to the theatre.
4 She said she wasn't interested in computer games.
5 Emily said she spent less than ten hours a week in front of a screen.

Exercise 5
1 **False** – Jack said that the survey wouldn't take longer than five minutes.
2 **True**
3 **False** – Emily said she had been to the theatre quite a few times.
4 **True**
5 **False** – Emily said she spent more than 15 hours a week in front of a screen.

Integrated skills
An entertainment survey

LESSON OBJECTIVES
In this lesson students will:
- work on all four skills
- read a survey
- watch or listen to people taking part in a survey
- practise a survey and report the results

WARMER
Write *survey* on the board. Ask what kind of things surveys are usually designed to find out (eg *shopping habits*, *political preferences*).

1 Read

1 • Students read the questions carefully. Check students understand the phrase in front of a screen (using a computer or similar device that has a screen or watching TV).
• They read the survey and note down their answers.
• Find out which students spend the most time in front of a screen and which the least.

2 • Students read the questions carefully first. They read the text again and find the information to fill the gaps. Check answers.

2 Listen

Video with audio option
The dialogue is also available to play as an audio file. If you prefer to present it this way, play the audio and follow the teacher's notes as for the video.

3 58 REC
• Students watch, read or listen to the extract from a survey. Elicit the answer to the question from the class (She goes out once or twice a week).

4 • Play the video again. Students watch and repeat to practise their intonation.

5 59
• Students read the sentences carefully first.
• Play the audio. Students listen to the complete survey. They decide if the sentences are true or false and correct the false sentences.
• Students compare their answers in pairs.
• Check answers as a class.

58 Audioscript, page 76, exercises 3, 4, 5 & 6

Jack: Hello Emily! I'm doing some research into entertainment. Could I ask you a few questions?
Emily: Sure, no problem.
Jack: Great, thanks. It won't take longer than five minutes. I'll be taking some notes – is that OK?
Emily: Yes, that's fine.
Jack: OK, let's get started! First, could you tell me how old you are, please?
Emily: Yes, I'm 15.
Jack: OK, and could you tell me how often you go out with your friends?
Emily: Oh, probably a couple of times a week – once at the weekend and once during the week.
Jack: So you go out about twice a week then, is that correct?
Emily: Yes, on average.

59 Audioscript, page 76, exercise 5 & 6

Jack: Can you tell me if you ever go to the cinema?
Emily: Er, not very often. Probably about once a month. But I watch films online quite a lot.
Jack: And have you ever been to the theatre?
Emily: Yes, I have, quite a few times. There are sometimes concerts at my local theatre.
Jack: OK, great. And would you mind telling me if you're interested in computer games?
Emily: Computer games? Er, not, not really. I'm not into computer games, no.
Jack: Do you know approximately how many hours you spend in front of a screen, each week?
Emily: Oh, let's think. Maybe two or three hours a day, either watching telly or on the tablet.
Jack: So, more than 15 hours a week?
Emily: Gosh! Yes, I guess so ...
Jack: OK. Is there anything else you'd like to add?
Emily: Er, no, I don't think so.
Jack: OK. Well, that's it! Thank you so much for taking part.
Emily: No worries.

6 • Students look at the Communication kit and read through the phrases.
• Ask which phrases are used in the complete survey. Play the audio again for students to check their answers.

3 Write

7 • Students read the survey in exercise 1 again and write down their own answers to the questions in their notebooks.
• Encourage them to add a comment after each answer, eg *Most of the time I spend in front of a screen is on the computer, but I sometimes watch TV too.*

LANGUAGE NOTE

Highlight that there is no inversion of subject / verb in indirect questions, eg *Can you tell me how old you are?* (not *Can you tell me how old are you?* which is a very common error when using indirect questions). The auxiliary verb *do / does / did* is not used in indirect questions.

8 • Show how the direct question in the survey is transformed into the indirect form after *Could you tell me* ...? Highlight the different word order and the fact that *do* is not used in the indirect part of the question.
• Students rewrite questions 2–5 as indirect questions using *Can / Could you tell me* ...? or *Would you mind telling me* ...? to introduce the indirect questions.
• Check answers as a class.

4 Communicate

9 • Students work in pairs and interview each other using the indirect questions from exercise 8.
• They record the answers in their notebooks.

10 • The purpose of this activity is for students to report their partner's answers using reported speech.
• Read the example sentence aloud to the class. Encourage students to report their partner's answers in the same way.

11 • This activity could either be done on the board with the whole class by finding out and recording how many students give certain answers or it could be done as a group project with each group producing a bar graph or pie chart to show the results for a particular question.
• Note that students will write a report on the results of this class survey in the next Writing lesson.

! COMMUNICATION TIP
ASKING INDIRECT QUESTIONS

Highlight the information in the Communication tip box and remind students which phrases in the Communication kit are used to ask indirect questions.

Integrated skills > Resource centre

Hello, Emily! I'm doing some research into entertainment. Could I ask you a few questions?	Sure, no problem.
Great, thanks. It won't take longer than five minutes. I'll be taking some notes – is that OK?	Yes, that's fine.
OK, let's get started! First, could you tell me how old you are, please?	Yes, I'm 15.
OK, and could you tell me how often you go out with your friends?	Oh, probably a couple of times a week – once at the weekend and once during the week.
So you go out about twice a week then – is that correct?	Yes, on average.

Communication kit

- I'm doing some research into ... • Could I ask you a few questions?
- It won't take longer than five minutes. • I'll be taking notes – is that OK?
- OK, let's get started! • Could you tell me ... • Would you mind telling me ...?

Exercise 6
All the phrases

6 Look at the Communication kit. Which phrases are used in the Speaking sketch? Watch or listen again to check your answers.

3 Write

Exercise 7
Students' own answers

7 Prepare your answers to the questions in the survey. Choose a, b or c and write your own comments in your notebook.

8 Prepare to interview your partner. Change survey questions 1–5 into indirect questions.

1 Could you tell me how often you usually go out with your friends?

Exercise 8
Possible answers:
2 Could you tell me if you ever go to the cinema?
3 Could you tell me if you have ever been to the theatre?
4 Would you mind telling me if you are interested in computer games?
5 Can you tell me how many hours you spend in front of a screen?

4 Communicate

Exercise 9
Students' own answers

9 Work in pairs. Interview your partner to find out his / her answers to the survey. Write the answers in your notebook.

I'm doing some research into ...

Exercise 10
Students' own answers

10 Tell the class about your interview. Use reported questions and reported speech.

I asked Javier how often he went out with his friends, and he told me that ...

Exercise 11
Students' own answers

11 Compile all the survey results in your class.

15 people said they usually went out twice a week ...

COMMUNICATION TIP
ASKING INDIRECT QUESTIONS

Use indirect questions to make questions or requests more polite. The word order in indirect questions is the same as in reported questions.

INTEGRATED SKILLS

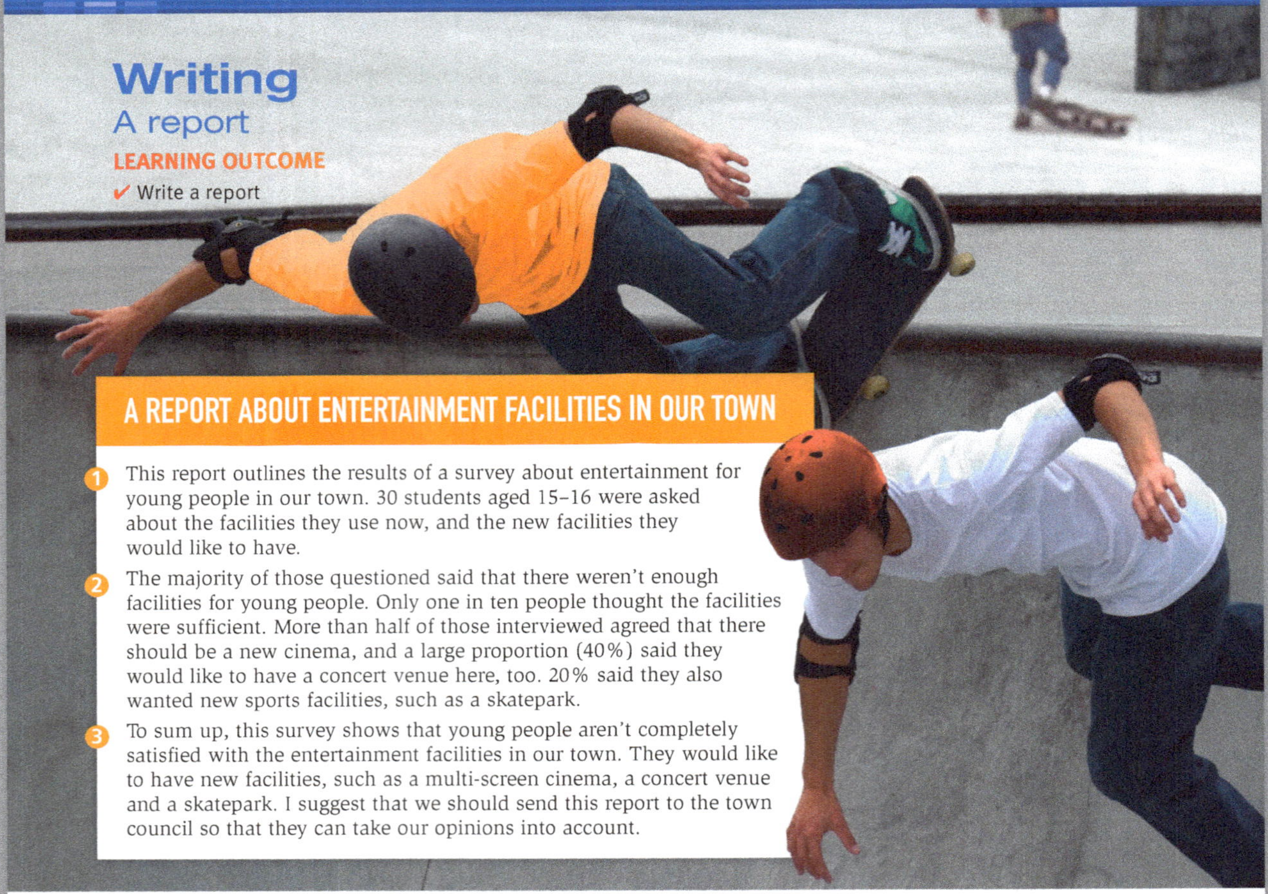

Writing

A report

LEARNING OUTCOME

✔ Write a report

A REPORT ABOUT ENTERTAINMENT FACILITIES IN OUR TOWN

1 This report outlines the results of a survey about entertainment for young people in our town. 30 students aged 15–16 were asked about the facilities they use now, and the new facilities they would like to have.

2 The majority of those questioned said that there weren't enough facilities for young people. Only one in ten people thought the facilities were sufficient. More than half of those interviewed agreed that there should be a new cinema, and a large proportion (40%) said they would like to have a concert venue here, too. 20% said they also wanted new sports facilities, such as a skatepark.

3 To sum up, this survey shows that young people aren't completely satisfied with the entertainment facilities in our town. They would like to have new facilities, such as a multi-screen cinema, a concert venue and a skatepark. I suggest that we should send this report to the town council so that they can take our opinions into account.

Exercise 1
a) 3
b) 1
c) 2

1 **Focus on content** Read the report. Which paragraph ...

a) has a summary of the results and provides recommendations?
b) introduces the purpose and content of the report?
c) gives some statistics from the survey?

Exercise 2
biggest: 9 out of 10
smallest: one in ten

2 **Focus on language** Read the information. Which expression refers to the biggest number? Which refers to the smallest number?

Expressing statistics

the majority   one in ten
nine out of ten
more than half
a large proportion   20%

Exercise 3
1 the majority
2 25%
3 seven out of ten
4 a minority / less than 50%
5 almost everyone
6 75%

3 Express each statistic in a different way.

30% = three out of ten

1 55%
2 one in four
3 70%
4 less than half
5 99%
6 three quarters

4 Write a report based on the results of your class survey from page 77.

Exercise 4
Students' own answers

Writing kit

1 **Plan** your report.

- Collect all the data from your class survey.
- Analyse the results.

2 **Write** your report using three paragraphs. Use the model report to help you.

1 introduction
2 results of the survey
3 conclusion and your recommendations

3 **Useful phrases**

This report outlines ...
... of those questioned said / thought / agreed ...
To sum up, ...
I suggest ...

4 **Check** your writing.

☑ phrases for expressing statistics
☑ use reporting verbs and the correct tenses in reported speech
☑ three paragraphs

Study guide > p105   Writing hub > Workbook p124

Writing

A report

LESSON OBJECTIVES
In this lesson students will:

- read a short report
- use different ways of expressing statistics
- write a report

WARMER
Write *entertainment facilities* on the board and check understanding. Ask students what entertainment facilities there are in their town or city (eg *cinema*, *sports centre*).

1 Focus on content

- Students read the report and match the paragraph summaries to the paragraphs. Check answers.

2 Focus on language

- Students look at expressions in the box.
- They work individually and decide which expression refers to the biggest number and which to the smallest.
- Check answers as a class. Ask them to express the phrases *one in ten* and *nine out of ten* as percentages (*10%* and *90%*).
- Point out that *the majority* means any number more than half. For any number of people less than half, we use a minority. A *large proportion* is *about 70% or more*.

3
- Show how *30%* can also be expressed as *three out of ten*. Ask how *four out of ten* is expressed as a percentage (*40%*).
- Students complete the task. Check answers.

4
- Explain the task. Ask students to follow the stages in the Writing Kit.
- Encourage them to use a variety of phrases for expressing statistics in their report.
- Monitor while they are writing and give help with vocabulary if necessary.
- At the check stage, ask them to swap notebooks and check each other's writing.

Writing kit
The aim of this activity is for students to write a report based on the results of the class survey in exercise 11 of the previous lesson that includes the correct use of phrases for expressing statistics. It also gives them practice in using reporting verbs and the correct tenses in reported speech, and in organizing paragraphs correctly.

Study guide > Student's Book page 105

Writing hub > Workbook page 124

UNIT **8**

PERSUADING PEOPLE

UNIT OBJECTIVES AND KEY COMPETENCES

In this unit the student will learn ...

- to recognize, understand and correctly use vocabulary related to advertising and a set of verbs that are often confused **CLC SCC CAE**
- to recognize, understand and correctly use relative and indefinite pronouns and use them in a short speaking activity **CLC L2L SIE**
- to recognize, understand and correctly use reflexive pronouns and use them in a short speaking activity **CLC L2L SIE**
- about advertising and how advertisers target young people **CLC CMST SCC CAE**
- about giving a persuasive presentation by watching a short video **CLC DC SCC CAE**

In this unit the student will learn how to ...

- guess meaning from context in a text about C.A.T.S. advertising service **CLC CMST SCC CAE**
- look online for more information about C.A.T.S. **CLC CMST DC SCC CAE SIE**
- understand numbers and prices in radio adverts **CLC CMST SCC CAE**
- read two charity adverts, listen to a pairwork presentation about funding for a charity, prepare for and give a persuasive presentation **CLC SCC CAE SIE**
- write a for and against essay **CLC SCC**

LINGUISTIC CONTENTS

Main vocabulary

- Advertising: *advertising campaign*, *target audience*, *peer pressure*, etc
- Easily confused verbs: *borrow*, *earn*, *hope*, *lend*, *remember*, *remind*, *see*, *spend*, *wait*, *waste*, *watch*, *win*

Extra vocabulary

- Words in context: *bombard*, *billboard*, *raise (money)*, *supporter*, *infrastructure*; *catchy*, *swipe*, *mood*, *bargain*, *gender*
- Word builder: Compound nouns and adjectives; Verb + noun collocations

Grammar

- Relative pronouns
- Indefinite pronouns
- Reflexive pronouns

Functional language

- Phrases for persuading

Pronunciation

- Difficult sounds: s + consonant
- Difficult sounds: /ð/ and /θ/

SKILLS

Reading

- Read an online article about advertising
- Read a text about analysing adverts
- Read an online for and against essay about banning adverts for unhealthy food

Writing: Interaction and production

- Write notes to prepare for a persuasive presentation about fundraising for a charity
- Write a for and against essay in three steps
- Learn how to use connectors of addition and contrast

Listening

- Listen to five adverts
- Listen to a persuasive presentation about charity fundraising

Spoken interaction

- Ask and answer questions about advertising
- Ask and answer questions using easily confused verbs

Spoken production

- Prepare and give a persuasive presentation

LIFELONG LEARNING SKILLS

Self-study and self-evaluation

- Study guide: Student's Book page 108
- Progress check: Workbook page 70
- Extension: Workbook page 71
- Grammar reference and practice: Workbook pages 98–99
- Wordlist: Workbook pages 151–157

Learning strategies and thinking skills

- Guessing meaning from context
- Critical thinking: categorising

Life skills

- Critical thinking

Cross-curricular contents

- Advertising, advertising in the London underground
- Literature: *The Pearl* by John Steinbeck
- Literature task: searching the internet for further information about John Steinbeck

EVALUATION

- Unit 8 End of unit test: Basic, Standard and Extra
- CEFR Skills Exam Generator

KEY COMPETENCES

CLC	Competence in linguistic communication
CMST	Competence in mathematics, science and technology
DC	Digital competence
SCC	Social and civic competence
CAE	Cultural awareness and expression
L2L	Learning to learn
SIE	Sense of initiative and entrepreneurship

DIGITAL MATERIAL

New Pulse Digital Course including:

- Interactive vocabulary presentation
- Grammar and Vocabulary basics exercises
- Getting started video
- Flipped classroom grammar video: relative pronouns
- Speaking sketch video: a persuasive presentation

DIGITAL COMPETENCE

- Web quest: Find out more information about advertising in the London underground
- Digital competence worksheet: Web-based voice-recording tools

REINFORCEMENT MATERIAL

- New Pulse Basics: Teacher's Resource Centre
- Vocabulary and grammar consolidation worksheets: Teacher's Resource Centre
- Grammar and Vocabulary basics exercises: Teacher's Presentation Kit

EXTENSION MATERIAL

- Vocabulary and grammar extension worksheets: Teacher's Resource Centre
- Advance your vocabulary: Workbook page 110
- The longer read: Teacher's Resource Centre
- Writing hub: Workbook page 126

TEACHER'S RESOURCE CENTRE

- Translation and dictation worksheets
- Evaluation rubrics
- Key competences worksheets
- Culture and CLIL worksheets
- Digital competence worksheets
- Macmillan Readers worksheets
- Integrated Skills

Vocabulary
Advertising

LESSON OBJECTIVES
In this lesson students will:
- learn words related to advertising
- learn how compound nouns and compound adjectives are formed

VIDEO: GETTING STARTED

In this video the speakers answer the question *Tell us where you can find adverts.*

- Focus the students on the unit title *Persuading People.*
- Write these statements on the board:
  1 Who thinks there are too many adverts?
  2 Who remembers adverts when they have a jingle? (2 speakers) **3** Who talks about the adverts around his / her school?
- Students watch the video and decide whether the statements are true or false.
- They watch the video again to check answers.
- At the end of the lesson, ask students to answer the question from the video: *Tell us where you can find adverts.*

Answer key: 1 Josh **2** Naomi, Harry **3** Emily

WARMER

Books closed. Introduce the topic by ask students if they can see any examples of advertising in their everyday life. What ads can they see every day on the way from home to school?

1
- Ask students to work individually and note all the places they see adverts. They compare their answers with a partner.
- Highlight that *advert* and *ad* are short forms of *advertisement*. Then elicit the verb *advertise* and the word for a person who advertises (*advertiser*). Highlight the difference in the pronunciation of the syllable *-ise* and the difference in stress between the verb *advertise* /ˈædvɜːtaɪz/ and the noun *advertisement* /ədˈvɜːtɪsmənt/.
- If you are using the TPK and your students need more work on the meaning of the words, do the Vocabulary basics exercise.

Vocabulary basics

Answer key Down: 1 advert **2** jingle **3** celebrity
Across: 3 consumer **4** hype **5** brand

2 60
- Students read the words in the box.
- They work in pairs and discuss the meaning of the words. Students use dictionaries to check the meaning of unknown words.
- Highlight that if something is eye-catching, it is attractive and unusual and therefore people notice it.
- Elicit from the class which of the words are nouns, which are verbs and which are adjectives.
- Play the audio. Students listen to the words and repeat them. Make sure students pronounce *persuasive* /pəˈsweɪsɪv/ correctly.

3 Word builder
- Ask students to read the information in the Word builder box. Point out that compound words can be either compound nouns or compound adjectives.
- Ask students to find other compound words in the word pool in exercise 2.
- Point out that *go viral* is not a compound word as it is a verb phrase made up of a verb + an adjective. Check answers.

4
- Ask students to find the words in exercise 2 that match the definitions.
- Check answers as a class.

5
- Ask students to work individually and choose the correct words.
- They compare answers in pairs.
- Check answers as a class.

6
- Put students into pairs to ask and answer the questions in exercise 5.
- Listen to their ideas as a class.

PERSUADING PEOPLE

UNIT 8

LEARNING OUTCOMES IN THIS UNIT

- Guess meaning from context in a text
- Understand numbers and prices in radio adverts
- Use persuasion in a presentation
- Write a for and against essay about online advertising

VIDEO: GETTING STARTED

WATCH Watch the teenagers talking about advertising and answer the question.

Vocabulary
Advertising

1 **Make a list of all the places where you see adverts. How many ads* do you think you see every day?**

on the internet, in magazines, …

* ad = advert = advertisement

> **Exercise 1**
> Students' own answers

2 **Check the meaning of the words in the box. Use a dictionary to help you. Are they nouns, verbs or adjectives? Listen and repeat.** 60

ad agency advert advertising campaign brand celebrity consumer eye-catching go viral hype jingle online ads peer pressure persuasive target audience

> **Exercise 2**
> **nouns:** ad agency, advert, advertising campaign, brand, celebrity, consumer, hype, jingle, online ads, peer pressure, target audience
> **verbs:** go viral
> **adjectives:** eye-catching, persuasive

3 **Word builder** **Read the information and answer the questions.**

COMPOUND NOUNS AND ADJECTIVES
We make compound nouns and adjectives when we put two words together. The two words are sometimes written separately and sometimes with a hyphen.

eye-catching (adjective)
ad agency (noun)

1 Which other expressions in exercise 2 are compound words?
2 Are they compound nouns or compound adjectives?

> **Exercise 3**
> 1 advertising campaign online ads peer pressure target audience
> 2 compound nouns

4 **Find words in exercise 2 that mean …**

1 a famous person, especially in entertainment
2 someone who buys and uses products or services
3 a short slogan or tune designed to be easily remembered
4 a product or group of products that are made by one particular company
5 the use of intensive publicity or promotion to create interest
6 the influence that other people of your age have on the way you behave or dress
7 attractive or unusual, so you notice it
8 good at making people believe what you want them to

> **Exercise 4**
> 1 celebrity
> 2 consumer
> 3 jingle
> 4 brand
> 5 hype
> 6 peer pressure
> 7 eye-catching
> 8 persuasive

5 **Choose the correct words.**

> **Exercise 5**
> 1 advert
> 2 jingle
> 3 ad agency
> 4 celebrity
> 5 viral

6 **Work in pairs. Ask and answer the questions in exercise 5.**

Can you remember …? *Yes, I can. I remember …*

> **Exercise 6**
> Students' own answers

Exercise 1

Clapham Common Underground Station (London); It's the station where the billboards were replaced for two weeks.

Virginia (USA); A supporter of the campaign flew to London from there.

Atlanta (USA), Barcelona (Spain) and Cape Town (South Africa); Copy-cat campaigns are planned there.

Times Square; It's a famous place in New York that has many adverts.

Reading

An article with comments

LEARNING OUTCOME

✔ Guess meaning from context in a text

1 **Read and listen to the text. Do you know where these places are? How are they relevant to the article?** 61

- Clapham Common Underground Station
- Virginia
- Atlanta, Barcelona and Cape Town
- Times Square

Exercise 2

a) infrastructure (noun)
b) bombard (verb)
c) supporter (noun)
d) raise (money) (verb)
e) billboard (noun)

2 **Words in context** **Find these words in the text. Are they nouns or verbs? Match them with definitions a–e from the text.**

bombard billboard raise (money) supporter infrastructure

a) the structures and facilities needed for society to operate
b) to give someone so much information that it is difficult to deal with
c) someone who supports a particular idea or cause
d) to collect money for a particular purpose
e) a large board for adverts in an outside public place

Exercise 3

Suggested answers

advertising takeover = a situation where advertising takes control of a place
rescue cat = a cat that has been saved from a bad situation
marketing stunt = something done to get attention, in this case related to marketing
cat-crazy = unusually interested in or enthusiastic about cats
copy-cat campaign = a similar campaign, a copy of it
captive audience = a group of people who can't leave or look away

3 **Read the information. Then guess the meaning of these words and expressions from the text.**

- advertising takeover
- rescue cat
- marketing stunt
- cat-crazy
- copy-cat campaign
- captive audience

GUESS MEANING FROM CONTEXT

It isn't always possible to check a word in the dictionary (for example, in an exam), so it's important to guess its meaning using the context of the sentence and text.

- Think about the meaning of the words around it, and the type of word it is.
- Think about what you already know about the subject of the text.

4 **Copy and complete the sentences to make definitions for these cat-related words.**

1 C.A.T.S. is an acronym which means ...
2 A rescue cat is a cat that needs ...
3 A cat-crazy person is a person who ...
4 A copy-cat campaign is a campaign which ...

HOME BLOG RECENT FORUM

PURRFECTLY

FELINE FRIENDS TAKE OVER

Nowadays it seems we can't go anywhere without being bombarded with adverts for things we don't need. That's why a group of friends in London formed 'C.A.T.S.' (the Citizens Advertising Takeover Service), to create a space where people could take a break from all the ads. For two whole weeks, they replaced all 68 billboards at Clapham Common Underground Station with pictures of cats, cats … and more cats! They chose cats because they thought it would help the story to go viral. Plus, most of the cats on the billboards were real rescue cats which needed new homes, so this was a good way to lend a hand.

James Turner, founder of Glimpse, the group that organized the campaign, explained that they weren't trying to make money or sell anything. 'This isn't a clever marketing stunt for a pet food brand,' he told *The Independent* newspaper. 'The people behind it are volunteers who raised the money using Kickstarter.' In total, more than 700 people donated £23,000 to the crowd-funding campaign. Every supporter received a reward – from a cat-themed app for a £5 donation, to a photographic portrait of the pet whose owner gave £2,500. One cat-crazy supporter even flew to London from Virginia, USA, to see his pet on the giant billboard in the station!

WHAT DO YOU THINK? SHOULD ADVERTISING

Anny03 22 May @ 16:30

Yes – it's ugly to see ads everywhere. And it isn't fair because we can't choose whether to look at them or not – we're a captive audience!

CityBoy 22 May @ 16:52

Because of the fact that money from advertising is used to pay for public infrastructure, I think it's something which we have to accept. It benefits consumers as well as companies.

5 **Answer the questions.**

1 How many billboards at the tube station were replaced with pictures of cats?
2 How long were the cat pictures in the station?
3 Who is James Turner?
4 How much money was raised by the crowd-funding campaign?
5 How much money did supporters have to give to get a photographic portrait of their own pet?

Exercise 5

1 68
2 two weeks
3 the founder of Glimpse, the group that organized the campaign
4 £23,000
5 £2,500

Exercise 4

1 ... the Citizens Advertising Takeover Service.
2 ... a new home.
3 ... is very enthusiastic about cats.
4 ... will be the same.

Reading
An article with comments

LESSON OBJECTIVES
In this lesson students will:
- read an internet article with comments
- guess meaning from context

WARMER
Write *advertisement* on the board. Put students into pairs. They have to come up with as many words derived from it and use them in grammatically correct sentences as possible. The pair that produces more grammatically correct sentences in two minutes is the winner.

1 61
- Students read through the list of places first. Ask them to say where these places are.
- Read the second question to the class and ask them to read and listen and note down the answers.
- Play the audio. Students complete the task individually.
- Check answers as a class.

EXTRA ACTIVITY
Write these words from the text on the left of the board: **1** *stunt* **2** *donate* **3** *giant* **4** *volunteer*. Write definitions **a–d** on the right of the board: **a)** *something silly that people do in order to attract attention or impress other people* **b)** *someone who offers to help without being paid* **c)** *extremely large* **d)** *to give money to an organisation such as a charity*. Students work in pairs and match the words and definitions. (**Answer key: 1** a, **2** d, **3** c, **4** b)

CULTURE NOTE
The London underground (also known as the Tube), is the oldest underground railway in the world. The first line was opened in 1863 and it now consists of 11 main underground lines, plus six train lines and carries nearly 5 million passengers every day.

2 Words in context
- Ask students to find the words in the text. Encourage them to use the context to help them with the meaning and the word class of each word.
- They work individually to match the words with their definitions.
- They compare answers in pairs.
- Check answers as a class.

FINISHED?
Ask fast finishers to find examples of compound nouns and compound adjectives in the text on page 80, eg *crowd-funding*, *pet food*, *public space*, *peer pressure*.

READING STRATEGY
Guess meaning from context
Explain to students that being able to guess meaning from context is a key skill, as they won't always have access to a dictionary to check the meaning. The *Words in context* boxes on the Reading pages of *New Pulse* are specifically designed to help students develop this skill.

3
- Ask students to read the information from the Reading Strategy box and emphasize its importance for efficient reading.
- Put students into pairs. Ask them to read the text, find the given words and expressions and guess their meaning by using the context.
- Check answers as a class.

4
- Ask students to copy the sentence beginnings into their notebooks.
- They work individually and complete the sentences using the information in the text.
- They compare their answers in pairs.
- Check answers as a class.

5
- Ask students to read the questions carefully first and check they understand them all.
- They work individually and note down the answers.
- Check answers as a class.

6 • Point out that each answer should begin with *Because*.
- Students work individually and write the answers in their notebooks using the information in the text.
- Check answers as a class.

7 Word builder
- Ask students to read the information and highlight the importance of remembering *verb + noun collocations*. Give one or two further examples if necessary (eg *make a suggestion*, *do one's homework*, *take notes*).
- Students work individually. They find the examples in the text and match them to definitions a-c. Then they choose the best verbs to form collocations in question 2.
- Check answers as a class.

8 • Ask students to read the questions first and note down some ideas.
- Put them into pairs to ask and answer the questions.
- Listen to their ideas as a class.

DID YOU KNOW?

Highlight the *Did you know?* box. Students read about the magnitude of the exposure of the average American to adverts every day. Ask students if they are surprised by these figures.

CRITICAL THINKING

- Students draw two columns in their notebooks and label them *For* and *Against*. They decide which column the four comments belong to.
- They write a comment of their own and add it to the appropriate column.
- Listen to their ideas as a class.

WEB QUEST

Students search for more information about the C.A.T.S. stunt at the underground station.

1 **Investigate** Students open a search engine (eg Google) and search for information (including images and videos) about the C.A.T.S. takeover of the station.

2 **Communicate** Students share the information they found with a partner. They show their images and videos to the rest of the class.

TIP! Remind students that to look specifically for "images" or "videos" they should use the options under the search bar.

VIDEO: FLIPPED CLASSROOM

You may want to ask students to watch the Flipped classroom video for unit 8 as homework in preparation for the following grammar lesson. The Flipped grammar presentation focuses on relative pronouns.

The longer read > Resource centre

DID YOU KNOW?
Studies show that the average American is exposed to between 4,000 and 10,000 brand adverts every day.

PERSUASIVE… LONDON UNDERGROUND

The people behind C.A.T.S. just want us all to think about the power that ad agencies and brands have over us. They would like us to imagine a world where public spaces make us feel positive. 'We know this is a silly project,' adds James. 'But what if we did this in every major city in the world? Cats everywhere! From all this madness something amazing could happen.' And apparently, 'copy-cat' campaigns are planned in Atlanta, Barcelona and Cape Town!

BE BANNED IN PUBLIC SPACES?

GreenGreg 22 May @ 17:13
Ads can be so persuasive. They definitely shouldn't target young kids at an age when they're much too susceptible to peer pressure.

CatLover 22 May @ 18:22
No way! Not only do adverts make you smile, but they also add colour to ugly places. Imagine Times Square without those huge eye-catching signs!

6 **Answer the *Why …?* questions with *because* and ideas from the text.**
1 Why did a group of friends form C.A.T.S.?
2 Why did they choose to put photos of cats on the billboards?
3 Why did people donate to the campaign?
4 Why did one supporter fly to London?
5 Why do the people at C.A.T.S. want us to think about advertising?

Exercise 6
1 Because they thought people can't go anywhere without being bombarded with adverts for things we don't need.
2 Because they thought it would help the campaign go viral, plus most of the cats were rescue cats that needed new homes.
3 Because they received rewards for their donations.
4 Because they wanted to see their own cat on one of the giant billboards.
5 Because they want to bring awareness to the power ad agencies and brands have over us.

7 **Word builder** **Read the information and answer the questions.**

VERB + NOUN COLLOCATIONS
Certain verbs and nouns are often used together, for example:
take a break lend a hand receive a reward

1 **Find the examples in the text. Match them with definitions a–c.**
a) get a prize or gift
b) have a rest
c) help someone
2 **Which other verbs collocate with the nouns above? Choose the correct verbs.**
1 **be** / **have** a break
2 **give** / **take** (someone) a hand
3 **have** / **get** a reward

Exercise 7
1 a) receive a reward
b) take a break
c) lend a hand
2 1) have
2) give
3) get

8 **In pairs, ask and answer the questions.**
1 Are there adverts on public transport where you live?
2 Where do you see ads on an average day in your town?
3 Do you think it was a good idea to have pictures of cats instead of ads? Why (not)?

Exercise 8
Students' own answers

CRITICAL THINKING
CATEGORIZE
Read the comments. Categorize the arguments *for* and *against* banning ads in public places. Can you think of any more arguments?
Decide whether you are for or against banning ads in public places. Compose your own comment for the Comments section.

WEB QUEST
Works in pairs. Find images and videos about the C.A.T.S. takeover at Clapham Common tube station.
1 **Investigate** Each choose either images or videos. Search online specifically for either images or videos.
2 **Communicate** Share your results with your partner. Select the best images and videos to show to the class.

TIP! Remember to use the options under the search bar to look specifically for 'images' or 'videos'.

Grammar
Relative pronouns

VIDEO: FLIPPED CLASSROOM

WATCH

Watch the grammar presentation and do the task.

Exercise 1
1 after
2 whose
3 people – who, things – which, places – where, time – when
4 instead of who or which

1 Read sentences a–e in the table. Check the meaning of the relative pronouns. Then answer the questions.

who, which, where, when, whose

a) C.A.T.S. was a campaign **which** / **that** replaced adverts with photos of cats.
b) It was set up by a group of friends **who** / **that** lived in London.
c) They wanted to create a space **where** people could take a break from adverts.
d) We're bombarded with adverts **whose** slogans have become part of popular culture.
e) Advertisers shouldn't target children at an age **when** they're susceptible to peer pressure.

1 Do relative pronouns come before or after the noun they describe?
2 Which relative pronoun do we use for possession?
3 Which relative pronoun do we use for ... people? things? places? time?
4 When can we use *that*?

Exercise 2
1 where
2 which
3 whose
4 who
5 which
6 where

2 Copy and complete the questions with the correct relative pronouns. Then listen and check. Ask and answer the quiz questions. 62

What's the name of ...

QUIZ

- the country (1) ... H&M was set up?
- the South Korean brand (2) ... produces Galaxy phones?
- the tech company (3) ... logo is a fruit?
- the actor (4) ... promotes Nespresso coffee?
- the company (5) ... owns YouTube?
- the city (6) ... you can see the Piccadilly Circus adverts?

Indefinite pronouns

Exercise 3
1 affirmative
2 negative
3 affirmative

3 Look at the sentences in the table. Then choose the correct words in rules a–c.

some-, any-, no- compounds

You can't go **anywhere** without seeing adverts.
There's **nowhere** you can go to avoid the ads.
There should be **somewhere** you can go without advertising.
Is there **anywhere** you can go without seeing adverts?

a) We usually use *some-* in **affirmative** / **negative** sentences.
b) We use *any-* in **affirmative** / **negative** sentences and questions.
c) We use *no-* with **affirmative** / **negative** verbs.

Exercise 4
1 b
2 c
3 a
We use *anything*, *anyone* and *anywhere* in questions.

4 Match 1–3 with a–c. Which pronouns do we use in questions?

1 people	a) something, nothing, anything
2 places	b) someone, no one, anyone
3 things	c) somewhere, nowhere, anywhere

Exercise 5
1 anything
2 Nothing
3 something
4 somewhere
5 Someone

5 Copy and complete the dialogue with the pronouns in exercise 4.

A: Hi, Ben! Are you doing (1) ... on Saturday afternoon?
B: No, I don't think so. (2) ... in particular!
A: Do you want to come shopping with me? I need to buy (3) ... for Rob's birthday.
B: OK. Let's meet (4) ... for a coffee first.
A: Let's meet at the Green Café. (5) ... told me their cupcakes are delicious.
B: Sounds great! See you there at three o'clock?

Exercise 6
Students' own answers

6 Complete the sentences so they are true for you. Talk about your sentences with your partner.

1 ... is somewhere I often go shopping.
2 I never buy anything which ...
3 I don't know anyone who ...
4 ... is someone who I really admire.

ANALYSE

In English, we don't use 'double negatives'.
~~There isn't nothing to do.~~ ✗
There's nothing to do. ✓
What about in your language?

Grammar

Relative pronouns

LESSON OBJECTIVES

In this lesson students will:

- learn the use of different relative pronouns
- learn a set of indefinite pronouns
- do a speaking activity using indefinite pronouns

VIDEO: FLIPPED CLASSROOM

- If you set the video for homework, ask students to compare their Task time! answers and then check the answers as a class.
- If you didn't set it for homework, watch the video in class and answer the Task time! questions at the end of the presentation.

Answer key: **1** False **2** True **3** True

WARMER

Write the letters *wh-* on the board. Ask students to work in pairs and write six question words that begin with these letters. Elicit examples from the class and write them on the board: *who, what, which, when, where, whose*. Point out that five of these words can also be used as relative pronouns but that one cannot. Tell them that they will find out which word cannot be used as a relative pronoun (*what*) after doing the next exercise.

1
- Students read the examples. Check students understand the meaning of the relative pronouns.
- They answer questions 1–4.
- Check answers as a class.
- Highlight the fact that both *who* and *that* can be used to refer to people and *which* and *that* to things.
- If you are using the TPK and your students need more practice of the grammar, do the Grammar basics exercise.

Grammar basics

Answer key: **1** after **2** that **3** who **4** where **5** whose **6** when

2 62
- Encourage students to refer to exercise 1 to help them do the activity.
- They compare answers in pairs.
- Play the audio. Students check their answers.
- Students work in pairs and ask and answer the questions.

Indefinite pronouns

3
- Ask students to look at the examples in the table. They choose the correct words to complete the rules.
- Check answers as a class.
- If you are using the TPK and your students need more practice of the grammar, do the Grammar basics exercise.

Grammar basics

Answer key: **1** something **2** anything **3** nothing **4** somewhere **5** anywhere **6** nowhere **7** someone **8** anyone **9** no one

4
- Explain the task. Students match the pronouns with the words they refer to.
- Point out that we use indefinite pronouns to refer to people, places and things.
- Check answers. Highlight that *any-* is used in negative sentences and questions, eg *I can't see anything. Can you see anything?*

5
- Complete the first gap with the whole class as an example. Elicit that *anything* is used because it is a question.
- Check answers as a class.

6
- Complete the first sentence yourself as an example, eg *El Corte Inglés is somewhere I often go shopping.*
- Students complete the sentences with words and phrases that are true for them.
- They talk about sentences with a partner.
- Listen to some sentences as a class.

ANALYSE

Point out that affirmative verbs are used with indefinite pronouns beginning with *no-* because double negatives are not used in English. Students answer the question about double negatives in their language.

Grammar reference > Workbook page 98

Pronunciation lab > Difficult sounds: /s/ + consonant > Student's Book page 125

Vocabulary and listening

Easily confused verbs

LESSON OBJECTIVES

In this lesson students will:

- learn verbs that are often confused
- understand numbers and prices in radio adverts

WARMER

Explain that one of the two sentences you are going to write on the board is incorrect. Write: *He said he was tired* and *He told he was tired.* Elicit from the class that the second sentence is incorrect. Ask why and elicit that *tell* must be followed by an indirect object eg *He told me he was tired* or *He told the teacher he was tired.* Point out that *say* and *tell* are often confused.

DIGITAL VOCABULARY FLASHCARDS

In this digital presentation, students match the vocabulary with definitions.

- Do the digital presentation with the class.
- Encourage students to repeat the words.

1 63

- Do the first question with the whole class to demonstrate the activity.
- Students work individually and match the other verbs with the definitions.
- They compare answers in pairs. Check answers as a class.
- Play the audio. Students listen and repeat the words in blue.
- If you are using the TPK and your students need more work on the meaning of the words, do the Vocabulary basics exercise.

Vocabulary basics

Answer key: 1 waste **2** wait **3** earn **4** lend **5** watch **6** remind

2 • Ask students to choose the correct verbs. Encourage them to refer back to the definitions in exercise 1 to help them. Check answers.

- They write true answers for each of the questions.
- Do not ask students for their answers to the questions at this stage.

LANGUAGE NOTE

Remind can be used in two ways. If you say *Can you remind me to phone my brother later?* you are asking someone to tell you to do this so that you do not forget to do it. If you say *She reminds me of that famous actress on TV*, this means that she looks like the actress, so you think of that actress when you see her.

3 • Students work in pairs and ask and answer the questions from exercise 2.

- Ask different students each question and listen to some of their answers as a class.

4 • Ask students to look at the pictures. Elicit from the class what products or services the pictures show. Check answers.

5 64

- Explain that students will hear adverts for five of the items in exercise 4.
- Play the audio. Students do the task.

For audioscript, see page T84

6 • Ask students to read the example and explain that the numbers they will hear refer to different things and they should note these items down.

- Play the audio. Students do the task.
- Check answers as a class

7 • Ask students to read the questions first. Point out that they should answer with the number of the extract. Check answers.

EXTRA ACTIVITY

Use part of the audioscript as a dictation. Read advert 2 sentence by sentence. Students write down what they hear. Then invite individual students to come to the board to write each sentence. If there are mistakes, invite other students to come to the board and correct them.

Advance your vocabulary > Workbook page 110

Vocabulary and Listening

Easily confused verbs

LEARNING OUTCOME

✔ Understand numbers and prices in radio adverts

DIGITAL VOCABULARY FLASHCARDS

Do the matching exercise to discover the new vocabulary.

borrow earn hope lend remember remind see spend wait waste watch win

Exercise 1
1 **spend:** a) **waste:** b)
2 **wait:** a) **hope:** b)
3 **earn:** a) **win:** b)
4 **borrow:** a) **lend:** b)
5 **watch:** a) **see:** b)
6 **remind:** a) **remember:** b)

1 Match the verbs with meanings a) and b). Listen and repeat the words in blue. 63

1 spend / waste
a) use money to pay for things
b) use more of something than is necessary

2 hope / wait
a) stay in one place because something is going to happen
b) want or expect something to happen

3 win / earn
a) receive money for work that you do
b) finish first in a competition

4 borrow / lend
a) use something that belongs to someone else, and promise to return it later
b) give someone something for a short period of time

5 see / watch
a) look at something for a period of time
b) notice something or someone

6 remember / remind
a) tell someone again about something that they used to know
b) bring to mind a fact you knew before

Exercise 2
1 won
2 watch
3 borrow
4 wait
5 remember
6 spend

2 Choose the correct verbs. Then write true answers.

1 Have you ever **won** / **earned** a prize?
2 Did you **see** / **watch** anything on TV last night?
3 Do you ever **borrow** / **lend** books from the library?
4 How long would you **hope** / **wait** for friends if they were late?
5 How do you **remember** / **remind** new English words that you learn?
6 How much do you **spend** / **waste** on your mobile phone every month?

Exercise 3
Students' own answers

3 Work in pairs. Ask and answer the questions in exercise 2.

Have you ever ...?
Yes, I have. I ...

4 Look at pictures a–f. What kind of product or service are they related to?

Exercise 4
a) space travel
b) health/skin
c) technology/ computers
d) mobile phones/ communi- cation
e) entertainment/theme parks/ fun fairs
f) food/ eating/ hospitality

5 Listen to adverts 1–5. Match them with five of the pictures in exercise 4. 64

Exercise 5
1 f
2 d
3 e
4 c
5 a

6 Listen to the adverts again. What do these numbers and prices refer to?

14.99 = pounds (the price of a mega-pizza)

1 20 2 300 3 40
4 30 5 3

7 Answer the questions.

Which advert ...
a) is trying to persuade you to change your behaviour?
b) explains that you can order online or by phone?
c) is promoting something that you can't do / buy yet?
d) is selling a product with a 50% discount?
e) mentions a promotion where you can win something?

Exercise 7
a) 2
b) 1
c) 5
d) 4
e) 3

Vocabulary basics | Advance your vocabulary > Workbook p110

Exercise 6
1 minutes – under 20 minutes is the guaranteed pizza delivery time
2 mobiles – more than 300 mobile phones are stolen in London every day
3 pounds – a family ticket at the theme park costs only £40
4 per cent – about 30% of all PCs are infected with a virus
5 dimensions – you can watch the film in 3D

Life skills
Critical thinking

FACT! Some web browsers allow you to control the ads you see.

Exercise 1
Students' own answers

1 **Think about adverts you remember. What makes them memorable? Write a list.**

slogans, humour, jingles, ...

Exercise 2
Students' own answers

2 **Read the text. How many of your words in exercise 1 did you find?**

3 **Words in context** **Find these words in the text. What do they mean?**

catchy swipe mood bargain gender

Exercise 3
catchy: a tune or phrase that attracts your attention and is easy to remember.
swipe: to move your finger across the screen of a smartphone or tablet.
mood: the way somebody is feeling
bargain: something that costs much less than normal
gender: traditional division into male and female

4 **Match questions a–e with the key words in the text.**

- type
- tone
- focus
- attraction
- objective

a) Who is the target audience?
b) Is it an audio / video / interactive ad?
c) What attracts the consumer's attention?
d) Is it funny / emotional / serious?
e) Is the ad for a specific product or a brand?

Exercise 4
a) objective
b) type
c) attraction
d) tone
e) focus

5 **Work in pairs. Choose an advert from a magazine or website. Analyse your ads using the questions in the text. In your opinion, do the ads achieve their objectives?**

Exercise 5
Students' own answers

Analysing adverts

Have you ever seen an ad that suddenly appeared on your screen to remind you about something you were looking at the day before?

Now, adverts are increasingly integrated into our daily lives, and targeted to specific users. Advertisers 'track' our movements every time we interact online – clicking on links, talking to 'chatbots', helping ourselves to 'free' content.

The internet is so full of advertising that we need to put our critical thinking skills into action! Next time you see an ad, ask yourself the following questions ...

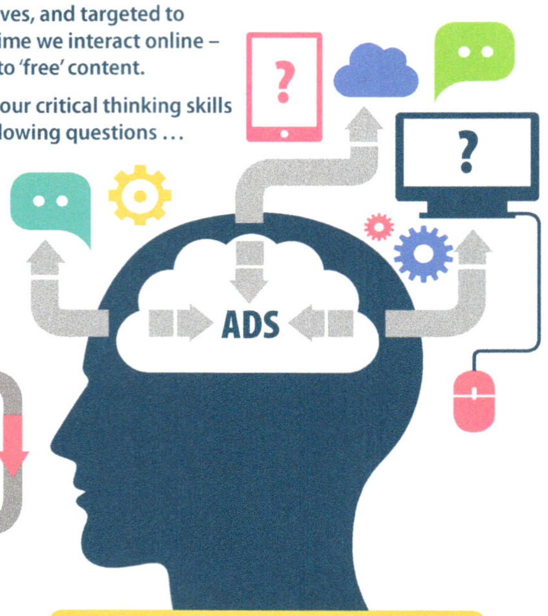

1 What TYPE of advert is it?
What can you see / hear? Are there any eye-catching images, logos or catchy jingles? Is it interactive – can you click / swipe / play?

2 What's the TONE?
What's the general 'mood' of the ad – is it funny or serious, silly or stylish? Is the language informative, emotional or both? Is there a bigger 'story', such as ambition, adventure or love?

3 What's the FOCUS?
Is the company hoping to earn your trust and persuade you to commit to the brand over time? Or are they just selling this product?

4 What's the ATTRACTION?
Does the ad make you feel that you're getting a bargain (e.g. 'buy one get one free')? Or do you identify yourself with the people in the ad ('cool', 'eco-friendly', etc)? If there are celebrities in the ad, why might that be?

5 What's the OBJECTIVE?
Does the ad target you specifically (for example, by age / gender / location)? If you use this product, will you become a 'walking advert' (e.g. by wearing clothing with a logo or carrying a particular brand of technology)?

Do you think the advert achieves its objectives? Does it make you want to spend money, and will you remember the advert and / or the brand?

Life skills
Critical thinking

LESSON OBJECTIVES
In this lesson students will:
- read a text about advertising
- analyse advertisements

WARMER

Write on the board the first two letters of four of the compound words from earlier lessons in this unit, eg *pe____ pr____, ad____ ca____, ey____ -ca____, ca____ au____.* Students work in pairs and complete the spelling of each of the compound words. Elicit the correct spelling from the class, making sure they pronounce the letters correctly in English. Write the complete compound words on the board. (**Answer key:** peer pressure, advertising campaign, eye-catching, captive audience)

FACT!

Students read the information in the Fact! box. Ask if they think that controlling the ads they can see is useful?

1 • Ask students to think about what makes adverts memorable. Read the examples and ask them to work individually and write a list. Do not check answers at this stage.

2 • Students read the text and see how many of the words in their list from exercise 1 they can find.
• Check answers as a class.

3 Words in context
• Read the words in the box aloud to the class.
• Students work individually to find the words in the text and guess their meaning from context.
• They compare answers in pairs.
• Check answers as a class.

4 • Explain that these five questions match the key words for different categories for analysing adverts.
• Students work individually and match the questions with the key words.
• They compare their answers in pairs.
• Check answers as a class.

5 • Put students into pairs.
• They choose and advert and analyse it using the five questions in the text.
• Listen to their ideas as a class.

64 Audioscript, page 83, exercises 5 and 6

1 **Man 1:** Why is Pizza Night the most popular pizza takeaway in town? Let us remind you! Could it be our delicious 18-inch mega-pizzas with extra toppings ... for only £14.99? Could it be the free soft drinks ... which come with every order? Could it be the guaranteed delivery ... in under 20 minutes?
Woman 1: Mmm ... nothing beats Pizza Night!
Man 1: Call 0880 1499, or order online at PizzaNight.com. And don't forget – you earn bonus points every time you spend!
Woman 1: Mmm ... it's Pizza Night!

2 **Man 2:** Would you walk down the street with £400 in your hand? Probably not! So why walk down the street with something worth £400 in your hand?! Not a good idea!
Woman 2: Don't let everyone see your phone. You can't see them but thieves are watching you ... More than 300 mobiles are stolen in London every day!
Man 2: Remember! Take care of your possessions! Don't be a target for thieves.

3 **Children:** Top Valley Towers – it's a whole new experience!
Woman 3: Top Valley Towers is now open for the new season! And this year we'll be celebrating fifty years of great family fun with three completely new rides and lots of fantastic special events!
Children: ... Big rides ... big thrills ... spend hours and hours ... at Top Valley Towers!
Woman 3: Top Valley Towers – the place where you get big fun with little prices! Don't wait till summer! Top Valley Towers is now open – hope to see you here soon!
Man 3: Limited offer ... Family ticket only £40 ... visit now for a chance to win a free annual pass!

4 **Woman 4:** Do I really need an anti-virus?
Sales assistant: Well – about 30% of all PCs are infected ... and at only £24.99, it's half price!
Woman 4: Great!
Man 4: Don't wait for a virus to attack your computer. Put a stop to online scams and phishing. For a limited period, our anti-virus software is only £24.99! Bug Attack anti-virus software. Don't waste money on cheap imitations! Bug Attack – the people who care ...
Woman 4: No-one's phishing in my PC!!

5 **Man 5:** Did you ever imagine you could be somewhere this beautiful?
Woman 5: It's unimaginable! I can't even begin to describe it ...
Man 6: Studio Film presents *The Red Planet*. Coming soon to a cinema near you.
Woman 5: What would happen to us ... you know, if something went wrong?
Man 5: Don't even think about it!
Man 6: From acclaimed director Petra Stone. Starring George Rooney and Melissa Miles. *The Red Planet*.
Man 5: Oh no, we're losing control ... we're going down ... Planet Earth? Can you hear me?
Man 6: Outer space as you've never seen it before. An adventure that goes beyond the boundaries of your imagination ... *The Red Planet*. See it soon in 3D.

Grammar
Reflexive pronouns

LESSON OBJECTIVES
In this lesson students will:
- learn reflexive pronouns
- read a text about a novel

WARMER
Write the question *Do you identify yourself with the people in the ad?* on the board with the words in the wrong order: *people yourself you do the ad in with identify the?* Students work in pairs and write the question in the correct order. Write the correct sentence on the board.

1 • Students read the examples.
- They work individually and complete the sentences in the table with singular and plural reflexive pronouns.
- They compare answers in pairs.
- Check answers as a class. Point out that indirect pronouns are formed by adding *-self* or *-selves* to object personal pronouns.
- If you are using the TPK and your students need more work on the meaning of the words, do the Grammar basics exercise.

Grammar basics
Answer key: 2 √ 3 √ 5 √

LANGUAGE NOTE
Point out that *buy* and *earn* can also be used without reflexive pronouns but that if you say *I bought myself a new phone*, you emphasize that you bought it and not someone else.

ANALYSE
Students answer the questions about reflexive verbs in their language. Point out that we can say *I washed myself* in English but if we do, we emphasize that we did it, not somebody else, so it is quite unusual to say this.

2 • Do the first sentence with the whole class as an example.
- Students work individually and complete the exercise using exercise 1 to help them.
- They compare answers in pairs.
- Check answers as a class.

3 • Explain the task. Point out that the reflexive pronoun in questions 5 will depend on whether the teacher is a man or a woman.
- Students work individually to complete the exercise.
- They compare answers in pairs.
- Check answers as a class. If you treat yourself to something, you buy something special to make you feel happy.

4 • Students work individually and write true answers to questions 1–6 in exercise 3.
- They work in pairs and ask and answer the questions.
- Check students' answers as a class by asking different students to answer each of the questions.

CLIL
Grammar in context: Literature

5 65
- This activity practises reflexive pronouns from this lesson and relative and indefinite pronouns from the previous grammar lesson.
- Ask students to read the whole text before they choose the correct answers.
- Students work individually to complete the exercise.
- They compare answers in pairs.
- Play the audio. Students listen and check their answers.

LITERATURE TASK
Students use the internet to find out more about John Steinbeck and answer the questions. Check answers.

Grammar reference > Workbook page 98

Pronunciation lab > Difficult sounds /ð/ and /θ/ > Student's Book page 125

Grammar
Reflexive pronouns

Exercise 1
1 himself
2 herself
3 ourselves
4 themselves

1 Copy and complete 1–4 in the table with *himself*, *herself*, *themselves* and *ourselves*.

singular	
I	I treated **myself** to a new T-shirt.
you	Ask **yourself** these questions.
he	My brother earned (1) ... £1,000.
she	My sister taught (2) ... Italian.
it	This TV turns **itself** off.
plural	
we	We enjoyed (3) ... at the party.
you	Did you behave **yourselves**?
they	They hurt (4) ... in an accident.

ANALYSE
How do you use reflexive verbs in your language? Is the form different for each subject?

Exercise 2
1 c
2 a
3 e
4 d
5 b

2 Match sentence beginnings 1–5 with endings a–e.

1 You could earn
2 David enjoyed
3 Babies can't look
4 Sandra saw
5 I didn't hurt

a) himself a lot.
b) myself.
c) yourself €100.
d) herself on TV.
e) after themselves.

Exercise 3
1 treat yourself
2 enjoy themselves
3 hurt yourself
4 behave themselves
5 talk to himself / herself
6 taught yourself

3 Copy and complete the questions with the correct form of the verbs in brackets and a reflexive pronoun.

1 If you had €100, what would you ... (treat) ... to?
2 Where do young people go to ... (enjoy) ... in your town?
3 Have you ever ... (hurt) ... in an accident?
4 Do your classmates always ... (behave) ...?
5 Does your teacher ever ... (talk to) ...?
6 Have you ever ... (teach) ... a new skill?

Exercise 4
Students' own answers

4 Write answers to the questions in exercise 3 so they are true for you.

If I had €100, I would treat myself and buy some new clothes.

CLIL
Grammar in context: Literature

5 Read the text and choose the correct answers. Then listen and check. 65

Exercise 5
1 B
2 C
3 B
4 B
5 A
6 B
7 B
8 C

The Pearl
by John Steinbeck

CAN POSSESSIONS MAKE US HAPPY?

John Steinbeck (1902–1968) was an American writer (1) … other novels include *The Grapes of Wrath* and *Of Mice and Men*. In *The Pearl*, Steinbeck considers how we persuade (2) … that material possessions will make us happy. It's a story (3) … considers themes like greed and exploitation. This book was published in 1947, at a time (4) … life was very difficult for many working people.

The story is about a man called Kino (5) … finds a huge pearl. At first, he's very happy because he plans to sell the pearl for a lot of money. But then (6) … in the village finds out about the pearl, and life becomes very difficult for Kino and his wife Juana. But I'm not going to tell you (7) … that happens – you'll have to read it for (8) … !

	A	B	C
1	who	whose	which
2	us	myself	ourselves
3	where	that	who
4	which	when	where
5	who	which	whose
6	no one	someone	anyone
7	everywhere	everything	nothing
8	myself	itself	yourself

LITERATURE TASK
Find out more about John Steinbeck.
- Where was he born?
- When did he win the Nobel Prize for Literature?
- Who was Charley in Steinbeck's book *Travels with Charley*?

INTEGRATED SKILLS

Charity adverts

LEARNING OUTCOME

✔ Use persuasion in a presentation

Today we're looking at the language of persuasion. We're preparing a group presentation to persuade people to support our charity fundraising.

TASK Use emotive language in a presentation

1 Read some adverts
2 Understand a team presentation
3 Write a presentation
4 Give a persuasive presentation

1 Read

1 Look at the adverts and answer the questions.

1 Which two charities have produced these adverts?
2 Which charity is fighting against censorship?
3 Which charity provides food and water to people in need?
4 How does each advert attract your attention? Think about:
- colours
- design
- language

5 In your opinion, which advert is more persuasive? Why?

Exercise 1
1 Oxfam and Amnesty International
2 Amnesty International
3 Oxfam
4 Students' own answers
5 Students' own answers

2 Read the adverts again. Find words or expressions that mean …

a) make you angry.
b) care about something.
c) the ability to say what you want.
d) the rights that everyone should have in a society.
e) when personal expression is not allowed for moral, religious or political reasons.

Exercise 2
a) drive you up the wall
b) give a monkey's
c) freedom of speech
d) human rights
e) censored

2 Listen

3 Read and listen to the presentation on page 87. Complete 1–5 with five of these words. 66

- £1 • 50p • 90% • 100%
- agree • disagree • poverty
- themselves • yourselves

Exercise 3
1 poverty
2 agree
3 50p
4 yourselves
5 100%

4 Listen again and repeat. Practise your intonation.

Exercise 4
Students' own answers

5 Watch or listen to another presentation by Oliver and Jack. Choose the correct answers. 67

1 Oliver and Jack are selling **notebooks** / **socks** / **T-shirts**.
2 Amnesty International was set up in **1961** / **1981** / **1996**.
3 Amnesty has got about **300,000** / **3 million** / **30 million** members.
4 Their product costs **£2.99** / **£5.00** / **£7.50**.

Exercise 5
1 T-shirts
2 1961
3 3 million
4 £5

6 Look at the Communication kit on page 87. Which phrases are used in the Speaking sketch? Watch or listen again to check your answers.

Exercise 6
We're sure you'll agree that …
Don't they look …?
Go on – treat yourselves!
We guarantee that …
Please …

Integrated skills
Charity adverts

LESSON OBJECTIVES
In this lesson students will:
- work on all four skills
- read two charity adverts
- watch or listen to a presentation persuading people to support a charity
- write and give a persuasive presentation

WARMER
Write *charity* on the board. Elicit some well-known charities from both the students' country and around the world, eg *WWF*, *UNICEF*. Elicit the kind of things charities often do.

1 Read

1
- Students read the questions carefully first. Check students understand censorship (the process of removing parts of books, films, newspapers, etc that are considered unsuitable for moral, religious or political reasons).
- They read the adverts and note down their answers. They compare answers.
- Check answers as a class.

CULTURE NOTE
Oxfam was originally founded in 1942 as the Oxford Committee for Famine Relief. It is now an international confederation of 17 organizations working in approximately 94 countries worldwide to find solutions to poverty and what it considers to be injustice around the world.

Amnesty International was founded in London in 1961 following a newspaper article about the abuse of prisoners in different countries. It draws attention to human rights abuses and campaigns for compliance with international laws and standards. Amnesty International was awarded the Nobel Peace Prize in 1977.

2
- Students to read the definitions carefully.
- They read the text again and find words or expressions that match these definitions.
- Check answers as a class. Point out that *drive you up the wall* is an idiom and *give a monkey's* is a slang expression that should not be used in formal speech or writing.

2 Listen

Video with audio option
The dialogue is also available to play as an audio file. If you prefer to present it this way, play the audio and follow the teacher's notes as for the video.

3 66 REC
- Students watch, read and listen to the presentation. They complete the presentation on page 87 with five of the words in the box.
- Check answers as a class.

For audioscript 66, see page T87

4
- Play the video again. Students watch and repeat and practise their intonation.

5 67
- Ask students to read the sentences and the different possible answers carefully first.
- Play the audio of another presentation by Oliver and Jack.
- Students listen and choose the correct answers.
- They compare answers in pairs.
- Check answers as a class.

6
- Ask students to look at the Communication kit on page 87 and read through the phrases.
- Play the audio again for students to check their answers.

67 Audioscript, page 86, exercise 5

Oliver: Hello! We're Oliver and Jack, and we're taking part in our school's Charity Fundraising Event this week. We're raising money for Amnesty International - a charity which promotes human rights around the world. Amnesty International supports freedom of speech and is against censorship on moral, religious or political grounds.
Jack: Yes – around the world there are countries which censor newspapers and magazines, the internet and even people's personal communications on social media. Amnesty International is a non-governmental organization which was set up in 1961, and it's now got more than 3 million members around the world. We're sure you'll agree that this is a fantastic cause!
Oliver: So that's why we've made these amazing T-shirts to persuade you to part with your cash and raise money for Amnesty! Don't they look fabulous? As you can see, they're available in two colours - black or white - and you can get them in three sizes (small, medium or large). They only cost £5 each, so go on, treat yourselves to a bargain!
Jack: Yes, and we guarantee that all our profits will go directly to Amnesty International. So, please buy a T-shirt today, and help promote human rights for everyone!

3 Write

7 • Ask students to work in pairs and decide which product they are going to sell to raise money for that charity and which charity they wish to support.
• Ask them to note down the product and the charity.

8 • Students work in pairs and prepare their presentation. Make sure they write two or three sentences for each of the four parts.
• Encourage them to use emotive language and the expressions in the Communication kit.

4 Communicate

9 • Read the example aloud to the class.
• Ask students to practise their presentations in pairs, with each person taking an equal part in the presentation.
• Monitor while they are working and give help if necessary.

10 • Each pair gives their presentation to the whole class.
• Ask students to decide which presentation was the most persuasive by taking a class vote.

! COMMUNICATION TIP
EMOTIVE LANGUAGE

Ask students to read the information in the Communication tip box. Highlight that extreme adjectives are often used in emotive language and point out that *People are starving* is much more emotive than *People are hungry.*

66 Audioscript, exercises 3, 4 and 6

Oliver: Hello! We're Oliver and Jack, and we're taking part in our school's Charity Fundraising Event this week. We're raising money for Amnesty International – a charity which promotes human rights around the world. Amnesty International supports freedom of speech and is against censorship on moral, religious or political grounds.
Jack: Yes – around the world there are countries which censor newspapers and magazines, the Internet, and even people's personal communications on social media. Amnesty International is a non-governmental organization which was set up in 1961, and it's now got more than 3 million members around the world. We're sure you'll agree that this is a fantastic cause!
Oliver: So that's why we've made these amazing T-shirts to persuade you to part with your cash and raise money for Amnesty! Don't they look fabulous? As you can see, they're available in two colours – black or white – and you can get them in three sizes (small, medium or large). They only cost £5 each, so go on – treat yourselves to a bargain!
Jack: Yes, and we guarantee that all our profits will go directly to Amnesty International. So, please buy a T-shirt today, and help promote human rights for everyone!
Katy: Hello! We're Katy and Emily, and we're taking part in the Charity Fundraising Event this week. We're raising money for Oxfam - a charity which fights poverty worldwide.
Emily: All around the world there are people who have nothing to eat, and nowhere to get clean water. We're sure you'll agree that helping them is a fantastic cause.
Katy: That's why we've made these delicious cupcakes to persuade you to part with your cash! Don't they look amazing? And they only cost 50p each. Go on – treat yourselves!
Emily: We guarantee that 100% of our profits will go directly to Oxfam. So, please buy a cupcake today, and help fight famine around the world!

Integrated skills > Resource centre

SPEAKING SKETCH

Hello! We're Katy and Emily, and we're taking part in the Charity Fundraising Event this week. We're raising money for Oxfam – a charity which fights (1) ... worldwide.

That's why we've made these delicious cupcakes to persuade you to part with your cash! Don't they look amazing? And they only cost (3) ... each. Go on – treat (4) ...!

All around the world there are people who have nothing to eat, and nowhere to get clean water. We're sure you'll (2) ... that helping them is a fantastic cause.

We guarantee that (5) ... of our profits will go directly to Oxfam. So, please buy a cupcake today, and help fight famine around the world!

Communication kit

- We're sure you'll agree that ...
- Don't they look ...?
- Go on – treat yourselves!
- We guarantee that ...
- Please ...
- You really should / ought to ...

3 Write

Exercise 7
Students' own answers

7 Work in pairs. Decide and make notes about:

- the product which you're going to sell
- the charity which you're going to support

Exercise 8
Students' own answers

8 Prepare your presentation. Write two or three sentences for each of the four parts of the presentation.

about you ▸ about your charity ▸ about your product ▸ final summary

4 Communicate

Exercise 9
Students' own answers

9 In pairs, practise your presentation. Work together and divide the presentation between you equally. Try to make improvements.

Hello! We're Marta and Javier, and we're ...

Exercise 10
Students' own answers

10 Now listen to all the presentations. Whose is the most persuasive?

! COMMUNICATION TIP
EMOTIVE LANGUAGE

Use emotive language to persuade people to do or buy something. Emotive language causes people to feel a strong emotion, like excitement or hunger.

Writing

A for and against essay

LEARNING OUTCOME

✔ Write a for and against essay about online advertising

debates online | HOME | DEBATES | OPINIONS | HEALTH

Should all adverts for unhealthy food be banned? Yes or No

1. In Britain, adverts for junk food and fizzy drinks are banned during children's TV programmes, although there are still ads on posters and the internet. Some doctors say that all these adverts should be banned, but there are arguments for and against this position.

2. One of the main arguments for banning these adverts is that they are contributing to childhood obesity. Britain has got one of the highest rates of childhood obesity in Europe. Furthermore, adverts for other unhealthy habits (such as smoking) are already banned.

3. On the other hand, companies have the right to advertise their products in order to promote their business. In addition, perhaps it is the responsibility of consumers to make their own decisions about buying the products which are advertised.

4. To sum up, I am in favour of banning adverts for unhealthy food, not only on TV, but also on the internet. Nevertheless, it is also important to educate people to make good decisions about the food which they choose to eat.

Exercise 1
1 c
2 d
3 b
4 a

1 **Focus on content** Read the essay and match paragraphs 1–4 with a–d.

a) conclusion
b) arguments against banning adverts
c) introduction
d) arguments for banning ads

Exercise 2
Addition: furthermore, ... in addition, ...
Contrast: although but on the other, hand ... nevertheless, ...

2 **Focus on language** Read the information. Copy and complete the table with the underlined words from the text.

Connectors of addition and contrast

addition	contrast
Moreover, ... not only ... but also ...	However, ...

Exercise 3
1 but
2 Furthermore
3 On the other hand
4 not only can you

3 Choose the correct connectors.

1. Online adverts are annoying, **but** / **moreover** they keep the content free.
2. Pop-up ads are a distraction. **Furthermore** / **Nevertheless**, they can be sexist.
3. On the one hand, online ads can be fun. **On the other hand** / **In addition**, they can waste time when you want to watch video clips.
4. On the internet, **although you can** / **not only can you** get ads which are targeted at you, but you can also click on them immediately.

4 Write a for and against essay about online advertising.

Exercise 4
Students' own answers

Writing kit

1 **Plan** your essay. Which of these arguments are *for* online advertising and which are *against*? How many more arguments can you think of?

- Pop-up ads are really annoying.
- They keep the content free.
- You get ads which are targeted at you.

2 **Write** four paragraphs. Use the model essay to help you.

1. introduce the topic
2. advantages of online advertising
3. disadvantages of online advertising
4. conclude with your personal opinion

3 **Useful phrases**

There are arguments for and against this position
One of the main arguments for ...
On the other hand, ...
To sum up, ...

4 **Check** your writing.

- ✔ connectors of addition and contrast
- ✔ vocabulary for advertising
- ✔ at least one relative pronoun
- ✔ four paragraphs

Study guide > p106 Writing hub > Workbook p126

Writing

A for and against essay

Study guide > Student's book page 106

Writing hub > Workbook page 126

LESSON OBJECTIVES

In this lesson students will:

- read a short for and against essay
- use connectors of addition and contrast
- write a for and against essay

WARMER

Write *TV advert* on the board. Ask students what kind of products are commonly advertised on TV. Elicit examples, eg *food*, *cars*. Ask if any products are not allowed in TV adverts in their country, eg *cigarettes*.

1 Focus on content

- Students read the for and against essay and match a–d to the paragraphs.
- Check answers as a class.

2 Focus on language

- Ask students to look at expressions in the table. Highlight the different functions of addition and contrast. If necessary, ask students to translate the expressions into their language.
- Students complete the table with the underlined words from the text.
- Check answers as a class.

3

- Students complete the task.
- Check answers as a class. Point out the inversion of subject/verb that occurs after *not only* and highlight that this does not happen after *but also*.

4

- Ask the students to follow the stages in the Student's Book.
- Encourage them to use the model essay for ideas.
- Monitor while they are writing and give help with vocabulary if necessary.
- At the Check stage, ask them to swap notebooks and check each other's writing.

Writing kit

The aim of this activity is for students to write a for and against essay using connectors of addition and contrast, and vocabulary for advertising. It also gives them practice in organizing paragraphs correctly.

UNIT 9

GET READY FOR YOUR EXAMS!

UNIT OBJECTIVES AND KEY COMPETENCES

In this unit the student will learn ...

- about what not to do in exams CLC SCC L2L
- good exam technique CLC SCC L2L
- about managing stress CLC SCC CAE L2L
- about improving your memory CLC SCC CMST
- about what memory is CLC CMST SCC
- about participating in a class debate by watching a short video CLC SCC CAE

In this unit the student will prepare for exams and learn how to ...

- revise vocabulary presented throughout the book CLC L2L
- revise vocabulary word-building techniques presented throughout the book CLC L2L
- revise reading strategies presented throughout the book CLC L2L
- revise grammatical structures and verb tenses studied throughout the book CLC L2L
- read an online forum about whether exams are the best way to assess people, listen to a class debate, prepare for and have a class debate CLC L2L SCC CAE
- write a formal email CLC CAE

LINGUISTIC CONTENTS

Main vocabulary

- Reporting verbs (revision)
- Phrasal verbs (revision)
- Adjectives and adverbs (revision)
- Easily confused words (revision)
- Noun suffixes (revision)

Grammar

- Tense review
- Gerunds and infinitives (revision)
- Conditionals (revision)
- Reported speech (revision)
- Verb tenses (revision)
- The passive (revision)

Functional language

- Expressing opinions

SKILLS

Reading

- Read a text about exam fraud
- Read a leaflet about managing exam stress
- Read a web debate about exams
- Read an informal email and a formal email

Writing: Interaction and production

- Write notes to prepare for a group debate about exams
- Write an email in three steps
- Revise techniques for improving writing skills

Listening

- Listen to a group debate about exams

Spoken interaction

- Ask and answer questions about what to do before, during and after an exam

Spoken production

- Prepare and participate in a group debate

LIFELONG LEARNING SKILLS

Self-study and self-evaluation

- Study guide: Student's Book page 107
- Progress check: Workbook page 78
- Extension: Workbook page 79
- Grammar reference and practice: Workbook pages 100–101
- Wordlist: Workbook pages 151–157

Learning strategies and thinking skills

- Revision of reading, listening and communication strategies
- Critical thinking: summarising and evaluating information
- Revision of writing techniques studied throughout the book
- Study strategies for effective revision and developing efficient study habits

Cross-curricular contents

- Exams
- Literature: information about Charles Dickens and his novels
- ICT: searching the internet for information

EVALUATION

- Unit 9 End-of-unit test: Basic, Standard and Extra
- CEFR Skills Exam Generator
- End-of-term test, Units 7–9: Basic, Standard and Extra
- End-of-year test: Basic, Standard and Extra

KEY COMPETENCES

CLC Competence in linguistic communication
CMST Competence in mathematics, science and technology
DC Digital competence
SCC Social and civic competence
CAE Cultural awareness and expression
L2L Learning to learn
SIE Sense of initiative and entrepreneurship

DIGITAL MATERIAL

New Pulse Digital Course including:

- Interactive vocabulary presentation
- Grammar and Vocabulary basics exercises
- Getting started video
- Flipped classroom grammar video
- Culture byte video: Revision rap
- Speaking sketch video: A formal interview

DIGITAL COMPETENCE

- Digital competence worksheet: Mind maps and word clouds

REINFORCEMENT MATERIAL

- New Pulse Basics: Teacher's Resource Centre
- Vocabulary and grammar consolidation worksheets: Teacher's Resource Centre
- Grammar and Vocabulary basics exercises: Teacher's Presentation Kit

EXTENSION MATERIAL

- Vocabulary and grammar extension worksheets: Teacher's Resource Centre
- Advance your vocabulary: Workbook page 111
- The longer read: Teacher's Resource Centre
- Writing hub: Workbook page 128

TEACHER'S RESOURCE MATERIAL

- Translation and dictation worksheets
- Evaluation rubrics
- Key competences worksheets
- Culture and CLIL worksheets
- Culture byte video worksheets
- Digital competence worksheets
- Macmillan Readers worksheets
- Integrated Skills

Review quiz
TEST YOURSELF!

LESSON OBJECTIVES

In this lesson students will:

- test themselves to see how much they remember about the content of the lessons they read in New Pulse 4.

VIDEO: GETTING STARTED

In this video, two students answer the question *What do you think is the best way to prepare for exams?*

- Focus the students on the unit title *Get Ready for Your Exams!*
  Write these gapped sentences on the board: **1** Who thinks removing distractions is important? **2** Who says it is important to eat and sleep well before an exam? **3** Who usually studies with his / her friends?
  Students watch the video and complete the gapped sentences.
- They watch the video again to check their answers.

At the end of the lesson, ask students to answer the question from the video: *What do you think is the best way to prepare for exams?*

Answer key: 1 Olivia **2** Josh **3** Harry

WARMER

Books closed. Ask: *Which was your favourite Unit? Why?* Start a class discussion. Which was the class favourite unit?

1
- Ask students to work individually and answer as many questions as they can without looking back in the book.
- Encourage them to guess the answers to multiple choice questions if they do not remember the answer.
- Ask students to check their answers in pairs. Allow them to include any missing answers by going through the book.
- Check answers as a class.

FINISHED?

Ask fast finishers to write three more questions for the quiz. They could do this individually or in pairs. Check their questions before asking them to the rest of the class.

GET READY FOR YOUR EXAMS!

UNIT 9

LEARNING OUTCOMES IN THIS UNIT

- Review grammar, vocabulary and topics from the course
- Practise reading strategies
- Participate in a debate
- Write to an institution

VIDEO: GETTING STARTED

WATCH

Watch the teenagers talking about exam preparation and answer the question.

Exercise 1

1 c) Frida
2 A young magician; Sarah Jade
3 Royal National Lifeboat Institution; save lives at sea
4 An affordable, flat-pack 3D printer
5 True
6 Casino Royale
7 b) Turkey
8 **Possible answers:** things you upload online; emails you send; websites you visit
9 Canada
10 430 km/hr
11 a) Henry Ford
12 True
13 Trap House
14 c) Clapham Common
15 Nepal
16 £4.20
17 Huntsville, Alabama
18 False – it was in 1989
19 British Films Institute; courses related to all areas of film-making
20 William Shakespeare

Review quiz

1 Read the quiz and answer the questions. How much of New Pulse can you remember?

TEST YOURSELF!

How much do you remember from New Pulse 4?

1. Which rescue dog found 12 survivors in Mexico City?
   a) Bonny
   b) Little
   c) Frida
2. Who is Leah Mae Devine and what is her sister's name?
3. What does the acronym RNLI mean, and what does this organization do?
4. Young engineer Josh Mitchell won an award at 'The Big Bang' STEM fair. What kind of machine did he design?
5. True or false? More than 2 billion people around the world use a smartphone.
6. What's the name of the first James Bond Story?
7. In which country are the unusual rock formations of Cappadocia?
   a) Russia
   b) Turkey
   c) Peru
8. Give three examples of things that make up your digital footprint.
9. Which country is the young activist and blogger Hannah Alper from?
10. How fast does a Maglev train travel?

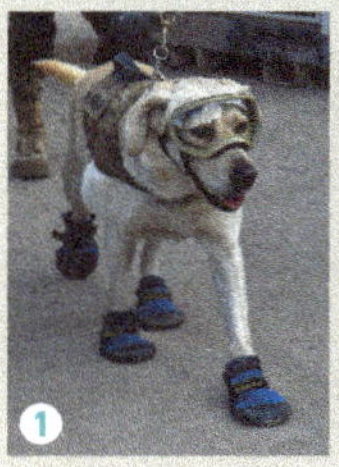

1

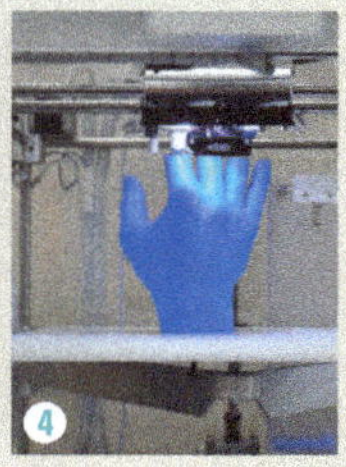

4

7

10

14

17

11. Who opened the first car factories in the USA in 1908?
    a) Henry Ford
    b) Mercedes Benz
    c) Toyota Yaris
12. True or false? About 90,000 15–17-year-olds take part in NCS (National Citizen Service) in the UK every year.
13. With which rap star did Isaiah Acosta collaborate on the song *Oxygen to Fly*?
14. Which London underground station was taken over by cats for two weeks?
    a) Piccadilly Circus
    b) Baker Street
    c) Clapham Common
15. In which country was Matt Moniz climbing when an earthquake caused a huge avalanche?
16. What's the national minimum wage per hour for 16-year-olds in the UK?
17. Where does the Space Academy summer camp take place?
18. True or false? The World Wide Web was invented in 1999.
19. What does the acronym BFI mean, and what kind of courses do they organize?
20. Who wrote the comedy *A Midsummer Night's Dream*?

Vocabulary review

Revision

TIP!

During the course, you've learnt lots of new vocabulary. You've also studied different word-building techniques to expand your vocabulary. Review them regularly!

Exercise 1
1 c
2 e
3 b
4 d
5 f
6 a

1 Match 1–6 with a–f.

1 reporting verbs
2 phrasal verbs
3 extreme adjectives
4 adverbs of degree
5 adverbs of manner
6 noun suffixes

a) endings (eg -*ness*) that are added to words to make new nouns
b) words that are stronger than normal adjectives
c) verbs that are used to report what someone said previously
d) words that tell us the intensity of something
e) a verb and a particle that have a different meaning together than the verb alone
f) words that modify a verb to tell us how something is done

Exercise 2
1 fill in
2 huge
3 apply to
4 appearance
5 asked, admitted, said
6 quietly / successfully, well

2 Read the text and find ...

1 a phrasal verb.
2 an extreme adjective.
3 a verb that collocates with 'university'.
4 one noun suffix.
5 at least two reporting verbs.
6 one regular and one irregular adverb of manner.

Reporting verbs

Exercise 3
1 told
2 said
3 complained
4 asked
5 agreed
6 suggested

3 Choose the correct words.

1 Our teacher **promised** / **told** / **suggested** us to revise for a test tomorrow.
2 She **asked** / **refused** / **said** that we had to learn all the vocabulary.
3 We **complained** / **offered** / **convinced** that there wasn't enough time.
4 We **admitted** / **asked** / **said** her to give us time to revise.
5 She **suggested** / **agreed** / **invited** to postpone the test until Monday.
6 They **convinced** / **told** / **suggested** that we bring an extra pencil.

Phrasal verbs

Exercise 4
1 after
2 up, on
3 out
4 out
5 off

4 Copy and complete the sentences with these words. There is one extra word.

• on • up • in • out • out • after • off

1 Look ... yourself during the exam period. Make sure you eat and sleep well.
2 Meet ... with the classmates you get ... with best and study together.
3 Revising is hard work! Make sure you also allow time to hang ... with your friends and family.
4 Don't go ... the night before an exam.
5 Turn ... your mobile during the exam.

Exams ... what NOT to do!

A 52-year-old French woman posed as her 19-year-old daughter to take part of the Baccalaureat exam for her. The woman, identified as 'Caroline D', dressed in jeans and trainers, and wore make-up in an attempt to change her appearance. She managed to enter the exam hall and fill in her daughter's personal information on the examination paper. She then began the three-hour English exam.

Things were going well for the fraudster until an invigilator became suspicious. He alerted the police and quietly asked the woman to leave. She was taken to a police station, where she admitted that she had cheated and said that she only wanted to help her daughter.

The Baccalaureat is the final exam which French students must complete successfully before applying to university. Stress can be a huge problem for teenagers taking the 'Bac', and some parents are prepared to take desperate measures!

Vocabulary review

Revision

LESSON OBJECTIVES

In this lesson students will:

- revise reporting verbs, phrasal verbs, extreme adjectives, adverbs of frequency, adverbs of degree, adverbs of manner, easily confused words and noun suffixes

WARMER

Introduce the topic. Write *exam* on the board. Ask students what this word is short for and elicit the word examination. Ask students to find four verbs that collocate with the word exam. Elicit *take an exam*, *sit an exam*, *pass an exam* and *fail an exam*. Point out that *sit an exam* and *take an exam* have the same meaning.

1
- Highlight the Tip! box.
- Explain that 1–6 are different areas of vocabulary that have been studied in this book.
- Students work individually and match examples a–f with the different vocabulary categories 1–6.
- They compare answers in pairs.
- Check answers as a class.

2
- Remind students that when words collocate, they go together. Give one or two examples, eg *do homework*, *make friends*.
- Explain the task. Students work individually and find examples of the different word categories in the text.
- Check answers as a class.

CULTURE NOTE

The Baccalaureat (Bac) is an academic qualification which French students take at the end of their secondary education. It was introduced by Napoleon in 1808 and is the main diploma that students need if they want to study at university. The International Baccalaureate (IB) is a set of exams that is used in many countries as a qualification for going to university.

Reporting verbs

3
- Point out that there is a choice of three reporting verbs in each sentence and only one is correct.
- Students work individually to complete the task.
- They compare answers in pairs.
- Check answers as a class. Point out that if you tell someone to do something, this is an instruction.

Phrasal verbs

4
- Note that some of the given words are from the set of phrasal verbs in Unit 4, but others are general revision.
- Read the instructions aloud to the class and highlight that three of the particles are not used, but that two are used twice.
- Students work individually to complete the task.
- They compare answers in pairs.
- Check answers as a class.

Adjectives and adverbs

5 • Ask students to read all the words in the word pool.
• Students choose the correct words to fill the gaps in the sentences.
• They compare answers in pairs.
• Check answers as a class. Remind students that we use *absolutely* with extreme adjectives, eg *absolutely terrifying* and *very* with ordinary adjectives, eg *very nice*.

FINISHED?

Write these adverbs and adjectives on the board: *extremely, thoroughly, seldom, worrying, really*. Ask students to complete the sentences in exercise 5 using these adverbs. Note that in sentence 4, the word carefully should be replaced by one of these adverbs. (**Answer key**: **1** seldom **2** really **3** worrying **4** thoroughly **5** extremely)

Easily confused words

6 • Remind students that they studied these words in the Starter unit and in Unit 8 and that they are words that are often confused.
• Students choose the correct words to fill the gaps in the sentences.
• Check answers as a class. Highlight that *lend* = *give* and *borrow* = *take*.

FINISHED?

Ask fast finishers to write five sentences using the words that are not used in each pair in exercise 6, eg *I watched an interesting film last night.*

Noun suffixes

7 • If you think this might be too difficult for some students, write the different suffixes in random order on the board: *-ment*, *-ship*, *-ness*, *-ance*, *-ion*.
• Students work individually and write the nouns with suffixes in the table.
• They compare answers in pairs.
• Check answers as a class.

8 • Point out that the words used to fill the gaps can either be from the root word column in the table or from the noun with suffix column.
• Encourage students to read the whole text before they begin.
• They work individually and complete the exercise.
• Check answers as a class.

9 68
• Highlight the Tip! box and encourage students to get apps to help them with the pronunciation of new vocabulary.
• Ask students to read the title of the text. Elicit that the text contains good advice about exams.
• Encourage students to read the whole text before they begin.
• They work individually and choose the correct words 1–10.
• They compare answers in pairs.
• Play the audio. Students listen and check their answers.
• If you are using the TPK and your students need more work on the meaning of words, do the Vocabulary basics exercise.

Vocabulary basics

Answer key: 1 A **2** C **3** B **4** A **5** B **6** C **7** A **8** A

Advance your vocabulary > Workbook page 111

Adjectives and adverbs

Exercise 5
1 rarely
2 absolutely
3 terrifying
4 Always
5 very
adjective: terrifying
adverb of **frequency:** rarely
adverb of **manner:** carefully
adverbs of degree: very, absolutely

5 **Copy and complete the sentences with these words. Which one is an adjective? Are the other words adverbs of frequency, manner or degree?**

- very
- absolutely
- terrifying
- rarely
- always

1. People ... cheat in exams – it's too risky.
2. The exam didn't finish until 4pm. I was ... starving at the end!
3. Exams can be ... for people who suffer from exam phobia.
4. ... read all the exam questions carefully before you try to answer them.
5. The test was ... difficult – will I pass?

Easily confused words

Exercise 6
1 wait
2 borrow
3 waste
4 see
5 trip

6 **Copy and complete the sentences with one word from each pair.**

- wait / hope
- see / watch
- lend / borrow
- trip / voyage
- spend / waste

1. Plan your revision now. Don't ... until the day before the exam!
2. It's useful to ... revision guides from the library.
3. Don't ... time. Stick to your study goals!
4. Take notes while you're revising. It's helpful to ... the information in your own handwriting.
5. Enjoy your end-of-year ... after the exams!

Noun suffixes

Exercise 7
1 awareness
2 education
3 employment
4 importance
5 citizenship

7 **Copy and complete the table.**

root word	noun with suffix
national (adj)	*nationality*
aware (adj)	(1) ...
educate (v)	(2) ...
employ (v)	(3) ...
important (adj)	(4) ...
citizen (n)	(5) ...

Exercise 8
2 awareness
3 education
4 employment
5 important
6 citizen

8 **Copy and complete the text with words in exercise 7.**

To obtain citizenship in the UK, immigrants of another (1) *nationality* have to take an exam called 'Life in the UK'. Candidates must learn about British culture. For example, you must have an (2) ... of the British (3) ... system (schools and universities) and (4) ... regulations (such as workers' rights). Knowledge of the English language is also very (5) ... There are 24 questions, and you must answer 18 correctly. Then you can become a British (6) ...!

TIP!
You can get apps to help you practise the pronunciation of new vocabulary. Try downloading 'Sounds: the Pronunciation app' to your smartphone or tablet.

9 **Choose the correct words. Then listen and check.** 68

Exercise 9
1 absolutely
2 found out
3 aware
4 hoped
5 take
6 remembered
7 tell
8 to cancel
9 complained
10 noisy

Exam horrors

A monstrous mistake

A Level students at Newmarket College in Suffolk, England, were (1) **very / absolutely** horrified when they (2) **found out / gave up** that they had been taught the wrong book. Apparently, teachers weren't (3) **awareness / aware** that the exam text was *Frankenstein* not *Dracula*. Students received a five-hour intensive class days before the exam, and then (4) **waited / hoped** that the questions would be easy!

Singing socks

A student at Sheffield University was about to (5) **take / make** his final exam when he realized that he didn't have any clean socks to wear. Then he (6) **remembered / recorded** that he had received a pair of funny Rudolph socks for Christmas. The invigilator had to (7) **say / tell** him to take them off when they started playing the *Rudolph the Red-Nosed Reindeer* song half-way through the exam!

Pigeons cause chaos

Officials decided (8) **cancelling / to cancel** a final exam at Bangor University in Wales when pigeons flew into the exam room. Students (9) **complained / convinced** that it was impossible to concentrate because the birds were very (10) **noisy / noisily**. The university apologized to students and the exam was rescheduled.

Vocabulary basics
Advance your vocabulary > Workbook p111

Reading

A leaflet

LEARNING OUTCOME

✔ Practise reading strategies

Exercise 1
time management, healthy eating, taking exams

TIP!

During the course, you've studied different strategies to improve your reading, and you've done many different types of comprehension activity. Keep practising these different techniques!

Reading strategies

Predicting content

Exercise 2
1 b
2 a
3 e
4 c

1 Read the title of the text and look at the photo. Which three of these things do you think you'll read about?

- time management
- assertiveness
- healthy eating
- advertising
- taking exams
- identity theft

Skimming the text

Exercise 3
1 manage your time effectively, plan ahead, make a revision timetable, vary the subjects so you don't get bored
2 snack on bananas instead of sweets, drink plenty of water, avoid coffee, aim to sleep eight to ten hours a night
3 a teacher, doctor or counsellor
4 find out where the exam is and how to get there, prepare your bag, set your alarm

2 Read the text quickly. Complete 1–4 with headings from a–e. There is one extra heading that you don't need.

a) How to stay healthy and beat exam nerves
b) How to revise
c) What to do during and after the exam
d) How to obtain sample papers
e) What to do the day before and the morning of your exam

Scanning for specific information

3 Read and listen to the text. Then find: 69

1 at least four things to help you revise
2 at least four ways of keeping healthy
3 three people you could ask for help
4 three things you should do the night before an exam

4 Words in context Find these words in the text. Then write definitions using *who*, *which* or *where* and the words in brackets.

A revision timetable is a plan which helps you to revise.

revision timetable (plan)
revision app (mobile application)
sample papers (practice exams)
gym (place) counsellor (person)
invigilator (person)

HOW TO … keep calm and pass exams!

Follow these tips before, during and after the exam.

Before the exam: revision and preparation

1 …

Managing your time effectively is essential for good revision. Plan ahead – don't wait until the last minute! Make a revision timetable and find the revision techniques that work for you, varying the subjects so that you don't get bored. Online revision apps can be useful, but remember that people still used to pass exams before mobile phones were invented! So try turning off your phone to avoid getting distracted.

TOP TIP:
Find out exactly what type of activities will be in the exam, and do sample papers if possible.

2 …

A healthy diet and plenty of sleep are essential to exam success. Instead of snacking on sweets, experts suggest bananas for a sustained energy boost. You'll lose concentration if you're dehydrated, so drink plenty of water – but avoid coffee because caffeine is no substitute for proper rest. You should aim to sleep eight to ten hours a night, and stop studying two hours before bedtime. Physical exercise is also important – not only does it improve concentration, but it also reduces stress. So keep a good study / life balance – you don't have to give up the gym or time with friends. Take regular breaks and use those activities as motivational 'treats'.

TOP TIP:
If you're feeling anxious about exams, ask a teacher, doctor or counsellor for help.

Exercise 4
A **revision app** is a mobile application which can be useful.
Sample papers are practice exams which you could use to practice different types of activities.
The **gym** is a place where you can do physical exercise.
A **counsellor** is a person who you can talk to if you're feeling anxious.
An **invigilator** is a person who watches over the students sitting the exam.

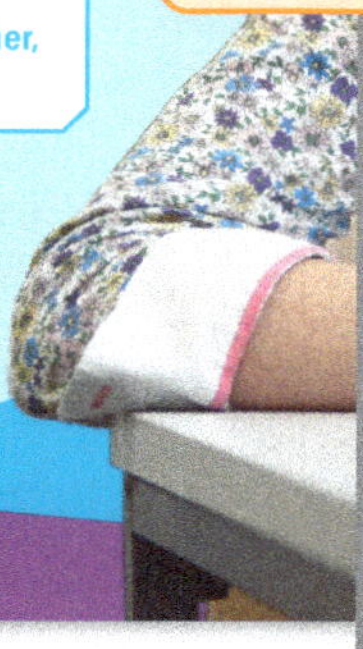

Reading
A leaflet

LESSON OBJECTIVES
In this lesson students will:
- revise reading strategies
- read a text about the key to success in exams

WARMER
Books closed. Write these reading strategies on the left of the board: **1** *predicting* **2** *skimming* **3** *scanning* **4** *words in context.* On the right of the board, write definitions **a–d: a)** *working out the meaning of unknown words* **b)** *using pictures, titles, etc to imagine what the text will be about* **c)** *reading the text quickly to get a general idea* **d)** *reading the text quickly to find specific information.* Ask students to work in pairs and match the reading strategies and the definitions. Check answers as a class. (**Answer key: 1** b, **2** c, **3** d, **4** a)

Reading strategies
Predicting content

1
- Highlight the Tip! box.
- Ask students to read the title of the text and look at the photo.
- They read the six topics and choose the three things they predict they will read about in the text.
- They compare answers in pairs.
- Check answers as a class.

Skimming the text

2
- Remind students that skimming the text means reading quickly to get a general idea of content from key words.
- Students read the text and match the headings with the paragraphs.
- Check answers as a class.

EXTRA ACTIVITY
Write these words from the text on the left of the board: **1** *vary* **2** *dehydrated* **3** *oversleep* **4** *alarm.* Write definitions **a–d** on the right of the board: **a)** *a clock that wakes you up at a particular time* **b)** *feeling weak or ill because you don't have enough water in your body* **c)** *to make changes to something to make it more interesting* **d)** *to wake up later than you intended to.* Students work in pairs and match the words and meanings. (**Answer key: 1** c, **2** b, **3** d, **4** a)

Scanning for specific information

3 69
- Ask students to read the things they need to find carefully first.
- Play the audio. Students listen and follow the text in their books.
- They note down the answers.
- Check answers as a class.

4 Words in context
- Read the example definition aloud to the class and show how the definition is formed using the word in brackets.
- Students find the other words in the text and write definitions for them.
- Monitor while they are writing and give help if necessary.
- They compare answers in pairs.
- Check answers as a class.

Comprehension activities

5
- Ask students to read the questions and the different answers carefully first.
- They read the text again and choose the correct answers, noting down words or phrases that helped them choose the correct answers.
- Check answers as a class. Make sure students give evidence for each answer.

6
- Ask students to read all the sentences carefully first.
- Point out that some may not be mentioned at all in the text.
- Students work individually to complete the exercise.
- They compare answers in pairs.
- Check answers as a class.

7
- Emphasize that students should answer these questions in their own words and not simply copy sections of text.
- Monitor while they are writing and give help if necessary.
- Listen to their answers as a class. Nominate different students to read out their answers.

CRITICAL THINKING

- Students work individually and choose three pieces of advice from each paragraph.
- They decide which four of these pieces of advice are the most important. Ask students to compare their list with a partner and then listen to their ideas as a class.

VIDEO: CULTURE BYTE

This video is about traditional methods versus modern, fun and effective ways to revise. For exploitation and comprehension practice based on this video, see the Culture byte video worksheets on the Resource Centre.

VIDEO: FLIPPED CLASSROOM

You may want to ask students to watch the Flipped classroom video for unit 9 as homework in preparation for the following grammar lesson. The Flipped grammar presentation focuses on revision of grammatical forms.

The longer read > Resource centre

Are you ready for exam day?

3 ...

Make sure you know exactly when the exam will be held, and find out how to get there if it isn't at your school. Prepare your bag the night before – you'll sleep better if you know that everything is ready. It goes without saying that you shouldn't go out the night before your exam, but neither should you stay up late revising! Try to switch off and have an early night, and set your alarm to avoid oversleeping.

TOP TIP:
Be sure to double-check the start time of your exam!

4 ...

When you're about to start the exam, read all the questions carefully and calculate how much time to dedicate to each section. If you don't understand the instructions, tell the invigilator straight away. After the exam, don't waste time comparing answers – it would be more effective if you had a good rest before preparing for your next exam.

TOP TIP:
Think positively and don't give up. Good luck!

Comprehension activities

5 Choose the correct answers. Find evidence in the text to support your choices.

1 Mobile phones ...
a) should be used in exams.
b) are a good way of preparing for exams.
c) can be a distraction during revision.

2 Caffeine ...
a) is not recommended.
b) is a substitute for sleep.
c) causes dehydration.

3 The night before an exam, you should ...
a) revise as much as possible.
b) remember to set your alarm.
c) go out with your friends.

4 After an exam you should ...
a) read the questions carefully.
b) check the answers.
c) have a rest.

6 Is the information true, false or not mentioned in the text?

1 It's a good idea to do sample papers before an exam.
2 Sweets are a good snack because they provide a sustained energy boost.
3 You shouldn't talk to your friends the night before an exam.
4 You should ask another student if you don't understand the instructions.

7 Answer the questions in your own words. Write full sentences.

1 Does the writer recommend using apps?
2 How much sleep should you try to get while you're doing exams?
3 What should you double-check the night before an exam?
4 What's the first thing you should do in an exam?

CRITICAL THINKING

SUMMARIZE AND EVALUATE INFORMATION

Summarize the advice given in the text. Write a list of three important pieces of advice from each paragraph.
Evaluate the advice. Which four would *you* choose for the 'Top Tips'?

VIDEO: CULTURE BYTE

WATCH
Watch the video supplied by BBC.

Exercise 5
1 **c** – 'people still used to pass exams before mobile phones were invented! So try turning off your phone to avoid getting distracted.'
2 **a** – 'avoid coffee because caffeine is no substitute for proper rest.'
3 **b** – 'set your alarm to avoid over sleeping.'
4 **c** – 'it would be more effective if you had a good rest before preparing for your next exam.'

Exercise 6
1 True
2 False
3 Not mentioned
4 False

Exercise 7
Students' own answers

Grammar
Revision

VIDEO: FLIPPED CLASSROOM

WATCH — Watch the grammar presentation and do the task.

Review of grammar forms

Exercise 1
1 d
2 c
3 b
4 e
5 j
6 a
7 i
8 h
9 g
10 f

1 Match questions 1–10 with grammar forms a–j. Then write answers. Remember to use the correct tenses and grammatical structures.

YOUR SCHOOL DAYS ... HAPPY MEMORIES?

1 Which primary school did you use to go to before this school?
2 Had you already learnt to read before you started school?
3 Which year of your education have you enjoyed the most?
4 Were you ever told off by one of your teachers?
5 If you had had the opportunity to go to any school, where would you have gone?
6 Are you studying any subjects this year which you really enjoy?
7 If you could change one thing about your school, what would it be?
8 Do you think you might stay at this school next year?
9 When will you be taking your last obligatory exam?
10 Which of your teacher(s) will you always remember?

a) present continuous
b) present perfect
c) past perfect
d) *used to*
e) past passive
f) *will / won't*
g) future continuous
h) modals
i) second conditional
j) third conditional

Exercise 2
Students' own answers

2 In pairs, ask and answer the questions in exercise 1. Make notes using reported speech.

I asked Fatima which primary school she used to go to, and she told me ...

Gerunds and infinitives

3 Complete the text with the infinitive with *to* or gerund form of the verbs in brackets.

Exercise 3
1 to improve
2 to exercise
3 learning
4 to keep
5 Spending
6 eating
7 to remember
8 to get

HOW TO IMPROVE YOUR MEMORY!

A good memory depends on the health of your brain. Here are some things you can do (1) … (improve) your mental performance:

GIVE YOUR BRAIN A WORKOUT
Like muscles, you need (2) … (exercise) your brain! Do this by (3) … (learn) new things and getting out of your comfort zone.

BEAT STRESS
Did you know that chronic stress can destroy brain cells? Avoid stress if you want (4) … (keep) your brain healthy!

FUN AND LAUGHTER
(5) … (spend) time with friends has cognitive benefits. Did you know that laughter is good for the brain?

SUPERFOODS
Boost your brain power with plenty of fruit, vegetables and whole grains. Avoid (6) … (eat) too much sugar and saturated fat.

DEEP SLEEP
It's easier (7) … (remember) things after a good night's sleep. It's important (8) … (get) eight hours every night!

Conditionals

4 Copy and complete the sentences with the correct form of the verbs in brackets. Use the first, second or third conditional.

1 If you ... (avoid) stress, your brain will be much healthier.
2 If I'd known that laughter is good for the brain, I ... (spend) more time with my friends.
3 I ... (sleep) better if I didn't have to get up so early in the morning.
4 I ... (not fail) the test if I had revised more.
5 If I were you, I ... (not worry) about it!

Exercise 4
1 avoid
2 'd have spent
3 'd sleep
4 wouldn't have failed
5 wouldn't worry

Grammar reference > Workbook p100

Grammar
Revision

LESSON OBJECTIVES
In this lesson students will:
- revise the tenses covered in this book
- revise gerunds and infinitives
- revise conditionals
- revise reported speech
- revise the passive voice
- read about a writer and his novels

WARMER

Write the first letters of grammar features covered in this book on the board: *1 r____ s____ 2 p____ v____ 3 f____ c____ 4 s____c ____5 t____ c____ 6 m____v____* . Ask students to work in pairs and write the full forms of each grammar feature. Invite different students to come to the board and complete the full forms. (**Answer key: 1** reported speech **2** passive voice **3** first conditional **4** second conditional **5** third conditional **6** modal verbs)

VIDEO: FLIPPED CLASSROOM

- If you set the video for homework, ask students to compare their Task time! answers and then check the answers as a class.
- If you didn't set it for homework, watch the video in class and answer the Task time! questions at the end of the presentation.

Answer key: 1 just **2** past perfect **3** third conditional

Review of grammar forms

1 • Explain the task. Students should read and identify the grammar area in each question. They should then write a true answer for each question.
- Students work individually to complete the exercise.
- They compare answers in pairs.
- Check answers as a class.

2 • Read the example aloud to the class. Elicit a possible ending and point out that *used to* doesn't change in reported speech but that the verbs used when reporting the other answers might.
- Students work in pairs and ask and answer the questions from exercise 1. They note down their partner's answers.
- Students report back to the class. Make sure they report their partner's answers correctly, eg *Elena said she had enjoyed the third year of her education the most.*

Gerunds and infinitives

3 • Ask students to match the two pictures with two of the headings in the text (*Fun and laughter*, *Superfoods*).
- Explain the task. Students should choose the infinitive with *to* or the gerund (*-ing form of the verb*) of the verbs in brackets to complete the exercise.
- Students complete the task individually.
- They compare answers in pairs.
- Check answers as a class.

CULTURE NOTE

Some experts dispute the idea that everyone should get eight hours sleep a night. Some people are able to function on much less sleep. For example, Barack Obama, the former US president, is said to go to bed at 1am and get up at 7am. Sometimes, he has much less sleep than that. Sir Isaac Newton, the scientist who discovered gravity, slept for only two hours a night.

Conditionals

4 • Explain the task.
- Students work individually to write the correct form of the verb in brackets in each sentence.
- They compare answers in pairs.
- Check answers as a class.

Reported speech

5 • Remind students that time expressions also change in reported speech, eg *tomorrow* changes to *the next day*.
• If necessary, do the first sentence with the whole class as an example (*Ana said that she was taking her English exam the next day*).
• Students work individually and rewrite the sentences with reported speech.
• Check answers as a class. Note that both verbs change in question 3.

FINISHED?

Ask fast finishers to close their books and rewrite the reported answers to exercise 5 in direct speech without looking at the original direct speech examples.

Verb tenses

6 • The aim of this exercise is to revise some of the tenses students have covered so far.
• Encourage students to read through the whole text first.
• They work individually and write the correct forms of the verbs in brackets.
• They compare answers in pairs.
• Check answers as a class.

The passive

7 • Remind students that *by* and the agent are not used if the person who did the action is unknown or not important.
• Students work individually and rewrite the sentences in the passive voice (present, past and future).
• They compare answers in pairs.
• Check answers as a class.
• If you are using the TPK and your students need more practice of the grammar, do the Grammar basics exercise.

Grammar basics

Answer key: 1 wouldn't **2** told **3** to organise **4** spent **5** Getting **6** will take place **7** were corrected **8** study

CLIL

Grammar in context: Literature

CULTURE NOTE

Charles Dickens is often regarded as the greatest Victorian novelist and amongst the finest British writers of all time. His novels were serialised in weekly or monthly instalments in journals and was very popular at the time. They were later reprinted in book form. Most of his works have been adapted for TV and cinema and contain some of the world's best-loved literary characters.

8 • Students work individually and complete the exercise choosing the correct word in each case.
• They compare answers in pairs.
• Play the audio. Students listen and check their answers.

9 70

LITERATURE TASK

Students choose one of the four books by Charles Dickens. They use the internet to find out about the main characters and the story of the book they have chosen. They write a list of the main characters and a short summary of the story.

Grammar reference > Workbook page 100

Exercise 5
1 Ana said that she was taking her English exam the next day.
2 She told me she had revised all the grammar the day before.
3 She admitted she had forgotten what time the exam started.
4 She told me she was a bit nervous that day.
5 She said that she hoped she would pass.

Reported speech

5 Rewrite the sentences with reported speech. Change the tenses and the time expressions.

1 'I'm taking my English exam tomorrow.'
Ana said that …
2 'I revised all the grammar yesterday.'
She told me …
3 'I've forgotten what time the exam starts.'
She admitted …
4 'I'm a bit nervous today.'
She told me …
5 'I hope I'll pass.'
She said that …

Verb tenses

6 Copy and complete the text with the correct form of the verbs in brackets.

What is memory?

Nowadays psychologists (1) … (describe) memory as the way the human brain obtains, stores and retrieves information. People (2) … (be) fascinated by memory for thousands of years. In fact, the study of memory (3) … (begin) more than 2,000 years ago, when the Greek philosopher Aristotle (4) … (write) his book *On Memory and Reminiscence*. But a scientific approach to memory (5) … (not exist) until the 1880s, when the psychologist Hermann Ebbinghaus (6) … (classify) the three types of memory: short-term, long-term and sensory memory. We still (7) … (use) this classification today. By the 1960s, computer scientists (8) … (begin) to compare the way memories are stored by humans and machines. If doctors and computer scientists work together, perhaps they (9) … (invent) a memory chip for humans in the future. Imagine that if you (10) … (have) an exam in a particular subject, you could simply insert the relevant memory card!

Exercise 6
1 describe
2 have been
3 began
4 wrote
5 didn't exist
6 classified
7 use
8 had begun
9 will invent
10 had

The passive

7 Rewrite the active sentences in the passive voice. Use *by* only when necessary.

The brain stores our memories.
Our memories are stored by the brain.

1 Psychologists study the process of memory.
2 Aristotle wrote *On Memory and Reminiscence*.
3 They improved computer memory in the 1980s.
4 Perhaps they will invent a memory chip for humans in the future.
5 A lot of students will use it!

Exercise 7
1 The process of memory is studied by psychologists.
2 *On Memory and Reminiscence* was written by Aristotle.
3 Computer memory was improved in the 1980s.
4 Perhaps a memory chip for humans will be invented in the future.
5 It will be used by a lot of students!

CLIL Grammar in context: Literature

8 Read the text and choose the correct answers below.

Exercise 8
1 B
2 A
3 B
4 A
5 B
6 C
7 B
8 A
9 C
10 B

Charles Dickens
(1812–1870)

Charles Dickens was an English writer (1) … novels are still popular today. He (2) … born in 1812. 12 years later, his father (3) … to prison because he couldn't (4) … his debts. Suddenly, Dickens (5) … to leave school and start working in a factory. He experienced terrible conditions, which he remembered all his life. Later, these experiences influenced his work. He probably (6) … have written novels such as *Oliver Twist* and *David Copperfield* if he hadn't experienced poverty (7) … . Dickens (8) … a successful journalist and a great philanthropist, campaigning for children's rights and social reform. By the time he died at the age of 58, Dickens (9) … 15 novels and hundreds of short stories. (10) … you read any of them yet?

	A	B	C
1	who	whose	which
2	was	were	is
3	sent	was sent	were sent
4	pay	to pay	paid
5	must	had	didn't have
6	won't	would	wouldn't
7	herself	himself	themselves
8	became	has become	was becoming
9	wrote	has written	had written
10	Do	Have	Had

9 Listen and check your answers. 70

LITERATURE TASK

Choose one of these books, and write:
- a list of the main characters
- a short summary of the story

Oliver Twist *Great Expectations*
A Tale of Two Cities *David Copperfield*

Literature task
Students' own answers

Assessment methods

LEARNING OUTCOME

✔ Participate in a debate

Today we're going to debate whether exams are the best way to assess people. What do you think?

TASK Express your opinion

1 Read contrasting opinions

2 Identify opinions

3 Write a list of arguments

4 Participate in a debate

Home | Forums | GCSE | A Level | IB | University | Careers

ARE EXAMS THE BEST WAY TO ASSESS STUDENTS?

Until recently, most GCSE subjects in England were assessed by coursework throughout the year, or a combination of coursework and exams. But this is changing, and now most assessment for GCSEs is mainly by final exams only. Do you think this is a good idea?

50% SAY YES

I think that exams are the best kind of assessment, because they motivate you to work harder. Passing exams and getting good grades is an incentive like earning money when you have a job!

Like Comment Share **Posted by Amy**

In my opinion, exams are the fairest assessment because you can't cheat. Someone else could do coursework for you, so it isn't a true test of your ability. But I also think we should be allowed to take reference materials into exams. In the real world, you can always check things online.

Like Comment Share **Posted by Brendan**

The way I see it is that exams are the only really objective way to test people. It wouldn't be practical for teachers to assess everyone individually – it would take too long, and the teacher could be biased.

Like Comment Share **Posted by Caitlin**

50% SAY NO

Exams are terrible for people who get stressed. It's not fair to judge someone's ability entirely on their performance in a single exam, is it? What if you're feeling ill or just having a bad day?

Like Comment Share **Posted by David**

Everyone has different ways of learning, so there should be different ways of assessing people, too. Some people are more effective giving presentations, for example, or doing practical tasks or projects. I'm definitely in favour of continuous assessment throughout the course.

Like Comment Share **Posted by Eleanor**

I don't think exams are a true test of knowledge and understanding. They only really test if you've got a good memory. When teachers just want you to pass exams, it makes school boring and limits creativity.

Like Comment Share **Posted by Freddie**

1 Read

1 Read the text. Find words that mean …

1 schoolwork you do, where the mark is part of your final exam result.
2 numbers or letters that show the quality of a student's work.
3 to behave dishonestly in an exam.
4 giving someone special treatment.
5 all the facts you know about something.

Exercise 1
1 coursework
2 grades
3 cheat
4 biased
5 knowledge

2 Read the text again. Who thinks that …

1 you should be able to use books in exams?
2 some people are better at projects?
3 exams can be hard for people who get nervous?
4 exams are an incentive to study more?
5 exams only test whether you can memorize information?

Exercise 2
1 Brendan
2 Eleanor
3 David
4 Amy
5 Freddie

2 Listen

3 Read and listen to the extract from a group debate on page 97. Who is in favour of exams? 71

Exercise 3
Emily

4 Listen again and repeat. Practise your intonation.

Exercise 4
Students' own answers

5 Watch or listen to the complete debate. Which three arguments are used in favour of exams? 72

1 Exams are fair because nobody can cheat.
2 Exams are like real life because you have to solve problems alone.
3 Preparing for exams helps you to understand what you've studied.
4 Preparing for exams helps to improve your memory.
5 Exams are objective when they're marked by an external assessor.

Exercise 5
1, 3, 5

Integrated skills
Assessment methods

LESSON OBJECTIVES
In this lesson students will:
- work on all four skills
- read a web debate
- watch or listen to a group debate
- prepare and participate in a debate

WARMER

Introduce the topic. Elicit *assessment* from students by writing lines for each letter in the word: _ _ _ _ _ _ _ _ _ _. Ask students to call out letters. If a letter is correct, write it on the correct line in the word. Keep a record of the number of incorrect suggestions. If students guess the word before they have suggested ten letters, they have won. If ten suggestions are incorrect, you have won.

1 Read

1
- Highlight the speech bubble. Explain that students will discuss and answer the question in this lesson.
- Explain the task. Students should find the words in the text that match the five definitions.
- They read the definitions carefully first and then look in the text and find the words.
- They compare their answers in pairs.
- Check answers as a class.

2
- Ask students to read the questions carefully first. Point out that they need to find the person in the debate who said each of these things.
- They read the text again and note down the answers.
- They compare answers in pairs.
- Check answers as a class.

2 Listen

Video with audio option

The dialogue is also available to watch as an audio file. If you prefer to present it this way, play the audio and follow the teacher's notes as for the video.

3 71 REC
- Students watch, read or listen to the extract from a group debate about exams. Elicit the answer to the question from the class.

4
- Play the video again. Students watch and repeat and practise their intonation.

5 72
- Ask students to read the statements first and point out that only three of the five arguments are used in the complete debate.
- Play the audio.
- Students listen and note down the answers.
- Check progress. If necessary, play the audio again.
- Check answers as a class.

71 & 72 Audioscript, page 96, exercises 3, 4 and 5

Teacher: OK, so, today we're going to discuss whether exams are the best way to assess students. Who would like to start the debate?
Emily: In my opinion, exams are the most effective type of assessment. I think the main argument is that exams are fairer because nobody can cheat.
Jack: It's an interesting point, but it's not really true, is it? I mean, some people cheat in exams, don't they?
Emily: Well, I suppose so, but not many, I don't think. Another argument is that preparing for exams helps you to learn. It forces you to understand everything that you've studied during the year.
Oliver: I'm sorry, but I completely disagree. In my view, exams don't necessarily show that you've understood things. They just show that you can memorize lots of facts and information!
Emily: Well, my third point is that exams are more objective. I mean, if the exams are corrected by an external assessor, then there isn't any personal bias or prejudice. The examiner doesn't even know who you are!
Jack: Yes, I suppose that's true. But what about all the stress caused by exams? I mean, it's not really objective to compare the results of people who are really calm about exams, and people who get stressed. I think exams are incredibly stressful.
Oliver: Yes, so do I. The way I see it is that ...

3 Write

6
- Explain that the debate will be about exams and whether students are for them or against them.
- Students work individually and make a list of arguments for or against. Encourage them to use the ideas on page 96 and to add their own ideas.

7
- Ask them to look at the expressions in the Communication kit and match them with 1–5.
- They compare answers in pairs.
- Check answers as a class.

4 Communicate

8
- Highlight the Communication tip box. Remind students that they have studied these communication strategies in this book.
- Students work in pairs and prepare for the debate.
- Encourage them to use the expressions in the Communication kit.

9
- Write the topic of the debate on the board: Exams are the best way to assess students.
- Nominate one student to present the argument for the proposal and another to support the first student.
- Nominate one student to present the argument against the proposal and another to support him or her.
- Then allow the rest of the class to contribute to the debate.
- At the end of the debate, take a class vote and find out if the majority are for or against exams.

! COMMUNICATION TIP
REVISE AND PRACTICE

Remind students that revising and practising communication strategies like giving opinions, agreeing and disagreeing, or using question tags is a way of integrating those strategies so that they become natural when they have a debate or a discussion.

Integrated skills > Resource centre

Teacher: OK, so, today we're going to discuss whether exams are the best way to assess students. Who would like to start the debate?

Emily: In my opinion, exams are the most effective type of assessment. I think the main argument is that exams are fairer because nobody can cheat.

Jack: It's an interesting point, but it's not really true, is it? I mean, some people cheat in exams, don't they?

Emily: Well, I suppose so, but not many, I don't think. Another argument is that preparing for exams helps you to learn. It makes sure that you understand everything you've studied during the year.

Oliver: I'm sorry, but I completely disagree. In my view, exams don't necessarily show that you've understood things. They just show that you can memorize lots of facts and information!

Communication kit

- In my opinion, ...
- It's an interesting point, but ...
- That's not really true, is it?
- Another argument is that ...
- I'm sorry, but I completely disagree.

3 Write

6 Prepare your argument for the debate. Are you for or against exams? Write a list of arguments. Use the ideas on page 96 and your own ideas.

Exercise 6
Students' own answers

! COMMUNICATION TIP
REVISE AND PRACTISE

Periodically revise and practise communication strategies you learn during the course, such as giving opinions, agreeing and disagreeing and using question tags.

7 Look at the Communication kit. Find an example for 1–5.

1 using question tags
2 disagreeing with someone
3 sequencing your arguments
4 presenting your opinion
5 giving a counter-argument

Exercise 7
1 That's not really true, is it?
2 I'm sorry, but I completely disagree.
3 Another argument is that ...
4 In my opinion, ...
5 It's an interesting point, but ...

4 Communicate

8 In pairs, prepare for the debate. Practise giving your opinions and agreeing or disagreeing.

In my opinion, ...
It's an interesting point, but ...

Exercise 8
Students' own answers

9 Have a class debate. At the end, have a class vote. Are the majority for or against exams?

Exercise 9
Students' own answers

Writing

Formal emails

LEARNING OUTCOME

✔ Write to an institution

Hi Oliver,

How are things? Hope your exams are going OK!

Here's that info I promised to send you about the grant to study abroad. You should definitely apply – you'll have an amazing time!

Good luck!

Paul

STUDY ABROAD
PROGRAMME

Apply now!

Complete the online grant application and email it to Ms Travis at secretary@iba.eu

To: secretary@iba.eu

Subject: Grant application for 'Study Abroad Programme'

Dear Ms Travis,

Please find attached my completed application form for a grant from the Study Abroad Programme. As you will see, I am particularly interested in studying in Spain during the next academic year.

I am currently a student at Highton School in Newville. This year I am taking GCSE exams in nine subjects, and I am expected to pass with good grades. I have studied Spanish for four years and my level is B1. I went on a school exchange to Spain last year, so I already have some experience of living there.

I can assure you that I will make the most of this fantastic opportunity if I receive a grant to study abroad. After the Baccalaureate I hope to study modern languages at university, so it would be a great advantage if I could improve my language skills.

Thank you for considering my application. I look forward to hearing from you.

With best wishes,

Oliver Khan

1 **Read Paul and Oliver's emails. Which is more formal?**

Exercise 1
Oliver's

2 **Focus on language** **Write *formal* or *informal* for rules a–f.**

Start with 'Hi' or 'Hello'. *informal*

a) Use exclamations.
b) Start with 'Dear ...'.
c) Use contractions.
d) Use everyday expressions.
e) End with 'With best wishes'.
f) Ask personal questions.

Exercise 2
a) informal
b) formal
c) informal
d) informal
e) formal
f) informal

3 **Focus on content** **Read Oliver's email again. Find at least one example for 1–8.**

1 present simple
2 present continuous
3 past simple
4 present perfect
5 present passive
6 future simple
7 first conditional
8 second conditional

Exercise 3
1 I am currently a student...
2 I am taking ...
3 I went on a school exchange to Spain...
4 I have studied ...
5 I am expected ...
6 As you will see,...
7 I will make the most of... if I receive ...
8 it would be a great advantage if I could ....

TIP!

In a writing exam, you must show the examiner that you can use a variety of grammatical structures. Make a list (like the one in exercise 3) and try to include at least one example of each.

4 **Imagine you're applying for a grant to study abroad. Write an email to send with your application form.**

Exercise 4
Students' own answers

Writing kit

1 **Plan** your email. Answer these questions.

- Who are you writing to?
- What are you applying for?
- Where do you want to go? Have you been there before?
- What are you studying at the moment?
- What language skills have you got now?
- What are you planning to do in the future?

2 **Write** your email. Use the model email and the notes from your plan to help you.

3 **Check** your writing.

☑ use a variety of tenses and grammatical structures
☑ use formal language appropriately
☑ check your composition carefully

Study guide > p107 | Collaborative project 3 > p112 | Writing hub > Workbook p128

Writing
Formal emails

LESSON OBJECTIVES
In this lesson students will:
- read two emails
- revise formal and informal language
- write a formal email

WARMER
Elicit from the class the different things they have practised writing in the writing skills sections of the units of this book. Make a list on the board: *a blog*, *a news report*, *a CV*, *an instant message*, *a formal letter of complaint*, *a profile of a person*, *a report based on the results of a survey*, *a for and against essay*.

1
- Ask students to read the two emails.
- They decide which of the two emails is the more formal.
- Check answers as a class.

2 Focus on language
- Remind students that they have studied formal and informal language in this book.
- Demonstrate the task by writing *Hi* on the board. Ask students if this is used in formal or informal emails.
- They work individually and complete the task.
- Check answers as a class. Note the use of a comma after a connector of sequence at the beginning of a sentence.

3 Focus on content
- Highlight the Tip! box. Remind students of the importance of using a variety of grammatical structures in a writing exam (not just the present simple, for example).
- They read the formal email again and find an example of each of the grammatical structures and write them in their notebooks.
- Check answers as a class.

4
- Check students understand the term *grant* (money you get from the government or an organisation which you do not have to pay back).
- Ask the students to follow the stages in the Student's Book.
- Encourage them to use the model email and the notes from their plan for ideas.
- Monitor while they are writing and give help with vocabulary if necessary.
- At the Check stage, ask them to check their composition carefully before swapping notebooks and checking each other's writing.

Writing kit
The aim of this activity is for students to write an email to apply for the grant to study abroad using a variety of tenses, grammatical structures and formal language appropriately.

Study guide > Student's Book page 107

Collaborative project 3 > Student's Book page 112

Writing hub > Workbook page 128

Collaborative project 1

Giving a presentation

LESSON OBJECTIVES
In this lesson students will:

- give a presentation about an entrepreneur or an exciting new company
- read slides from a presentation and answer questions about them
- listen to a group planning a presentation
- read and complete a conversation extract
- discuss and decide what to do their presentation about
- write and then give a presentation

WARMER

Write *entrepreneur* on the board. Brainstorm famous entrepreneurs and discuss as a class what they have done.

TASK

Read the task with the class and check students understand. NOTE: If students do not have access to computers to create a presentation, they can make posters with photos and written texts instead of slides.

1 Think

1
- Discuss presentations with the class. Have they done or seen any? Which tools were used? What was good or bad about the presentations?
- Ask students to read the slides and answer the questions. Help with any vocabulary if necessary.
- Check answers as a class.
- Read the Digital Literacy box with the class and check students understand.

@ DIGITAL LITERACY

Read the information in the Digital literacy box with the class. Tell students, when we do a presentation, it is always best to get to wherever you are doing it early, if possible. This allows us time to set up and get prepared. This might also give us the chance to sort out any technical problems and helps to make us feel more confident.

Giving a presentation

TASK Work in groups to give a presentation about an entrepreneur or an exciting new company.

1 Think | 2 Listen and plan | 3 Create | 4 Evaluate

1 Think

Exercise 1
1 What the slide is about, who it is about and why
2 It has clear headings and bullet points.
3 By making sentences clear

1 **Look at the slides about *We Are Knitters* and answer the questions.**

1 What different information is in the slides?
2 How is the information easy to follow?
3 Could you improve the presentation? How?

a

YOUNG ENTREPRENEURS
OVERVIEW

1. Introduction
2. *We Are Knitters* – What? Who? Why?
3. More about We Are Knitters
4. About the products
5. Conclusion

b

We Are Knitters

WHAT?
- a knitting and fashion brand

WHO?
- María José Marín and Alberto Bravo, two young Spanish entrepreneurs

WHY?
- knitting really popular with many trendy people in Paris, New York & Hollywood – even film stars knitting! – wanted to make this traditional art cool everywhere
- company teaches people of all ages to knit

@ DIGITAL LITERACY

When you give a presentation:

DO
- include an overview, introduction and conclusion.
- practise giving the presentation.
- check the computer works properly.
- say you will answer questions at the end.

DON'T
- include too many slides – it's better to have a few clear slides.
- speak too fast or too quietly.
- talk for too long.

c

More about *We Are Knitters*

- María José and Alberto worked extremely hard to make their business a success
- overcame many practical problems, eg move to a bigger office and change suppliers
- learnt new business skills – how to delegate and how to launch product in new markets such as the USA
- appeared in a TV series about new entrepreneurs

d

About the products

- all designs are for the latest fashions – buy a kit from the website
- kits have everything you need – easy-to-follow instructions, needles, wool, accessories, designs from beginner to advanced
- videos on the website help you with any problems
- lots of people post pictures on Instagram when they finish!

Exercise 2
1 a knitting and fashion brand
2 two young Spanish entrepreneurs because they wanted to make this traditional art cool for everyone
3 practical problems like moving to a larger office and changing suppliers
4 new business skills
5 easy-to-follow instructions, needles, wool, accessories, designs

2 **Read the slides again and answer the questions.**

1 What kind of company is We Are Knitters?
2 Who started the company? Why?
3 What problems did they have to overcome?
4 What did they have to learn about?
5 What do the knitting kits include?

2 Listen and plan

Exercise 3
The correct order is: d, a, f, b, c, e

3 **Listen to Pablo, Gema and Luisa doing the task. In which order do they talk about these things?** 73

a) speaking more slowly
b) using your own words
c) varying your tone of voice
d) reading what's on the slide
e) repeating key words
f) pausing after important information

Exercise 4
1 exactly
2 more
3 pause
4 own
5 vary
6 too

4 **Complete the conversation extract with the words in the box. Listen again and check your answers.**

exactly more own pause too vary

Luisa: Wait a minute! You're reading (1) ... what's on the slide. That's really boring.
Pablo: I agree. And you're speaking too fast. I think it will help if you speak (2) ... slowly. And you didn't pause once!
Gema: OK, good idea. I'll try and (3) ... after important information, too.
Luisa: Perhaps you should use your (4) ... words and then put up each point after you've talked about it.
Gema: Yes, I think that will help.
Pablo: Another idea might be to (5) ... your voice tone. You could repeat some key words, too. We Are Knitters is one of Spain's most exciting new companies!
Gema: That sounds good. OK, so I could say: We Are Knitters is an exciting new company. This is definitely knitting for the 21st century! Two young Spanish entrepreneurs started the company.
Pablo: That's brilliant. Your voice is good and you're not speaking (6) ... fast.
Luisa: Yes and you've made it sound interesting. You're using your own words. You sound great!

5 **Work in groups. Plan and practise your presentation. Use the Useful language box to help you.**

- Choose the person or company you are going to do the presentation about.
- Decide what information to include.
- Decide how to share the work.
- Decide who is responsible for presenting each section.

Exercise 5
Students' own answers

3 Create

6 **Follow the steps to create your presentation.**

Exercise 6
Students' own answers

Share information
Read and listen to each other's work. Check these things:
- Is it in your own words?
- Have you got all the information you need?
- Are the grammar and vocabulary correct?
- Can you improve it?

Create the presentation
Write slides A–D of the presentation. Add titles, headings, photos and video clips. Then, edit the presentation. Check the grammar and vocabulary again. Can you make the presentation more attractive?

Practise giving the presentation
Practise your sections and then listen to each other. What can you improve?

Show and tell
Give your presentation to the class.

4 Evaluate

7 **Now ask your teacher for the group and individual assessment grids. Then complete the grids.**

Exercise 7
Students' own answers

Useful language
What about (speaking more slowly)?
I think it will help if you (pause after important information).
Perhaps you should (point at the photo).
Another idea might be to (ask the audience a question).
You could (repeat the important information).

2 • Ask students to read the questions carefully.
• Students read and answer the questions.
• Check answers as a class.

2 Listen and plan

3 73
• Ask students to read the information carefully.
• Play the CD. Students listen and put the things they talk about in the correct order.
• Check answers as a class.

4 • Read the Useful language box with the class and help with any vocabulary.
• Students read the conversation extract and complete it in pairs.
• Play the CD again. Students listen and check their answers.
• Check answers as a class. Students practise the extract in groups.

5 • Explain to the class that they are going to write their own presentation in groups.
• Ask students to read the list of things they need to do to plan their presentations.
• Students work in groups and plan and practise their presentations. Ask one or two groups to report back to the class to explain their plans.

3 Create

6 • Read the steps with the class to give students a clear idea of what they have to do. Encourage them to use the slides on page 108 to help them write their own presentations.

Share information

Students share their information in their groups. Then discuss their work and how to improve it. They check for errors.

Create the presentation

Each group creates their presentation. They write each slide of the presentation and add titles, headings, photos and video clips. They edit the presentation, check the language and discuss if they can make it more attractive.

Practise giving the presentation

Groups practise their presentations. They listen to each other, discuss what they can improve about giving the presentations and then practise their presentations again.

Show and tell

Each group gives their presentation to the class. Allow time for the other students to ask questions and comment on the presentation.

4 Evaluate

7 • Look at the evaluation grids with the class.
• Read through the different options and help with any vocabulary as necessary.
• Students complete their self-evaluation. Go round and help as necessary.

EXTRA ACTIVITY

Each group writes ten questions about their presentation and asks the whole class to answer their questions.

73 Audioscript, page 109, exercises 3 and 4

Gema: OK, I'm not sure about giving my part of the presentation. Is it OK? How can I improve? We Are Knitters is a knitting and fashion brand. It was started by María José Marín and Alberto Bravo, two young Spanish entrepreneurs. They realized that knitting was really popular with many trendy people in places like Paris, New York and Hollywood – even film stars were knitting! – and they wanted to make this traditional art cool everywhere ...
Luisa: Wait a minute! You're reading exactly what's on the slide. That's really boring.
Pablo: I agree. And you're speaking too fast. I think it will help if you speak more slowly. And you didn't pause once!
Gema: OK, good idea. I'll try and pause after important information too.
Luisa: Perhaps you should use your own words and then put up each point after you've talked about it.
Gema: Yes, I think that will help.
Pablo: Another idea might be to vary your voice tone. You could repeat some key words too.
We Are Knitters is one of Spain's most exciting new companies!
Gema: That sounds good. OK, so I could say:
We Are Knitters is an exciting new company. This is definitely knitting for the 21st century! Two young Spanish entrepreneurs started the company.
Pablo: That's brilliant. Your voice is good and you're not speaking too fast.
Luisa: Yes and you've made it sound interesting. You're using your own words. You sound great!
Gema: Thanks. I feel much more confident now! OK, Pablo, let's listen to your part and see if we can improve it.

Collaborative project 2

LESSON OBJECTIVES
In this lesson students will:

- create an app
- read descriptions of apps and answer questions about them
- listen to a group planning an app
- read and complete a conversation extract
- discuss and decide what kind of app to create

WARMER

Brainstorm the advantages and disadvantages of apps as a class.

TASK

Read the task with the class and check students understand. NOTE: If students do not have phones or computers to create apps, they can make posters about the app they would like to create, with a written description and visual information.

1 Think

1
- Discuss apps with the class. Do students use them? Are they useful or are they a waste of time? Which ones are most useful for learning? Have they ever made an app?
- Read the Digital Literacy box with the class and check students understand.
- Ask students to read the descriptions of the people and the apps, and to find a suitable app for each person.
- Check answers as a class.

@ DIGITAL LITERACY

- Read the information in the Digital literacy box with the class. Tell the students that it's a good idea to look at a range of different apps to get ideas about what they do/don't like, what they think does/doesn't work and which designs they think are best. Remind them that they must never copy another app, but think about how theirs will be different.

2
- Ask students to read the questions carefully.
- Students look at the description of the apps again.
- Discuss the answers to the questions as a class.

Developing an app

TASK Work in groups of three to develop a simple app. Prepare the app and a description of it.

1 Think **2** Listen and plan **3** Create **4** Evaluate

1 Think

Exercise 1
1 a
2 b
3 c

1 **Look at the apps below. Find an app for someone who:**

1 wants to practise a foreign language
2 wants to be more environmentally friendly
3 has decided to get fitter and do more exercise

@ DIGITAL LITERACY

When you develop an app, remember to:
- think about the target users (Who is going to use it? How?)
- think of a simple interesting idea (What will people use it for? When?)
- use software to develop your app

Reviews | Guides | Phones | TVs | Photography | Best deals | Search

TOP APP Reviews ★★★★★

a

L-Lingo

L-Lingo is a fun way to learn and practise a new language.

With this app you can also do lessons offline.

b

Energy Track

Are you concerned about the environment? **Energy Track** helps you reduce your carbon footprint by showing you information about the energy you use.

c

Fitgo

Fitgo records the exercise you do and encourages you to get fit through social networking. It includes simple exercise programmes to help you. It has a fantastic feature that shows local parks, cycle paths and walks.

Exercise 2
1 Students' own answers
2 Students' own answers
3 They tell you what the app does and what is good about each one.

2 **Look at the apps and descriptions again. Answer the questions.**

1 Have you used these apps or similar ones?
2 Which do you think is the most / least interesting and most / least useful? Why?
3 What kind of information is included in the descriptions?

PROJECT 2

2 Listen and plan

Exercise 3
1 a
2 c
3 a) Luisa
b) Pablo
c) Gema

3 **Listen to Pablo, Gema and Luisa doing the task. Choose the correct answers.** 74

1 They decide to create an app …
a) for organizing homework.
b) to check the spelling of English words.
c) to play a game.

2 They decide the app should be …
a) original.
b) complicated.
c) simple.

3 Who is going to …
a) draw the screen design?
b) research programs to write apps?
c) write the description of the app?

Exercise 4
1 best
2 like
3 should
4 mean
5 right
6 about
7 agree

4 **Complete the conversation extract with the words in the box. Listen again and check your answers.**

like mean about agree should best right

Pablo: OK, so we have to decide what kind of app we want to produce and how we're going to do it.
Luisa: Let's do a game app, maybe a fantasy game. That would be the (1) … thing.
Pablo: I don't see it (2) … that at all. I think we (3) … do an app related to learning English.
Gema: That's a great idea, but we have to decide who is going to use it and what they're going to use it for. I (4) … , there are lots of things you can do related to learning a language.
Pablo: Gema's (5) … . I think it should be for secondary school students, because we know a lot about them.
Gema: What (6) … a spellchecker for English words? That's really useful.
Luisa: Yes, that would be really helpful.
Pablo: I (7) … , but I think it's too complicated! This is our first app, so we should do something simple.

5 **Work in groups. Plan your app. Use the Useful language box to help you.**

- Decide who the app is for.
- Decide what exactly the app will do.
- Decide how to share the work.
- Decide when to meet again to share your information.

3 Create

6 **Follow the steps to create your app.**

Share information

Read or listen to each other's work. Discuss your work. Check these things:

- Can you improve the design and content of your app? Is the description attractive and interesting?
- Are the grammar and vocabulary correct?
- Are the spelling and punctuation correct?

Create the app

Finalize your design and create your app. Test your app. Then check the grammar, punctuation and spelling again.

Show and tell

Show the rest of the class your app. Answer any questions.

4 Evaluate

7 **Now ask your teacher for the group and individual assessment grids. Then complete the grids.**

Useful language

Suggesting
Let's (develop a music app).
Why don't we (add some music)?
What about (an app for revising vocabulary)?
What about (including a photo)?
We should (write an app for students).
Agreeing / Disagreeing
I agree / don't agree.
(Pablo) is right …
Clarifying
I mean …

2 Listen and plan

3 74

- Ask students to read the questions and the three possible answers carefully.
- Play the CD. Students listen and answer the questions. Check answers.

4
- Read the Useful language box with the class and help with any vocabulary.
- Students work individually to complete the conversation extract.
- Play the CD again. Students listen, check their answers and practise the conversation in groups.

5
- Explain to the class that they are going to create an app in groups.
- Students work in groups of three and plan their apps. Ask one or two groups to report back to the class to explain their plans.

3 Create

6
- Read the steps with the class to give students a clear idea of what they have to do. Encourage them to look at the descriptions on page 110 to help them.

Share information

Students share their information in groups. They discuss their work and how to improve it, and check for errors.

Create the app

Each group finalizes their design and creates their app. They test their app. Finally, they check their work carefully again.

Show and tell

Each group shows the rest of the class their app and tells the class about it.

4 Evaluate

7
- Look at the evaluation grids with the class.
- Read through the different options and help with any vocabulary as necessary.
- Students complete their self-evaluation.

EXTRA ACTIVITY

After trying out all the apps, students write a review of the best one, saying what it does and why they liked it. Alternatively, they write a review of their favourite app.

74 Audioscript, page 111, exercises 3 and 4

Pablo: OK, so we have to decide what kind of app we want to produce and how we're going to do it.
Luisa: Let's do a game app, maybe a fantasy game. That would be the best thing.
Pablo: I don't see it like that at all. I think we should do an app related to learning English.
Gema: That's a great idea, but we have to decide who is going to use it and what they're going to use it for. I mean, there are lots of things you can do related to learning a language.
Pablo: Gema's right. I think it should be for secondary school students, because we know a lot about them.
Gema: What about a spellchecker for English words? That's really useful.
Luisa: Yes, that would be really helpful.
Pablo: I agree, but I think it's too complicated! This is our first app, so we should do something simple. I'm sorry, but I disagree. Why shouldn't we try something more interesting? It's good to have a challenge.
Luisa: I agree with Pablo. Let's do something simple for this first app and then we can try and design a more complicated one. It doesn't have to be totally original!
Pablo: What about doing a homework diary? You know, it lets you write down all the homework you have to do and reminds you when you have to finish it.
Luisa: Brilliant. OK, so let's go and research different programmes to write apps.
Pablo: I can do that, I've already used some programmes, so I'll have a look and compare them.
Luisa: I can work on a design for how the app will look on screen and write the instructions.
Gema: And I'll write the description for the app.

Collaborative project 3
Making an advert

LESSON OBJECTIVES
In this lesson students will:

- make a TV or radio advert for a product
- read and answer questions about a storyboard and script for an advert
- listen to a group planning an advert
- read and complete a conversation extract
- plan an advert
- write and record their advert

WARMER

Ask students to describe their favourite advert and say why they like it.

TASK

Read the task with the class and check students understand. NOTE: If students are not able to record their adverts, they can act them out for the class.

1 Think

1
- Have a quick class discussion. What makes an advert interesting? What makes an advert boring? Why? How do students think people prepare an advert?
- Ask students to look at the storyboard and read the script to find out what the advert is for.
- Check the answer as a class. Help with any vocabulary if necessary.
- Read the Digital Literacy box with the class and check students understand.

@ DIGITAL LITERACY

- Read the information in the Digital literacy box with the class. Discuss the importance of everyone participating equally and saying what they do/don't like about any current adverts. This will make sure the whole team are motivated and can create a final product that everyone is proud of.

Making an advert

TASK Work in groups of three to make a TV or radio advert for a T-shirt printing business.

1 Think | 2 Listen and plan | 3 Create | 4 Evaluate

1 Think

Exercise 1
1 an advert for car washing

1 Look at the storyboard and the script. What is this advert for?

@ DIGITAL LITERACY

When you make a TV or radio advert, remember to:

- watch and listen to adverts to get ideas for creating your own.
- organize your ideas and prepare a detailed script. If you make a TV advert, prepare a simple storyboard.
- pay attention to speed and pronunciation while you are recording the advert.

STORYBOARD

Scene 1 – Script

Time	Who / What	Script
0.00	Dramatic music, camera shots of dirty car	–
0.10	Chloe	My car is dirty, but I haven't got time to clean it. I've got to pick my manager up in an hour. What shall I do? I know! I'll take it to Teen Clean!

Scene 2 – Script

Time	Who / What	Script
0.45	Camera shots of Teen Clean team cleaning the car Narrator 1 (David) Narrator 2 (Maria)	At Teen Clean we clean your car so well it looks new. We have the best prices in town! You'll be glad you called Teen Clean!
1.15	Camera shots of very clean car Chloe	Yes, I'll see you in five minutes.

Scene 3 – Script

Time	Who / What	Script
1.20	Outside the restaurant in clean car Chloe Marta Chloe (thinking – voice over) Narrator 1 (David) Narrator 2 (Maria)	Hi, Marta! Hi, Chloe! Have you got a new car? It looks great! Yes, thanks to Teen Clean! Any time you need your car cleaned, call or text us on 07981 328823. Remember, with Teen Clean your car will be so clean everyone will think it's new! Phone us now on 07981 328823.

Exercise 2
1 the different screens and timings for each section
2 by screen, and time, then by character and their script. There are four people in total who take part.
3 repetition, talking about the benefits of the service, addressing the customer directly

Exercise 3
1 **True**
2 **False** – They discuss dressing up as different celebrities wearing T-shirts that they have printed.
3 **True**
4 **True**
5 **False** – They take the list of tips for creativity to read and make a list of more ideas.

Exercise 4
1 think
2 discuss
3 opinion
4 could
5 me
6 funny

2 Look at the storyboard and script again and answer the questions.

1 What does the storyboard show? Why is it useful?
2 How is the script organized? How many people take part?
3 Which of these advertising techniques do they use?

humour repetition
talking about the benefits of the service
addressing the customer directly
persuading celebrity endorsement

2 Listen and plan

3 Listen to Pablo, Luisa and Gema doing the task. Are the sentences true or false? Correct the false sentences. 75

1 They decide to write as many ideas as possible and then discuss them all.
2 They don't discuss any silly ideas.
3 They discuss using colours in the advert.
4 They look at some tips for creativity.
5 They finish by choosing the best ideas.

4 Complete the conversation extract with the words in the box. Listen again and check.

discuss funny opinion me think could

Luisa: Let's make a list of ideas. I (1) ... we should dress up as different celebrities wearing T-shirts we have printed.
Pablo: That's silly!
Gema: Let's make a list of all our ideas first, including the ones that seem silly. Then we can (2) ... them.
Pablo: Good idea. In my (3) ... , colours are important in adverts. For example, red is for action and youth. Green is for health and blue is for trust and security.
Gema: That's really interesting. We (4) ... use different coloured T-shirts with slogans related to those things.
Pablo: For (5) ... , the most important thing is that it's (6) .... People remember funny adverts. Maybe we could have a dog in a T-shirt!
Gema: That could be cool.
Pablo: Yeah, it could be part of a colour theme.

5 Work in groups. Plan your advert. Use the Useful language box to help you.

- Decide what kind of advert you are going to make.
- Decide on the content of the advert and how you are going to make it.
- Decide what each person is going to do.

Exercise 5
Students' own answers

3 Create

6 Follow the steps to create your advert.

Exercise 6
Students' own answers

Share information
Read or listen to each other's work. Discuss your work. Check these things:
- Have you chosen the best content ideas for the advert?
- Are the sentences clear? Do they get the listener's attention?
- Can you use a wider variety of words?

Create the script and storyboard
Write the final script and add the times.

Find any music or sounds you need to make the advert.

Make the advert
Film or record the advert as many times as necessary.

Edit the video or audio. Add any sound effects and music. Add any titles, subtitles, graphics or special effects.

Show and tell
Broadcast your advert to the class.

4 Evaluate

7 Now ask your teacher for the group and individual assessment grids. Then complete the grids.

Exercise 7
Students' own answers

Useful language
For me, the most important thing is ...
That could (work) / That won't (work) because ...
Should we (use celebrity endorsement)?
What do you think?
How should we (plan this)?
Let's (read these tips). / What about (reading the tips)?
We have to remember to (include some music).

2 • Ask students to read the questions carefully.
• Students look at the storyboard and script again and answer the questions.
• Check answers as a class.

2 Listen and plan

3 75
• Ask students to read the sentences carefully.
• Play the CD. Students listen and decide if the sentences are true or false. They correct the false sentences.
• Check the answers as a class.

75 Audioscript, page 113, exercises 3 and 4

Pablo: OK, so we're going to do an audio-visual advert for a T-shirt printing business.
Luisa: Let's make a list of ideas. I think we should dress up as different celebrities wearing T-shirts we have printed.
Pablo: That's silly!
Gema: Let's make a list of all our ideas first, including the ones that seem silly. Then we can discuss them.
Pablo: Good idea. In my opinion, colours are important in adverts. For example, red is for action and youth. Green is for health and blue is for trust, and security.
Gema: That's really interesting. We could use different coloured T-shirts with slogans related to those things.
Pablo: For me, the most important thing is that it's funny. People remember funny adverts. Maybe we could have a dog in a T-shirt!
Gema: That could be cool.
Pablo: Yeah, it could be part of a colour theme. What do you think?
Luisa: It could work ... We have to remember to include contact information. And what about prices, should we include them or not?
Pablo: I'm not sure.
Gema: What about other ideas?
Pablo: I found some tips for creativity on the internet. Here you are.
Luisa: OK, let's all read the tips and make a list of more ideas. I've written down today's ideas, but I'm sure we can think of more.
Pablo: Yes, why don't we meet again tomorrow and choose the best ideas? Then we can write the script and make the storyboard together.

4 • Read the Useful language box with the class and help with any vocabulary.
• Students read the conversation extract and complete it in pairs.
• Play the CD again. Students listen and check their answers.
• Check answers as a class. Students practise the conversation in groups.

5 • Explain to the class that they are going to write and record their own TV or radio advert for a T-shirt printing business.
• Students work in groups of three and plan their advert. Ask one or two groups to report back to the class to explain their plans.

3 Create

6 • Read the steps with the class to give students a clear idea of what they have to do. Encourage them to use the storyboard and script on page 112 to help them.
• Monitor while they are working and give help if necessary.

Share information
Students share their information. They discuss and check their work.

Create the script and storyboard
Each group creates their script and storyboard. They find any music or sounds they need.

Make the advert
Each group films or records their advert as many times as necessary. They edit it and add music, sounds, titles, graphics or special effects if they want to.

Show and tell
Each group broadcasts their advert to the class. Allow time for the other students to comment on each advert. If you like, the class can vote for their favourite advert.

4 Evaluate

7 • Look at the evaluation grids with the class.
• Read through the different options and help with any vocabulary as necessary.
• Students complete their self-evaluation. Go round and help as necessary.

EXTRA ACTIVITY
Each student finds an advert online. They show it to the class and say why they think it is a good or bad advert.

External exam trainer: Speaking Introducing yourself

Your exam preparation

LESSON OBJECTIVES
In this lesson students will:
- practise giving personal information
- practise having a simple conversation

TARGET EXAMS

This section will prepare your students for the following external exams:

- EOI speaking (B1)
- Trinity GESE Elementary stage (grade 4–6)
- Trinity ISE speaking (level 1)

ABOUT THE EXAM

Introducing yourself
Ask students to read the About the exam box. Point out to students that at this stage they will only talk to the examiner and not to another candidate. The opening part is an introduction and will test their ability to answer questions and have a basic conversation.

EXAM TIP: Answering *wh-* questions

Highlight the information in the Exam Tip box and the importance of not answering the examiner's questions with single word answers but always adding a bit more information, as in the example.

1 76
- Students read the Exam tip and listen to the Model exam.
- Make sure students understand the task first. Ask them to copy the list of topics into their notebooks. They should tick the topics that are mentioned.
- Play the audio. Students listen and read the questions and answers in the Model exam.
- Check answers as a class.

2
- Students read the questions in the Model exam again.
- They decide which question is not asking for personal information.
- Check the answer as a class.

3
- Students read Ana's answers to the questions in the Model exam carefully first.
- They decide if they are true or false.
- They check their answers by looking at the interview in the Model Exam again.

76 Audioscript, page 114, exercise 1

Examiner: What's your name?
Ana: My first name is Ana and my surname is Fernandez Garcia. In Spain we have two surnames!
Examiner: How old are you?
Ana: I'm 15, nearly 16. It's my birthday next month.
Examiner: Do you live in Madrid?
Ana: Yes, I live in a flat in the city centre.
Examiner: Who do you live with?
Ana: I live with my mother, my sister, Gabriella, and my grandmother. Oh yes, and my cat, Spotty.
Examiner: What do you enjoy doing in your free time?
Ana: Well, I spend a lot of time online with friends. And if it is not windy I like to play badminton with my brother.

External exam trainer: Speaking

Your exam preparation

Exercise 1
name, age, hobbies, family, pets

1 **Read and listen to the Model exam. Which topics does Ana mention? 76**

1 name
2 age
3 hobbies
4 places
5 likes / dislikes
6 family
7 pets

Exercise 2
Question 5

2 **Read questions 1–5 in the Model exam. Which question is asking about hobbies and leisure activities?**

Exercise 3
1 True
2 False
3 False
4 True

3 **Read Ana's answers to the questions. Are the sentences true or false?**

1 Ana has more than one surname.
2 She is 16.
3 She lives in a flat outside of the city.
4 She lives with three members of her family and a pet.

ABOUT THE EXAM

Introducing yourself
The examiner asks you for personal information – for example, your name, age, hobbies, where you live and who you live with. This tests your ability to give information about yourself and to have a simple conversation.

EXAM TIP: Answering *wh-* questions

When responding to *wh*-questions (questions that begin with *what*, *who*, *how*, etc) remember to give as much information as possible. Don't just give a one-word answer!

Do you live in this city?
Yes. ✘
Yes, I do. I live in a flat in the city centre. ✔

MODEL EXAM

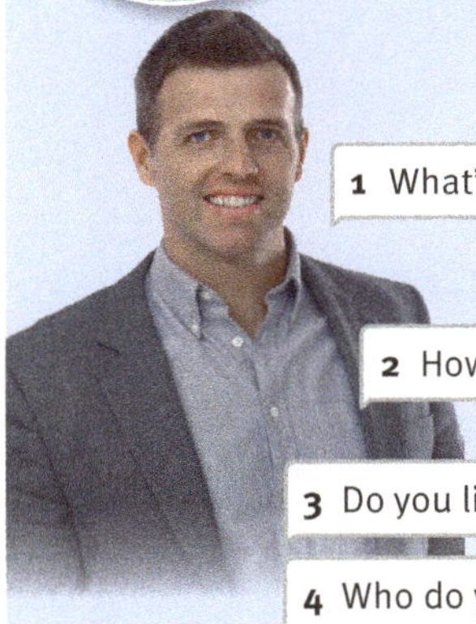

1 What's your name?
My first name is Ana and my surname is Fernandez Garcia. In Spain we have two surnames!

2 How old are you?
I'm 15, nearly 16. It's my birthday next month.

3 Do you live in Madrid?
Yes, I live in a flat in the city centre.

4 Who do you live with?
I live with my mother, my sister, Gabriella, and my grandmother. Oh yes, and my cat, Spotty.

5 What do you enjoy doing in your free time?
Well, I spend a lot of time online with friends. And if it is not windy I like to play badminton with my brother.

Introducing yourself

Your exam practice

Exercise 4
1 e
2 a
3 b
4 c
5 d

4 **Read questions 1–5 in Your exam. Match them with answers a–e.**

a) I'm 16.
b) No, I live in Amsterdam.
c) I live with my mum and dad and my younger brother, Axel.
d) I like inventing and preparing new recipes.
e) My name's Peter. My last name is Jansen.

Exercise 5
Students' own answers

5 **Add more information to the answers in exercise 4. You can invent the information!**

a) I'm 16. It was my birthday last week.

EXAM TIP: Give full answers to questions

Try to give as much information as possible when you answer a question. Remember that you have to give true answers about your name and age, but you can invent answers for other questions. This can be useful if you cannot remember a word or phrase.

Exercise 6
Students' own answers

6 **Answers questions 1–5 in Your exam with information that is true for you. Give as much information as possible.**

Exercise 7
Students' own answers

7 **Work in pairs. Ask and answer the questions in Your exam.**

YOUR EXAM

1 What's your name? And your surname?

2 How old are you?

3 Do you live in this city? Where?

4 Who do you live with?

5 What do you enjoy doing in your free time?

EXAM KIT: Useful language

Personal information
- My first name / surname is ...
- I'm (16).
- It's my birthday ...
- My birthday is on ...
- next week
- next month
- the first / second, etc of January, February, etc

Where you live
- I'm from ...
- I live in ...
- I live with ...
- a flat
- a house

Family and pets
- mum
- dad
- sister
- brother
- step-brother
- step-sister
- uncle
- aunt
- grandmother
- grandfather
- cousin
- dog
- cat
- hamster
- guinea pig
- gerbil
- fish
- reptile
- turtle

Free time
- youth club
- do magic tricks
- play in a band
- do voluntary work
- make new friends

Your exam practice

4
- Ask students to read the questions in the Your exam box.
- They match them with answers a-e.
- Check answers as a class.

EXAM TIP: Give full answers to questions

Ask students to read the information in the Exam tip. Point out that it is important for students not to simply give one word answers (eg *Where do you live? Madrid.*) as this can sound rude or abrupt in English. Encourage them to add information like in the example in exercise 5 (*How old are you? I'm 16. It was my birthday last week.*)

5
- Remind students of the importance of adding extra information and not just giving short answers. Refer them to the information in the Exam tip box.
- They work individually and add extra information to answers a-e in exercise 4.
- Listen to their ideas as a class.

6
- Students answer the questions in Your exam using information that is true for them. Remind them that they can also invent answers to some questions, eg question 5.
- Refer students to the useful language in the Exam kit box and encourage them to use some of this language when answering the questions.

7
- Put students into pairs. They take it in turns to ask and answer the questions in the Your exam box.
- Listen to some pairs as a class.

External exam trainer: Speaking Talking about yourself

Your exam preparation

LESSON OBJECTIVES

In this lesson students will:

- practice talking about their daily life, likes and dislikes
- practise using social language

TARGET EXAMS

This section will prepare your students for the following external exams:

- EOI speaking (B1)
- Trinity GESE Elementary stage (grade 4–6)
- Trinity ISE speaking (level 1)

ABOUT THE EXAM

Talking about yourself

Ask students to read the information about the exam carefully. Highlight the fact that this part of the exam requires students to answer questions about their daily life, interests and likes and dislikes. In terms of grammar, this will mainly require the use of present tenses. Students should think about their interests, hobbies, and have some ideas ready before the exam.

EXAM TIP: Think about the questions in advance

Remind students that even if it's better to have a list of hobbies, interests, like and dislikes ready, it's better not to memorize long replies that might sound unnatural.

1
- Explain the task. Students will listen to a model exam in which the examiner will ask about some of the items in the list. Highlight the example sentence by reading it aloud to the class.
- Put them into pairs to predict which of the topics on the list they think the examiner will ask about.
- Do not check answers at this stage as students will read and listen to the text in the next activity.

2 77
- Explain that students will hear someone answering questions. They should listen and check which of the topics in exercise 1 the examiner asks about.
- Play the audio. Students listen and note down their answers.
- Check answers as a class. Ask if any of the topics were surprising.

For audioscript, see page T117

3
- Encourage students to read through the information in the box carefully first and think about what type of words they might write for 1-10.
- Play the audio. Students listen and note down their answers.
- They read the Model exam again and find the answers.
- Check answers as a class.

4
- Point out that people often need time to think when answering questions. Refer students to the first section of the Exam kit on page 117 and the expressions used for this purpose.
- Play the audio again. Students listen and note down which of these expressions Pietro used in his answers in the Model exam.
- Check answers as a class.

External exam trainer: Speaking

Your exam preparation

Exercise 1
school subjects, places in your town, sport, holidays, food, months of the year, friends, TV

1 Work in pairs. Discuss which topics you think the examiner will ask about.

I'm sure they won't talk about school subjects.

- school subjects
- teachers
- places in your town
- friends
- family
- pets
- sport
- video games
- TV
- food
- holidays
- months of the year
- seasons
- health

Exercise 2
Students' own answers

2 Pietro is doing the Model exam. Listen and check your answers to exercise 1. Did any of the topics surprise you? 77

EXAM TIP: Think about questions in advance

Before the exam, think about the questions that the examiner might ask you and plan how you will answer them.

ABOUT THE EXAM

Talking about yourself
The examiner asks you questions about your daily life, your interests and the things you like. This tests your ability to have a conversation about the things that are important to you.

3 Listen to the conversation again. Complete the information about Pietro.

Likes: French, the town (1) … , football, spaghetti with (2) … sauce, the month of (3) …
Sport: PE at school (4) … a week, football training (5) … a week.
Holidays: Different place every (6) …
Last year (7), …
Best friend: Gabriel, aged (8) … , good at maths and (9) …
TV: Watches about (10) … hours per week.

Exercise 3
1 park
2 tomato
3 May
4 three times
5 twice
6 year
7 Greece
8 15
9 sport
10 eight

4 Listen to Pietro's answers again. Which language for 'Giving yourself time to think' from the Exam kit on page 117 does Pietro use in his answers?

Exercise 4
All of them

MODEL EXAM

1 Which school subject do you enjoy the most?

Well, I think the subject that I enjoy the most is French. The teacher is really good and I'm learning so much.

2 Tell me about a place in your town that you really like.

Let me think, somewhere in my town that I really like. I'd say the park. I often go there with my friends to play football.

'…'

3 How often do you do sport?

4 Where do you usually go on holiday?

5 What's your favourite food?

6 Which month of the year do you like best and why?

7 Tell me about your best friend.

8 Over a week, how much time do you spend watching TV?

Talking about yourself

Your exam practice

Exercise 5
1 e
2 b
3 a
4 h
5 c
6 f
7 g
8 d

5 **Read questions 1–8 in Your exam. Match them with the beginnings of answers a–h.**

a) Let's see. I do it every day of the week ...
b) Let me think, somewhere in my country that I really like ...
c) Well, that's a difficult question to answer because I like several different teams!
d) Well, I don't watch many videos, but I do watch ...
e) I think the sport that I enjoy the most is ...
f) Oh, that's an easy question for me to answer! I love Fridays because ...
g) OK, so, my favourite aunt is called ...
h) There isn't one place in particular that I go to.

6 **Prepare your answers to the questions in Your exam. Make notes and use these things to help you:**

- The beginnings of answers in exercise 5 where appropriate
- The Model exam on page 116
- The Useful language in the Exam kit

Exercise 6
Students' own answers

7 **Work in pairs. Ask and answer the questions in Your exam. Remember to include extra information.**

Exercise 7
Students' own answers

EXAM TIP: Repetition

If you didn't hear or understand the question, it's OK to ask the examiner or your partner to repeat it.

Sorry, can you repeat that, please?

YOUR EXAM

1 Which sports do you enjoy the most?
2 Tell me about a city in your country that you really like.
3 How often do you do homework?
4 Where do you usually go at the weekend?
5 What's your favourite football team?
6 Which day of the week do you like best and why?
7 Tell me about your favourite aunt or uncle.
8 Over a week, how much time do you spend using a screen?

EXAM KIT: Useful language

Giving yourself time to think
- Well, ... • Let me think ... • Let's see ...
- That's a difficult question to answer because ...
- Oh, that's an easy question for me to answer!
- OK, so ...

Adverbs and expressions of frequency
- never • rarely • sometimes • often
- usually • always • once / twice / three times a day / week / month / year

Likes and dislikes
- I (really) like / don't mind / enjoy / love / don't like / hate + noun / -ing
- My favourite / One of my favourite ... is ...

Describing people
- I've known him / her since ...
- She's / He's good / brilliant / great at ...

Your exam practice

5 • Ask students to read questions 1-8 in Your exam carefully first.
• They match them with answer beginnings a-h.
• Check answers as a class.

6 • Students work individually and prepare their answers to the questions in Your exam. Encourage them to use the answer beginnings in exercise 5 to help them.
• Explain that they can also refer to the Model exam on p 116 again as wll as the useful language in the Exam kit box.

7 • Before you put students into pairs, refer them to the Exam tip box and emphasize that it is perfectly acceptable to ask for repetition if you don't understand a question. Highlight the example sentence and read it aloud to the class.
• Put students into pairs to ask and answer the questions.
• Listen to some pairs as a class.

EXAM TIP: Repetition

Point out to students when they are not sure what the examiner or someone else said they should ask for repetition. Encourage them to learn polite phrases to do this like *Would you mind saying that again?*

77 Audioscript, page 116, exercises 2, 3, 4

Examiner: Which school subject do you enjoy the most?
Pietro: Well, I think the subject that I enjoy the most is French. The teacher is really good and I'm learning so much.
Examiner: Tell me about a place in your town that you really like.
Pietro: Let me think, somewhere in my town that I really like. I'd say the park. I often go there with my friends to play football.
Examiner: How often do you do sport?
Pietro: Let's see. I do it three times a week in PE lessons at school and I belong to a local football team, so I have to go to training twice a week for that, then play a match most weekends. So I'd say five to six times a week.
Examiner: Where do you usually go on holiday?
Pietro: There isn't one place in particular that I go to. My mum and dad like to choose somewhere different every summer. Last year, we went to Greece.
Examiner: What's your favourite food?
Pietro: Well, that's a difficult question to answer because I like so many different types of food! But one of my favourites is spaghetti with a tomato sauce.
Examiner: Which month of the year do you like best and why?
Pietro: Oh, that's an easy question for me to answer! I love May, when it stops being cold, but isn't yet really hot, and everything's really green and beautiful.
Examiner: Tell me about your best friend.
Pietro: OK, so, my best friend is called Gabriel. He's 15, like me, and I've known him since I was five. He's really clever – he's brilliant at maths – and he's also good at sport. He plays for the same football team as me.
Examiner: Over a week, how much time do you spend watching TV?
Pietro: Well, I don't watch very much TV – some days I don't watch any at all. I'd say that, over a week, I probably spend about eight hours watching TV.

External exam trainer: Speaking Describing photos

Your exam preparation

LESSON OBJECTIVES

In this lesson students will:

- describe where things are
- talk about a photo

TARGET EXAMS

This section will prepare your students for the following external exams:

- EOI speaking (B1)
- Trinity GESE Elementary stage (grade 4–6)
- Trinity ISE speaking (level 1)

ABOUT THE EXAM

Describing photos

Ask students to read the information about the exam carefully. Highlight the fact that this type of speaking test does not require students to interact. This time they should use appropriate vocabulary to describe what is / was happening, and grammatical structures such as *there is* / *are* or *there was* / *were* and the past continuous tense.

1
- Ask students to read the four statements carefully first.
- They look at photos A and B in the Model exam and match the sentences with the pictures.
- Check answers as a class.

EXAM TIP: Using narrative tenses

Ask students to read the exam tip. Emphasize the importance of using the correct narrative tense to describe past events.

2 78
- Explain the task. Students hear part of an exam in which a student is describing pictures A and B. They listen and answer the two questions.
- Play the audio. Students listen and follow the text in their books.
- They note down the answers.
- Check answers as a class.

78 Audioscript, page 118, exercise 2

Jannik: In these pictures, I can see a house on fire. In the first picture, there's a house with smoke coming out of it. It's seven o'clock in the evening, and I hope that the residents managed to get out and call the fire brigade! By eight o'clock, the firefighters had arrived. In the second picture, I can see two firefighters in the foreground, with a fire hose. They're wearing helmets and protective clothing. In the background you can see the burning house, with flames coming out of the window on the left of the picture.

3
- Refer students to the Useful vocabulary box and the Useful expressions box on page 119.
- Explain the task.
- They read the Model exam again and find the answers.
- They compare answers in pairs.
- Check answers as a class. Highlight the importance of expressions such as *in the foreground* and *on the left* when describing a photo.

External exam trainer: Speaking

Your exam preparation

Exercise 1
A 1, 3
B 2, 4

1 Look at the photos in the Model exam. Match sentences 1–4 with pictures A or B.

1 In the middle of the picture, I can see smoke coming out of the window.
2 In the foreground, there are two firefighters.
3 In the background, you can see the grey sky.
4 On the left, you can see flames coming out of the roof.

EXAM TIP: Using narrative tenses

When you describe past events, remember to use the past simple or past continuous after *at*, and the past perfect after *by*.

At six o'clock, I was watching the news.
At seven o'clock, someone called the fire brigade.
By eight o'clock, the firefighters had arrived.

ABOUT THE EXAM

Describing photos
The examiner will show you some photos, and ask you to describe them. This tests your range of vocabulary about different topics, and your ability to use narrative tenses to describe the photo effectively.

2 Read and listen to Jannik's Model exam. Answer the questions. 78

1 What was happening at 7pm?
2 What had happened by 8pm?

3 Read Jannik's Model exam again. How many examples can you find of:

- phrases from the Exam kit on page 119?
- verbs in the past perfect tense?

Exercise 2
1 There was smoke coming out of the building.
2 Fire fighters had arrived and flames were coming out of the window.

Exercise 3
Jannik uses seven phrases from the Exam kit: In these pictures ...; In the first picture ...; By eight o'clock ...; In the second picture ...; in the foreground ...; In the background ...; on the left ...
Jannik uses one verb in the past perfect tense: had arrived

MODEL EXAM

Jannik

In these pictures I can see a building on fire. In the first picture, there's a building with smoke coming out of it. It's seven o'clock in the evening, and I hope that all the people managed to get out and call the fire brigade! By eight o'clock, the firefighters had arrived. In the second picture, I can see two firefighters in the foreground, with a fire hose. They're wearing helmets and protective clothing. In the background you can see the burning building, with flames coming out of the window.

A 7pm

B 8pm

Describing photos

Your exam practice

Exercise 4
Suggested answers:
flood, flooded, rescuers, street, evacuate, In these pictures, In the first / second picture

Exercise 5
Suggested answers:
1 cars in a flooded street / rescuers evacuating victims of flooding.
2 many more cars in flood water / flood water up to the windows on a building.
3 a car driving down the flooded street / victims in a boat.
4 branches of a tree over the street / rescuers.

Exercise 6
Students' own answers

4 Look at photos A and B in Your exam. Which words from the Exam kit could you use to describe them?

5 Complete the sentences about the two photos.

1 In the foreground I can see ...
2 In the background I can see ...
3 In the middle there's ...
4 At the top of the picture, you can see ...

6 Prepare your description of photos A and B. Make notes and use these things to help you:

- the sentences in exercise 5
- the Model exam
- the Exam kit

EXAM TIP: Organize your time

When you have to talk about more than one photo, make sure you organize your time effectively. Don't talk too much about one photo. Try to talk about each photo for the same amount of time.

7 Work in pairs. Cover your description and describe photos A and B. If possible, record yourselves!

Exercise 7
Students' own answers

YOUR EXAM

A 10am

B 4pm

EXAM KIT: Useful language

Rescue and survival
- boat • branch • building • drive
- evacuate • float • flood • flooded
- parked • rescuers • safe • street
- victims • windows

Describing photos
- In these pictures ...
- In the first / second picture ...
- In the foreground / middle / background ...
- At the top / bottom ...
- On the left / right ...

Narrating events
- At ... o'clock, (+ past simple or continuous)
- By ... o'clock, (+ past perfect)

Your exam practice

4 • Ask students to look at the photos. Ask which words from the Exam kit they would need to describe these photos.
• Students compare answers in pairs.
• Check answers as a class.

5 • Students read the sentence beginnings carefully first.
• They work individually and complete the sentences using the vocabulary in the Exam kit and any other relevant vocabulary they know.
• Check answers as a class.

6 • Students work individually to prepare their description by using their answers from exercise 5.
• Encourage them to refer to the Exam kit and the Model exam to help them.
• Remind students to use the past simple or past continuous after at and the past perfect after by when discussing past events.

EXAM TIP: Organize your time

Read the information in the Exam tip box aloud to the whole class. Emphasize the importance of making sure they organize their time so that they speak about each photo for the same amount of time. Point out that there could be as many as three photos for them to describe.

7 • Students cover their description and describe photos A and B.
• If possible, ask students to record themselves.

TEACHING TIP

When students have completed the preparation stages in exercise 6, you can either listen to each description individually or ask students to work in small groups and practise describing the photos in turn first.
When assessing how well students have performed in exam practice of this type, consider the following:

- Was what they said clear and comprehensible?
- Did they use relevant vocabulary?
- Did they use grammatical structures accurately (eg the past simple, the past perfect)?
- Did they use phrases such as *in the background?*

External exam trainer: Speaking Collaborative task

Your exam preparation

LEARNING OUTCOMES

In this lesson students will:

- read and listen to a dialogue
- practise discussing a topic in pairs

TARGET EXAMS

This section will prepare your students for the following external exams:

- EOI speaking (B1)
- Trinity GESE Elementary stage (grade 4–6)
- Trinity ISE speaking (level 1)

ABOUT THE EXAM

Collaborative task

Ask students to read the instructions for the Model exam carefully. Highlight that this type of speaking test requires students to cooperate, express their opinions and try to reach an agreement.

1
- Ask students to read the three sentences carefully first.
- They read the instructions for the exam and decide if sentences 1–3 are true or false.
- They correct the false sentences.

2
- Explain the task. Students should read the notes about Javier and Inés and then the notes about each possible exchange partner. They should then decide which exchange partner would be the better one.
- Make sure that they give reasons for their choice, eg *They both like sports. They both like artistic activities.*

3
- 79
- Make sure students understand the task. They will hear Sophia and João discussing the same question. They should listen and see if Sophia and João's choices are the same as the choices they made in exercise 2.
- Play the audio. Students listen and follow the text in their books.
- They compare answers in pairs.
- Check answers as a class.

4
- Ask students to look at the expressions in the Exam kit on page 121.
- Ask them to read the dialogue again and find which of these expressions Sophia and Javier use.
- Check answers as a class.

EXAM TIP: Reaching an agreement

Read the information in the Exam tip box aloud to the whole class. Emphasize that it is possible for students to disagree during the discussion, giving reasons why they disagree, but that they should try to reach agreement by the end of the discussion. Elicit ways of agreeing and disagreeing and make a list on the board, eg *You're right. I agree. Sorry, I don't agree. I don't think so.*

79 Audioscript, page 120, exercise 3

Examiner: Javier and Inés are going on an exchange trip to Ireland. Read the information, then talk with your partner about which exchange partner you think they would get on best with. Try to reach an agreement, and give reasons for your choices.
João: What do you think, Sophia? Who would Javier get on best with?
Sophia: I'm not sure. Perhaps he'd get on well with Chris, because they're the same age.
João: I don't think so. Chris isn't into sport. I wonder if Javier would have more in common with Dan?
Sophia: Dan? Yes, perhaps. They're both into sport and music. I think he'd be the best exchange partner.
João: Yes, I agree. And what about Inés?
Sophia: I think Sally would be the best choice. She seems to be quite creative, too, so they'd probably get on well.
João: Yes, Emma is more sporty. I think Inés and Sally would enjoy hanging out together.

External exam trainer: Speaking

Your exam preparation

Exercise 1
1 False. You do the activity with a partner.
2 False. You should try to reach an agreement.
3 True

1 Read the instructions for the Model exam. Are sentences 1–3 true or false? Correct the false sentences.

1 You're going to do the activity with the examiner.
2 You don't have to reach an agreement.
3 You have to give reasons for your choices.

Exercise 2
Students' own answers

2 Read the information in the Model exam. Who do you think would make the best exchange partners for Javier and Inés? Why?

Exercise 3
Students' own answers

3 Sophia and João are doing the activity. Read and listen to their dialogue. Is their choice the same or different from yours? 79

ABOUT THE EXAM

Collaborative task
The examiner will explain an activity to you and your partner. He / She will give you some information, and ask you to try to reach an agreement together. This tests your ability to cooperate and express your opinions.

EXAM TIP: Reaching an agreement

You can agree and disagree with your partner during the discussion, but you must try to reach an agreement in the end. It doesn't matter if it isn't your true opinion! Don't forget to give reasons for your choices.

4 Read the dialogue again. Which phrases in the Exam kit on page 121 do Sophia and João use?

Exercise 4
Asking for opinions: What do you think?
Agreeing: Yes, I agree.
Disagreeing: I'm not sure, I don't think so.

MODEL EXAM

Examiner's instructions
Javier and Inés are going on an exchange trip to Ireland. Read the information, then talk with your partner about which exchange partner you think they would get on best with. Try to reach an agreement, and give reasons for your choices.

JAVIER (16)
Family: 2 brothers, 1 sister
Likes: sports, music, camping

CHRIS (16)
Family: only child, pet dog
Likes: cinema, reading, art

OR

DAN (15)
Family: 2 sisters
Likes: concerts, football, Scouts

INÉS (15)
Family: 1 brother
Likes: photography, drawing, hanging out with friends

SALLY (16)
Family: 1 sister, a pet cat
Likes: music, web design, galleries

OR

EMMA (15)
Family: 2 brothers, 1 sister
Likes: volleyball, swimming, skating

João: What do you think, Sophia? Who would Javier get on best with?

Sophia: I'm not sure. Perhaps he'd get on well with Chris, because they're the same age.

João: I don't think so. Chris isn't into sport. I wonder if Javier would have more in common with Dan?

Sophia: Dan? Yes, perhaps. They're both into sport and music. I think he'd be the best exchange partner.

João: Yes, I agree. And what about Inés?

Sophia: I think Sally would be the best choice. She seems to be quite creative, too, so they'd probably get on well.

João: Yes, Emma is more sporty. I think Inés and Sally would enjoy hanging out together.

Collaborative task

Your exam practice

Exercise 5
A presentation on the importance of water using the photos included.

5 Read the instructions in Your exam. What are you preparing?

Exercise 6
Students' own answers

6 Look at pictures A–G in Your exam. Why are these things important? Can you think of any more things that are important to consider?

- health
- water cycle
- weather

Exercise 7
Students' own answers

7 Look at options A–G again. What's your opinion? Give a reason.

I think that ... is the most important idea because ...

EXAM TIP: Involve your partner

Remember to build a conversation with your partner. Ask questions to get their opinion and listen carefully to their replies. This can give you more ideas to use.

Exercise 8
Students' own answers

8 Work in pairs. Discuss Your exam. Use these things to help you:

- your notes in exercises 5 and 6
- the Model exam on page 120
- the Useful language in the Exam kit

YOUR EXAM

Examiner's instructions
You and a classmate are preparing a presentation on the importance of water in our life. Talk together about the different uses of water and decide which ones you should include in your presentation.

EXAM KIT: Useful language

Talking about the uses of water
- drinking water
- extinguish fire
- ferryboat
- firehose
- have a shower
- hygiene
- mop and bucket
- transport
- water sports

Asking for opinions
- Do you agree with me?
- What's your view?
- What do you think?
- Are you OK with that?

Agreeing
- Yes, you're right
- That's a good point.
- Absolutely!
- Yes, I agree!

Disagreeing
- No, I don't think so.
- Absolutely not!
- I totally disagree.
- I'm not so sure about that.
- That's a nice idea, but ...

Your exam practice

5 • Read the question aloud to the class.
- Students read the exam instructions and find the answer.
- Check the answer as a class.

6 • Ask students to look at pictures A-G in Your exam. Ask them to say why health, the water cycle and the weather are important.
- Ask them to work individually and consider which other aspects of the use of water are important.

EXAM TIP: Involve your partner

Remind students that in collaborative tasks it is important that both students speak and contribute ideas. They should ask their partner questions and listen carefully to their replies because that may help them to get more ideas.

7 • Read the example sentence aloud to the class. Encourage them to give a reason for their choice.
- Students work individually and consider options A-G in Your exam.

8 • Students work in pairs and do the activity in Your exam, using their ideas from exercise 7.
- Encourage them to use the expressions in the Exam kit, their ideas from exercises 5 and 6, and to look again at the Model exam on p120 to help them.

TEACHING TIP

When assessing how well students have performed in exam practice of this type, consider the following:

- Was what they said clear and comprehensible?
- Did they use relevant vocabulary?
- Did they use grammatical structures accurately (eg conditional sentences)?
- Did they agree and disagree with their partner and reach agreement?

Your exam preparation

LEARNING OUTCOMES
In this lesson students will:
- read and listen to a student talking to an examiner about a prepared topic
- practise talking about a prepared topic

TARGET EXAMS

This section will prepare your students for the following external exams:

- EOI speaking (B1)
- Trinity GESE Elementary stage (grade 4–6)
- Trinity ISE speaking (level 1)

ABOUT THE EXAM

Discussing a topic
Ask students to read the information about the exam carefully. Highlight the fact that in this type of speaking test students may have to discuss the topic with the examiner and/or their partner, so good communication is important.

1 80
- Refer students to the Exam tip and the importance of giving examples of personal experiences and the experiences of others (friends or family members).
- Check students understand the task. They should read and listen to the discussion in the Model exam and decide who is discussing the topic.
- Play the CD. Students listen and follow the dialogue in their books. Check the answer as a class.

2
- Ask students to read all the questions carefully first.
- Play the CD again. Students listen and follow the text in their books.
- They note down the answers.
- Check answers as a class.

3
- Students read the examples in the Exam kit on page 123.
- They read the Model exam again and find which of the expressions are used.
- They compare answers in pairs.
- Check answers as a class.

80 Audioscript, page 122, exercises 1 and 2

Examiner: Would you like to go on an exchange trip to another country?
Amy: Yes, I'd love to if I got the chance. I think it would be really interesting to spend some time abroad staying with a family there and experiencing a different culture. What about you, Ben?
Ben: Yes, I completely agree. My older sister went on an exchange trip to Denmark a couple of years ago and she had a great time. She still keeps in touch with the family there. Do you think your school will organize an exchange trip in the future?
Amy: Well, actually, they are planning one with a school in France next year, but there are a limited number of places available. I really hope I can go!
Examiner: Who do you get on best with in your family?
Ben: Let's see. I think I get on pretty well with all of them, but, if I had to choose, I'd say my sister. Neither of us are into sport and we're both quite creative and enjoy hanging out together and doing things like drawing and photography. How about you, Amy?
Amy: Well, for me, I think it would be my mum, actually. I get on OK with my brothers, but, to be honest, I've got more in common with my mum. We both like skating, for example, and we both love cats! Do you get on with your mum?

External exam trainer: Speaking

Exercise 1
The candidates discuss the topic with the examiner and with each other.

Exercise 2
1 It would be interesting to spend some time abroad and to experience a different culture.
2 She went to Denmark. She had a great time. She still keeps in touch with the family there.
3 His sister, because neither of them are into sport, and they are both creative and enjoy hanging out together and doing photography and drawing.
4 Her mother because they have things in common, eg they both like skating and love cats.

Your exam preparation

1 **Read and listen to the Model exam below. Do the candidates discuss the topic only with the examiner or with each other as well?** 80

2 **Read and listen to the Model exam again. Answer the questions.**

1 Why would Amy like to go on an exchange trip abroad?
2 What does Ben say about his sister's experience of an exchange trip?
3 Who does Ben get on best with in his family and why?
4 Who does Amy get on best with in her family and why?

3 **Which language in the Exam kit on page 123 do Amy and Ben use?**

ABOUT THE EXAM

Discussing a topic
The examiner asks you questions related to the subject of the collaborative task which you will discuss with the examiner and / or your partner. This tests your ability to express your opinion and talk about your likes, dislikes, preferences and habits.

EXAM TIP: Using personal experiences

As well as giving personal opinions, give examples of your own personal experiences of the topic being discussed, or those of friends and family members.

My older sister went ...

For me, I think it would be ...

MODEL EXAM

Examiner's question 1
Would you like to go on an exchange trip to another country?

Amy: Yes, I'd love to if I had the chance. I think it would be really interesting to spend some time abroad staying with a family and experiencing a different culture. What about you, Ben?

Ben: Yes, I completely agree. My older sister went on an exchange trip to Denmark a couple of years ago and she had a great time. She still keeps in touch with the family there. Do you think your school will organize an exchange trip in the future?

Amy: Well, actually, they are planning one with a school in France next year, but there are a limited number of places. I really hope I can go!

Examiner's question 2
Who do you get on best with in your family?

Ben: Let's see. I think I get on pretty well with all of them, but if I had to choose, I'd say my sister. Neither of us are into sport and we're both quite creative. We enjoy hanging out together and doing things like drawing and photography. How about you, Amy?

Amy: Well, for me, I think it would be my mum, actually. I get on OK with my brothers, but, to be honest, I've got more in common with my mum. We both like skating, for example, and we both love cats!

Exercise 3
What / How about you ...?
Do you think ...?
I think ...
For me, ...
I'd say ...
I'm / We're (not) into ...
I / we enjoy ...
I / we (both) love ...

Discussing a topic

Your exam practice

Exercise 4
Students' own answers

Exercise 5
Students' own answers

Exercise 6
Students' own answers

Exercise 7
Students' own answers

4 Read the examiner's questions in Your exam below. What is the topic they are discussing?

5 Read the examiner's questions again. Which is the easiest question to answer, in your opinion? Which is the most difficult?

6 Work in pairs. Choose two questions from Your exam to ask each other. Think about your answers to the questions and make notes.

7 Ask and answer two questions from Your exam.

Use these things to help you:

- your notes in exercise 6
- the Model exam on page 122
- the Useful language in the Exam kit

EXAM TIP: Cooperation

To be successful in the exam, you must communicate well with the examiner and with your partner. Remember to ask questions and respond to what your partner says. Don't show off, talk all the time or interrupt your partner!

YOUR EXAM

1 Would you prefer to go hiking or to watch a football match?

2 Which sports do you think are the most interesting to watch?

3 Have you ever been to a music festival? If not, would you like to go?

4 Where would you take an exchange student who wanted to do something cultural in your town or city?

5 Is there a free-time activity that you have never done but would love to try? Why?

EXAM KIT: Useful language

Free-time activities
- go hiking
- get to know each other
- get to know the area
- do something cultural
- go to an art gallery
- go to a music festival
- have a great time
- watch a football match

Adjectives
- beautiful
- boring
- fun
- interesting
- noisy
- quiet
- sunny
- wet

Giving opinions
- I think ...
- I'd say ...
- In my opinion, ...
- For me ...

Asking your partner's opinion
- What / How about you?
- Do you think ...?
- Would you agree?

Talking about likes, dislikes and preferences
- I / We (both) love
- I / We enjoy ...
- I'm / We're (not) into
- I'm / We're (not) keen on ...
- I (really) don't like ...
- I / I'd prefer ... to ...

Your exam practice

4 • Ask students to read the questions in Your exam carefully first. They decide what the topic is.

5 • Ask them which question is the easiest and which the most difficult. Ask them to say why.

6 • Students work individually and note down their own answers to the questions in Your exam.
• Monitor while they are working and give help if necessary.

7 • Students work in pairs.
• They take it in turns to be the examiner and the student, and to ask and answer questions about two of the topics. Encourage them to use their notes from exercise 5, the Model exam on p122, and the language in the Exam kit.
• Listen to some pairs as a class.

EXAM TIP: Cooperation

Refer students to the Exam tip box and remind them of the importance of asking questions and also giving their partner time to speak.

TEACHING TIP

When assessing how well students have performed in exam practice of this type, consider the following:

- Was what they said clear and comprehensible?
- Did they use relevant vocabulary?
- Did they use grammatical structures accurately?
- Did they communicate well with their partner?

Pronunciation lab

Unit 1

-*tion* endings

1 81
- Play the audio, pausing after each word. Students repeat the words chorally.
- Play the audio again. Students repeat the words chorally and then individually.
- Highlight the –*tion* sound in each word.

2 82
- Play the audio, pausing after each word. Students write the words they hear.
- Play the audio again.
- Check answers as a class

Unit 2

Difficult sounds: /ʒ/ and /z/

1 83
- Play the audio. Students listen and repeat the words chorally.
- Play the audio again. Students repeat the words chorally and then individually.
- Highlight the /ʒ/ and /z/ sound in each word.

2 84
- Play the audio. Students decide which words have the /ʒ/ sound.
- Check answers as a class.

Word stress in multi-syllable words

1 85
- Play the audio, pausing after each word. Students repeat the words chorally.
- Play the audio again. Students decide which syllables are stressed.
- Check answers as a class.

2 86
- Students copy the table into their notebooks.
- Play the audio. Students complete the table with the words they hear. Check answers as a class.

Unit 3

Contractions: *'ll* and *won't*

1 87
- Play the audio. Students listen and repeat the short and full forms chorally.
- Play the audio again. Students repeat the words chorally and then individually.

2 88
- Play the audio. Students listen and write the sentences they hear.
- Play the recording again.
- Check answers as a class.

Unit 4

Intonation in conditional sentences

1 89
- Play the audio. Students listen and repeat the sentences chorally.
- Play the audio again and highlight the intonation in each sentence.

2 90
- Students copy the sentences into their notebooks. Tell them there is rising and falling intonation in each sentence.
- Play the audio. Students listen and mark the rising and falling intonation.
- Check answers as a class.

Diphthongs

1 91
- Students copy the table in their notebooks.
- Play the audio. Students listen and repeat the words chorally and individually. Highlight the pronunciation of each of the diphthongs.
- Play the audio again. Students check their answers.

2 92
- Students complete the table in exercise 1 with the words in the box.
- Play the audio. Students listen and repeat the words chorally.
- Play the audio again.
- Check answers as a class.

Pronunciation lab

Exercise 2
1 What'll you be doing in three years' time?
2 I'll be studying at university.
3 Will you be living in this town?
4 I won't be living in this country!

UNIT 1

-tion endings

1 Listen and repeat the words. 81

- resolution • cooperation • negotiation
- solution

Exercise 1
Students' own answers

2 Listen and write the words you hear. Practise your pronunciation. 82

Exercise 2
innovation
participation
communication
organization

UNIT 2

Difficult sounds: /ʒ/ and /z/

1 Listen and repeat the words. 83

/ʒ/	usually	casualty	decision
/z/	victims	capsize	disasters

Exercise 1
Students' own answers

2 Listen to the words. Which three have got the /ʒ/ sound? 84

1 television
2 zero
3 exposure
4 music
5 revision
6 please

Exercise 2
television, exposure, revision

Word stress in multi-syllable words

1 Listen and repeat the words. Which syllables are stressed? 85

gor•geous hor•rif•ic ab•so•lute•ly
starv•ing fu•ri•ous hil•ar•i•ous

Exercise 1
gorgeous
horrific
absolutely
starving
furious
hilarious

2 Copy the table into your notebook. Then listen and complete the table with the words you hear. Which syllables are stressed? 86

2 syllables	3 syllables	4 syllables
freez•ing		

Exercise 2
2 syllables: freezing, tiny
3 syllables: exhausted, disgusting
4 syllables: terrifying, fascinating

UNIT 3

Contractions: *'ll* and *won't*

1 Listen and repeat the short and full forms. 87

1 I will be going = I'll be going
2 He will not be studying = He won't be studying
3 What will you be doing? = What'll you be doing?

Exercise 1
Students' own answers

2 Listen and write the sentences. Do you hear the full or contracted forms? Practise your pronunciation. 88

UNIT 4

Intonation in conditional sentences

1 Listen and repeat. Pay attention to the intonation. 89

1 If you do your homework (↗), the teacher won't tell you off (↘).
2 If I were you (↗), I'd do it now (↘).
3 If I'd had time (↗), I would've done it (↘).

Exercise 1
Students' own answers

2 Copy the sentences into your notebook. Then listen. Does the intonation rise (↗) or fall (↘)? 90

1 I'll help you ( ) if you don't understand ( )!
2 I wouldn't do that ( ) if I were you ( ).
3 If I'd had your number ( ), I would have called you ( ).

Exercise 2
1 I'll help you (↘) if you don't understand (↗)!
2 I wouldn't do that (↘) if I were you (↗).
3 If I'd had your number (↗), I would have called you (↘).

Diphthongs

1 Copy the table into your notebook. Then listen and repeat the words. Pay attention to the pronunciation. 91

/aɪ/	/aʊ/	/eə/	/eɪ/
smile bite	frown out	stare hair	make raise

Exercise 1
Students' own answers

2 Add these words to the table in exercise 1. Then listen, check and repeat. 92

- my • their • say • brown • care
- shake • fine • thousand

Exercise 2
/aɪ/: my, fine
/aʊ/: brown, thousand
/eə/: their, care
/eɪ/: say, shake

UNIT 5

Linking words: Final consonant + vowel sound

1 Listen and repeat. Pay attention to the linking (‿) between the final consonant and the following vowel sound. 93

1 He was‿awarded the science prize.
2 How‿are the designs going to be improved?
3 She is‿often late.
4 When is‿the competition taking place?

Exercise 1
Students' own answers

Pronunciation lab

2 Copy the sentences into your notebook. Listen and draw the linking (‿) where you hear it. 94

1 What are you designing?
2 I don't know anyone who's eaten at that restaurant.
3 I think this was invented by a German company.
4 How often do you watch television?

Exercise 2
1 What‿are you designing?
2 I don't know‿anyone who's eaten at that restaurant.
3 I think this was‿invented by a German company.
4 How‿often do you watch television?

UNIT 6

/ə/ in *have to* / *had to*

1 Listen and repeat. Pay attention to the /ə/ sound at the end. 95

1 have to
2 has to
3 had to
4 didn't have to

Exercise 1
Students' own answers

2 Listen and repeat the sentences. 96

1 Do you have to be 18 to open a bank account?
2 You have to be careful when you use a wi-fi hotspot.
3 The fraudsters had to go to prison.

Exercise 2
Students' own answers

Silent letters

1 Listen and repeat the words. Pay attention to the silent letters. 97

1 debt
2 Wednesday
3 different
4 knife
5 half
6 government

Exercise 1
Students' own answers

2 Copy the words into your notebook. Then listen and underline the silent letters. 98

1 sandwich
2 would
3 thumb
4 autumn
5 vegetable
6 knee

Exercise 2
1 sandwich
2 would
3 thumb
4 autumn
5 vegetable
6 knee

UNIT 7

Intonation in reported speech

1 Listen and repeat the sentences in direct speech. Pay attention to the stressed words. 99

1 'We've arrived at the festival.'
2 'It's amazing!'
3 'I hope it won't rain.'

Exercise 1
Students' own answers

2 Copy the reported speech into your notebook. Listen and underline the stressed words. Are they the same as the direct speech or different? 100

1 They said they'd arrived at the festival.
2 She said it was amazing.
3 He hoped it wouldn't rain.

Exercise 2
1 They said they'd arrived at the festival.
2 She said it was amazing.
3 He hoped it wouldn't rain.

UNIT 8

Difficult sounds: /s/ + consonant

1 Listen and repeat. Pay attention to the pronunciation at the beginning of the words. 101

- slogan
- start
- school
- spend
- square
- spread

Exercise 1
Students' own answers

2 Listen. Practise saying the sentence. 102

Students in Spain speak Spanish.

Exercise 2
Students' own answers

Difficult sounds: /ð/ and /θ/

1 We can pronounce 'th' in two different ways. Copy the table into your notebook. Then listen and repeat the words. 103

/ð/	/θ/
this they with	thing nothing Thursday

Exercise 1
Students' own answers

2 Add these words to the table in exercise 1. Then listen, check and repeat. 104

- the
- something
- that
- think
- other
- everything

Exercise 2
/ð/: the, that, other
/θ/: something, think, everything

Unit 5

Linking words: Final consonant + vowel sound

1 93

- Play the audio. Students listen and repeat the sentences chorally.
- Point out the link between the final consonant and following vowel sound in each sentence.
- Play the audio again. Students repeat the sentences chorally and then individually.

2 94

- Students copy the sentences in their notebooks.
- Play the audio. Students listen and write the linking lines where they hear it.
- Play the audio again. Students compare their answers in pairs.
- Check answers as a class.

Unit 6

/ə/ in have to / had to

1 95

- Play the audio. Students listen and repeat the words chorally.
- Play the audio again. Students repeat the words chorally and then individually.
- Highlight the /ə/ sound at the end of the words.

2 96

- Play the audio. Students listen and repeat the sentences chorally.
- Play the audio again. Students listen and repeat the sentences.
- Again, highlight the /ə/ sounds at the end of words.

Silent letters

1 97

- Play the audio. Students listen and repeat the words chorally.
- Play the audio again.
- Students practise repeating the words in pairs.

2 98

- Students copy the words in their notebooks.
- Play the audio.
- Students underline the silent letters in each word and compare their answers in pairs.
- Check answers as a class.

Unit 7

Intonation in reported speech

1 99

- Play the audio.
- Play the audio again. Students listen and repeat the sentences individually.
- Check answers as a class.
- Highlight the stressed words in each sentence.

2 100

- Students copy the reported speech sentences into their notebooks.
- Play the audio. Students listen and underline the stressed words.
- Check answers as a class.

Unit 8

Difficult sounds: /s/ + consonant

1 101

- Play the audio. Students listen and repeat the words chorally.
- Play the audio again. Students repeat the words individually.
- Students work in pairs to practise the pronunciation of the beginning of the words.

2 102

- Play the audio. Students listen and repeat the sentence individually
- Students work in pairs to practise saying the sentence.

Difficult sounds: /ð/ and /θ/

1 103

- Play the audio. Students listen and repeat the words chorally.
- Play the audio again. Students repeat the words individually.
- Highlight the pronunciation of /ð/ and /θ/.

2 104

- Students add the words to their list from exercise 1.
- Play the audio. Students repeat the words chorally.
- Play the recording again.
- Check answers as a class.